Global Journalism Research

Global Journalism Research

Theories, Methods, Findings, Future

Edited by Martin Löffelholz and David Weaver
with the assistance of Andreas Schwarz

Blackwell
Publishing

© 2008 by Blackwell Publishing Ltd
except for editorial material and organization © 2008 by Martin Löffelholz and David Weaver

BLACKWELL PUBLISHING
350 Main Street, Malden, MA 02148-5020, USA
9600 Garsington Road, Oxford OX4 2DQ, UK
550 Swanston Street, Carlton, Victoria 3053, Australia

The right of Martin Löffelholz and David Weaver to be identified as the Authors of the Editorial
Material in this Work has been asserted in accordance with the UK Copyright, Designs, and
Patents Act 1988.

First published 2008 by Blackwell Publishing Ltd

1 2008

Library of Congress Cataloging-in-Publication Data

Global journalism research: theories, methods, findings, future / edited by Martin Löffelholz &
David Weaver; with the assistance of Andreas Schwarz.
     p. cm.
   Includes bibliographical references and index.
   ISBN 978-1-4051-5331-7 (hardcover: alk. paper) — ISBN 978-1-4051-5332-4 (pbk.: alk.
paper)
1. Journalism—Research. I. Löffelholz, Martin, 1959– II. Weaver, David H. (David Hugh), 1946–
   PN4784.R38G56 2008
   070.4'3—dc22

                                            2007028075

A catalogue record for this title is available from the British Library.

Set in 10/12.5 pt Sabon
by The Running Head Limited, Cambridge, www.therunninghead.com
Printed and bound in Singapore
by C. O. S. Printers Pte Ltd

The publisher's policy is to use permanent paper from mills that operate a sustainable forestry
policy, and which has been manufactured from pulp processed using acid-free and elementary
chlorine-free practices. Furthermore, the publisher ensures that the text paper and cover board
used have met acceptable environmental accreditation standards.

For further information on
Blackwell Publishing, visit our web site:
www.blackwellpublishing.com

Contents

Notes on Contributors

Klaus-Dieter Altmeppen, PhD, is Professor of Journalism at the Catholic University of Eichstaett-Ingolstadt (Germany). His latest publication is *Journalismus und Medien als Organisationen: Leistungen, Strukturen und Management* [*Journalism and media as organisations: Performance, structures, and management*] (2006).

Arnold S. de Beer is Professor Emeritus of the Department of Journalism at the Stellenbosch University (South Africa). He is editorial board member of different academic journals, including *Ecquid Novi: South African Journal for Journalism Research* and research director of Media Tenor SA and the Institute for Media Analysis in South Africa (Imasa). De Beer has written several works on news and journalism education and is co-editor of *Global journalism: Topical issues and media systems* (2004).

Joseph M. Chan is the Changjiang Chair Professor of the School of Journalism, Fudan University (China). He is also Professor at the School of Journalism and Communication, Chinese University of Hong Kong. The books he has co-authored or co-edited include *Mass media and political transition* (1991), *Global media spectacle* (2002), and *In search of boundaries* (2002).

Mark Deuze has a joint appointmentat Indiana University's Department of Telecommunications in Bloomington, United States, and is Professor of Journalism and New Media at Leiden, the Netherlands. Publications of his work include five books, including *Media Work* (Polity Press, 2007).

Wolfgang Donsbach is Professor of Communication at the Department of Communication at Dresden University, Germany, of which he has been the founding director. He was elected president of the International Communication Association (ICA) for the term 2004–5. Among numerous publications, he is currently the general editor of the forthcoming *International encyclopedia of communication* (Blackwell Publishing, 2007).

Bob Franklin is Professor of Journalism Studies in the Cardiff School of Journalism, Media and Cultural Studies, Cardiff University. Book length publications include: *Local journalism, local media: The local news in context* (2006) and *Television policy: The MacTaggart Lectures* (2005). He is co-editor of a new series of books to be published by Sage, entitled *Journalism studies: Key texts*.

Thomas Hanitzsch is Assistant Professor at the Institute of Mass Communication and Media Research at the University of Zürich and was the founding chair of the Journalism Studies Division of the International Communication Association. His research has been published in journals such as *Asian Journal of Communication, Communication Theory*, and *Journalism Studies*.

John Hartley is ARC Federation Fellow at the ARC Centre of Excellence for Creative Industries and Innovation (CCI) at the Queensland University of Technology (Brisbane, Australia). He is among the pioneers of media and cultural studies and has authored and co-authored over a dozen books in these areas. His works have been translated into 13 languages.

Ari Heinonen, PhD, is Senior Lecturer in Journalism at the University of Tampere in Finland. His research interests include journalism and new media, the changing journalism profession, and journalism ethics. He is the author of *Vahtikoiran omatunto* [*The conscience of the watchdog*] (1995), *Journalism in the age of the net* (1999), and co-author of *Loyalty in the global net* (2001).

María Elena Hernández Ramírez is Professor at the University of Guadalajara's Department of Social Communication Research, Mexico. She wrote articles in journals such as *Comunicación y Sociedad (Universidad de Guadalajara) and Revista Mexicana de Comunicación* and is the author of *La producción noticiosa*. [*News production*] (1995).

Christian Kolmer, PhD, is a media scientist and historian working with the Media Tenor Institute in Bonn, Germany. His fields of interest center on agenda-setting research and cross-country comparisons, especially in the field of national images. He is the author of *Die Treuhandanstalt. Theorien der Nachrichtenauswahl. Eine Input-Output-Analyse* [*The Treuhand (Trust). Theories of news selection. An input-output analysis*] (2000).

Ven-hwei Lo is Dean and Professor in the College of Communication at National Chengchi University, Taipei, Taiwan. He is the author of four books; his recent publications have appeared in journals such as *Journalism & Mass Communication Quarterly, Journal of Broadcasting and Electronic Media, The Harvard International Journal of Press/Public*, and *Asian Journal of Communication*.

Martin Löffelholz is Professor in Media Studies at Ilmenau University of Technology (Germany). He has edited or published 15 books and more than 100 journal articles and book chapters. His books include *Die Zukunft des Journalismus* [*The future of journalism*] (1994, co-author), *Krieg als Medienereignis II* [*War as media* *event II]* (2004, editor), and *Theorien des Journalismus [Theories of journalism]* (2004, editor).

Heikki Luostarinen is Professor of Journalism Studies at the University of Tampere in Finland. He is author of books such as *Perivihollinen [The Ancient Foe]* (1986), *Mielen kersantit [Sergeants of the mind]* (1994), and the co-author (with Wilhelm Kempf) of *Studying war and the media: Journalism and the new world order*, vol. 2 (2002).

Maja Malik, PhD, is a research associate at the Institute of Communication Science at the University of Münster, Germany. She is the author of *Journalismusjournalismus: Funktion, Strukturen und Strategien der journalistischen Selbstthematisierung [Journalism-journalism: Function, structures and strategies of journalistic self-reflection]* (2004) and co-author of *Die Souffleure der Mediengesellschaft: Report über die Journalisten in Deutschland [Prompters of the media society: Report about journalists in Germany]* (2006).

Zhongdang Pan is Professor in the Department of Communication Arts at the University of Wisconsin-Madison. He is a co-author of two books, *To see ourselves: Comparing traditional Chinese and American cultural values* (1994) and *Global media spectacle: News war over Hong Kong* (2002).

Thorsten Quandt, PhD, is Junior Professor of Communication Studies with a specialization in journalism at the Free University Berlin, Germany. He has written numerous books including *Journalisten im Netz: Eine Untersuchung journalistischen Handelns in Online-Redaktionen [Journalists on the net: A study onf journalistic action in online newsrooms]* (2005).

Stephen D. Reese, PhD, has been a member of the University of Texas at Austin faculty since 1982. He is co-author of *Mediating the message: Theories of influence on mass media content*, 2nd edition (1996) and co-editor of *Framing public life: Perspectives on media and our understanding of the social world* (2001).

Gertrude J. Robinson is Emeritus Professor and past Director of the Graduate Program in Communications at McGill University in Montreal. Her primary research focus has been on gender issues in the journalistic profession and her latest book is *Gender, journalism and equity: Canadian, US and European experiences* (2005).

Manfred Rühl is Emeritus Professor and former Chair at the University of Bamberg. His recent publications include *Vertrauen: kommunikationswissenschaftlich beobachtet [Trust: observed from a communications perspective]* (2005), *Globalisierung der Kommunikationswissenschaft [Globalizing communications]* (2006), and *Public relations methodology: Should we bother (if it exists)?* (2007). He is currently working on a theory of Communication Cultures in World Society.

Andreas Schwarz is an assistant researcher and PhD candidate at the Department of Media Studies at the Ilmenau University of Technology in Germany. His research interests include journalism, public relations, and cross-cultural communication research. Schwarz has recently published an article in *Communications* about the theory of newsworthiness applied to Mexico's press.

Jane B. Singer is an Associate Professor in the School of Journalism and Mass Communication, University of Iowa (USA), and the Johnston Press Chair in Digital Journalism in the Department of Journalism, University of Central Lancashire (UK). Her research has appeared in a variety of publications, including *Journalism & Mass Communication Quarterly*, *Journalism Studies*, and *Journalism: Theory, practice and criticism*.

Karin Wahl-Jorgensen is a Senior Lecturer at the Cardiff School of Journalism, Media and Cultural Studies, Cardiff University. She is the author of *Journalists and the public* (2006), and *Citizens or consumers?* (2005, with Sanna Inthorn and Justin Lewis). She is editor of *Mediated citizenships* (2007).

David H. Weaver is the Roy W. Howard Research Professor in the School of Journalism at Indiana University's Bloomington campus. He is the author of *The global journalist* (1998) and co-wrote several books about American journalists in recent decades, including lately *The American journalist in the 21st century* (2007).

Siegfried Weischenberg is Professor of Journalism and Communication Science and Head of the Department of Journalism and Mass Communication at Hamburg University, Germany. He has written or edited many books on journalism and journalism education. His latest publications include *Die Souffleure der Mediengesellschaft: Report über die Journalisten in Deutschland* [*Prompters of the media society: Report about journalists in Germany*] (2006, co-author) and *Handbuch Journalismus und Medien* [*Handbook of journalism and media*] (2005, co-editor).

Barbie Zelizer, PhD, is Professor of Communication and holds the Raymond Williams Chair of Communication at the University of Pennsylvania. She is most recently the author of *Taking journalism seriously: News and the academy* (2004) and co-editor of *Reporting war: Journalism in Wartime* (2004). She is founding co-editor of *Journalism: Theory, practice, criticism*.

Preface

We live in one world and, at the same time, we live in a world with 10,000 different societies that live in more than 200 states, as the World Commission for Culture and Development wrote in 1996. Thus, global journalism refers to the ongoing evolutionary homogenization of news production structures and standards ("one world") and, at the same time, to the totality of quite distinct journalism cultures representing the different societies of the world. *Global Journalism Research* takes into account both of these understandings of global journalism by widening the perspective from specific regional research to a global view. Increasingly, universal ("global") theoretical and methodological standards of academic inquiry, at least wide-ranging scholarly principles, are required to enable researchers to analyze the "journalisms" of the world comparatively as well as journalism as a global practice.

Consequently, *Global Journalism Research* is a compendium that, for the first time, brings together four main aspects in one book: (1) It introduces major theoretical approaches taking into consideration that journalism research can no longer operate within national or cultural borders. (2) It describes the methodology of comparative journalism research as well as the main tools for conducting empirical studies (survey, content analysis, and observation). (3) It provides a real global perspective by presenting relevant paradigms and findings of journalism research in Asia, Africa, Europe, and North and Latin America. (4) Finally, it raises questions of how globalization affects journalism research as a discipline and challenges traditional paradigms based on the concept of the nation-state and its boundaries. All in all, this book gives a comprehensive overview of journalism research worldwide and, therefore, is suitable to be used as a general introduction to global journalism research.

Global Journalism Research is based upon the conference "Journalism Research in an Era of Globalization" which was organized in 2004 at the old medieval city of Erfurt by the Institute of Media and Communication Science of Technische Universität Ilmenau (Germany) in association with the School of Journalism at Indiana University (USA) and the Journalism Studies Division of the German Communication Association (DGPuK). The editors express their gratitude to the Alexander von Humboldt Foundation as well as to the German Research Association (DFG) for providing travel grants and additional support to bring together well known scholars from around the globe to discuss the consequences of global-ization on journalism research. The editors thank the speakers of the conference as well as the authors of the book who contributed such thought-provoking and useful chapters and were willing to do the revisions we requested. It has been a pleasure to work with them throughout this long process and to see such a worth-while result from our joint efforts.

The editors also thank Andreas Schwarz of the Technische Universität Ilmenau in Germany for all his help in organizing the editing and revisions of the chapters as well as Indiana University doctoral student Yue Tan for her work in compiling the subject and name indexes for this book. Furthermore, David Weaver thanks former doctoral student Eunseong Kim for her assistance during the 2005–6 aca-demic year, and the Roy W. Howard Research Chair for its support during the entire process of editing this book. Martin Löffelholz is grateful to his secre-tarial assistant Alexandra Büttner as well as to his former research assistants Dr Klaus-Dieter Altmeppen (Catholic University of Eichstätt, Germany), Dr Thomas Hanitzsch (University of Zürich, Switzerland), and Dr Thorsten Quandt (Free University of Berlin, Germany) for their excellent support in organizing the 2004 Erfurt conference.

At the beginning of the 16th century, in the period of humanism, a group of Erfurt professors and students engaged frequently in a dispute against the dog-matic concepts of Cologne theologians. To encourage public attention, the Erfurt humanists issued the famous *epistolae obscurum virorum* – fictitious satirical letters against dogmatism. Those letters can be seen as early predecessors of crit-ical media. The rich Erfurt humanist tradition of openness, non-dogmatism, and scholarly skepticism has guided our conference in 2004 as well as the conceptual-ization of this book. Hopefully others will find *Global Journalism Research* useful and instructive in their own research on journalists and journalism and in teach-ing others to do such research.

Martin Löffelholz and David Weaver
Ilmenau/Erfurt (Germany) and Bloomington (Indiana, USA)
August 2007

Part I

Introduction to Journalism Research

Chapter 1

Questioning National, Cultural, and Disciplinary Boundaries

A Call for Global Journalism Research

David Weaver and Martin Löffelholz

In many countries the past few decades have witnessed an upsurge in interest in studying journalism. Some of the more visible signs of the increasing relevance of journalism studies include the publication of two new journals in this first decade of the 21st century – *Journalism Studies* in February 2000 and *Journalism: Theory, Practice and Criticism* in April 2000 – as well as the many books and articles that have focused on journalism in the past decade (e.g. Ettema and Glasser, 1998; Weaver, 1998; Heinonen, 1999; Deuze, 2002; Gans, 2003; Schudson, 2003; Hanitzsch, 2004; Löffelholz, 2004; Zelizer, 2004; de Burgh, 2005; Franklin et al., 2005; Quandt, 2005; Altmeppen, 2006; Hess, 2006; Weischenberg et al., 2006; Weaver et al., 2007).

Moreover, the International Communication Association (ICA) as well as the European Communication Research and Education Association (ECREA) recently launched specific divisions in order to provide better opportunities for researchers to study journalism comparatively and beyond narrow national paradigms. The ongoing institutionalization of internationalized or even globalized journalism studies is not only indicating a growing importance, but also demonstrating that journalism research can no longer operate within national or cultural borders only: Media industries, media corporations, and public institutions in the field of communication are "going global," computer-mediated communication spreads around the world, and cultural borderlines are becoming blurred by the hybridization of cultures (McPhail, 2006). In this increasingly global media environment, advertising, entertainment, public relations, and – last but not least – journalism are becoming global phenomena affecting media content, the process of news production and even the actual working background of journalists in many countries.

This insight provides a central starting point for our book of global journalism research. It aims to give a comprehensive overview on journalism research and its different approaches, methods, and paradigms around the world. Thus, the book brings together, for the first time, four main aspects in one volume. The first part introduces major theories of journalism research while the second part focuses on traditional research methods in the context of globalization. Aspects of comparative research are especially emphasized. In order to provide a real global perspective, for the third part we selected six contributions describing paradigmatically the state of journalism research in Asia, Africa, Europe, and North and Latin America, while the fourth part discusses important aspects of future journalism research in an era of globalization. In order to acknowledge the current trends of journalism research, it is, however, useful to briefly look back at the beginnings of a scholarly understanding of news production.

Early Steps in Journalism Research

In a sense, we have come full circle from the 1930s, when the emphasis was on broadening what was considered narrowly focused journalism research into the more general study of mass communication processes and effects. One of the early influential books of this movement, *Mass communications*, edited by Wilbur Schramm and published in 1960 by the University of Illinois Press, includes the following tribute: "This volume is dedicated to three pioneers in the study of mass communications through the social sciences: Paul F. Lazarsfeld, Harold D. Lasswell, and Carl I. Hovland" (Schramm, 1960, p. v). These three pioneers of mass communication research were known mainly for their studies of media effects, of course, not for studying the producers of media content, although Harold Lasswell (1948) did put more emphasis on analyzing actual content than did the other two. But none of these early pioneers were much concerned with studying media organizations or journalists. They tended to accept media messages as given, and they were not very interested in studying how and why these messages came to be what they were. In addition, many of the studies of journalists and journalism before the 1930s were mostly descriptive, often anecdotal and uncritical histories of printing, newspapers, and periodicals that focused on the lives of major editors and publishers.

From the 1930s to the 1950s, in the United States as well as in other countries, there were more interpretive histories of journalism that examined the relationships between societal forces and journalistic institutions, and there were also a few more systematic studies of journalists, including Leo Rosten's 1937 book on Washington correspondents (Rosten, 1937). Among those early research projects were David Manning White's study of the "gatekeeper" selecting the news (White, 1950), and Warren Breed's study of social control in the newsroom (Breed, 1955). Other studies of journalists during this period included one of the editorial staff of the *Milwaukee Journal*, of Oregon editorial writers, of Kansas weekly publishers, of American correspondents abroad, and of foreign correspondents in the United States (Schramm, 1957). This shows that there were studies of journalists and journalism before the 1970s, but they were few compared to the dozens of studies of media uses and effects. It was not until 1971 that, as far as we know, the first and truly large-scale national survey of journalists working for a variety of media was carried out by the sociologist John Johnstone and his colleagues at the University of Illinois Chicago Circle campus (Johnstone, Slawski, and Bowman, 1976).

Another important step of empirical journalism research is connected with the work of the German scholar Manfred Rühl. Based on a societal approach to journalism, Rühl conducted in the 1960s the first empirical study that focused on an organized social system instead of journalistic individuals. His case study of a German newspaper marked a radical change in perspective because he did not describe journalism by identifying characteristics and attitudes of journalists as individuals but by analyzing it as a rationalized production process taking place in an editorial setting that was defined as an organized social system (Rühl, 1969). It took, however, decades before the relevance of theoretically driven empirical journalism research was adequately recognized.

The Indistinct Relevance of Journalism Research in the 1970s and the 1980s

Some years after John Johnstone and Manfred Rühl conducted their influential studies, David Weaver and Richard Gray argued in a paper reviewing trends in mass communication research presented at the 1979 AEJ convention in Houston that many mass communication researchers had become more concerned with media audiences and the effects of media messages upon them than with journalism, journalists, and the actual production of messages (Weaver and Gray, 1979). They also argued that even though the programs of research on media uses and effects had some relevance to journalism education and journalism, it was limited. Weaver and Gray concluded that continued concern over media effects had resulted in little systematic research on the effects of society on the media, even though journalists are greatly influenced by societal and organizational constraints, and even though their training and values and news organizations are shaped by political and economic forces.

A dozen years later, in the first edition of their important book, *Mediating the message*, first published in 1991, Pamela Shoemaker and Stephen Reese made essentially this same point when they wrote that "Most books on mass media research mainly cover studies dealing with the process through which the audience receives mass media content or with the effects of content on people and society. We believe that it is equally important to understand the influences that shape content" (Shoemaker and Reese, 1996, p. 3).

Why was not there more systematic research on journalists and journalism compared to the outpouring of studies of media messages, audiences, uses, and effects? Shoemaker and Reese (1996) suggest that it was due to several factors, including the uncritical nature of mass communication research that rarely questioned media institutions themselves, dependence on media industry funding for large-scale surveys and the interest of large media organizations in their audiences (the so-called "dominant paradigm" exemplified by Paul Lazarsfeld and his Bureau of Applied Social Research at Columbia University), as well as the interest of governments worldwide (quite often significant funders of research) in media effects, especially the effects of propaganda in wartime and the possible harmful effects of films and television. These factors largely correspond with those discussed by David Weaver and Richard Gray in their 1979 paper on research trends (Weaver and Gray, 1979).

Another reason for fewer studies of journalists and news organizations has to do with limited access. It is still far easier to study media messages and audiences than it is to study journalists, media organizations or the entire process of structured news production, particularly from a comparative perspective. Experiences with the most recent national survey of US journalists (Weaver et al., 2007) or with the first comparative survey of German and American online journalists (Quandt et al., 2006), for instance, showed that getting access to journalists is still not an easy task. A comparison of the various national surveys of US journalists suggests that the responses of journalists to surveys are on the decline (Weaver et al., 2007). Getting access is even more difficult in newsroom observation studies because they require not only willingness of journalistic individuals but also acceptance within the entire news organization (Quandt, 2005). Hence, newsroom observation studies are perhaps the most difficult of any journalism studies, without personal connections that provide the needed access to the newsroom.

Linking the Diverse Levels of Journalism Research: The 1990s until Today

Although the relevance of journalism research is still being disputed in some countries and although empirical studies more than ever have to take into account the limited access to journalists and newsrooms, the overall number of studies on journalism and journalists is increasing steadily on a global scale. Above and beyond surveys, interviews with journalists or newsroom observations there are some very insightful and useful journalism studies that rely entirely on analysis of journalistic messages or that study the economics, culture, policies, and practices of media organizations from a more macro level (Schudson, 2003; Zelizer, 2004). But there are relatively few studies until today that try to link the characteristics and attitudes of journalists, the attributes of their news organizations, and societal influences with the kinds of messages journalists produce.

Certainly the surveys of journalists that the editors of this book on global journalism research have been involved with (Weaver and Wilhoit, 1986, 1991, 1996; Weischenberg, Löffelholz, and Scholl 1998; Quandt et al., 2006; Weaver et al., 2007) have done little in this regard, and the same is true for most other surveys of journalists that we know about. In the 1982 and 1992 surveys of American journalists and in the 1993 survey of German journalists, it was attempted to correlate the demographics and attitudes of journalists with samples of their best work (Weaver and Wilhoit, 1991, 1996; Weischenberg, Löffelholz, and Scholl, 1998), but in the most recent 2002 national study of US journalists (Weaver et al., 2007) and in the 2005 national study of German journalists (Weischenberg et al., 2006), there was no way of matching individual journalists in the survey with their samples of work, particularly due to increased privacy protections for survey respondents.

There is value in systematically studying representative samples of journalists to document their characteristics, backgrounds, attitudes, beliefs, and perceptions, but much of that information will always be descriptive rather than explanatory or predictive. Although this kind of descriptive baseline information is useful for documenting who journalists are and what they believe about their work and their organizations, especially over time and across national and cultural boundaries, it does not by itself contribute very much to explaining why news coverage is the way it is or why journalists do their work as they do.

There are some fairly recent exceptions, however, that hold out more promise for advances in theory than many of the more descriptive surveys of journalists. These include a growing number of integrative journalism theories searching for the micro–macro link in journalism research (see the chapter of Martin Löffelholz in this book) as well as empirical studies such as that by Stephanie Craft and Wayne Wanta (2004), which examines the influences of female editors and reporters on the news agenda, an article by Shelly Rodgers and Esther Thorson (2003) that examines the news coverage of male and female reporters at three US dailies, and a paper by Tim Vos (2002) that examined the correlation between journalists' perceived roles and the roles manifested in their news stories, building on the work that Lori Bergen (Weaver and Wilhoit, 1991) and Divya McMillin (Weaver and Wilhoit, 1996) did with the 1982 and 1992 surveys of American journalists and the samples of best work sent to the authors by these journalists. These studies that attempt to correlate the characteristics and beliefs of individual journalists with their news coverage often find rather weak relationships, especially between role perceptions and the roles evident in news coverage, but they are at least starting to examine relationships that could lead to more explanation and prediction.

We suspect that the attitudes of journalists do matter to the kind of reporting they do, but more so at the organizational level than the individual. For example, if most journalists in a particular news organization rate the adversarial role highly, it seems likely that more of the news articles produced by that organization will be adversarial in nature, and we think that the same is true for other roles such as neutral disseminator and interpreter. Because news media reporting is usually not the product of isolated individuals, we think that it is likely to be more fruitful to study the links between journalists' attitudes and news content at the organizational rather than the individual level.

This is true, we think, even for those studies that suggest that gender of journalists is correlated with reporting. As Kay Mills points out in her chapter on what difference women journalists make in Pippa Norris' book, *Women, media, and politics* (Mills, 1997, p. 45), women at some newspapers and broadcast media lack the "critical mass" to alter definitions of news and to change the agendas of news coverage. Katherine Graham of *The Washington Post* is quoted in another chapter in this book by Maurine Beasley as saying that there is "a difference between having the authority to make decisions and the power to make policy" (Beasley, 1997, p. 240). Thus it seems likely that this important individual characteristic may exert its influence indirectly through first influencing the priorities of a news organization, which then in turn influences the kind of news reporting produced by that organization, as Siegfried Weischenberg and Maja Malik argue in their chapter on journalism research in Germany.

It is possible to view these influences in the opposite order, of course, so that the organizational characteristics have their influence indirectly through individual journalists' characteristics and beliefs, as Wolfgang Donsbach is suggesting in his chapter of this book, but in the longer run the characteristics of news organizations are probably influenced by individuals, especially those who achieve positions of influence and power such as prominent editors, publishers, news directors, producers, and owners.

This example points out the importance of studying influences on news content not only at the individual level, but also at the organizational and even more abstract levels such as extramedia and societal, as Pamela Shoemaker and Stephen Reese (1996) have advocated. It is possible to aggregate individual level data from surveys of journalists into the organizational level, if one has enough cases from each organization, but studying extramedia factors such as the economic and political environments and societal ideologies cannot be done by surveying individual journalists in one country or culture. Comparative studies across national and cultural boundaries are necessary to assess these influences, as in the analysis of journalists from mainland China, Hong Kong, and the United States (Zhu et al., 1997).

Journalism Research in an Era of Globalization

The growing number of comparative studies indicates that journalism and journalism research no longer operate within national or cultural boundaries. As international events such as war, terrorism, international conferences etc. gain more attention in the media around the globe, research has to examine the new complex networks and institutions that produce news. This implies many challenges for practicing journalists as well as journalism researchers who will have to set up international cooperation if they do not want to lose a grip on the phenomena they try to explain. Comparative research and theories of wide scope are needed that take into account these developments. Therefore this book includes sections on journalism theories, methods, selected paradigms and findings from various regions of the world, as well as on the future of a globalized journalism research.

The theories that are needed to better understand journalism cultures, systems, structures, functions, and practices include those at different levels of analysis (psychological, organizational, societal, and cultural) and also those that focus on different dimensions of journalists, such as gender. The second section of this book is a comprehensive review including the most important theories of journalism research. While Martin Löffelholz gives an introductory overview of the approaches, the following contributors offer insights into various theories and approaches in the field. Manfred Rühl introduces the societal approach, followed by John Hartley, who draws on the cultural studies approach when he claims "everybody is a journalist." Klaus-Dieter Altmeppen points out the organizational aspects of journalistic institutions, their structures and processes. Besides structural factors, journalists as individuals and their decisions of what becomes news depend on psychological variables. Therefore, Wolfgang Donsbach presents a model that tries to integrate various theories about news decisions. Another central variable, of course, is gender, which Gertrude J. Robinson considers to be a constituting element of human society. As all interaction is influenced by it, journalism research has to analyze systemic gender biases within the journalistic profession as well.

Of course journalism research cannot be done without its tools. The classics among them are survey, content analysis and observation, so this book includes chapters on each of these by scholars who have done recent studies using them. But first, in an era of globalization, the methodology of comparative journalism research is one of the central issues. The difficulties and models of cross-national or cross-cultural research are the starting point of the first chapter in this section by Thomas Hanitzsch. The first method described in detail, survey research, is discussed by David Weaver and is based on the American Journalist surveys (Weaver and Wilhoit, 1986, 1991, 1996; Weaver et al., 2007) and his edited book, *The global journalist*, which brought together surveys of journalists from all over the world (Weaver, 1998). Christian Kolmer, of the Media Tenor organization, has specialized in news media and its contents. He presents insights into the analysis of the world *in* the media. The professional routines and working patterns as conditions of news production can also be observed directly, so Thorsten Quandt, who recently conducted a detailed study of online journalism, introduces a rarely applied, but very promising, method of journalism research: the systematic newsroom observation.

After discussing major theories and methods in journalism research, the book turns to selected paradigms and findings from studies of journalism and journalists in several different countries and regions, including China, Taiwan, and Hong Kong (by Zhongdang Pan, Joseph Man Chan, and Ven-hwei Lo), Germany (by Siegfried Weischenberg and Maja Malik), Great Britain (by Karin Wahl-Jorgensen and Bob Franklin), Mexico (by María Elena Hernández Ramírez and Andreas Schwarz), South Africa (by Arnold de Beer), and the United States of America (by Jane Singer). The central aim of this section is to bring together researchers who discuss approaches and main findings of journalism research in their countries in the context of globalization and its challenges.

Finally, the last section raises questions and challenges traditional paradigms based on the concept of the nation-state and its boundaries. The contributors discuss how globalization affects journalism itself as well as journalism research as a discipline and thus suggest new ways that scholars should go. Barbie Zelizer, for instance, argues that despite wide-ranging scholarship, few attempts are being made to share knowledge beyond disciplinary boundaries. She analyzes five main types of inquiry concerning journalism research – sociology, history, language studies, political science and cultural studies – and points out their limitations. However, Ari Heinonen and Heikki Luostarinen from Finland focus on the object of scholarly research, journalism, which is characterized by its changing nature. They outline the dual nature of journalism consisting of media-centric and society-centric dimensions and analyze the "signs of change" that can be observed in times of globalization. These changes, they argue, will affect journalism both internally and externally. Stephen Reese considers globalization as a process that extends beyond economic changes into political and cultural spheres. He describes the role of journalism in that process as crucial and raises the question of how it supports democratic life in a globalized society. Mark Deuze points out the lack of coherence in the field of journalism research as well as education and, as a consequence, suggests considering journalism as an occupational ideology.

The objective of this final section is to suggest a new orientation for journalism research, which needs to take into account the processes of globalization and how they affect all parts of society. Both national and disciplinary boundaries have to be overcome in this new approach, which is no easy task, as this book makes clear. Journalism is, of course, only one form of public communication, but it is one of the most important, if not the most important, for any democratic system of government. Advertising, public relations, and entertainment are all important and influential genres of public communication, but often their importance is measured more in economic terms than political terms. Therefore, some of the theories that are successful in describing and explaining these other forms of public communication are not likely to fully apply to the study of journalism. However, journalism is not so different from other forms of public communication that it needs completely different theories, as the agenda-setting theory is illustrating.

We hope that this book on global journalism research will stimulate and refine our thinking about the approaches and methods that will be most fruitful in studying journalists and journalism in this decade and beyond. And we hope that in our forthcoming discussions of old and new paradigms, theories, and methods for studying journalism we will keep in mind opportunities to link our studies with those about media uses and effects to produce a more unified, theoretical, and useful body of knowledge about the complex processes of this form of public communication known as journalism.

References

Altmeppen, K. D. (2006). *Journalismus und Medien als Organisationssysteme. Leistungen, Strukturen und Management* [*Journalism and media as organizational systems. Functions, structures and management*]. Wiesbaden: Verlag für Sozialwissenschaften.

Beasley, M. H. (1997). How can media coverage of women be improved? In P. Norris (ed.), *Women, media, and politics* (pp. 235–44). New York and Oxford: Oxford University Press.

Breed, W. (1955). Social control in the newsroom. *Social Forces*, 33, 326–35.

de Burgh, H. (2005). *Making journalists*. London and New York: Routledge.

Craft, S., and Wanta, W. (2004). Women in the newsroom: Influences of female editors and reporters on the news agenda. *Journalism & Mass Communication Quarterly*, 81, 124–38.

Deuze, M. (2002). *Journalists in the Netherlands*. Amsterdam: Aksant Academic Publishers.

Ettema, J. S., and Glasser, T. L. (1998). *Custodians of conscience: Investigative journalism and public virtue*. New York: Columbia University Press.

Franklin, B., Hamer, M., Hanna, M., Kinsey, M., and Richardson, J. E. (2005). *Key concepts in journalism studies*. London, Thousand Oaks, CA, and New Delhi: Sage.

Gans, H. J. (2003). *Democracy and the news*. New York: Oxford University Press.

Hanitzsch, T. (2004). *Journalismus in Indonesien. Akteure, Strukturen, Orientierungshorizonte, Journalismuskulturen [Journalism in Indonesia. Actors, structures, orientation horizons, journalism cultures]*. Wiesbaden: Deutscher Universitäts-Verlag.

Heinonen, A. (1999). *Journalism in the age of the net: Changing society, changing journalism*. Tampere, Finland: Acta Universitatis Tamperensis.

Hess, S. (2006). *Through their eyes: Foreign correspondents in the United States*. Washington, DC: Brookings Institution Press.

Johnstone, J. W. C., Slawski, E. J., and Bowman, W. W. (1976). *The news people: A sociological portrait of American journalists and their work*. Urbana, IL: University of Illinois Press.

Lasswell, H. D. (1948). The structure and function of communication in society. In L. Bryson (ed.), *The communication of ideas* (pp. 37–51). New York: Institute for Religious and Social Studies. Also reprinted in W. Schramm (ed.), *Mass communications*. 2nd edition (pp. 117–30). Urbana, IL: University of Illinois Press, 1960.

Löffelholz, M. (ed.) (2004). *Theorien des Journalismus [Theories of journalism]*. 2nd edition. Wiesbaden: Verlag für Sozialwissenschaften.

McPhail, T. L. (2006). *Global communication. Theories, stakeholders, and trends*. 2nd edition. Malden, Oxford, and Carlton: Blackwell Publishing.

Mills, K. (1997). What difference do women journalists make? In P. Norris (ed.), *Women, media, and politics* (pp. 41–55). New York and Oxford: Oxford University Press.

Quandt, T. (2005). *Journalisten im Netz. Eine Untersuchung journalistischen Handelns in Online-Redaktionen [Journalists in the net. A study of journalistic action in online newsrooms]*. Wiesbaden: Verlag für Sozialwissenschaften.

Quandt, T., Löffelholz, M., Weaver, D. H., Hanitzsch, T., and Altmeppen, K.-D. (2006). American and German online journalists at the beginning of the 21st century: A binational survey. *Journalism Studies*, 7(2), 171–86.

Rodgers, S., and Thorson, E. (2003). A socialization perspective on male and female reporting. *Journal of Communication*, 53, 658–75.

Rosten, Leo. (1974 [1937]). *The Washington correspondents*. New York: Harcourt, Brace. Reprint of 1937 edition published by Arno Press.

Rühl, M. (1969). *Die Zeitungsredaktion als organisiertes soziales System [The newspaper's editorial department as an organized social system]*. Bielefeld: Bertelsmann Universitätsverlag.

Schramm, W. (1957). Twenty years of journalism research. *Public Opinion Quarterly*, 21, 91–107.

Schramm, W. (1960). *Mass communications*. Urbana, IL: University of Illinois Press.

Schudson, M. (2003). *The sociology of news*. New York: Norton.

Shoemaker, P. J., and Reese, S. D. (1996). *Mediating the message: Theories of influences on mass media content*. 2nd edition. White Plains, NY: Longman.

Vos, Tim P. (August 9, 2002). *Role enactment: The influence of journalists' role conceptions on news content*. Paper presented to the Association for Education in Journalism and Mass Communication. Miami, FL.

Weaver, D. H. (1998). *The global journalist: News people around the world*. Cresskill, NJ: Hampton Press.

Weaver, D. H., Beam, R. A., Brownlee, B. J., Voakes, P. S., and Wilhoit, G. C. (2007). *The American journalist in the 21st century: US news people at the dawn of a new millennium*. Mahwah, NJ: Lawrence Erlbaum Associates.

Weaver, D. H., and Gray, R. G. (1979). *Journalism and mass communication research in the United States: Past, present and future*. Paper presented to the Association for Education in Journalism. Houston, Texas. Also published in G. C. Wilhoit and H. de Bock (eds.) (1980) *Mass communication review yearbook*, 1 (pp. 124–51). Beverly Hills, CA: Sage.

Weaver, D. H., and Wilhoit, G. C. (1986). *The American journalist: A portrait of US news people and their work*. Bloomington, IN: Indiana University Press.

Weaver, D. H., and Wilhoit, G. C. (1991). *The American journalist: A portrait of US news people and their work*. 2nd edition. Bloomington, IN: Indiana University Press.

Weaver, D. H., and Wilhoit, G. C. (1996). *The American journalist in the 1990s: US news people at the end of an era*. Mahwah, NJ: Lawrence Erlbaum Associates.

Weischenberg, S., Löffelholz, M., and Scholl, A. (1998). Journalism in Germany. In D. H. Weaver (ed.), *The global journalist: Studies of news people around the world* (pp. 229–56). Cresskill, NJ: Hampton Press.

Weischenberg, S., Malik, M., and Scholl, A. (2006). *Souffleure der Mediengesellschaft. Report über die Journalisten in Deutschland* [*Prompters of the media society. Report about journalists in Germany*]. Konstanz: UVK.

White, D. M. (1950). The "gatekeeper": A case study in the selection of news. *Journalism Quarterly*, 27, 383–90.

Zelizer, B. (2004). *Taking journalism seriously: News and the academy*. Thousand Oaks, CA: Sage.

Zhu, J., Weaver, D. H., Lo, V., Chen, C., and Wu, W. (1997). Individual, organizational, and societal influences on media role perceptions: A comparative study of journalists in China, Taiwan, and the United States. *Journalism & Mass Communication Quarterly*, 74, 84–96. Reprinted in M. Prosser and K. Sitaram (eds.) (1999), *Civic discourse: Intercultural, international, and global media*. Vol. 2 (pp. 361–74). Stamford, CT: Ablex.

Part II

Theories of Journalism Research

Chapter 2

Heterogeneous – Multidimensional – Competing

Theoretical Approaches to Journalism – An Overview

Martin Löffelholz

Why do newspapers and other media worldwide every now and then report on the same events, and why are there quite often astonishing differences? How do political, economic, technological, or cultural factors influence the everyday work of journalists in Brazil, China, Great Britain, Kenya, Mexico, Philippines, South Africa, the United States or elsewhere? Does the increasingly global media environment change the working background of journalists? Is the distinction between entertainment and news disappearing with the emergence of new communication forms on the Internet? Journalism researchers from all over the world are trying to answer such questions by conducting empirical studies – and by creating theories on the structures and functions of journalism in diverse societies and cultures. Theoretical approaches give us a sense of how journalists are organizing their work, why they are selecting certain kinds of news, or how political, economic, technological, or cultural changes are affecting journalism as a whole. In many countries, therefore, researchers are trying to describe journalism from a theoretical viewpoint.

Today, journalism studies is a pluralistic, differentiated, and dynamic field of research in the broader area of communication science. The current theoretical discourse on journalism is heterogeneous, multidimensional, and full of competing ideas – some of them are considerably elaborate. The theoretical perspectives range from normative approaches and middle-range theories, to organizational and integrative social theories as well as gender and cultural studies, to name a few. The large number and heterogeneity of the theoretical approaches that developed due to the growing relevance of communicator research worldwide, make it quite difficult to give a consistent overview of theories and perspectives. Based upon previous work of the author (Löffelholz, 2004a; Löffelholz and Quandt, 2005), however, this chapter gives some insight into the emergence of and the current debate on some of the most significant journalism theories.

The Beginnings: Normative and Individualistic
Descriptions of Journalism

The beginnings of the theoretical description of journalism are linked to the works of Robert Eduard Prutz (1816–72), who published a history of German journalism (Prutz, 1971 [1845]) more than 160 years ago – long before journalism became an academic subject. This is astonishing insofar as Prutz already focused on "journalism," and not on such "media" as newspapers and magazines. Prutz also identified journalism as a social area that operates in relation to other social areas, and did not reduce it to the work of individual journalists. In this respect, he was very much ahead of his time (and ahead of many later approaches to journalism), although his ideas did not produce a significant echo in the 19th century's humanities.

Besides Prutz, only a few researchers showed any interest in theoretical work at this early stage of academic development. Although an institutional basis existed in several countries with the establishment of full professorships and university institutes since the early 1900s, researchers in this field did not use their resources for research in contemporary journalism. American universities primarily were interested in teaching journalism, while the so-called newspaper studies in other countries considered journalism first as a historical subject. However, the head of the journalism school at the University of Wisconsin, the ex-journalist turned academic Willard Bleyer, insisted vocational training was not sufficient, and that history was a largely descriptive field. The journalism curriculum that Bleyer created therefore contained a clear research orientation (Zelizer, 2004, pp. 15–19).

Nevertheless, most of the early researchers worldwide viewed journalism in a historical and normative way, and analyzed the field through the individual journalist's personality. The journalist, in this view, had to be a special person with outstanding character and talent. The perspective of this "normative individualism" is based on ideas that can be traced back to the very early roots of journalism research. Normative ideas (e.g. how journalists should work, what kind of personal characteristics are considered journalistic, etc.) were very common at the beginning of the 20th century, and can still be found in current discussions about journalism, for example "peace journalism," "development journalism," and "civic journalism."

In general, the normative perspective began at the end of the 18th century, and was the basis for the socio-philosophical teachings of utilitarianism (which says that usefulness is the category and source of moral behavior). By virtue of this normative basis, a journalistic ideology of personal talent developed, according to which the journalist must be a "gifted" person. Due to its concentration on the character and talent of the individual journalist, "normative individualism" as a theoretical concept features only a very low complexity. Societal and organizational aspects, such as, political constraints and the editorial work process, are not recognized as important aspects of journalistic production, which, instead, is reduced to actions of individual journalists.

Still, some critics, such as the German sociologists Max Weber (1864–1920) and Ferdinand Tönnies (1855–1936), and Robert E. Park (1864–1944) at the University of Chicago, challenged these narrow normative, historical, or individualistic views of journalism. Their sociological concepts emphasized the necessity of theoretical pluralism, the relevance of empirical research, and the notion that journalism can only be adequately described by analyzing the relationship between individuals and society. Weber even suggested a survey of the "sociology of newspapership" (Weber, 1924), with special attention paid to journalistic production and work context. It took decades, however, before American scholars who conducted the first representative surveys of journalists brought his ideas into reality (Johnstone, Slawski, and Bowman, 1976; Weaver and Wilhoit, 1986). Nevertheless, normative and individualistic ideas of journalism can be found even today across the globe in both journalistic practice and theoretical approaches to the field.

A normative perspective on journalism, once influential particularly in the former Soviet Union and its allies, disappeared after the cold war ended: The materialistic media theory derived from theoretical ideas of Marx, Engels, and Lenin. This approach described journalism as a class-defined institution to guide and organize communication under the inclusion of large masses in the class struggle. The normative ideological shaping of this approach reduced its theoretical complexity as well as its empirical relevance. In contrast to that of the 1970s and the 1980s, the academic debate at the beginning of the 21st century is no longer oriented toward the materialistic perspective.

Max Weber, Ferdinand Tönnies, and Robert E. Park may be considered predecessors of a modern theoretical understanding of journalism. However, their influence on the development of journalism theories in other world regions was quite limited. Comparing the emergence of journalism studies, particularly its theoretical impulses in Europe, Asia, Africa, and the United States, Barbie Zelizer (2004, p. 19) concluded, "journalism's study borrowed unevenly from both the humanities and the social sciences." From a global perspective, different academic traditions and the diverse cultural and societal roots of journalism and journalism studies have led to a discontinuous, multi-perspective emergence of journalism theories. Apparently, the theoretical discourses on journalism worldwide follow neither the same pattern nor clearly arranged continuous stages.

As a result, the reader may look upon the following phases not as a representation of a historical process but as a simplified heuristic model describing roughly the development of journalism theories:

- from the discovery of empiricism to middle-range theories of journalism;
- from journalism as an organized system to integrative social approaches;
- from journalism as popular culture to growing theoretical pluralism.

Martin Löffelholz

From the Discovery of Empiricism to
Middle-Range Theories of Journalism

When researchers such as Wilbur Schramm at the University of Iowa began to utilize social sciences (particularly the work of Paul Lazarsfeld in sociology, Harold Lasswell in political science, and Carl Hovland in social psychology) to enhance journalism studies, normative ideas were quickly losing their dominant role. The success of empiricism, first in the United States and afterwards in other parts of the world, led to a reorientation in journalism studies, and journalism researchers were focusing more and more on empirical research. Their fields of interest included the journalist's behavior and decision-making processes – a research tradition introduced by David Manning White's "gatekeeper approach" (1950). Early gatekeeper studies did feature methodological individualism, but soon the researchers realized that news production is a complex process, relying not only on the work of individuals. This led to an inclusion of organizations and systematic influences in the theoretical frameworks, and an opening up of theories toward a pluralism of ideas and approaches.

Since then, empirical research was (and is) of central importance for journalism studies across the globe and, accordingly, most of the theoretical approaches can be seen as "theories of a middle range" (Merton, 1957, p. 5), based on and confirmed by empirical data. Middle-range theories were mostly introduced by American researchers and then "imported" into the theoretical debates in other parts of the world. The success of this perspective is based on the adoption of the premises of empiricism, (neo)-positivism, and analytical philosophy (e.g. inter-subjective crosscheck of data as a quality standard), as well as the intense development and critical testing of middle-range theories, such as the gatekeeper theory or the agenda-setting approach. Middle-range theories do not primarily aim toward the social taxonomy of journalism as a whole, but try to describe and explain specific aspects of journalism.

Several conditions are central for a consistent theory, according to the empirical-analytical perspective. A theory should combine two or more variables, and the variables and concepts must be defined. Analytical concepts must be linked to observation through transformation rules – rules that connect variables and indexes to the meaning of analytical concepts. Finally, restrictions on the application of the theory must be indicated (Löffelholz, 2004a, pp. 23–5).

Today, obviously empiricism still remains the central paradigm of journalism research. However, to speak of *the* empirical-analytical journalism research would be misleading, as an enormous theoretical, methodological and thematic bandwidth has developed since the 1940s. In the 1970s, three different research traditions were identified: the emergence of journalistic messages, the professionalization approach (influenced by the sociology of professions), and the gatekeeper research. Today, fields of research include many more aspects such as the journalists' professional attitudes and structures of consciousness, professionalization and socialization in media companies, editorial structures and working conditions, the consequences of the introduction of new technologies, and the working conditions for women in journalism (Shoemaker and Reese, 1996; Schudson, 2003).

Empirical-analytical journalism studies cannot be identified as a single theoretical concept, because other perspectives on journalism have adopted some methodological premises of the approach. Many methods of and data from journalism studies are based on the premises of the empirical-analytical perspective, particularly those descriptions of journalism using (implicitly) sociological theories of action. The basic concepts of action theories can be traced back to ideas developed by sociologists such as Max Weber, Alfred Schütz, and Thomas Luckmann. The central concepts of this perspective are social actors, their actions, and the meaning of these actions. It is hypothesized that social action is formed by rules, which develop during the process of human interaction. Journalism research based on this perspective, such as the description and analysis of editorial decision-making processes, primarily focuses on a typology of journalistic action forms, patterns, and rules. However, one could argue that journalism research – in contrast to other areas of communication science, such as media effects research – simply uses, often implicitly, some terms of action theory without yet fully exploring the depth of this approach.

Furthermore, the expansion of empiricism in journalism studies does not imply the end of normative concepts. Some representatives of an empirical approach to journalism even explicitly emphasize the importance of normative ideas as starting points for empirical research. Wolfgang Donsbach for instance, former president of the International Communication Association, began a study on the legitimacy of journalism with the assumption of a certain political bias in journalism, and tried to reconstruct this ideological view through empirical research. Donsbach, a former student of Elizabeth Noelle-Neumann ("The Spiral of Silence"), connected theoretical ideas on the profession of journalism with the ideas of Noelle-Neumann, who said that the large influence of mass media could only be adequately explained if media effects research turns to the communicators themselves.

Therefore, the question of how journalistic attitudes are legitimized is crucial, that is, the question of "whether those who exert the largest influence on the contents of mass communication deal with this power in such a way that no damage arises to the community as a result" (Donsbach, 1982, p. 10). Donsbach argues that journalists are a social power, a privileged occupational group with far greater chances of political participation than the remaining citizens have, but with no appropriate social authentication. Journalists are an unusually homogeneous occupational group with similar political attitudes; but they by no means represent the population at large with their features, interests, and opinions. Journalists do not limit themselves to the mere role of mediators of information, but predominantly practice (politically) biased journalism, thereby gaining political influence (Donsbach, 1982, p. 218).

Critics of this normatively driven empirical perspective note that it primarily focuses on the non-standard attitudes of journalists, but ignores the structural conditions of media production, for instance the time- and source-dependency of journalistic work. Equating journalism with media can also be criticized, because it does not take into account the dependency of journalistic work on economic, organizational, and technological structures. Besides, it is not proven, but only assumed, that the intentions of journalists and their attitudes are relevant for message production and journalistic output (Altmeppen and Löffelholz, 1998, p. 105).

In addition to normative approaches and action theories, an empirical-analytical understanding of journalism can also be found in theoretical concepts using a "systems" perspective of journalism.

From Journalism as an Organized System to Integrative Social Approaches

The elaboration of functional systems theories as a perspective for describing journalism began with an empirical study of a newspaper's editorial department as an organized social system. Based on ideas of the sociologists Talcott Parsons (1902–79) and Niklas Luhmann (1927–98), the German scholar Manfred Rühl conducted in the 1960s the first empirical study that focused on an organized social system instead of journalistic individuals. Rühl's case study on the structures and function of the newsroom marked a radical change in perspective and initiated a paradigm shift:

> Editorial action, in the form of producing newspapers in a highly industrially developed society system, is not only carried out by some editors collecting messages, correcting, and writing, but is rather a fully rationalized production process in an equally rationalized and differentiated organization.
>
> (Rühl, 1969, p. 13)

Thus, Rühl turned against the normative and individualistic tradition of journalism research and outlined an alternative: "The person as a paradigm is a much too complex and inelastic term to serve as a unit of analysis for journalism. In response to this, the term 'social system' is suggested, which permits differentiation between journalism and its environments" (Rühl, 1980, pp. 435–9). The substantial building blocks of functional systems theories include the system/environment paradigm as an order principle of a general theory of journalism and the identification of a journalism-specific function. According to Rühl, this function lies in the production and supply of topics for public communication. Further important aspects of a functional system's perspective on journalism are the development and differentiation of decision structures in journalism as well as its social embedding. In this view, journalism is always dependent on a broader societal system, which can be socio-historically identified.

In the course of recent decades, many scholars, particularly in the German-speaking countries, have adapted Rühl's basic notions, criticized them, attempt to develop them further and described the advantages of a systems approach for an international audience (Görke and Scholl, 2006). The separation of journalists as persons from journalism as a social system promised to overcome the oversimplifying concepts of the early period of journalism research, as well as being the link to the sociological debate, without having to give up the requirement of an empirical check of theory.

The term "system," however, is by no means uniformly used in journalism studies. Some approaches operate within the term "system," but show the legacy of the individualistic tradition conceptualizing journalism as a system of actors. Different approaches are also pursued within functional systems theories. A central question revolves around systemic integration. Is journalism a functional system *within* society, as Rühl (1980) assumes, or does it operate as a subsystem within a larger functional system such as "public" or "mass media"? Diverging views also exist regarding the structures that constitute the internal order of the system, and the (primary) function of journalism (Görke and Scholl, 2006).

Criticism of functional systems theories comes from different sources. Critics note that these approaches underestimate the relevance of journalistic subjects for the execution of journalistic actions. Furthermore, they charge that functional systems theories ignore the extensive interrelationships between media-specific (especially economic) and journalistic procedures. They also criticize the dichotomy of system and subject, in which the perspective of action theory is reduced to one of a micro-structural actor, although theories of action concern themselves expressly with dynamic social structures (Löffelholz, 2004a, pp. 57–8). Given this background, it is not surprising that in journalism research during the 1990s, not only was the systems theoretical approach refined, but also the search for social "integration" theories begun – theories that could overcome the dichotomy of system and subject, and of structure and action.

The hierarchy-of-influences model, for instance, developed by American scholars Pamela Shoemaker and Stephen D. Reese, links individual, structural, and normative factors in order to describe how media content is produced. In their view, influences on news production could be systematized by differentiating between five dimensions, which they call the individual level, routines level, organizational level, extramedia level, and ideological level. Consequently, the actions of individuals, the organized process of news production, and factors outside of media organizations influence journalistic content (Shoemaker and Reese, 1996). A similar perspective is pursued by the Hamburg-based researcher Siegfried Weischenberg (1992). His model for the systematic identification of factors that constitute journalism systems consists of four levels: media system (norms), media institutions (structures), media content (functions), and journalistic actors (roles).

The hierarchy-of-influences model and other similar descriptions are helpful to reduce the complexity of journalism studies by offering heuristic frameworks to categorize the field and organize empirical data. However, these models do not provide consistent theoretical descriptions of journalism. For example, why should factors outside of media organizations influence journalistic actors and their attitudes, whereas the actors themselves cannot influence the other dimensions of news production? It is likewise doubtful, whether catalogs of research objects can serve as theoretical models for journalism's relationships to its environment. Besides these "stand-alone approaches," which are not sufficiently connected to general sociological theories, there is a growing number of journalism theories using approaches created to describe social phenomena in general. They share the assumption that the social structures of journalism may not be as unique as stand-alone approaches claim.

Promising sociological approaches used as starting points for social integrative journalism theories are the theory of structuration, introduced by the British sociologist Anthony Giddens, the habitus concept of the French sociologist Pierre Bourdieu, the theory of communicative action of the philosopher Jürgen Habermas and the concept of actor-structure dynamics, pioneered by the German sociologist Uwe Schimank (Löffelholz, 2004b). In Schimank's perspective, for instance, elements of institutional, systems, and action theories are connected. Journalistic organizations such as editorial departments can be analyzed as both institutional complexes and collective actors. The different levels of journalistic functions, institutions, and actions refer to each other in this approach, but are not directly linked. Thus, interactions are not solely derived from structural imperatives, but can lead to their own generation of structure. Maximilian Gottschlich (1980), an Austrian scholar, analyzes, with reference to the works of Jürgen Habermas, the role of journalism in social discourse and the legitimacy of journalists' influence on society. On this basis, he develops a normative framework for the analysis of journalism. His aim is to overcome the journalistic "loss of orientation" that he identifies as an outcome of the discrepancy between subjective conceptions of work and objective reality in the profession.

So far, none of these approaches seems to provide a complete and consistent theory for the description of journalism. Nevertheless, one day these integrative social theories may offer sophisticated theory architectures, essentially connected to certain sociological reorientations. We have just started on the long path toward an integration theory in which the links between macro-, meso-, and micro-levels of journalism are consistently explained. In the future, substantial integration potential might come also from other approaches emphasizing cultural rather than societal aspects.

From Journalism as Popular Culture to Growing Theoretical Pluralism

Barbie Zelizer has pointed out that "An interest in the cultural dimensions of journalism was part of journalistic inquiry since its inception" (Zelizer, 2004, p. 178). The starting point of the cultural studies' perspectives primarily in the United States and in Great Britain were concepts derived from such diverse approaches as Marxism, critical theory, semiotics, linguistics, and theories of action. Cultural studies focus on contextual research in and modification of the relationship between culture, media, and power. In numerous research projects, cultural studies have concentrated on the reception of media, especially television entertainment programs, while the interest in journalism was less developed.

However, researchers such as Robert Park from the University of Chicago and, decades later, James Carey from the University of Illinois, stressed the importance of understanding journalistic practice by analyzing collective codes of knowledge by which journalists typically structure their world. Representatives of a cultural approach to journalism view culture as "one of the resources journalists draw upon to coordinate their activities as reporters and editors. However, news itself is seen as cultural, ultimately relative to the givens of the groups and individuals engaged in its production" (Zelizer, 2004, p. 176). Journalism as an area of everyday culture serves as a sphere for the (re)production of meaning, sense, and consciousness. For cultural studies, it does not seem so important how journalistic messages are produced. Journalism is rather seen from the recipient's perspective as an everyday life resource, which serves the social circulation of meaning. Media are interpreted as a structure of meaning, as literary and visual constructs that apply symbolic ways and means and are shaped by certain rules, standards, conventions, and traditions.

The British-Australian scholar John Hartley describes journalism as part of popular reality:

> While journalism is produced in conditions of present-tense organized chaos and consumed in the routine expectation of being thrown away and forgotten, it is neither reinvented anew each day nor necessarily very different from what was being done decades and even lifetimes ago. Since my focus is on journalism from the readership's point of view, it follows that what journalism is "made of," as it were, is not only or even primarily its industrial productive apparatus – technology, corporations, finance, work practices, occupational ideologies, institutional policies and so on – but also, and perhaps more fundamentally, it is "made of" something at once more modest and elusive, namely meanings, and more pervasive and general, namely readership themselves – the public.
>
> (Hartley, 1996, p. 1)

Undoubtedly, cultural approaches to journalism offer a multitude of theoretical ideas. The concept of culture is gaining further significance because, in a globalized world, what separates people also connects them: the possibility of perceiving oneself as culturally distinct. In the course of globalization, transnational cultures are developing, which increasingly shape the production of media content. In the light of the concept's various origins, it is not surprising, however, that cultural studies do not represent a closed theoretical architecture; even the definition of the term "culture" varies greatly among works of cultural studies researchers. Nevertheless, due to the radical changes of global journalism and journalism cultures, a further multiplication of ideas in theorizing journalism is quite likely.

Martin Löffelholz

Globalization, the Internet, and the
Future of Journalism Theories

it is obvious that the Internet has brought and will bring further
. The Internet allows the distribution of information to large masses
ing a mass medium in the traditional sense of the word. It combines
aspects of interpersonal and mass communication (Morris and Ogan, 1996) with
unknown consequences for both traditional and new media. Considering this, it is
not plausible that one can simply transfer journalism theories from the traditional
media to the Internet. At the very least, a rethinking of the term "mass medium" is
necessary, and so is a reevaluation of established theories.

With the advent of the Internet, communication structures and economic
environments have been changing worldwide. The ongoing development called
globalization also has an impact on media companies and audiences. The larger
companies are now competing in a global media market, and company mergers
affect markets that were formerly divided – by nation, medium, or audience seg-
mentation. Globalization means that borderlines are dissolving, in both a positive
and a negative sense. Borders signify not only an artificial line delimiting freedom,
but also a necessary and meaningful distinction. With the disappearance of language barriers primarily based on traditional national borders, new differences
will develop – of subcultures or companies. Journalism must cope with structural changes as well as audience changes, and there is no easy solution or simple
answer.

While some large media companies aim at a global market, most of the other
"medium" and "small" companies act within a smaller environment. Nevertheless,
there are some other borderlines that may also be crossed, namely those between
journalism and PR, and between journalism and entertainment. Even though one
can argue that these differences were just a projection of a certain "purist" understanding of journalism, it is very certain that at least this understanding is at stake.
Does journalism still provide the audience with current, factual information, or
does it have a stronger orientation toward entertainment and "self-centered" communication (such as public relations) today? Surely, a certain amount of criticism
that journalism is becoming entertainment is exaggerated, but there are still some
changes in company structures that foster such development. If media companies
merge with other large companies, and if the trend toward (diagonal) concentration continues, the idea of journalism with no interest except the production of
news, might no longer be valid.

Given these challenges, journalism will have to adapt to the new situation. This
means that theoretical work in journalism may also change, although this is not
necessarily the case. A social theory of communication might not be directly influenced by a change in technology, for example. However, if the change in technology corresponds to a change in the social embedding of communication, the theory
must consider this. Quite a few of the above-mentioned theories are not up to the
task of modeling change adequately, nor are they interested in this. Especially nor-

mative ideas seem to be not flexible enough to cope with the new media and communication world. Their political undertone reflects a different historical situation; therefore, the normative basis of these approaches has an – arguably – shrinking relevance nowadays.

In contrast to these normative ideas, analytical empiricism will definitely generate new ideas of how to model communication; although limited in range, it is very flexible and always follows empirical development. The other perspectives (theories of action, functional systems theory, integrative social theories, cultural studies; see Table 2.1) have considerable room for new ideas and the improvement of concepts; they are in no way finished business. They offer some interesting ideas and insights not covered by analytical empiricism, especially due to their more global approach. Whether they will promote more research in the future is still in question, but they at least offer several starting points for new, creative ways of thinking about journalism.

Overall, it may be concluded that the development of journalism theories follows neither the linear-cumulative understanding of theoretical emergence introduced by the English philosopher Francis Bacon (1561–1626), nor the regular sequence of normal and revolutionary phases proposed by Thomas Kuhn. Journalism studies is rather an intermittent development of a multiple perspective. Progress is not

Synopsis of basic theoretical concepts in journalism studies

Concept	Context	Focus
Normative individualism	Individualism, normative media studies	Journalism as an addition of talented individuals
Analytical empiricism	Empiricism, neo-positivism, analytical philosophy, middle-range theories	Journalism as gatekeeping, news selection, agenda-setting, etc.
Theories of action	Theories deriving from general sociology	Journalism as social action
Systems theories	Logic of difference, theory of social systems	Journalism as social system
Integrative social theories	Structuration theory, habitus concept, theory of communicative action	Journalism as micro-meso-macro-integration
Cultural studies	Critical theory, semiotics, linguistics, theory of action, materialism	Journalism as popular culture

based on the substitution of "outdated" theories, but on the gain in complexity through the emergence of new theories and modification of older theories. Journalism studies is neither a homogeneous field, nor are there any "main" trends in theoretical work. This multi-perspective approach may be seen negatively as a lack of focus – as it is criticized by some researchers who say there is no academic discipline without a clear core of ideas – or, on the other hand, as the necessary answer to the many challenges of a social scientific description of journalism.

References

Altmeppen, K. D., and Löffelholz, M. (1998). Zwischen Verlautbarungsorgan und, vierter Gewalt. Strukturen, Abhängigkeiten und Perspektiven des politischen Journalismus' [Between announcement organ and fourth estate. Structures, dependencies and perspectives of political journalism]. In U. Sarcinelli (ed.), *Politikvermittlung und Demokratie in der Mediengesellschaft* [*Mediating politics and democracy in the media society*] (pp. 97–123). Opladen and Wiesbaden: Westdeutscher Verlag.

Donsbach, W. (1982). *Legitimationsprobleme des Journalismus: gesellschaftliche Rolle der Massenmedien und berufliche Einstellungen von Journalisten* [*Authentication problems of journalism: The social role of the mass media and vocational attitudes of journalists*]. Freiburg and Munich: Albers.

Görke, A., and Scholl, A. (2006). Niklas Luhmann's theory of social systems and journalism research. *Journalism Studies*, 7(4), 645–56.

Gottschlich, M. (1980). *Journalismus und Orientierungsverlust. Grundprobleme öffentlich-kommunikativen Handelns* [*Journalism and the loss of orientation. Basic problems of public communicative action*]. Vienna, Cologne, and Graz: Böhlau.

Hartley, J. (1996). *Popular reality. Journalism, modernity, popular culture*. London: Arnold.

Johnstone, J. W. C., Slawski, E. J., and Bowman, W. W. (1976). *The news people: A sociological portrait of American journalists and their work*. Urbana, IL: University of Illinois Press.

Löffelholz, M. (2004a). Theorien des Journalismus. Eine historische, metatheoretische und synoptische Einführung [Theories of journalism. A historical, metatheoretical and synoptical introduction]. In M. Löffelholz (ed.), *Theorien des Journalismus* [*Theories of journalism*] (pp. 17–63). Wiesbaden: Verlag für Sozialwissenschaften.

Löffelholz, M. (ed.) (2004b). *Theorien des Journalismus* [*Theories of journalism*]. Wiesbaden: Verlag für Sozialwissenschaften.

Löffelholz, M., and Quandt, T. (2005). Journalism theory: Developments in German speaking countries. *Equid Novi. South African Journal for Journalism Research*, 26(2), 228–46.

Merton, R. K. (1957). *Social theory and social structure*. 2nd, revised edition. Glencoe, IL: Free Press.

Morris, M., and Ogan, C. (1996). The Internet as mass medium. *Journal of Communication*, 46(1), 39–50.

Prutz, R. E. (1971 [1845]). *Geschichte des deutschen Journalismus* [*History of German journalism*]. Göttingen: Vandenhoeck und Ruprecht.

Rühl, M. (1980). *Journalismus und Gesellschaft. Bestandsaufnahme und Theorieentwurf* [*Journalism and society. Status quo and theory design*]. Mainz: Hase und Koehler.

Rühl, Manfred (1969). *Die Zeitungsredaktion als organisiertes soziales System* [*The news-*

paper's editorial department as an organized social system]. Bielefeld: Bertelsmann Universitätsverlag.

Schudson, M. (2003). *The sociology of news*. New York: Norton.

Shoemaker, P. J., and Reese, S. D. (1996). *Mediating the message. Theories of influence on mass media content*. White Plains, NY: Longman.

Weaver, D. H., and Wilhoit, G. C. (1986). *The American journalist: A portrait of US news people and their work*, Bloomington, IN: Indiana University Press.

Weber, M. (1924). *Gesammelte Aufsätze zur Soziologie und Sozialpolitik* [*Collected essays on sociology and social politics*]. Tübingen: Mohr.

Weischenberg, S. (1992). *Journalistik. Theorie und Praxis aktueller Medienkommunikation. Bd. 1: Mediensysteme, Medienethik, Medieninstitutionen* [*Journalism studies. Theory and practice of current media communication. Volume 1: Media systems, media ethics, media institutions*]. Opladen: Westdeutscher Verlag.

White, D. M. (1950). The "gatekeeper": A case study in the selection of news. *Journalism Quarterly*, 27, 383–90.

Zelizer, B. (2004): *Taking journalism seriously. News and the academy*. Thousand Oaks, CA, London, and New Delhi: Sage.

Chapter 3

Journalism in a Globalizing World Society
A Societal Approach to Journalism Research

Manfred Rühl

For journalism research in a globalizing world society, macro conceptions like social system approaches are unavoidable in order to understand better the function of journalism in society and its difference to other forms of public communication, e.g. propaganda, public relations, advertising, entertainment. Societal system theories are an invitation to open up the study of journalism as a system of society, as decision-making organizations and as performing and achieving markets. Unlike approaches focusing entirely on journalists as total individuals, societal system theories are decribing journalistic producers and journalistic recipients as social role structures in world society's journalism.

The old Greek word systema stands for a whole divided into parts, without environmental relations. This whole/parts system idea was able to maintain its position for two and a half thousand years (Riedel, 1990). It was used in the phase called *Zeitungswissenschaft* in early German communications, when "real" newspapers and "real" journals were described, classified, compared, and systemized as journalistic parts (objects) of a sum total (Wagner, 1965). This whole/parts system view was dropped, when problems replaced objects in journalism research. Since the 1940s, several system theories emerged in social sciences, some of them used in journalism research.

Why Societal Approaches Are Needed:
The Case of the Gatekeeper

Current usage of "system theory" (in the singular) is a catchall concept for very different denotations in various disciplines. Some journalism researchers comment on "system theory" to be a settled thing (Russ-Mohl, 1997). We oppose this statement with the thesis that without a sufficiently complex system theoretical architecture, no journalism research can be successful. Let us have a look at an example – the way the so-called gatekeepers were studied by journalism reasearchers.

Social psychologist Kurt Lewin (1947) used the term gatekeeper first, to describe housewives deciding which foods are to end up on the dinner table of their families. Concerning the activities of the gatekeeper, Lewin wrote: "This situation holds not only for food channels but also for the traveling of a news item through certain communication channels in a group" (Lewin, 1951, p. 187). A journalistic gatekeeper study was conducted "to examine closely the way one of the 'gatekeepers' in the complex channels of communication operates his 'gate'." David Manning White (1950/1964, p. 162) seized upon Lewin's concept, observing the activities of one decision-making wire editor of a small Midwestern newspaper, filtering copy and news stories, from inception to publication. Unlike the housewives in Lewin's study, "Mr Gates" was deciding upon subjective criteria, explicitly on his personnel prejudices (Rogers, 1994, p. 335). White's gatekeeper was an individual, and the study did not problemize organizational structures, decision-making programs, occupational and working roles, hierarchical positions, legal and moral norms, or enforceable values, typical social structures in journalism research.

Methodologically, White's and most other journalistic gatekeeper studies rely upon the doctrine of methodological individualism. This method maintains that statements on social matters are completely reducible to statements about individuals, finding interpretive access to underlying motives of those individuals. Max Weber, elaborating on this method, requests that before looking into factual acting of individuals, scholars should know the individual's social and cultural background – whether he is a "king," a "civil servant," an "entrepreneur," a "pimp," or a "magician" (Weber, 1968, p. 15). Aside from some demographic data, we do not know much about the social and cultural background of "Mr Gates."

For more than a quarter of a century, the term gatekeeper stood for the production side of journalism, although the scholarly perspectives of interest have changed to institutional and organizational problems (Robinson, 1973; Weiss, 1977). Individuality kept its research priority, when determinations and dependencies of journalists to editors-in-chief and to publishers were studied (Breed, 1952, 1955; Schulz, 1974). Interviews served to collect data and researchers did not expound problems of journalism as objective, social, and temporal problems in newsrooms. When journalism researchers became interested in the making and manufacturing of news as journalism's reality (Roshcoe, 1975; Tuchman, 1978), they referred to newsrooms in the traditional bipartite way, viewing organizations as courses of events and as hierarchies of positions, without explaining, whether these two parts can be checked empirically, and how they operate in making and manufacturing news. It may be concluded that gatekeeper studies sufficiently did not take into consideration the social and cultural background of journalists and journalistic organizations. The societal dimension of journalism was neglected.

Social Systems Theories

There is a saying that it takes two to tango. Although journalism is considered to be a major societal and cultural achievement, emerging in 19th-century Europe and North America, journalism researchers usually study only the production side. When classical social scientists prepared ground for the study of making, buying, and reading journalistic products, the societal problems of the time, especially industrialization, urbanization, migration, literacy, and democratization came into the game.

Émile Durkheim (1893/1968) conceived social facts as basic elements of social life, and elaborated on division of labor affecting the evolution of modern society. Georg Simmel, intensely affected by the cross-currents of up-and-coming metropolis, operated in many social intersections, examining especially social differentiation (Frisby and Featherstone, 1997). Simmel had a profound impact on Robert E. Park, who emphasized urban journalism and practiced "publicity," that is, public relations, for years (Rühl, 1999), before becoming the sociologist as city editor of the Chicago School (Lindner, 1996). Max Weber (1968) developed new ideas and new methodological approaches for social research, and some of his many interests were directed to domestic and foreign "press cultures," to the newspaper reading of farm workers and industrial workers. Albert Schäffle (1875), Karl Bücher (1896, 1915), Charles Horton Cooley (1909/1972, 1918), and Robert Ezra Park (1903/1972, 1922) reconstructed independently a field of scholarly interests emphasizing the press, journalism, public relations, with social action and forms of communication as basic processes. All of these scholars differed greatly in their reflections and research on journalism, but they all recognized journalism's linkages to society, studying and evaluating societal components such as publishing, journalistic and editorial work, publics and public opinion, media and technologies, readership, advertisement, ideologies, and so on.

At this time, it was fashionable to describe society as an organism in the historical steps of birth, maturity, and death. However, when Schäffle (1875) described society, he used organic terms without putting societal structures into organismic analogies. Immanuel Kant, Georg W. F. Hegel, and Karl Marx designed theories of history with a recognizable system paradigm. Before becoming professor of philosophy, Hegel was a rather successful and well-paid all-round-editor of the daily Bamberger Zeitung. During his eighteen months' stay in Bamberg, his first major work, *Phenomenology of Spirit* (1807/1978), was published, explaining his system paradigm (Rühl, 1999). Unfortunately, Hegel never wrote a book on journalism.

Only in the mid-1940s, when the terms media, mass media and mass communication came up in the United States, they were employed first to criticize American "mass media culture," that is, film, radio, magazines, etc. as a system effecting "mass deceit" in the service of "culture industry" (Adorno, 2001). Theodor W. Adorno claims that products of culture industry are intended to function as goods for economic markets, primarily, tailored to affecting the masses, without attempting to differentiate between media and journalism.

At the time, again almost exclusively in the United States, several cybernetic and communication science system/environment theories are taking shape. The first order cybernetics of observed systems (Wiener, 1946; Ashby, 1956; von Bertalanffy, 1962/1968) stimulate a macro-communication system study in Germany (Reimann, 1968); second order cybernetics of observing systems (von Foerster, 1982) inspired reflections on a variety of communication problems (Krippendorff, 1979). Another theoretical system approach of generalized assumptions and functional relations is known by the collective title Structural Functionalism. Usually, the American sociologist Talcott Parsons is called the best known representative of Structural Functionalism. But we lean to the assumption that Parsons has designed a world society theory of his own, while parts of his theories found entrance in structural functional system theories, particularly developed and promoted by the German sociologist Niklas Luhmann.

More than others, Talcott Parsons and Niklas Luhmann pioneered the analysis (and synthesis) of world society theory. For the purposes of this chapter, we shall focus on the ideas of Luhmann and briefly sketch a few important features of his work. Luhmann is not known as a journalism researcher in a narrower understanding of the concept. But he has an impact on present day journalism research worldwide.

Basic Ideas of Niklas Luhmann

In the preface to the English edition of his first major work, *Social Systems*, Niklas Luhmann confesses: "This is not an easy book. It does not accommodate those who prefer a quick and easy read" and "this holds for the German text, too" (Luhmann, 1995, p. xxxvii). When we try to open up Luhmann's complex thinking for the sake of this chapter, we are convinced to offer a suitable theory of reflections for macro-, meso-, and micro-perspective journalism research.

Luhmann worked out decisive and coherent thoughts for a functional theory of world society, conceived as communication system theory. Entering social sciences in the 1960s and studying with Parsons, Niklas Luhmann began as an action system theorist (Luhmann, 1964, p. 23). When reconstructing a world societal communication theory, the Parsonian world societal action system theory was no longer inspiring. Luhmann noticed inconsistencies, and especially "subject" and "action" were found to be irredeemable for describing world society (Luhmann, 1995, pp. xxxvii–xliv). Instead, Luhmann assumes that the complexity of world society is reduced by social systems. The political system or the economic system, to name just a few, are considered subsystems of world society that were set up to solve particular societal problems. Social systems "are by no means given objects, but constitute their identity by drawing a distinction between the system and its environment and by setting boundaries against their environment" (Görke and Scholl, 2006, p. 646). As basic elements of social systems, Luhmann identifies neither actors nor specific individuals but communication. Individual actors such as journalists are not constituents of social systems but important external co-performers for communication systems.

In the 1970s, Luhmann found communication to be the most sophisticated expression of human abilities. Although mankind practices communication every day and experiences communication as something self-evident, Luhmann advises scholars to start from the premise that communication is improbable, and improbability is not a given phenomenon (Luhmann, 1995, p. 154). Early American sociologists (Albion W. Small, George E. Vincent) likened a "social nervous system" to society's communication apparatus, whereas Robert K. Merton explicitly codified and paradigmatically presented a teleological functional analysis, credited to advance the study of mass communication (Wright, 1989). Luhmann's work does away with notions of system in traditional wording. He reconstructed law, science, religion, economy, politics, media, and art as functional systems of world society (Luhmann, 1997). World society's journalism system, however, was not found on his research agenda.

Problems of Journalism System Research

Reviewing research on journalism as a world societal system, we find approaches with Luhmannian, Parsonian, and Structural-Functionalism impacts (Rühl, 1980; Blöbaum, 1994; Kohring, 1997; Scholl and Weischenberg, 1998; Görke, 1999; Malik, 2004). Some of these empirical journalism-and-society or journalism-in-society studies, however, are not tested with the help of functionally generated data, but with data generated in behavioral-positivist manners. Empirical studies taking into account the societal dimension of journalism and using systems theoretical approaches to define journalism are still rare (Scholl, 2002). In order to identify journalism and to differentiate between journalism and other highly complex social systems such as public relations, advertisement, or propaganda, a unique function of journalism has to be defined (Rühl, 2001). A quarter of a century ago, I described performance and provision of themes for public communication as the specific journalistic function (Rühl, 1980, p. 322).

In the meantime, there have been many changes in state and field of journalism research. Re-entering this definition in interrelation to current world society, journalism's function can be described as asserting selected and varied themes of persuasive (sometimes manipulative) communication, deliberately improving world populations readability, comprehensiveness, and transparency (Rühl, 2004, p. 82). Journalism research works on preserved journalism theories. Primarily journalism re-analyzes sensemaking themes and information in interdependence with societally accepted norms and values, professionalizing labor and challenging problems of literacy, in past, present, and future.

In our days, the populations of constitutional societes around the globe belong to journalism as readers, listeners, and viewers, combining these with the social roles as parents, youth, citizens (or immigrants), consumers, traffic participants, patients, sports fans, tourists, and so on. In different areas of world society, with or without democratic governments, journalism is still growing as urban journalism in mega cities, suburbia, ghettos, country-sides and holiday resorts. Journalism is not a unique achievement. In early 17th-century France there were newspapers and press-related institutions with features and attributes, later on differentiated as journalism, public relations, advertising, or propaganda (Solomon, 1972; Rühl, 1999). Efforts to differentiate between journalism, public relations, advertising and propaganda with the help of specific functions, performances, and tasks, are rather new. But all these persuasive systems can be analyzed on three social levels, on an organizational level (Rühl, 1969, 2002), a market level (Rühl, 1978), and a societal level (Rühl, 1980).

Realigning journalism research is a significant conceptual and theoretical break with gaining information about journalism from collectives of journalistic practitioners. In case studies of newsrooms as organizations with a specific social environment, journalistic operations are steered by pre-programmed decision-making (Rühl, 1969; Dygutsch-Lorenz, 1971; Hienzsch, 1990; Neumann, 1997). Operating journalism starts with obtaining resources in short supply. Producing, distributing, and receiving of journalism causes different costs, not only time and money, but professional work, enforceable topics, sensemaking information, public attention, stabilizing laws, consented ethical principles, public trust, and private confidence. Journalistic resources are divisible and obtainable via markets of politics, economy, labor, lawmaking. Not all journalistic resources can be paid for by money.

The major benefit of this approach is: Journalism cannot be reduced, neither to single journalists nor to life systems (operating brains) or consciousness systems (active thinking). Journalism systems operate circularly, without a known beginning and without a foreseeable end. Journalistic repertoires of possibilities in social memories are texts produced in agencies and other journalistic organizations, in Internet, journals, books, archives, libraries, realized through psychic memories. Journalism systems construct and sustain themselves in this way.

As an academic undertaking, journalism research can be observed as an intersection of world society's journalism system and world society's science system, forming a self-descriptive system containing its own descriptions. Journalism research deserves more attention. Many theoreticians believe that older journalism theories are obsolete. Quite the reverse! In the past two hundred years, families, sciences, economies, politics, religions, journalism also have changed their semantics, sometimes rapidly (Koselleck, 1972). There is no standardized journalism, and our knowledge of journalism is always a selection, variation, and retention in interrelations to changing families, sciences, economies, etc.

Globalization in Journalism Research

For several thousands of years, face-to-face-communication determined mankind. In the middle of the 15th century, typography offered chances for radical changes, when books, newspapers, and journals printed by a letterpress became readable works in vernacular languages, and goods to be evaluated and traded on markets. Different from Latin texts, handwritten and read in medieval monastaries for the order's own use, books, newspapers, and journals are produced for markets, addressing potentially everybody, prompting telecommunication worldwide.

As a researchable concept, globalization implies a theoretical history. The term came up to describe wishful thinking of emperors for a united world, built by secular or religious power. In current issues and controversies, globalization is used more often as an umbrella term for a complex series of _economic, social, political, technological_ and _cultural_ changes, standing for increasing _interdependence_, integration and interaction between peoples and countries in disparate locations. "Global players" are said to dominate markets for goods, money, credits, personnel, and the Internet, being suspect to oppress areas of remote culture or tending to concentrate the sources of energy and knowledge.

Definitions of globalization discussed in communications are highly subjective, depending on political-ideological premises, most of them narrowly related to political-economic problems. When media scholars describe a media globalization, they refer to processes of adapting software applications and web sites, seemingly suitable for global use. Discussed in combined wordings of engineering, economics, culture, marketing, and communications, media globalization is not explicitly referring to journalistic problems, modelling communication as transport of something (Hepp et al., 2005).

Analyzing globalization as changes and confrontations between journalism and other societal systems (politics, economy, religion, law, etc.), world society expresses the foremost comprehensive system of human communication, and as a public communication system journalism is attainable worldwide, second to none. Journalism's sensemaking informations can reach all of us, and we all are well advised to be concerned with what's in the paper, what's on television, or online. There is no centralized journalism but a variety of productions and receptions, diversified locally, regionally, and nationally, bound to different values, norms, themes, and texts. Freedom of the press and voluntary self-control of the press, film, radio, and television are not fixed and standardized frontiers, but borderlines relating journalism's freedom of expression to politics, economy, religion, etc.

For centuries, mankind fixed boundaries between territories, powers, religions, languages, or currencies areas. Modern borderlines are endless horizons, moving themselves at every approach. Yet, all navigators use endless horizons for orientation and guidance (Husserl, 1999), and everything journalism observes as distinguishable, forms, schemes, frames, themes, informations, genres, headlines, decision-making programs, and so forth, they happen on this side of the horizon, not beyond. Concepts and schemes of journalism are known worldwide, but journalism varies structurally – hopefully in the future, too.

Globalizing journalism refers to sensemaking as the ultimate horizon of world society, permeable for new possibilities, drawing up limits for orientation. Journalism responds to globalization with renewing networks of production, organizations, marketing, house-holding, re-entering preserved journalism cultures. A unity of journalism education is not worthwhile. Time costs for googled journalism go down extremely. But what about news offered anonymously, without a traditional newspaper title. Do we trust it (Rühl, 2005)?

References

Adorno, Th. W. (2001). _The culture industry: selected essays on mass culture_; edited and with an introduction by J. M. Bernstein. London and New York: Routledge.

Ashby, W. R. (1956). *An introduction to cybernetics.* New York: Wiley and Sons.

Bertalanffy, L. v. (1962/1968). General system theory: a critical review. *General System Theory*, VII, 1–20. Reprint in W. Buckley (ed.) (1968) *Modern systems research for the behavioral scientist* (pp. 11–30). Chicago, IL: Aldine.

Blöbaum, B. (1994). *Journalismus als soziales System [Journalism as social system].* Opladen: Westdeutscher Verlag.

Breed, W. (1952). The newspaperman, news, and society. PhD dissertation, Columbia University.

Breed, W. (1955). Social control in the newsroom: a functional analysis. *Social Forces*, 33, 326–55.

Bücher, K. (1896). *Arbeit und Rhythmus [Work and rhythm].* Leipzig: Reinicke.

Bücher, K. (1915). *Die deutsche Tagespresse und die Kritik [The German daily press and criticism].* Tübingen: Mohr (Siebeck).

Cooley, C. H. (1909/1972). *Social organization. A study of the larger mind.* New York: Schocken.

Cooley, C. H. (1918). *Social process.* Introduction by Roscoe C. Hinkle. Carbondale, IL: Southern Illinois University Press.

Durkheim, É. (1893/1968). *The division of labor in society.* New York: Free Press.

Dygutsch-Lorenz, I. (1971). *Die Rundfunkanstalt als Organisationsproblem [The broadcasting institution as organizational problem].* Düsseldorf: Bertelsmann Universitätsverlag.

Foerster, H. v. (1982). *Observing systems.* Salinas, CA: Intersystems Publications

Frisby, D., and Featherstone, M. (1997). *Simmel on Culture: Selected Writings.* London: Sage.

Görke, A. (1999). *Risikojournalismus und Risikogesellschaft. Sondierung und Theorieentwurf [Risk journalism and risk society. Analysis and theoretical draft].* Opladen and Wiesbaden: Westdeutscher Verlag.

Görke, A., and Scholl, A. (2006). Niklas Luhmann's theory of social systems and journalism research. *Journalism Studies*, 7(4), 645–56.

Hegel, G. W. F. (1807/1978). *Phenomenology of spirit.* Translation by A. V. Miller, with analysis of the text and Foreword by J. N. Findlay. Oxford: Clarendon Press.

Hepp, A., Krotz, F., and Winter, C. (eds.) (2005). *Globalisierung der Medienkommunikation. Eine Einführung [Globalization and media communication. An introduction].* Wiesbaden: Verlag für Sozialwissenschaften.

Hienzsch, U. (1990). *Journalismus als Restgröße. Redaktionelle Rationalisierung und publizistischer Leistungsverlust [Journalism as residual. Editorial rationalization and loss of "publizistische" performance].* Wiesbaden: Deutscher Universitäts-Verlag.

Husserl, E. (1999). *The idea of phenomenology: A translation of Die Idee der Phänomenologie.* Translation and Introduction by Lee Hardy. Collected works no. 8. Dordrecht: Kluwer.

Kohring, M. (1997). *Die Funktion des Wissenschaftsjournalismus. Ein systemtheoretischer Entwurf [The function of science journalism. A systems theoretical approach].* Opladen: Westdeutscher Verlag.

Koselleck, R. (1972). Einleitung [Introduction]. In O. Brunner, W. Conze, and R. Koselleck, (eds.), *Geschichtliche Grundbegriffe. Historisches Lexikon zur politisch-sozialen Sprache in Deutschland [Basic terms of history. Historical encyclopedia of political-social language in Germany].* Vol. 1 (pp. xiii–xxvii). Stuttgart: Klett-Cotta.

Krippendorff, K. (ed.) (1979). *Communication and control in society.* New York: Gordon and Breach.

Lewin, K. (1947). Frontiers in group dynamics I. Concept, method, and reality in social science, social equilibria, and social change. *Human Relations*, 1(1), 5–42.

Lewin, K. (1951). *Field theory in social science: Selected theoretical papers*. D. Cartwright (ed.) New York: Harper and Row.

Lindner, R. (1996). *The reportage of urban culture: Robert Park and the Chicago school*. Translation by A. Morris with J. Gaines and M. Chalmers. Cambridge, UK: Cambridge University Press.

Luhmann, N. (1964). *Funktionen und Folgen formaler Organisation* [*Function and consequences of formal organization*]. Berlin: Duncker and Humblot.

Luhmann, N. (1995). *Social systems*. Translation by J. Bednarz, Jr., with D. Baecker. Foreword by E. M. Knodt. Stanford, CA: Stanford University Press.

Luhmann, N. (1997). *Die Gesellschaft der Gesellschaft* [*The society of society*]. Two vols. Frankfurt/Main: Suhrkamp.

Malik, M. (2004). *Journalismusjournalismus. Funktion, Strukturen und Strategien der journalistischen Selbstthematisierung* [*"Journalimsjournalism." Function, structures and strategies of journalistic self reporting*]. Wiesbaden: Verlag für Sozialwissenschaften.

Neumann, S. (1997). *Redaktionsmanagement in den USA: Fallbeispiel "Seattle Times"* [*Newsroom management in the USA: The case of "Seattle Times"*]. Munich: Saur.

Park, R. E. (1903/1972). *The crowd and the public, and other essays*. Edited and with an introduction by H. Elsner, Jr. Chicago, IL: University of Chicago Press.

Park, R. E. (1922). *The immigrant press and its control*. New York and London: Harper and Brothers.

Reimann, H. (1968). *Kommunikations-Systeme. Umrisse einer Soziologie der Vermittlungs- und Mitteilungsprozesse* [*Communication systems. Outline of a sociology of mediation and communication processes*]. Tübingen: Mohr (Siebeck).

Riedel, M. (1990). System, Struktur [System, structure]. In O. Brunner, W. Conze, and R. Koselleck (eds.), *Geschichtliche Grundbegriffe. Historisches Lexikon zur politisch-sozialen Sprache in Deutschland* [*Basic terms of history. Historical encyclopedia of political-social language in Germany*]. Vol. 4 (pp. 285–322). Stuttgart: Klett-Cotta.

Robinson, G. J. (1973). Fünfundzwanzig Jahre "Gatekeeper"-Forschung: Eine kritische Rückschau und Bewertung [Twenty-five years of "gatekeeper" research. A critical review and evaluation]. In J. Aufermann, H. Bohrmann, and R. Sülzer (eds.), *Gesellschaftliche Kommunikation und Information. Forschungsrichtungen und Problemstellungen*. Vol. 1 (pp. 344–55). Frankfurt/Main: Athenäum Fischer.

Rogers, E. M. (1994). *A history of communication study. A biographical approach*. New York: The Free Press.

Roshcoe, B. (1975). *Newsmaking*. Chicago, IL, and London: Chicago University Press.

Rühl, M. (1969). *Die Zeitungsredaktion als organisiertes soziales System* [*The newspaper newsroom as organized social system*]. 2nd edition, 1979. Fribourg/Switzerland: Universitätsverlag.

Rühl, M. (1978). Markt und Journalismus [*Market and journalism*]. In M. Rühl and J. Walchshöfer (eds.), *Politik und Kommunikation. Festgabe für Franz Ronneberger zum 65. Geburtstag* [*Politics and communication*] (pp. 237–71). Nuremberg: Verlag der Nürnberger Forschungsvereinigung.

Rühl, M. (1980). *Journalismus und Gesellschaft. Bestandsaufnahme und Theorieentwurf* [*Journalism and society. Review and theoretical groundwork*]. Mainz: v. Hase und Koehler.

Rühl, M. (1999). *Publizieren. Eine Sinngeschichte der öffentlichen Kommunikation* [*Pub-*

lishing. A history of making sense in public communication]. Opladen and Wiesbaden: Westdeutscher Verlag.

Rühl, M. (2001). Alltagspublizistik. Eine kommunikationswissenschaftliche Wiederbeschreibung [Everyday- public communication. A scholarly redescription]. *Publizistik*, 46, 249–76.

Rühl, M. (2002). Organisatorischer Journalismus. Tendenzen der Redaktionsforschung [Organized journalism. Trends of newsroom research]. In I. Neverla, E. Grittmann, and M. Pater (eds.), *Grundlagentexte zur Journalistik* [*Basic texts in journalism studies*] (pp. 303–20). Konstanz: UVK.

Rühl, M. (2004). Des Journalismus vergangene Zukunft. Zur Emergenz der Journalistik [The past future of journalism. The emergence of journalism studies]. In M. Löffelholz (ed.), *Theorien des Journalismus. Ein diskursives Handbuch* [*Theories of journalism. A discourse handbook*]. 2nd edition (pp. 69–85). Wiesbaden: Verlag für Sozialwissenschaften.

Rühl, M. (2005). Vertrauen: kommunikationswissenschaftlich beobachtet [Trust: Observed from a communications perspective]. In B. Dernbach and M. Meyer (eds.), *Vertrauen und Glaubwürdigkeit. Interdisziplinäre Perspektiven* [*Trust and credibility. Multidisciplinary perspectives*] (pp. 121–34). Wiesbaden: Verlag für Sozialwissenschaften.

Russ-Mohl, S. (1997). Arrivederci Luhmann? Vorwärts zu Schumpeter! Transparenz und Selbstreflexivität: Überlegungen zum Medienjournalismus und zur PR-Arbeit von Medienunternehmen [Arrivederci Luhmann? Ahead Schumpeter! Transparency and self reflexivity: Thoughts about media journalism and PR of media companies]. In H. Fünfgeld and C. Mast (eds.), *Massenkommunikation. Ergebnisse und Perspektiven* [*Mass communication. Results and perspectives*] (pp. 193–211). Opladen: Westdeutscher Verlag.

Schäffle, A. (1875). *Bau und Leben des socialen Körpers* [*Structure and life of the social body*]. Vol. 1. Tübingen: Laupp.

Scholl, A. (ed.) (2002). *Systemtheorie und Konstruktivismus in der Kommunikationswissenschaft* [*Systems theory and constructionism in communication studies*]. Konstanz: UVK.

Scholl, A., and Weischenberg, S. (1998). *Journalismus in der Gesellschaft. Theorie, Methodologie und Empirie* [*Journalism in society. Theory, methodology and empiricism*]. Opladen: Westdeutscher Verlag.

Schulz, R. (1974). *Entscheidungsstrukturen der Redaktionsarbeit. Eine vergleichende empirische Analyse des redaktionellen Entscheidungshandelns bei regionalen Abonnementzeitungen unter besonderer Berücksichtigung der Einflußbeziehungen zwischen Verleger und Redaktion* [*Decision structures of newsroom work. A comparative empirical analysis of newsroom decisions of regional newspapers with special consideration of the relationship between publisher and newsroom*]. Rer. pol. Diss. Mainz.

Solomon, H. M. (1972). *Public welfare, science, and propaganda in seventeenth-century France. The innovations of Théophraste Renaudot*. Princeton, NJ: Princeton University Press.

Tuchman, G. (1978). *Making news. A study in the construction of reality*. New York: Free Press, London: Macmillan.

Wagner, H. (1965). Ansätze zur Zeitungswissenschaft. Faktoren und Theorien [Approaches in newspaper studies. Factors and theories]. *Publizistik*, 10, 33–54.

Weber, M. (1968). *Economy and society*. G. Roth and C. Wittich (eds.). Berkeley, CA: University of California Press.

Weiss, H.-J. (1977). *Synopse "Journalismus als Beruf": Schlussbericht* [*Synopsis "journalism as occupation": final report*]. Munich: Arbeitsgemeinschaft für Kommunikationsforschung.

White, D. M. (1950/1964). The "gatekeeper": A case study in the selection of news. *Journalism Quarterly*, 27, 383–90. Reprint in L. A. Dexter and D. M. White (eds.), *People, society and mass communications* (pp. 160–72). London: Free Press.

Wiener, N. (1946). *Cybernetics or control and communication in the animal and the machine*. Cambridge, MA: MIT Press.

Wright, Ch. R. (1989). Functional analysis. In *International encyclopedia of communications*. Vol. 2 (pp. 203–6). New York: Oxford University Press.

Chapter 4

Journalism as a Human Right

The Cultural Approach to Journalism

John Hartley

Cultural studies and journalism overlap in important respects. They are both interested in the mediation of meanings through technology in complex societies. Both investigate ordinary everyday life: journalism from the point of view of reportable events; cultural studies from that of ordinary lived experience. They both display emancipationist tendencies: journalism as part of the modern tradition of liberal freedoms, cultural studies as part of a critical discourse developed around struggles over identity, power, and representation. But the tradition of journalism *research* that has grown up within university programs has tended to focus less on the overall purpose of journalism in modern societies and more on its purpose as a professional occupation in an industrialized and corporate mode of production (Gans, 2004). Cultural approaches have played only a minor role in this tradition. Indeed there is a tendency for cultural and journalistic approaches to be seen as either adversarial or mutually exclusive, despite (or because of) the fact that they share a common interest in the communication of meaning within societies characterized by conflict (Green and Sykes, 2004).

This chapter seeks to perform as well as to describe a cultural approach to journalism. It opens with an account of how cultural studies has approached journalism as an object of study. It is the overall approach – which is critical not quantitative – that is important, rather than any specific set of research findings. The chapter goes on to perform a cultural approach by proposing that journalism should not be seen as a professional practice at all but as a human right.

The Cultural Approach to Journalism

Cultural studies emerged in the 1960s as a critical, intellectual, and educational enterprise. Its purpose was critical, not professional. It was founded on teaching, not research. As an oppositional discourse it was not devoted to improving the expertise of practitioners; it sought to empower *readers and audiences*, not journalists. Therefore, journalism research performed on behalf of the profession, or for news organizations, or as part of the PR industry, was not its main priority.

British cultural studies (Turner, 2002; Lee, 2003) grew directly out of a perceived inadequacy of modern frameworks of knowledge, whether disciplinary (e.g. political science, economics, sociology, and literary studies), or activist (e.g. Marxism), to explain how social change occurred or how it could be encouraged, and for whose benefit. Existing frameworks were based upon *economics* and *politics*, characterizing the human "subject" of modernity as the *worker* and the *voter*, and focusing emancipationist struggles on the workplace by way of the labour movement and trade unionism (economics), and the ballot box by way of Labour Parties in parliaments (politics). But by the mid-20th century, neither of these struggles had precipitated the predicted social transformation and popular emancipation.

Meanwhile, established explanations of the role of culture in society (e.g. literary studies) seemed to ignore culture's impact on both economic and political developments, focusing instead on aesthetic matters. Culture was seen by modernist political and economic analysts as an epiphenomenon, an effect not a cause of change; and by modernist cultural theorists as an antidote to the political and economic direction of the day, not an engine of it. For literary-based approaches, the "subject" of modernity was not the worker or voter but the *reader*.

There was a split between politico-economic and literary-aesthetic approaches to culture, which found institutional form in the division between social sciences and humanities. It is noteworthy that journalism programs in higher education are to be found on both sides of that divide. Early college-based journalism training schemes were largely literary (Hartley, 1996, pp. 247–8), their purpose being to turn out professional writers. But journalism programs are now likely to be located in social science faculties (somewhere between communications and business) or in departments of politics and government. Journalism research is the progeny of these disciplines.

The project of cultural studies too was to integrate the economic (worker), political (voter) and cultural (reader) spheres as a coherent object of study, and to investigate why and how culture may affect the apparently determinant spheres of economics and politics. If working-class people did not behave as their economic and political class interests dictated they should, was there something about their culture that promoted conformism or could promote change? Was culture – after all – causal? (Williams, 1961).

It was at this point that cultural analysts interested in social change started to look in detail at the concept of subjectivity, shifting attention from *the worker* and *voter* (or masses) to *the consumer* in the communicative form of *audiences*. In order to understand why social change did not follow from activism at the factory gate or through the ballot box, the impact of industrialized forms of communication (popular publishing, newspapers, cinema, and broadcasting) on the subjectivity and consciousness of popular readers and audiences was quickly identified as a potential stumbling block. Was journalism, which from its own perspective was a beacon of liberal-democratic freedom, in fact an impediment to the emancipation of classed, raced, gendered, and otherwise "othered" subjects? Was the nightly news part of an apparatus of power and control (Hall et al., 1978; Ericson, Baranek, and Chan, 1987)?

The cultural approach to journalism was interested in the subjectivity of readers and audiences of popular media in order to assess the ideological, political, and economic impact of news media, as part of the apparatus of global corporate communications. However, the social-science/humanities disciplinary divide kicked in again here. The structural and institutional aspects of that apparatus – the operations of the state, corporations, and power-elites – were taken up in studies of the political economy of the culture industries, news media among them. Some critics have regarded political economy as part of the project of cultural studies, while others have seen it as a distinct tendency (Miller, 2001). Meanwhile, cultural analysts have drawn on literary, linguistic, and semiotic traditions to investigate how subjectivity is fixed in language, and how unequal power relations in modern societies are conducted on a day-to-day basis, both in everyday life and through the mass media. They were interested in the production and circulation of meaning in society, in order to answer this question: if power operates to "subject" people in various ways, how is it done communicatively? How is power transmitted through texts such as newspapers and television broadcasts? This led to the practice of "critical readings" or "demystification" of media texts including journalism (Hartley, 1982). The cultural approach to journalism has therefore been interested from the start in the *textual* relations between a powerful "addresser" (media corporations, government agencies) and emancipation-seeking "addressees" (audiences, readers). Such textual relations of "encoding" and "decoding" (Hall, 1973; Hall, Connell, and Curti, 1977) were investigated in detail to try to understand how meaning was conveyed or constructed in large-scale media, what some of the dominant meanings were, and what needed to be done to emancipate subordinate groups from being "subject" to them.

Cultural studies' founding interest in economic and political determinants of change entailed a focus on social class, especially the working class, but over time this extended to gender, ethnicity, race, first peoples, sexual orientation, nation, age group, and to identities formed around taste cultures such as music (mods, punk) or fanship (Trekkies). This attention to identity among consumers and audiences in popular culture has produced much of what is recognized as cultural studies. Journalism *as such* was not its object of study. However, it was in the context of identity politics that user-led and consumer-created journalism first became a significant topic, by way of the zines of subcultures and countercultures, and the counterpublic spheres proclaimed in the feminist, anti-war and environmental movements (Felski, 1989).

Journalism was incorporated into cultural studies not as a *professional* but as an *ideological* practice. News texts (including photos and audio-visual forms of reporting) were *analyzed* for their semiotic, narrative, and other communicational properties, in order to identify what causes the political or social impact that critics believe they have observed; and what resources ordinary people may have or build to resist the same, or to pose and create alternatives. The context of reception is as important in this assessment of journalism as is the context of production. That context is seen as a community (culture), not as a market (economics) nor as a constituency (politics).

The cultural approach to journalism is not a disciplinary project and is not associated with an agreed methodology. Because of its heterogenous and inter-disciplinary nature, one of its distinctive features over the years has been "reflexivity," which in brief means recognizing the position of the investigator both politically and as a knowing subject. Indeed, it is an interventionist form of analysis; its proponents want to change the world, not merely to understand it; many of its writers seek to produce activists.

Journalism as a Human Right

In order to perform – reflexively – the cultural approach, and to show that the universalist ambitions of liberal journalism can be integrated with the emanci-pationist claims of cultural studies, the rest of this chapter takes up the challenge of the bold hypothesis advanced in Article 19 of the Universal Declaration of Human Rights (UDHR), especially that of the radically utopian-liberal idea that "everyone" (no exceptions!) has the right not only to seek and receive but to "impart" (communicate) "information and ideas":

> *Article 19:* Everyone has the right to freedom of opinion and expression; this right includes freedom to hold opinions without interference and to seek, receive and impart information and ideas through any media and regardless of frontiers.
>
> (United Nations, 1948)

As the influential British journalist and editor Ian Hargreaves has also put it: "In a democracy everyone is a journalist. This is because, in a democracy, everyone has the right to *communicate* a fact or a point of view, however trivial, however hide-ous" (Hargreaves, 1999, p. 4).

Hargreaves' real challenge, like that of the UDHR itself, is to society at large. But it is also a challenge to journalists and journalism educators; therefore to journalism research. If "*everyone* is a journalist," then how can journalism be *professed*? If its real extent is "everyone in a democracy," then journalism research needs to extend its horizons beyond the occupation of journalist or the news industry as presently constituted.

If "everyone is a journalist," then there is a challenge to cultural studies here too. For the *consumer* (reading public) is transformed into the *producer* (jour-nalist). What happens when the "reading public" (audience or consumer) of modernity turns into the "writing public" (user, "prosumer" or "ProAm") of global interactive media (Leadbeater and Miller, 2004; Bruns, 2005)?

Journalism as an Ethnicity

Until recently, the means have not been available to turn the UDHR's univer-sal human right into a right that can be exercised by humans in general. Instead, *journalism* has exercised that right on behalf of the public. In representative democracies, we have grown used to "representative journalism" – our freedom to impart is exercised by them on everyone's behalf (in the public interest). Like representative politics, this has become an increasingly professionalized, corporatized, and specialized occupation, and increasingly remote from the common life and lay population it represents.

Meanwhile, journalism has grown up throughout the modern period as an occupation with a strong culture of separation between insiders and outsiders. Indeed, what with their "nose for news," their "gut feeling" for a story, and the idea that good journalists are "born not made" (Given, 1907, p. 148), there is a sneaking suspicion that journalism may be experienced by insiders more as an *ethnicity* than as a human right. Indeed, journalists are beginning to conform to the definitional status used in Australia and elsewhere to identify Aboriginal people: to qualify as such, you need to: (i) be descended from; (ii) identify and live as; and (iii) be accepted by a particular community which wants to recognize, preserve, and transmit its unique cultural heritage (ADAA, 1981, p. 8). In their own eyes, journalists are literally a tribe.

A corollary of this distinction between journalism's "we" community and its outside is that journalism research is routinely confined to the study of the insider perspective. Journalism education, likewise, means training for jobs in existing newsroom organizations. Few if any journalism schools educate for journalism as a human right; but many assume that anyone who has not practiced journalism as a newsroom employee is not competent to profess journalism, nor should they be allowed to educate those for whom it will become a primary occupation. The result of this is that journalism research and education have become part of a *restrictive practice*. They are designed to keep outsiders *out* of journalism.

It may be protested at this point that that is a highly desirable situation, because journalists ought to be trained to high standards, and entry into the profession ought to be restricted to those who can do a good job, as in other professions such as medicine and the law. That is a persuasive argument, but unfortunately it conforms neither to the facts of journalism as practiced in many countries (where the way someone looks can trump good training), nor to the interests of societies that espouse individual freedom and liberal democracy. The societal objection to professionalism is that restricting journalism to those who have qualified by whatever process is tantamount to licensing the expression of ideas, which is simply antidemocratic. In some countries, training itself is viewed with suspicion by editors, owners, and even many senior journalists, for whom it is not a profession but a trade to be learnt on the job. As a result, it is still possible to work as a journalist without any professional training. At the same time, the majority of journalism graduates do not go on to work in newsrooms. The laudable desire to have competent practitioners and an explicit understanding of the practice is directly at odds with both industry and democratic imperatives.

Journalism schools' own consumers, meanwhile, suggest a very different possibility. Many undergraduates take journalism degrees as a new form of the general arts degree, one with practical skills and engagement with political and business applications. They may have no intention of gaining entry to the (increasingly bureaucratized and proletarianized) corporate newsroom. They are already acting as though everyone is a journalist, and honing some critical skills without wanting to "be" journalists.

Journalism as a Transitional Form

Scholarship about the production side of news has obscured the fact that despite its longevity (about 400 years), journalism "as we know it" may be a *transitional form*, constructed upon the technical impossibility of achieving its full democratic potential, namely that *everyone* has a right to *practice* it. During the mechanical and broadcast phases of modernity, journalism depended on the printing press or electronic media production techniques, where increasingly heavy capital investment was needed to achieve wide-scale reach and ratings. It developed a *one-to-many* model of *mass* communication; the antithesis of the right to individual freedom of expression which it purported to represent.

But now the interactive phase of modernity has begun to take technical shape and unsurprisingly journalism has become one of the first victims of post-broadcast interactive media, starting with the Internet (Matt Drudge), but quickly burgeoning to encompass various user-led forms regardless of technological platform including e-zines, blogging and what Axel Bruns (2005) calls "collaborative" online journalism. Journalism has transferred from modern expert system to contemporary open innovation – from "one-to-many" to "many-to-many" communication.

So, out with journalism as an ethnicity; in with journalism as a human right. If journalism is a *human* right then it is necessary not only to theorize it as a craft that everybody can practice, but also to extend what counts as journalism beyond the democratic-process model to encompass much more of what it means to be human; especially the world of private life and experience, and the humanity of those lying outside favored gender, ethnic, national, age or economic profiles that are targeted by corporate news media. Such an eventuality has been thoroughly rehearsed, as it were, in the alternative and social-movements media, the underground or countercultural press, community broadcasting, fanzines; and also in cultural or entertainment forms of mainstream journalism including fashion, lifestyle, consumer, and leisure reporting (Lumby, 1999). These forms employ many of the world's journalists, but they barely rate a mention *as journalism* in journalism schools, which remain wedded to watchdog, fourth estate or First-Amendment models of journalism as the representation – and representative – of the democratic process (Gans, 2004), and concomitantly dismissive of non-news or lifestyle journalism which is equated with feminized consumption and for that reason despised.

Journalism and Culture

Research into journalism as a human right, a *general capacity for communicative action*, has not yet been established. But it too has been rehearsed, in a branch of inquiry that focuses on the media consumer and the context within which the commodity form of news is taken up into people's everyday lives to become culture. This is the very place where cultural studies first came in (Hoggart, 1957; Hall et al., 1978). Cultural approaches to journalism start where the latter becomes *meaningful*. They are interested in the moment when political economy, textual system, cultural form and ideology converge upon the point of consciousness, the point where cultural identities are forged in an alloy of symbolic and economic values. Cultural studies wants to know what journalism means in the context of its social and cultural uptake. But in contemporary society (mechanico-electronic modernity) journalism as a *practice* is separated from journalism as *meaning*. There has thus been a division of intellectual labour, where journalism research concentrates on the producer and practice (public affairs), and cultural studies on the consumer and meaning (private life), and both tend not to dwell on the fact that the practice and meaning of journalism ought to be understood as the same object of study.

In cultural studies, consumers are not conceptualized as passive or behavioral. Like journalists they too are agents – in fact their *sense-making practices* are what make journalism meaningful *as* social uptake. Such practices begin with decoding and may end at the ballot box, the bargain or the barricade. Everyone's position is structural and governed in many ways, but at the same time it is creative, productive, and causal; it is *action* not *behavior*. Here then, in a cultural context, are found *actions constrained by power*, the *making* of sense using classed, raced, gendered, and socioeconomically shaped subjectivity within everyday life. So the cultural approach to journalism starts from the "wrong" end of the value chain. Instead of beginning with origination – the ownership, manufacture or authorship of corporate news – the cultural approach typically starts at its destination, with the readers/audience or consumers of news media, understood as part of culture. From this cultural perspective, consumers may be seen as a multimedia "reading public," successors to the early modern "republic of letters" (Hartley 2004a, 2004b). They are not reduced to the status of an effect of marketing, media or political campaigning. In the cultural approach, ordinary people's interactions with journalism and news media are investigated within the rhythms and "personal politics" of everyday life, in order to study the anthropological process of sense making and identity formation in modern societies, including cultural struggles and identity politics that frequently do not even rate a mention in mainstream news media, much less in journalism schools.

Everyone Is a Journalist

The UN Declaration of journalism as a human right is aspirational; a challenge to action, not a description of facts. It represents an ideal type of liberal democratic polities. If it is to mean anything in practice it needs to be championed, extended, used, and defended. As Aboriginal lawyer Mick Dodson said in reference to the right of indigenous peoples to self-determination: "in the world of the real-politic, neither the existence nor even the legal recognition of a right are sufficient to guarantee its enjoyment" (Dodson, 1994). Many of the most progressive and important initiatives in journalism since Milton (1644) were undertaken by men and women who claimed journalism as a human right *by practicing it*. Without permission they started to publish journals. From this point of view, journalistic history is an accrual of discourses and practices organized around the simple *exercise* of that right. But there are many forces or powers working to limit the realization of the UN Declaration, including most of what counts as contemporary journalism, which from this perspective is an *impediment* to its aspirations.

For if everyone is a journalist, there can be no theory of journalism based on its *professional* production, on its *industrial* organization (including ownership and control), its *textual* form (from news to PR) or even its *reception*, for none of these is essential.

- The *professionalization* of journalism is among other things a restrictive practice designed to create scarcity of labor and therefore work for the already professionalized.
- The *industrialization* of media limits those who can communicate on a society-wide basis to the tiny number who can afford the cost of entry into "mass" media.
- As a *textual system* accrued by custom and practice over several centuries, journalism has taken on some generic characteristics that work powerfully to exclude various forms of expression from what counts as journalism.
- The *regulation* of media is used both correctively and protectively to limit journalism – to redress defamation, obscenity, and the like, or to protect identities and minorities from opinions that are legislatively deemed too hideous to be allowed journalistic expression.
- The right to express opinion or to gain information has been *constrained by power* – in practice it is not neutral as to gender, class, race, age, etc. The "logic of democratic equivalence" may inspire struggles by various social movements to extend the right to women, workers, people of color, children, etc., but universality is never achieved in practice and even small extensions require struggle and leadership.

Quite a few entrepreneurs have found work and wealth, and some have exercised political or cultural power, by increasing the scale, efficiency, and productivity of media communication. Such achievements – even up to the scale of media empires – cannot be excluded from a theory of journalism but neither can they be its foundation, for the model of journalism that is commercially definitive now can be countermanded by someone having a different idea that catches on, as witness the current ascendancy of personal journalism (blogs) and search-engine journalism (Google News).

A Writing Public

Opinion and information become journalism only when they are circulated among a public. Media technologies and a literate reading public are both needed to "impart" them, which is why journalism is a modern phenomenon, unknown in premodern societies. Historically, in direct opposition to the Declaration, access and even capability have not been generally distributed. While modern mass media, both print and broadcasting, have been very efficient at gathering populations to "read" on page and on screen, such that more or less everyone in the old democracies is at least exposed to journalism, they have been less successful in extending the *practice* of journalism so widely. Modernity has been a "read-only" era, not a "read-write" era for most citizens. However, consideration of just this problem demonstrates the importance of the UN Declaration because it makes clear that modernity remains an incomplete project, as Habermas has said. Effort is required to extend the practice of journalism to "everyone." However, when that is done, or even imagined, the nature of what we habitually understand to be journalism changes completely. Journalism research therefore has to look toward the *history* of ways in which "everyone" has – or has not – been brought into the public domain of information and opinion, and toward the *culture* in which "everyone" is located in order to practice their right to communicate. It has to investigate the *uses* of public information and opinion in democratic or democratizing societies.

The reading public or republic of letters was one of early journalism's great creations, dating from the age of Johnson, Addison, and Tom Paine in the modernizing 18th century (Hartley, 1996, 2004b). It was extended to a mass reading public during the industrializing 19th century. For its part, cultural studies was launched by Richard Hoggart's *Uses of literacy* (1957), a study of the reading public when the latter had reached mass scale and the information media had achieved mass entertainment status. Ever since, cultural studies has been preoccupied with the moment at which media production becomes communication and culture – the moment of *use* in the circumstances of ordinary life.

Now the time has come when the idea of a multimedia reading public can be seen for what it really is – a halfway house toward full "read-write" literacy. The time has come, in short, to think about a *writing public*. Journalism's interest in the democratic process, factual reporting and compelling stories about the real can be combined with cultural studies' interest in critical activism within the context of power, lived experience and ordinary life. Thence it is possible to re-found journalism studies to address the "writing public."

Globalization and a Redactional Society

A problem yet to be faced here is that unless a reading public is formed around it, the right to "impart" information may not be realizable, because in some forms of expression there are more people writing than reading. If everyone is speaking, then who is listening, and on what kind of apparatus? That problem resolves itself into the question of creative editing or "redaction" – a journalistic practice that is swiftly becoming the defining art form of the age. I conceptualize contemporary society as "redactional" (Hartley, 2000). The editorial practices of the media, for example, may reveal presuppositions about the culture and the various groups within it, enabling conclusions to be drawn about how meaning is sourced, and explaining differences in the treatment of identities from business leaders and celebrities to foreigners and indigenous youth. Generalizing from such investigations, a "redactional society" is one in which *editorial* practices determine what is understood to be true and what policies and beliefs should follow from that; and what is the contemporary equivalent of beautiful (e.g. innovative, artistic, sexy, dark, entertaining, cool, original or strange) and how desires should be ordered around that. Such a scenario has emerged out of the combination of late-20th-century economic and technical ingredients – the globalization of media and entertainment content and the beginnings of mass scale in the use of interactive communication. Editorial practices are required to make the potentially overwhelming and chaotic possibilities of such plenitude into coherent packages for users, whether these are individuals, businesses or even nations.

This is part of a larger argument about long-term shifts along the "value chain" of meanings (Hartley, 2004a), where what was accepted socially as the source of meaning – and thence legitimacy – has drifted from author (medieval), via text (modern), to consumer (now). In medieval times, the source of meaning was God, the ultimate author(ity). In the modern era meaning was sourced to the empirical object or document, the observable evidence. But now, meaning is sourced to popular readerships or audiences, and is determined by the plebiscite (Hartley, 2006).

In contemporary societies, where values, truths, and meanings are fragmented into the number of sovereign citizens or consumers that make up a total population or market, there is no explicit or agreed mechanism (authority) for deciding which should prevail apart from weight of numbers. So elaborate mechanisms have evolved to *scale up* the myriad sources of meaning, and these are proliferating across many areas of public and mediated life. They include *redaction* and *the plebiscite* (Hartley, 2006). Redaction is the art form of editing, where existing materials are brought together into a new form. Journalism has begun to change from news gathering to a redactional function: a prime job of the journalist is to sift existing data and make sense of that for readers, not to generate new information. The process is evident in Google News, which edits thousands of news web sites into one, presenting the top stories around the world via an algorithm (not a journalist but a sort of automated plebiscite) that ranks them a by number of occurrences on the Internet and by recency (news value).

Globalization of digital content consumption also entails a society in which "everyone is a journalist" or can be. Not only can they express an opinion or circulate information via read-write media forms such as email, blogs, web sites, SMS, and the like, but their views can be gathered and processed into collective forms, ranging from the question of the day on Sky News to "best of . . ." competitions run by media organizations such as the BBC.

But in the meantime, *journalism* has so massively expanded that it is unrecognizable as *news*. No longer confined to the investigation of wrongdoing in politics, decision-making in government and business, or achievement in sport and entertainment, journalism in non-news areas has rapidly outgrown its parent. Corporate communication, PR, and marketing are routinely performed by journalists and as journalism. Fashion, travel, celebrity, makeover, and lifestyle shows on television are among the most envied jobs for aspiring journalists and among the most popular cultural forms. Magazines are more dynamic than newspapers, which have begun to function as magazines, at least at weekends. Information exchange in specialist areas, the traditional province of magazines, has migrated to the web, where there is so much information on any given special interest – genealogy, for instance – that new web sites and magazines are spawned to help people navigate it. In short, a society in which everybody is a journalist begins to be imaginable, whether their practice is direct or sampled or mashed-up via some *plebiscitary* or *redactional* representation. This is the terrain that a cultural theory of journalism needs to investigate.

Immediately, questions arise, all of which are good for further *research*:

1 How to *access* the right to write – questions of *literacy* in new media and not only technical skills but the full array of creative competence that goes beyond self-*expression* to *communication*, and thence to objective *description* and *argumentation*, extending literacy from "read only" to "read and write".
2 How to *organize* and edit the billions of pages of writing – not just technical questions about scaling, data-mining and archiving, but deeper questions about how to edit them for a media-saturated population who are producers as well as consumers; these are questions of *redaction* that need to be answered in an "economy of attention" (Lanham, 2006).
3 How to *represent* facts and opinions back to society – questions about how opinions can be scaled up; which are questions of the *plebiscite*.
4 How to *tell* the truth, and how to tell when it is being *told* – questions of communicational *ethics*.
5 How to hold together the "top" and "bottom" of a stratified society? – linking diverse and even conflictual readerships in a truth-seeking discourse about what is happening now? This requires research into the practice of *readership* in a context where utterance is valued above understanding (the collective hive over authorized wisdom).
6 In an era when *everyone* is a journalist, where are the greats and how do they emerge into visibility? This raises the question of journalism's appeal and communicability as a textual experience for readers – what used to be called "*literariness.*" What is good journalism; how can that be *universally* promoted?

If everybody is a *journalist*, then everyone has a right not just to express but also to *circulate* information and opinions that they actually hold, even when these are seen by others as harmful, "hideous" or wrong-headed (Hargreaves, 1999). So-called user-led innovation will reinvent journalism, bringing it closer to the aspirational ideal of a right for everyone. Journalism will be reinvented, but judging by what is currently done in journalism schools and in the name of journalism studies, the last people to know may be professional journalists.

References

ADAA (Australian Department of Aboriginal Affairs), Constitutional Section (1981). *Report on a review of the administration of the working definition of Aboriginal and Torres Strait Islander*. Canberra: AGP.

Bruns, A. (2005). *Gatewatching: Collaborative online news production*. New York: Peter Lang.

Dodson, M. (1994). The end in the beginning: redefining Aboriginality. Retreived June 2, 2006, from hreoc.gov.au/speeches/social_justice/end_in_the_beginning.html

Ericson, R., Baranek, P., and Chan, J. (1987). *Visualizing deviance: A study of news organizations*. Milton Keynes: Open University Press.

Felski, R. (1989). *Beyond feminist aesthetics*. Cambridge, MA: Harvard University Press.

Gans, H. (2004). Journalism, journalism education, and democracy. *Journalism and Mass Communication Educator*, 59(1), 10–17.

Given, J. L. (1907). *Making a newspaper*. New York: Henry Holt.

Green, K., and Sykes, J. (2004). Australia needs journalism education accreditation. *Jour-Net international conference on Professional Education for the Media*. Retrieved June 2, 2006, from portal.unesco.org/ci/en/ev.php-URL_ID=19074&URL_DO=DO_TOPIC&URL_SECTION=201.html

Hall, S. (1973). *Encoding and decoding in the media discourse*. Stencilled paper no. 7, Birmingham, CCCS.

Hall, S., Connell, I., and Curti, L. (1977). The "unity" of current affairs television. *Working Papers in Cultural Studies*, 9, 51–93.

Hall, S., Critcher, C., Jefferson, T., Clarke, J., and Robert, B. (1978). *Policing the crisis: Mugging, the state and law and order*. London: Hutchinson.

Hargreaves, I. (1999). The ethical boundaries of reporting. In M. Ungersma (ed.), *Reporters and the reported: The 1999 Vauxhall Lectures on Contemporary Issues in British Journalism* (pp. 1–15). Cardiff: Centre for Journalism Studies.

Hartley, J. (1982). *Understanding news*. London: Routledge.

Hartley. J. (1996). *Popular reality: Journalism, modernity, popular culture*. London: Edward Arnold.

Hartley, J. (2000). Communicational democracy in a redactional society: The future of journalism studies. *Journalism: Theory, Practice, Criticism*, 1(1), 39–47.

Hartley, J. (2004a). The "value chain of meaning" and the new economy. *International Journal of Cultural Studies*, 7(1), 129–41.

Hartley, J. (2004b). "Republic of letters" to "television republic"? Citizen readers in the era of broadcast television. In L. Spigel and J. Olsson (eds.), *Television after TV: Essays on a medium in transition* (pp. 386–417). Durham, NC, and London: Duke University Press.

Hartley, J. (2006). "Reality" and the plebiscite. In K. Riegert (ed.), *Reality politics: The entertainment of politics in television programming*. New York: Peter Lang.

Hoggart, R. (1957). *The uses of literacy*. London: Chatto and Windus.

Lanham, R. (2006). *The economics of attention: Style and substance in the age of information*. Chicago, IL: University of Chicago Press.

Leadbeater, C., and Miller, P. (1994). *The "Pro-Am" revolution*. London: Demos. Retrieved June 2, 2006, from demos.co.uk/catalogue/proameconomy/

Lee, R. E. (2003). *Life and times of cultural studies: The politics and transformation of the structures of knowledge*. Durham, NC: Duke University Press.

Lumby, C. (1999). *Gotcha. Life in a tabloid world*. Sydney: Allen and Unwin.

Miller, T. (ed.) (2001). *A companion to cultural studies*. Oxford: Blackwell.

Turner, G. (2002). *British cultural studies*. 3rd edition. London: Routledge.

United Nations. (1948). *Universal declaration of human rights*: Adopted by the General Assembly of the UN, December 10. Retrieved June 2, 2006 from www.unhchr.ch/udhr/miscinfo/carta.htm

Williams, R. (1961). *Culture and society 1780–1950*. Harmondsworth: Penguin.

Chapter 5

The Structure of News Production
The Organizational Approach to Journalism Research

Klaus-Dieter Altmeppen

Why an Organizational Approach to Journalism?

Organization has attended the newsroom since its beginning. Over time, occupational structures were outpaced, the roles of journalists changed, further divisions of labor, such as departments and sections, were established, and industrial disciplines aiming at a more routine organization of news production were introduced into the newsroom (Nerone and Barnhurst, 2003). Structures, roles, departments, and routines are typical terms of an organizational approach in general, including in journalism.

When journalists start their daily work, many parts of their job are already predetermined. The internal structure of the newsroom (e.g. departments, sections) is fixed; journalists know what is involved with gathering and selecting news in their roles as reporters or editors; they know about their work routines in respect to the criteria of news selection and investigation; they know about the work flow, hierarchies, and communication in the newsroom. The newsroom as an organization is the entity that enables groups of journalists to produce a newspaper, a magazine, a news web site, or a radio or television program.

News coverage is not the result of the work of individual journalists, as early findings in journalism research suggested. It depends much more on the specific organizational details in the newsroom, on the different occupational roles, on the inherent structure determined by the goals of the journalistic organization, on the influences of various technologies, and on the repercussions of media markets and competition between media companies. Even though, for example, the individual level and the analysis of role perception are important, the individual journalist is always embedded in organizational patterns which, as prearranged structures, influence the journalist's work and behavior in every newsroom.

Whereas a large part of research in journalism focuses on the role conceptions, attitudes, and beliefs of the individual journalist, the organizational approach to journalism is, contrariwise, concentrated on tracing the impact of the superordinate level of organization with its roles, its structures, and the policy and governance of the media organizations' leadership. Due to this, the organizational patterns indicate the distinguishing aspects of newsroom organization. Generally, both of these perspectives confirm the findings of Shoemaker and Reese (1996,

p. 140), who emphasize that, at the organizational level, "we are dealing with larger, more complicated, more macro structures."

All of these structures contribute in a greater or lesser degree to the shape of the organization, which in turn influences journalistic work, which, at the very least, alters the mass media content. Thus, knowledge about the organizational influence on journalism is of importance when reviewing the causes for the outcome of the journalists' work. For journalism research, the organization is an important factor in identifying the conditions under which news is produced. Researchers are interested in revealing what happens before the story is written, and wish to be able to analyze the forces behind the headlines. The question, how news coverage is produced, leads straight to the organizational level. In the long run, the organizational approach to journalism enables tracing the development of media organizations, and especially the newsroom, and enables comparisons of how journalism emerges (Nerone and Barnhurst, 2003).

Organizational approaches to journalism focus on three different levels. The first is the relationship between the individual journalist and the newsroom. The central point at this level is the range of mutual expectations between the individual and the organization, ranging from hard facts, such as salary, to softer criteria, such as job satisfaction. The second level deals with the relationships between the news organization and other organizations. Here, the media competition is one focal point; others are the interplay between public relations and journalism, and between journalism and the news wires. At the third level, the relationship between news organization and society is a topic where certain influences of society on journalism, and vice versa, are analyzed.

The organizational approach to journalism is less based on a single coherent model but rather characterized by a great variety of different, and sometimes competing, approaches. But there are certain terms such as organization, structures, and management that play a greater or lesser role in every analysis of newsrooms. These terms are explained in more detail in the second part of this chapter. The third part exemplifies the application of organizational studies in journalism research. The fourth part gives a forecast of future challenges in organizational journalism research.

Vertices of the Organizational Approach to Journalism: Organization, Structures, and Management

Organization, the first important vertex, is one of the crucial elements of all societies. Political parties, tax offices, the National Basketball Association (NBA), and finally all commercial companies, including the media, are organizations. The reason is that every time when people work together to solve specific problems or to accomplish a particular aim, they have to coordinate their collaboration and motivate each other to achieve that aim. Hence, the prior function of an organization is to coordinate and motivate the work and the tasks of the members of that organization.

All organizations are characterized by three specific features. First, organizations are oriented toward achieving specific aims over the long term. This goal direction is of great importance for the entire organization because the goals formulated by the management determine the work of all the staff. The main goal of an organization is "to make a profit" (Shoemaker and Reese, 1996, p. 145). The value of an organization depends on money to pay the staff, to allocate newsrooms and their equipment, and to satisfy the needs of the owners or stakeholders in general, and the stockholders in particular.

Due to the economic goal, the management imposes a structure on the organization. Thus, the second feature of an organization is that it has an established and accepted order and structure. The most popular way to describe the structure of an organization is through the organizational chart which indicates the departments (for example, editor, advertising, circulation), and the different roles in the departments, e.g. the executive editor, who oversees other editors, who in turn supervise reporters, photographers, etc. (Shoemaker and Reese, 1996, p. 143).

The more complex an organization is, the more complex the third feature will be. An organization coordinates its activities and available resources in such a way that it can ensure the achievement of its (economic) goals for long-term survival. Complex organizational structures enhance the task of coordination as they enforce the number of business units, departments, and occupational roles. New technologies, for example, confront the organization with changing demands that upset the existing structure in the way it would require new types of work flow. Decreasing revenues minimize available resources and lead to the restructuring of organizational patterns. Often, management must respond to new challenges by cutting costs and establishing new means of coordination. —

Since the response of an organization to upcoming challenges is to restructure itself, structure is then the second most important term after organization. The most important structures of an organization are the departments and roles. Concerning the roles of journalists, the different roles in the horizontal (editor, reporter, correspondent, and photographer) and vertical direction (editor-in-chief, senior editor) are crucial as they "show who does what" (Shoemaker and Reese, 1996, p. 142). Every different role designates what is expected of the individuals hired into these roles, and the lines of authority. The editor-in-chief is responsible for the entire coordination of the newsroom for producing a complete newspaper, while reporters have to coordinate the processes that they use in gathering the news.

But moreover, the organizational approach claims to analyze not only the structure inside certain departments of a media organization, but also attempts to reveal the intersections between such different departments as the newsroom and advertising or circulation department. To produce a newspaper or a 24-hour television program, all the departments of an organization have to be coordinated with respect to this goal. Finally the organizational approach enables research into the competition between media organizations for resources (e.g. an exclusive story, or the highest circulation) and the relationship between media organizations and society. The latter relationship deals with the societal functions of media organizations, such as public services, a goal that is often built into the overarching objective of profit margins.

The institution responsible for making decisions about goals is the management. Hence, media management is another important term that has to be considered when analyzing media organizations. When an organization has to solve problems and achieve aims, the question is, who defines these problems and aims? This is the task of the media managers, for example within the entire organization, it should be the owner, the sales manager, and advertising manager. In the newsroom, at the middle management level, editors, producers, and coordinators comprise the organizational roles. At the top level, corporate and news executives such as the editor-in-chief "make organization policy, set budgets, make important personnel decisions, protect commercial and political interests of the firm" (Shoemaker and Reese, 1996, p. 151). The field of media management deals with questions about how management sets policy and the governance of the organization; it addresses questions of leadership and decision-makers in the organization; and it studies the work of the media managers who organize, set budget, and work with people while being engaged in market analyses, product planning, promotion, production, and distribution. Altogether, management bridges the shape of the organizational structure with the question who manages the structure in what preferred way.

These structures affect the way news is produced because they influence what journalists report, what news an editor writes, and also the decisions about what should be published. Organizational structures represent constitutional conditions for producing news, because news

> does not merely come to be. It is produced by people, working in complex organizations embedded in a larger socio-cultural and historical context. News work is a social process, undertaken by occupants of roles, organized into social structures which serve to link individual occupational efforts in a way that allows the individual performers to function as members of a team which turns out a single, conjointly produced performance for the audience.
>
> (Gassaway, 1984, p. 16)

Definition, characteristics, and differences of media organizations and newsrooms

So far, we have pointed out a few examples of what media organization is, but we have not exactly defined the term "media organization." And furthermore, we have not argued whether media organizations as a whole are comparable to other organizations, or whether there are significant distinctions. There are a couple of aspects that indicate differences between media and other organizations. One of these aspects is the societal role of the media that is expressed through the specific protection of media by certain laws and amendments. This protection tends to ensure the public role of media by being watchdogs and interpreters of public issues and events. However, such protection implicates responsibilities that media managers should keep in mind when deciding the aims of the organization. Those responsibilities are, for instance, the public expectation that reporting should be credible and trustworthy. These responsibilities distinguish media products from other products such as shirts, cars, and food. Media products have a twofold orientation. They have to maintain the media's business while still performing the societal functions of media.

The economic goals of media organizations and the public role might be a cause for conflicts between owners and the newsroom staff, although most of the time the profit margin is the stronger argument. For this reason, the definition of media organization is dictated much more heavily by the economic view. "An organization can be defined as the social, formal, usually economic entity that employs the media worker in order to produce media content" (Shoemaker and Reese, 1996, p. 144). The production process of media content can be divided into at least three steps: gathering information, producing finished copies, and distributing the message (Lavine and Wackman, 1988, p. 11). Gathering information comprises the work of the reporters who investigate and check sources, and the work of the writers who package the raw material. In the second step of production the articles or broadcast reports have to be transformed into entire newspapers or broadcasts. Distribution entails transporting the message to the audience. Journalists perform only the first step and parts of the second step as these are the tasks of the newsroom, whereas production is supported by technicians such as typesetters and cameramen.

This division of labor reveals that the organizational approach to journalism should concentrate on two aspects. The first is the internal organization in the newsroom, whereas the second comprises the newsroom as a department of the entire media organization. The newsroom's internal structure strikes the coordination between different departments and the specific roles of journalists. The second aspect is related to the function and performance of the newsroom in the interplay of all departments that enables media organizations to assemble entire newspapers, magazines, radio and television broadcasts, and web sites.

Journalists are first and foremost members of the newsroom, where they have to perform the tasks expected of them in their roles as reporters, writers, and producers. The function of journalism is to select, to edit, and to disseminate topics that are informative as well as relevant for selected target groups (Löffelholz, 2003, p. 42). The newsroom, too, is the organizational background for the public roles of journalists, such as disseminators or interpreters of issues and events, or as watchdogs who observe the incidents under the surface of the political or economic system. Most of the time, the societal role of journalists is in conflict with the second aspect, the role of journalists as members of a media organization. Inside the media, the journalists also have to meet the expectations of the entire organization. This means that they have to yield certain to benefits for the organization. For the same reason that journalists are employees of the media organization that pays their salaries and provides the resources for the journalists' work, the organization also expects a specific amount of services in return, with priority, of course, to the completion of the tasks ascertained in the labor contract.

Whereas writers, editors, and reporters as front-line employees have no day-to-day contact with the owners of media organizations, middle- and top-level management do have such contact. The editor-in-chief and his representatives are integrated into the top-level management of the media organization, and represent the needs of their newsroom department in the management's decision-making process. In often-difficult negotiations, they struggle for scarce resources with other managers from the advertising and distribution departments, and also with the owners. Even though the newsroom and its staff are crucial within media organizations, decreasing resources often also lead to lowering newsroom budgets. Lower budgets and cost reductions usually have a direct effect on the media content because the editorial decisions are changed when the work has to be conducted by fewer staff, or when less money is available for investigation.

The new demand is to balance business with journalism. "As profit margin pressures have persisted, newspaper executives have found themselves under pressure not only to improve editorial quality and offer niche products, but also to restructure their organizations for innovation" (Lewis, 1997, p. 103). Newsroom management is involved in decisions about how to balance business with journalism, as it is the crucial hinge that links the boundaries between the newsroom and the media organization. The newsroom management coordinates the internal work flow while being involved in the management of the entire media organization because in both organizations, "the components must work together" (Shoemaker and Reese, 1996, p. 140) in order to accomplish the business goals successfully. The components, more precisely the structure of the newsroom, are the subjects for the next part of this chapter.

The structures of the newsroom

The organizational structure influences the way news is produced because this substantially represents the conditions for news production. In general, the organizational context can be regarded as the prestructured arrangement that both enables and restricts the journalists' jobs. However, the question is: What are these structural arrangements in the newsroom? Structures, in the simplest definition, are elements that constitute an entity (e.g. a newsroom) and the manner in which the elements are linked together. Structures, on one hand, bring order to the organization and provide stability and constancy. This occurs when the members of the organization (e.g. the journalists) work with respect to certain rules and they need specific resources in order to complete their work. The routine process of writing news, for example, takes place with regard to the rules of news selection. On the other hand, the journalists need certain resources such as news wires, technical support, and their own competence and experience for their job.

But structures are neither stable nor are they as invariant as the above-mentioned definition may suggest. Of course, management intends to establish long-term structures as it promises to minimize risk and uncertainty. But, as the current turbulent times in the media industry have indicated, change rather than stagnancy is more challenging. Media markets are highly dynamic and media organizations regularly have to adjust their business to changing competition, to new technologies, and to the changing needs of their audiences. To alter the structure in an appropriate way is therefore the priority. Hence, it might be better to discuss organizing journalism as an ongoing process rather than static organization of journalism.

The challenge for journalism researchers is to establish adequate theories for describing and analyzing these change processes. Since the change is above all structural, it seems necessary to specify this term precisely. Because in numerous organizational approaches to journalism structures are described using the terms "rules" and "resources," it might be appropriate to refer to the structurization theory developed by Giddens (1984). He understands structures as the interplay of rules and resources, a model that explains the amendment of rules (e.g. the change from departments to topic teams), the reasons for the change (e.g. the prerequisite of cost cutting), and how the allocation of resources is renewed in change processes. Rules in general are proceedings that enable journalists to do things properly. Rules of signification mean interpretative schemes, which, for instance, give journalists a precise meaning to their work (Giddens, 1984, p. 29). They might pursue certain role conceptions or, on the other hand, conduct market-driven journalism and concentrate on reaching the widest possible audience. Rules of signification explain the reasons for what is done and provide the normative grounds. The goals of the media organization are the most important kind of signification. The rules of domination deal with different facilities enabling and constraining power. Hierarchy is such a facility and the relationship between the newsroom employees and the media management belongs to the rules of domination. Finally, the rules of legitimation constitute the normative base of rules, and they allow certain sanctioning actions (Giddens, 1984, p. 29).

For instance, journalists not only know the rules for their daily work (news selection, treatment of sources), but they also know the rules made by the media company, in particular for the achievement of the company's goals. Furthermore, they know about the social demands regarding journalism, and they have to bring together these different factors in order to work successfully and professionally. Hence, rules are substantial for the social practices of journalists as they both enable (e.g. "sense making," professional skills) and constrain (e.g. economic goals, environmental conditions) the practices.

Resource, as the second term that constitutes structure in a broader meaning, can be split into two types. The first type is that of allocative resources that "refer to capabilities . . . generating command over objects, goods or material phenomena" and the second type is that of authoritative resources which generate "command over persons or actors" (Giddens, 1984, p. 33). When Shoemaker and Reese (1996, p. 147) state that the "skyrocketing salaries paid to star anchors and correspondents . . . have cut the resources available for newsgathering," they provide a well-known example for the types of distinguishable resources. The anchors are only able to request skyrocketing salaries due to their outstanding position as a "brand" that commits the audience to the broadcasting station. To put it in the words of the structuration theory, the anchors have the power to mobilize their authoritative resources (brand, image), which is why they earn such outstanding salaries. However, the salary sought after depends on the available economic resources and the willingness of the media management to pay it. Hence, when management and journalists negotiate salaries, they are negotiating rules and resources and their changes. This interplay demonstrates how the understanding of structure as a set of rules and resources allows analyses of how the organization works and what kind of influences play important roles.

Methods of organizational research on journalism

The question of how the newsroom works is becoming increasingly widespread in journalism research, especially in the turbulent times the media industry has undergone over the past decade. Stagnant ratings, growing media competition, and dropping advertising rates are endangering the existence of media organizations. Their reactions consist of intervention into organizational structures by cutting payrolls, simplifying chains of command, reducing the number of news managers, and flattening newsroom hierarchies to get back to satisfying profit margins. However, this reaction has consequences for the structures of the work flow in the newsroom.

New, versatile demands have emerged from the changed newsrooms. Researchers have found that working in project teams instead of individually is a future trend (for an overview, see Gade, 2004; Altmeppen, 2006). The researchers pinpoint the fact that journalists are requested to keep an eye on the management of the newsrooms and the costs of news production. In addition, journalists have to be aware of the target groups and they are requested to market the journalistic products.

The methods that researchers use to explore such organizational settings vary widely. In most cases, the usual methods of media and communication science are applied and adjusted to the prioritized research question. Thus, the questionnaire is the most commonly used instrument to learn about journalists' attitudes to structural change. When a research question deals with a new and unexplored field, in-depth interviews or case studies are employed. Case studies too are sometimes based on observation. A further reason for using the case study is to overcome a disadvantage of questionnaires resulting from biases from the self-estimation of interviewees. In a few cases, researchers apply triangulation, which means that multiple methods are adopted in combination. For example, in-depth interviews are followed by observation. The in-depth interviews provide a first insight into the research subject and they pave the way for the observation.

In nearly all cases of organizational research on journalism, researchers attempt comparisons. This might be a before-and-after comparison that focuses on what has changed in a single newsroom. This might further be a comparison to reveal differences between newsrooms in different media, between two or more newspapers, or between newspapers and television, for example. Finally, the organizational approach supports the comparison of specific newsrooms in different countries although this is a very rare case. The following section introduces some selected examples of current organizational approaches into journalism research.

Revealing Structures and Tracing the Changes: Findings on Organizational Journalism

Organizational research on journalism is widespread in media and communication science. The research aims are, roughly speaking, to reveal structural changes in newsrooms as well as to find out more about the attitudes and opinions of journalists toward structural change. Whereas former studies were more strictly concentrated on the central conditions and processes of gatekeeping and news-making (e.g. Gans, 1979), the research at present is more strongly focused on the causes and consequences of structural change induced through new requirements for the newsroom, such as marketing orientation, and being more conscious of the needs of audiences. The reasons are somewhat obvious: as a whole the media industry has to face exceptional challenges coming from both economic and technological developments. The new competition with the Internet and increasing economic pressure primarily affect the organizational structure as the media owners search for new and more cost-effective ways of meeting profit goals.

There is some evidence that the organization of journalism is currently changing in a way that has not happened since photosetting appeared in the 1970s. The findings of organizational research into journalism show significant structural changes in how news is gathered and presented, and how newsrooms are organized and managed. The new phenomena are flattened newsroom hierarchies with simplified chains of command, cross-departmental teams organized around topics rather than geography, and established news and copy desks referring to computerization and the new competition from the Internet.

The individual journalist and the organization of the newsroom

Whereas some journalism researchers are interested in better understanding the phenomena of the significant structural changes and therefore observe processes in the newsroom in order to answer the question of what happens, other researchers are much more interested in the attitudes and opinions of management and journalists toward organizational change. These researches would like to find answers to the question of journalists' own assessment of the changing processes.

Gade, for example (2004, p. 25), sent a multi-statement survey to a sample of rank-and-file journalists as well as to top newsroom managers. He aimed at answering research questions such as: What are the attitudes and opinions of management and journalists toward organizational change? How do management and journalists perceive changes? Are there differences in perceiving changes between management and journalists? Are there differences of perception between staff that are related to the organization's size (measured by circulation)?

Gade embeds his study in the theoretical framework of organizational development as the study of how organizations evolve, learn, and adapt. Organizational development focuses on variables that impact the success of organizational change in newsrooms, and in that way seek to determine whether employees understand

and accept new structural rules (such as topic teams and revised job descriptions) and changed resources. Since he surveyed managers and journalists, Gade (2004, p. 25) assumed differences in the assessment of organizational change between these two groups.

Gade found his hypothesis was confirmed in relation to the surveyed groups and, all in all, he reveals a greater extent of disagreement between management and journalists. Whereas the management's role is to "see the big picture" and "to do what should be done to enable change to succeed" (Gade, 2004, p. 40), the journalists "understand restructuring as a mechanism that affords them fewer resources to practice journalism" (p. 42). Journalists rank organizational change much more negatively than do the managers. Only in one score did the managers and journalists agree in their assessments. Both groups perceive the change processes "as both market and profit driven" (Gade, 2004, p. 43), a clear indicator for the economic dominance in the media industry as Shoemaker and Reese (1996, pp. 145–50) stated.

Among the suggestions for future research, Gade approves analysis to determine whether team-based structures impact the ways in which journalists work with one another. This question was the focus of a study concerning organizational changes in commercial radio journalism. Altmeppen, Donges, and Engels (1998) pursued the question of journalists' competences: What kind of skills and knowledge do journalists need for their work? They used triangulation for the research design: in-depth interviews with managers, a survey of journalists, and observations in selected newsrooms to reveal the amount of time the journalists spent at different tasks. Basically, they found that the radio journalism analyzed is shifting to a large extent toward more entertaining programs with a decreasing share of news, and new patterns of creation and presentation of the program content. As for newspapers, the departments and sections were dissolved, the journalists worked in teams that changed daily rather than in stable departments. This means that a journalist who is producing a comedy one day might be responsible for the editorial organization the next day; today's reporter might function as tomorrow's news editor; the head of the entertainment department will do the reporter's job when the latter is on leave. The low level of hierarchical and horizontal structure puts more workload on the shoulders of the individual journalist. The authors name this phenomenon of altered rules as the ideology of "everybody has to do everything" (Altmeppen, Donges, and Engels, 1998, p. 150). According to this, journalists have more responsibility for certain tasks unrelated to the usual professional newsroom practices, such as investigation and reporting, but more toward marketing and target-group-oriented content.

The reason for this is the goal of maintaining maximum profit or, at least, ensuring the survival of the stations. As the program directors admitted in the additional in-depth interviews, the stations' goals primarily consist of reaching the widest possible audience and the highest profit margin. All of the organizational resources were subordinated to this goal; even the structure of the production processes and the work routines.

Comparison of organizational patterns in the newsroom

One of the rare international empirical comparison studies of the organization of newsrooms comes from Esser (1998). He compared German and "Anglo-Saxon" newspaper newsrooms and aimed to "examine the influence of the organizational settings and the established routines in newspaper offices" (Esser, 1998, p. 376). On the base of participant observation, Esser found out that in the UK, the organizational principles are the division of labor and the central newsroom, whereas in Germany, the organizational principles constitute a low degree of division of labor and decentralization. One consequence is that editorial control in Germany is lower and journalistic autonomy is higher. These different principles influence not only the job profiles but also the understanding of the journalists' roles, a clear statement that organizational rules have far-reaching effects. Furthermore, the UK newsroom organization requires more staff, which might be "a waste of resources" (Esser, 1998, p. 396). This indicates an interplay between the organizational rules (e.g. the arrangement of work in the newsroom) and the resources (e.g. the staff).

Society and the organizational change in the newsroom

The analysis of the relationship between media organizations and society is one of the most difficult parts in the organizational approach. In Western countries, the media is mainly commercial companies that claim the freedom of the press. Nevertheless, the media is requested to yield to societal function and media owners insist on a free and politically unaffected economic development. The economic goals overarch the societal requirements, and accordingly organizing the newsroom is solely the job of the media owners and management.

In contrast, in communist countries, the political parties determine the reporting and their impact on the media includes the organization too. But many of the former communist countries are in transition to more or less democratic systems, and media ownership and structures are changing accordingly. The consequences of this process, particularly to the organizational pattern in China, are described by Wu and Chen (2005). They studied the organizational charts of different media in China and perceived a shift of responsibility and power away from the editor-in-chief, as being solely responsible, toward a management committee. Whereas in former times, the Communist Party supervised the editor-in-chief, since 1996, when newspaper industry groups were founded in China, the Communist Party has comprised only one of the three committees managing the media. The other committees are the management and the editing committee (Wu and Chen, 2005, p. 92).

Despite the opening of the Chinese newspaper industry to more market-driven companies, the committee leadership of the Chinese Communist Party "is still the highest policy-making agency" (Wu and Chen, 2005, p. 93). But this opening-up has enhanced competition among the newspapers and has established a first step toward a division of labor, especially the separation of newsroom from business departments. Thus, the societal environment and the organization of the newsroom are mutually dependent with regard to the most important aspects of news coverage in every society.

Future Organizational Research into Journalism

The organizational approach to journalism focuses on both the newsroom and the entire media organization because the newsroom is indeed part of the media organization. With organizational studies, both the internal structure of the newsroom and the environmental structures will be analyzed. The organizational approach aims to reveal the structures of how news is produced and attempts to determine the manner and degree of structural impact. Thus, it analyzes the level of organization and individual journalists, the relationship between the newsroom and other organizations, and that between journalism and society.

Nevertheless there is not only one dominating or outstanding organizational approach. Organizational approaches to journalism can revert to a widespread corpus of organization theories and approaches to organizational development. What unifies them is the use of central terms such as "organization," "structure," and "management," however they are applied. The same can be said for the methods of organizational studies, in which most of the methods often adopted in communication science are applied.

In general, it seems to be necessary to complete the organizational approach to journalism research by conducting more studies using multi-method designs and developing theoretical foundations. A theory-driven design, perhaps based on the structuration theory, generates more exact definitions of what the structure of journalism is. Putting these definitions into variables enables the researcher to reconstruct the organizational reality and allows "looking behind the scenes" of organizational charts – where organizational life actually happens.

One major advantage of organizational research on journalism definitely lies in the comparability of the underlying terms, for example, "organization," "structure," and "management." This especially facilitates international comparisons that are missing for the journalistic organization, whereas other global aspects of media organizations have already been analyzed, for instance the role of global media players and the challenges of transnational media management. The organizational approach understands the use of a large range of methods and theories for designing a differentiated picture of the worldwide differences and similarities in journalism.

References

Altmeppen, K.-D. (2006). *Journalismus und Medien als Organisationen. Leistungen, Strukturen und Management* [*Journalism and media as organizations. Performance, structures, and management*]. Wiesbaden: Verlag für Sozialwissenschaften.

Altmeppen, K.-D., Donges, P., and Engels, K. (1998). *Transformation im Journalismus* [*Transformation in journalism*]. Opladen and Wiesbaden: Westdeutscher Verlag.

Esser, F. (1998). Editorial structures and work principles in British and German newsrooms. *European Journal of Communication*, 3, 375–405.

Gade, P. J. (2004). Newspapers and organizational development: Management and journalist perceptions of newroom cultural change. *Journalism and Communication Monographs*, 6(1).

Gans, H. J. (1979). *Deciding what's news. A study of CBS Evening News, NBC Nightly News, Newsweek and Time*. New York: Pantheon.

Gassaway, B. M. (1984). The social construction of journalistic reality. Unpublished doctoral dissertation: University of Missouri.

Giddens, A. (1984). *The constitution of society. Outline of the theory of structuration*. Cambridge: Polity Press.

Lavine, J. M., and Wackman, D. B. (1988). *Managing media organizations. Effective leadership of the media*. White Plains: Longman.

Lewis, R. (1997). How managerial evolution affects newspaper firms. *Newspaper Research Journal*, 1–2, 103–25.

Löffelholz, M. (2003). Kommunikatorforschung: Journalistik [Communicator research: Journalistic]. In G. Bentele, H.-B. Brosius, and O. Jarren (eds.), *Öffentliche Kommunikation. Handbuch Kommunikations- und Medienwissenschaft [Public communication. Handbook communication and media science]* (pp. 28–53). Wiesbaden: Westdeutscher Verlag.

Nerone, J., and Barnhurst, K. G. (2003). US newspaper types, the newsroom, and the division of labor, 1750–2000. *Journalism Studies*, 4, 435–49.

Shoemaker, P. J., and Reese, S. D. (1996). *Mediating the message. Theories of influences on mass media content*. 2nd edition. White Plains, NY: Longman.

Wu, X. X., and Chen, J. Y. (2005). The changing structure of media organizations and its meaning during the transformation of the social and economic system in China. In C. del Zotto (ed.), *New economy coming of age: Growth and dynamics of maturing new media companies* (pp. 87–99). Jönköping: JIBS Research Reports.

Chapter 6

Factors behind Journalists' Professional Behavior

A Psychological Approach to Journalism Research[1]

Wolfgang Donsbach

Introduction: A Normative Bias in Communication Research

Theories of news decisions are of central relevance to communication research. They try to explain how nonfictional media content is created and, thus, how the pictures in our heads about areas beyond direct experience come about. But journalists' news decisions are a highly complex phenomenon and a challenge to communication research. Several authors have proposed models for the various factors involved in this process (Donsbach, 1987; Kepplinger, 1989; Schudson, 1991; Shoemaker and Reese, 1991; Weischenberg, 1992; Donsbach and Gattwinkel, 1998). These models, although different in aims and scope, all have their heuristic merits. However, we still await an empirical theory that is able to integrate all these factors – and probably building such a theory is not possible due to the complexity of the process. Instead, we have developed theories which try to assess the influence of individual factors in the news flow, the most important theories in this context being the theory of news values (Schulz, 1976; Staab, 1990; Kepplinger and Rouwen, 2000), the theory of instrumental actualization (Kepplinger et al., 1991), theories of social interaction (Tuchman, 1978; Gans, 1979), the theory of deviance and significance (Shoemaker, 1996), system theories (Rühl, 1969; Meckel, 1999), or the "hypothesis theory" of news research (Stocking and LaMarca, 1990).

However, contrary to their application in reception and effects analysis, when it comes to explaining journalists' news decisions, cognitive psychological and sociopsychological approaches have so far received little attention by the scientific community. Although psychological factors are often explicitly and, very much more so, implicitly built into these approaches, they do not have the status of causal explanations. This is even more astonishing as one of the earliest communication models by Westley and McLean (1957) focused on cognitive-psychological factors in the communication process and could have served as a heuristic model in research on news decisions.

This chapter attempts to make use of the evidence in psychology, particularly social and cognitive psychology, in order to improve our understanding of the news process. However, I am far from advocating a psychological monopoly. As in most cases, there are several ways to the truth and it is the combination or integration of different approaches and different disciplines that can improve our knowledge. Instead, this chapter describes the basic processes that might influence the way journalists look at and make their selection from what is going on in the real world.

Most of journalists' work is about perceptions, conclusions, and judgments: to see reality; to infer from it to developments and relationships; and to evaluate reality. It is my main hypothesis that two general needs or "functions" involving specific psychological processes can explain news decisions: a need for social validation of perceptions and a need to preserve one's existing predispositions. The former rests more in the social nature of men, the latter relates primarily to their individual cognitions. Of course, both factors are intertwined. But for analytical reasons, I treat them separately. Most, if not all, other factors discussed earlier, and many others that have been proposed as influencing the news process, can be regarded as an offspring of these two.

Social Validation of Judgments: The Function of Shared Reality

"The facts are not simple, and not at all obvious, but subject to choice and opinion" (Lippmann, 1922, p. 218). This characteristic of news makes journalism a risky business. Journalists have to decide what is true, what is relevant, and what is, in a moral sense, good or bad. In other words, they must constantly make factual and evaluative decisions. As this is a feature of many professions, journalists face four additional problems. They have to make these decisions usually under severe time constraints and under the pressure of competition. For many news decisions, they lack objective criteria and their decision becomes immediately public, that is, visible to many others, which carries the risk of public failure.

The lack of objective criteria does not, however, apply to all kinds and objects of reporting. Decisions of truth can often be verified objectively, and good and professional news reporting can be distinguished from poor reporting by the extent to which available sources and data have been exploited. This is a question of research activity, of professional knowledge about sources and the readiness to "falsify" one's own assumptions and hypotheses (Stocking and LaMarca, 1990). For instance, in many cases reporters can prove the truth of a spokesperson's assertions by asking the right experts or digging into the relevant databanks, thus building their final decision about the legitimacy of a particular assertion on an objective basis.

But often such criteria for evaluation do not exist or cannot be supplied under the typical constraints of the business. Other than factual decisions, evaluative judgments such as the news value of an event or the moral acceptability of a political actor's behavior lack, by definition, such objective criteria. They are always based on value judgments that can neither be verified nor falsified (Popper, 1977; Albert, 1980).

Walter Lippmann described this dilemma when he compared journalism with other professions:

> There is no discipline in applied psychology, as there is a discipline in medicine, engineering, or even law, which has authority to direct the journalist's mind when he passes from the news to the vague realm of truth . . . His version of truth is always his version.
>
> (Lippmann, 1922, p. 227)

Thus, journalists often find themselves in what psychologists call uncertain or undetermined situations.

In his "social comparison theory," Leon Festinger (1954) also suggested that an opinion, a belief or an attitude is "correct," "valid," and "proper" only to the extent to which it is anchored in a group of people with similar beliefs, opinions, and attitudes. He then describes three conditions under which people are most dependent on others: when external reality is ambiguous and difficult to assess, when there is a dualism between physical and social reality, and when physical reality takes precedence over social reality.

Hardin and Higgins (1996) have extended this hypothesis to all kinds of perceptions of reality. In their "shared reality" theory, they combine the theory of symbolic interaction with empirical evidence on the communication process. They assume that even basic cognitive processes are defined by the social activities in which they are manifested.

> In particular we suggest that in the absence of social verification, experience is transitory, random, and ephemeral, like the flicker of a firefly. But once recognized by others and shared in an ongoing, dynamic process of social verification we term "shared reality," experience is no longer subjective; instead it achieves the phenomenological status of objective reality. That is, experience is established as valid and reliable to the extent that it is shared with others.
>
> (Hardin and Higgins, 1996, p. 28)

In other words: sharing one's experience and beliefs with others makes them intersubjective, that is, reliable, valid, generalizable, and predictable, a metaphor from the philosophy of science that the authors use explicitly (p. 35). Such shared reality is reliable because it is reproduced by others, it is valid because it refers to a certain aspect of reality, and it is generalizable because it is valid for several individuals, times, and situations. It is also able to make predictions because it helps to control one's own behavior in the environment. Although shared reality might not necessarily yield the "truth" in every instance, it is the best the individual can get in order to validate his/her own perception of reality. The channel for achieving shared reality is communication: "a hold on reality requires cooperative social activity; in particular, consensually validated social roles and relationships are required for the mutual creation, monitoring, and maintenance of the individual experience of reality" (p. 38). Once a shared reality is established, it can survive even under the conditions of competing shared realities. It has crucial functions

in the building and maintaining of stereotypes and for the socialization of individuals (see Hardin and Higgins, 1996, p. 64). It is obvious that journalists are
constantly in undetermined, uncertain situations. To report from a news conference what nobody else has reported or not to report what everybody else reports
can be embarrassing and jeopardize a reporter's professional standing. Of course,
the editors' desire not to be the only news outlet with a story that nobody else
prints or broadcasts and vice versa is also sponsored by the professional norm to
confirm and double-check the news and by the influence of competition. But it is
the reporters on the "reality front," in particular, who are much more guided by
the need to make, under severe constraints, a pseudo-objective decision on what is
newsworthy – and who, therefore, seek the "shared reality" with others.

Ways of In-Group Orientation

I believe that this general theory about reality perception can help us understand
decision-making processes in the journalistic profession. The risky situation of
making decisions that become public requires that the perception of what is true
(facts), relevant (agenda), and acceptable (opinions) is validated by the help of
others. But who are these others? Of course, journalists interact with many groups
as part of the profession as well as in the private sphere. But if it really comes to
decision-making there is, for two reasons, only one group that counts: other journalists, that is, the "in-group." First, they are the easiest to access. Second, they
are their peers and, as such, represent professional norms. Therefore, they are,
from the journalist's point of view, perceived as the most legitimate influence on
his or her decision-making.

There are many ways in which journalists can communicate with their peers in
order to assess a shared reality. First, there is social interaction on the job. Usually
several journalists cover the same event. Crouse (1972) has described how the "boys
on the bus" on the 1972 campaign trail interact and observe each other before they
make a decision as to what aspects over a primary campaign event they would
report to their editors. Tuchman (1978) and Gans (1979) have reported insights
into newsroom social interaction. The importance of colleagues is also supported by
data from comparative cross-national surveys among news journalists in five countries (Patterson and Donsbach, 1996).

Second, journalists observe what other news media report and how they report
their stories. Wire services and leading national media play an important role in
deciding the media's shared reality (Patterson and Donsbach, 1996). This confirms Breed's (1965) evidence on the role of "opinion leaders" in the press.

Third, even social interaction with their fellows away from the job is a way journalists can assess shared reality. In the USA, three out of four and, in Germany, two
out of three news journalists stated that at least "one of their three best friends"
is also a journalist (Patterson and Donsbach, 1996). Thus, the process of setting a
group opinion is not restricted to newsrooms or press conferences. More research
on the social networks of journalists is needed to underpin these observations.

Media Consonance as an Indicator of Shared Reality

Communication research has long dealt with the "consonance" in media coverage. One of the most illuminating examples from research has been the coverage of an anti-Vietnam war demonstration in the city of London before and after the event. Halloran et al. (1970) described how the media built up a common expectation toward the event (the likeliness of violent acts and a leading role of foreign demonstrators). Although the event itself turned out to be very different from these expectations, the coverage still concentrated on the few minor happenings during the demonstration that seemed to confirm them. Thus, the coverage stayed within the "frame of reference" built up before the event. The authors explain their results mainly through the media's bias toward the activist groups. However, another explanation is the strength of the commonly shared reality of what is newsworthy.

So called "key events" are another illuminating example of how strong the assessment of such a shared reality can influence news decisions. After events with a high visibility, such as disasters, reports about similar events increase significantly compared to the previous coverage of the same type of events (Brosius and Weimann, 1991; Kepplinger and Habermeier, 1995). Although we lack a conclusive causal explanation, it seems plausible that such patterns of reporting can, at least to a certain extent, be explained by journalists' need to validate their professional decisions about what is newsworthy: because similar events have been covered before, something that fits the pattern will be covered with higher priority at a later stage.

In a longitudinal perspective, these commonly shared perspectives can change news values for good. The increasing proportion of negative news is an indicator for these long-term shared realities. This is what Westerstahl and Johansson (1986) have labeled changes in "news ideologies." News ideologies are news factors at a higher level. They are not only criteria for deciding about the newsworthiness of an event or statement but also reflect how journalists see their general role in society and toward the political system.

The concept of "news frames" can also be regarded as another by-product of journalists' shared reality. Kerbel and Ross (1999) see frames as the consequence of commonly shared scripts that journalists develop. Scripts embody the journalist's working assumptions through which they understand the political world. Whereas frames are the tangible product of journalists, scripts are the internalized, often implicit, understanding news workers use to interpret the world (Kerbel and Ross, 1999, p. 3). In politics these scripts often relate to the motives and goals of political figures. In their analysis of US campaign coverage from 1984 to 1996, Kerbel and Ross found that media content very often impugned the motivation of the candidates.

Bennett holds that a "small set of rules accounts for a large share of political content in the news . . . and gathering, sorting, shading, and packaging the day's political information reflect the application of creative decision rules based on, or rationalized by, these norms" (Bennett, 1996, p. 378). In the light of shared-reality theory, such "rules" are nothing other than condensations and generalizations

from journalists' prevailing perception of reality. According to Kepplinger, in processes of scandalization, journalists are often subject to two errors. First, they
falsely believe that they have achieved their judgments independently. Second,
they falsely believe that the convergence of the judgments among the group of colleagues over time is proof of the validity of these judgments (Kepplinger, 2001).
The Sherif experiment (Sherif, 1966) is a typical situation for news journalists:
making decisions in undetermined situations. The decision about reality, therefore,
represents group dynamics and group norms rather than reality. As journalists
have similar values and attitudes, more than members of most other professions,
it is rather easy for them to develop a shared reality.

Organizational Influences and PR
as Processes of Social Validation

Although they are the most important, colleagues are not the only reference group
for journalists. I argue that we can also conceptualize the influence of organizational roles and of public relations as part of this socio-psychological process of
defining the news in undetermined situations. These roles contribute – with their
own goals and with different degrees of influence – to the journalists' judgments.

In democratic societies, journalism is an independent profession where the professionals – at least in a physical or legal sense – cannot be forced to make decisions
against their own judgments. Nevertheless, pressure from seniors, management,
and owners to make specific news decisions does exist. Its impact is, however, more
a psychological impact. Cases where journalists consciously make news decisions
against their better knowledge are the exception rather than the rule. In most cases
their professional decisions are made deliberately. The influence of organizational
roles rather consists of persuasive processes than forced compliance. This does not
mean that there are no real threats. Not reacting to these influences might still
jeopardize a journalist's economic and professional situation.

In many countries, experts complain about increasing commercial influence on
news decisions. Indeed, more soft news and more tabloid news formats cater for
anticipated audience taste (Kalb, 1998; Esser, 1999). As this "new news" (Kalb) is
very likely not a product of the professional orientation and ethics of journalists
themselves, it is probably a consequence of subtle influence from seniors, managers, and proprietors. However, we obviously do not realize this influence.

The influence of sources and their public relations strategies is another factor
that I suggest should be regarded from this socio-psychological perspective. The
definition of what is important, for example in a political leader's major speech, is
the result of communication not only among reporters but also between reporters,
on the one side, and PR officers or spin doctors, on the other side. Here, again,
Walter Lippmann clearly described this process when he pointed to the beneficial
effect of "the publicity man" who "saves the reporter much trouble by presenting
him a clear picture of a situation out of which he might otherwise make neither
head nor tail" (Lippmann, 1922, p. 218).

Measures of the real influence of public relations on news decisions vary in methods and results. Results also differ quite considerably when journalists themselves attribute the influence of public officials on their news decisions. In Germany, and even more so in Italy, a slight majority holds that public officials determine the news agenda (Patterson and Donsbach, 1996). Although the respective questions are not really comparative, the results suggest that journalists perceive the influence of PR sources to be bigger than the influence of management.

Of course, a third group that influences news decisions is the audience. Some of this influence is picked up by the institutional objectives to cater for audience taste as described earlier. But journalists have their own conceptions of the audience and its taste. Although direct interaction with audience members is scarce, feedback through letters to the editor, call-ins, or data from market research lead to a more or less coherent picture of the average audience member. Some scholars have described journalists' news decisions as the result of a symbolic interaction with this picture of the audience (Früh and Schönbach, 1982). This, too, would be a communication process leading to a specific definition of reality and of the newsworthy. However, the majority of journalists do not believe subjectively that the expectations of their audience threaten their professional performance (Flegel and Chaffee, 1971; Patterson and Donsbach, 1996).

The Power of Predispositions: Selectivity in the Process of Perception

The second major psychological factor that influences journalists' perceptions and, thus, their news decisions is the journalist's existing knowledge and attitudes. These predispositions come into play in three different phases of journalistic work: in the exposure to statements and events in their environment, the processing of such information within the cognitive system, and their activation in reproduction. Here is not the place to go into details of the psychology of perceptions. However, a few aspects must be mentioned.

Perception is a process of gaining information from the environment as well as from inside the cognitive and physical system, including emotional processes involved in these activities. The result of perceptional processes is always a coproduct of stimuli, mainly in the environment, and prior experiences stored in long-term memory. In other words, different individuals can perceive the same object differently (Fröhlich, 1991; Flade, 1994). Thus, a major characteristic of the perceptional process is its high degree of selectivity. Selectivity happens on different levels which can be distinguished into selective attention, selective perception, and selective retention. In the process of selective attention, individuals decide to which of the innumerable stimuli in the outside world they address their perceptional system. A high degree of selectivity is necessary ("automaticity"; see Donohew et al., 1984) in order to act in the environment, for instance, in selecting the relevant visual and auditory signals out of millions of other signals when driving a car.

Here, too, the characteristics of the stimuli (e.g. colors, noises) and the characteristics of the individual (e.g. prior experience) come into play.

In the second phase, selective perception, we decide how we will process and store the information which we have adapted to our cognitive system. In the "hypothesis theory" of perception, it is assumed that each perception starts with a hypothesis by the individual. This hypothesis is based on prior perceptions and includes assumptions about the probability of certain signals and information. The strength of this hypothesis is itself based on prior verifications, the number and strength of alternative hypotheses and the motivational support for the respective hypothesis (Bruner and Postman, 1949; Hoffmann, 1994).

Hypothesis theory is closely linked to schema theory (Axelrod, 1973; Brosius, 1991). Schemata can be regarded as "drawers" into which new information is stored. Information for which we lack schemata cannot be processed and stored the way they are but have to be adjusted. Information supporting existing predispositions receives higher salience than non-supportive information. Doris Graber has described, for instance, how schemata influence the way citizens perceive political information in a campaign (Graber, 1984). The "hostile media phenomenon" can be regarded as another indirect proof of the existence of such schemata. Audience members with strong attitudes usually perceive neutral reports as biased against their own viewpoint (Vallone et al., 1985; Perloff, 1989). The greater the existing knowledge and the stronger the attitudes toward an issue were, the more selectively viewers perceived a news report.

Finally, in the process of selective retention, our cognitive system makes decisions as to which of the prior stored information it will keep the memory path alive. As we all know, this is again a highly selective process. It is again strongly influenced by predispositions, attitudes, and motivations. It becomes clear that the existence and characteristics of prior cognitions strongly influence to which signals in our environment we address our attention, which of those we process further, how we process them and what happens to them in memory. Integrating into this simple model of perception the previously mentioned socio-psychological theory of shared reality leads to a three-component model of perception: characteristics of the object, predispositions of the individual, and communication with others.

Journalists' Perceptions

In communication research, the application of psychological evidence on perceptions has been restricted mainly to recipients' behavior. This is particularly true for research on selective exposure to mass communication which has been primarily based on theories of consistency (see Zillmann and Bryant, 1985; Donsbach, 1991). Their common denominator is the assumption that the individual tends to hold consistent cognitions and, thus, is highly selective in his or her exposure to news content. If dissonance still arises, the individual will try to reduce it by avoiding situations and information which is likely to increase dissonance or by actively seeking consonant information. According to more recent evidence, the effect of the consistency motivation has been overrated. Editorial emphasis on news and its valence (negativity) can override the "protective shield" of selective exposure (Donsbach, 1991). For the audience, a strong selectivity would also be dysfunctional. An individual's exposure to news is mainly guided by the motivation to survey the environment and it would be counterproductive to take out large parts of the news only because it does not fit the predispositions.

However, journalists are in a slightly different position from their audience. Their reservoir of potential news is almost unlimited and their need to be selective, therefore, is much greater than that of the audience. On average, newspaper readers read about half of the news items in a daily newspaper, at least their headlines. Their selectivity rate is accordingly roughly one in two. Journalists, in contrast, have to drop at least about nine in ten news items from the news supplied only by the wire services. In addition, they have to make choices from what their correspondents supply, from other news sources such as press releases and spokespersons, and from their own, almost unlimited possibilities to do their own research on any topic. Although journalists' decisions are guided and thus de facto limited by professional conventions of what is newsworthy, it becomes clear that the likelihood of their decisions being influenced by their own predispositions is bigger just from the statistics. This applies, for instance, to the topics chosen, their selective attention to aspects of a political speech or text, the observation of non-verbal behavior in a televised debate, or the spontaneous judgment of the newsworthiness of an incoming story.

In his theory of instrumental actualization, Kepplinger has empirically investigated how journalists' predispositions affect their judgment on the newsworthiness of a controversial story (see Kepplinger et al., 1991). In his quasi-experimental study, news items supporting the journalist's own opinion on the issue at hand were attributed a higher news value than those which ran counter to these opinions. About one third in the variance of news decisions could be explained by this "instrumentality" to the journalist's predispositions. Obviously, the application of major professional norms (double checking, on the one hand, and timeliness, on the other hand) depends to a great degree on journalists' predispositions toward the news issue at hand.

Several other studies have proven, at least for Germany, that the news is often selected according to whether or not it matches the editorial slant of a news organization as measured in the editorials ("synchronization" of news with editorials (Schönbach, 1977; Donsbach, 1997)). This also applies to the citation of sources such as experts and spokespersons (Hagen, 1992). Mann (1974) found similar results for newspapers in the United States when they reported the figures of how many people participated in rallies on controversial issues.

In journalism, the process of selective perception can hardly be separated from selective attention as described previously. When journalists attribute a certain news value to a news item, this can be regarded as a decision of attention as well as of perception. Stocking and LaMarca (1990) have applied the hypothesis theory of perception to journalism. With intensive interviews, they proved that journalists also start their research with a "hypothesis," that is, an assumption about the truth, valence or meaning of a case at hand. The question is how many precautions a system provides to secure a neutral and valid test of these hypotheses.

The theoretical concept of news framing can also be applied to journalists' perceptions of issues, events and statements. According to Entman (1993, p. 52), to frame is to select some aspect of a perceived reality and make it more salient in a communicating text, in such a way as to promote a particular problem definition, causal interpretation, moral evaluation and/or recommendation for treatment for the item described. Such more or less stable and homogeneous news frames played out in the coverage of the German federal elections of 1998 (Kepplinger, 1999).

Conclusions

I have emphasized two psychological factors affecting news decisions: the socio-psychological concept of social validation of judgments through social interaction and the cognitive-psychological concept of stabilizing existing attitudes and cognitions. Both are phenomena that are not singular to journalism but describe general patterns of human behavior. But in journalism they are, first, more present and, second, more relevant. They are more present because journalists, unlike most other professions, constantly have to make perceptional decisions (truth, relevance, acceptability of facts and issues). They are more relevant because these decisions form the input of much of the perception of reality by citizens. In this combination, our picture of the world outside (Lippmann) is mainly the result of journalists' perceptions and group-dynamic processes within the profession.

Can the profession of journalism learn something from other professions? Judges and scientists are two other professions whose core function can be described in terms of relevant perceptional decisions. Judges also have to make factual and evaluative assertions about reality. For instance, in a criminal case, they have to decide whether a certain fact is true (e.g. a homicide), which circumstances are relevant for the procedures and how the behavior of the defendant has to be evaluated and punished according to these circumstances. In order to ensure the best possible trial, codes of procedures prescribe for judges what they have to do before making their verdict.

Science, in contrast, is about the acceptance of hypotheses and theories. According to modern epistemology, scientific statements are limited to empirically provable assertions. There is no place for value judgments in scientific discovery. A dispute over the acceptability of a hypothesis is decided by empirical evidence, that is, the result of a validly designed and systematic study.

For this purpose, the scientific community has developed rules of conduct (methodology) and rules of acceptance (e.g. peer review). In other words, both these professions work on the basis of systems of rules which are designed to bring about the best possible approximation to truth. The most important function of these rules, therefore, is to redress the influence of subjective predispositions (the prejudices of a judge, the pet theories of a scholar) and group dynamic processes (e.g. personal relations between judges and jurors or attorneys, insider relationships and "school building" in science).

It is possible that journalism needs a stronger elaboration of such systems of rules that are primarily designed to redress the influence of predispositions and group dynamics. Our results so far show that both factors have a strong and related influence on news decisions. As journalists very often have similar political and ideological viewpoints, their influence on news decisions is multiplied.

The implementation of checks and balances in order to protect against these influences has to start in journalism education. We need more integration of the relevant knowledge from journalism research – parts of which have been presented in this chapter – into the journalism curricula. Journalists must be aware of such influences on their own behavior in order to realize these factors when they come into play on the job. However, changes in education and training will not be sufficient. It is possible that we will have to reopen the discussion about a professionalization of journalism which was put to rest in the 1980s (McLeod and Hawley, 1964; Donsbach, 1981). Professions trade a high degree of the quality of their services to society – including rigid systems of quality control – with a high degree of professional autonomy and usually societal reputation. A process of professionalization would thus not only open discussions about the ways in which the quality of news can be secured in the face of subjectivity and group dynamics within the profession, but also would offer the possibility of fending off illegitimate influences from outside, for instance from commercial interests.

Note

1 A more detailed version of this chapter was published in *Journalism*: Wolfgang Donsbach (2004). Psychology of news decisions. Factors behind journalists' professional behavior. *Journalism*, 5(2), 131–57.

References

Albert, H. (1980). Die Wissenschaft und die Suche nach der Wahrheit [Science and the search for the truth]. In G. Radnitzky and G. Andersson (eds.), *Fortschritt und Rationalität in der Wissenschaft* [*Progress and rationality in science*] (pp. 221–45). Tübingen: Mohr.

Axelrod, R. (1973). Schema Theory: An information processing model of perception and cognition. *American Political Science Review*, 67, 1248–66.

Bennett, W. L. (1996). An introduction to journalism norms and representations of politics. *Political Communication*, 13, 373–84.

Breed, W. (1965). Newspaper opinion leaders and processes of standardization. *Journalism Quarterly*, 32, 277–84.

Brosius, H. B. (1991). Schema-Theorie. Ein brauchbarer Ansatz für die Wirkungsforschung? [Schema theory. A useful approach for media effects research?]. *Publizistik*, 36, 285–97.

Brosius, H. B., and Weimann, G. (1991). The contagiousness of mass mediated terrorism. *European Journal of Communication*, 6, 63–75.

Bruner, J. S., and Postman, L. (1949). Perception, cognition, and behavior. *Journal of Personality*, 18, 14–31.

Crouse, T. (1972). *The Boys on the bus: Riding with the campaign press corps*. New York: Random House.

Donohew, L. A., Nair, M., and Finn, S. (1984). Automaticity, arousal, and information exposure. In R. N. Bostrom and B. H. Westley (eds.), *Communication Yearbook*. Vol. 8 (pp. 267–84). Beverly Hills, CA: Sage.

Donsbach, W. (1981). Legitimacy through competence rather than value judgements. The concept of professionalization re-considered. *Gazette*, 27, 47–67.

Donsbach, W. (1987). Journalismusforschung in der Bundesrepublik. Offene Fragen trotz "Forschungsboom" [Journalism research in the Federal Republic of Germany. Open questions in spite of "research boom"]. In J. Wilke (ed.), *Zwischenbilanz der Journalistenausbildung* [*"Interim balance sheet" of journalism education*] (pp. 105–42). Munich: Olschläger.

Donsbach, W. (1991). Exposure to political content in newspapers: The impact of cognitive dissonance on readers' selectivity. *European Journal of Communication*, 6, 155–86.

Donsbach, W. (1997). Media Thrust in the German Bundestag Election, 1994: News values and professional norms in political communication. *Political Communication*, 14, 149–70.

Donsbach, W., and Gattwinkel, D. (1998). *Öl ins Feuer. Die publizistische Inszenierung des Skandals um die Rolle der Ölkonzerne in Nigeria* [*Petrol into the fire. The media's staging of the scandal with regard to the role of the oil companies in Nigeria*]. Dresden: Dresden University Press.

Entman, R. (1993). Framing: toward a clarification of a fractured paradigm. *Journal of Communication*, 43(4), 51–8.

Esser, F. (1999). Tabloidization of News. A comparative analysis of Anglo-American and German press journalism. *European Journal of Communication*, 14, 291–324.

Festinger, L. (1954). A theory of social comparison processes. *Human Relations*, 7, 17–140.

Flade, A. (1994). Wahrnehmung [Perception]. In R. Asanger and G. Wenninger (eds.), *Handwörterbuch Psychologie* [*Concise dictionary of psychology*], 5th edition (pp. 833–8). Weinheim: Beltz.

Flegel, R. C., and Chaffee, S. H. (1971). Influences of editors, readers and personal opinions on reporters. *Journalism Quarterly*, 48, 645–51.

Fröhlich, W. D. (1991). *Wörterbuch zur Psychologie* [*Dictionary of psychology*], 18th edition. Munich: dtv.

Früh, W., and Schönbach, K. (1982). Der dynamisch-transaktionale Ansatz. Ein neues Paradigma der Medienwirkungen [The dynamic-transactional approach. A new paradigm of media effects]. *Publizistik*, 27, 74–88.

Gans, H. (1979). *Deciding what's news*. New York: Vintage Books.

Graber, D. A. (1984). *Processing the news: How people tame the information tide*. New York: Longman.

Hagen, L. (1992). Die opportunen Zeugen. Konstruktionsmechanismen von Bias in der Zeitungsberichterstattung über die Volkszählungsdiskussion [The opportune witnesses. Menchanisms of construction of bias in the newspaper reporting about the census discussion]. *Publizistik*, 37, 444–60.

Halloran, J. D., Elliot, P., and Murdock, G. (1970). *Demonstrations and communication: A case study.* Harmondsworth: Penguin.

Hardin, C. D., and Higgins, E. T. (1996). Shared reality. How social verification makes the subjective objective. In R. M. Sorrentino and E. T. Higgins (eds.), *Handbook of Motivation and Cognition,* Vol. 3 (pp. 28–84). New York: Guilford.

Hoffmann, J. (1994). Kognitive Psychologie [Cognitive psychology]. In R. Asanger and G. Wenninger (eds.), *Handwörterbuch Psychologie* [*Concise dictionary of psychology*], 5th edition (pp. 352–6). Weinheim: Beltz.

Kalb, M. (1998). *The rise of the new news. A case study of two root causes of the modern scandal coverage: Press, politics – public policy.* Discussion paper D-34, October. Cambridge, MA: Shorenstein Center for the Press, Politics and Public Policy.

Kepplinger, H. M. (1989). Theorien der Nachrichtenauswahl als Theorien der Realität [Theories of news selection as theories of reality]. *Aus Politik und Zeitgeschichte,* 15, 3–16.

Kepplinger, H. M. (1999). Deutschland vor der Wahl. Eine Frame-Analyse der Fernsehnachrichten [Germany before the elections. A frame analysis of TV news]. In E. Noelle-Neumann, H. M. Kepplinger, and W. Donsbach (eds.), *Kampa. Meinungsklima und Medienwirkung im Bundestagswahlkampf 1998* [*Kampa. Opinion climate and media effects during the election campaign of 1998*] (pp. 78–107). Freiburg and Munich: Alber.

Kepplinger, H. M. (2001). *Die Kunst der Skandalierung und die Illusion der Wahrheit* [*The art of "scandalization" and the illusion of the truth*]. Munich: Olzog.

Kepplinger, H. M., and Habermeier, J. (1995). The impact of key events on the presentation of reality. *European Journal of Communication,* 10, 371–90.

Kepplinger, H. M., and Rouwen, B. (2000). Der prognostische Gehalt der Nachrichtenwert-Theorie [The prognostic power of the theory of newsworthiness]. *Publizistik,* 45, 462–75.

Kepplinger, H. M., Brosius, H. B., and Staab, J. F. (1991). Instrumental Actualization. A theory of mediated conflicts. *European Journal of Communication,* 6, 263–90.

Kerbel, M. R., and Ross, M. H. (1999). A longitudinal analysis of television news frames in US Elections: Some preliminary observations. Unpublished paper.

Lippmann, W. (1922). *Public Opinion.* New York: Harcourt Brace. (Reprint 1965.)

Mann, L. (1974). Counting the crowd: Effects of editorial policy on estimates. *Journalism Quarterly,* 55, 278–85.

McLeod, J. M., and Hawley, S. E. (1964). Professionalization among newsmen. *Journalism Quarterly,* 41, 529–39.

Meckel, M. (1999). *Redaktionsmanagement. Ansätze aus Theorie und Praxis* [*Newsroom management. Approaches in theory and practice*]. Opladen and Wiesbaden: Westdeutscher Verlag.

Patterson, T. E., and Donsbach, W. (1996). News decisions: Journalists as partisan actors. *Political Communication,* 13, 455–68.

Perloff, R. M. (1989). Ego-involvement and third-person effects of televised news coverage. *Communication Research,* 16, 236–62.

Popper, K. R. (1977). *The logic of scientific discovery.* 14th printing. London: Routledge. (First English edition. London: Hutchinson, 1959.)

Rühl, M. (1969). *Die Zeitungsredaktion als organisiertes soziales System* [*The newspaper newsroom as organized social system*]. Bielefeld: Bertelsmann Universitätsverlag.

Schönbach, K. (1977). *Trennung von Nachricht und Meinung. Empirische Untersuchung eines publizistischen Qualitätskriteriums* [*The separation of news and opinion. Empirical study of a journalistic criterion of quality*]. Freiburg and Munich: Alber.

Schudson, Michael (1991). The sociology of news production revisited. In J. Curran and M. Gurevitch (eds.), *Mass media and society* (pp. 141–59). London: Edward Arnold.

Schulz, W. (1976). *Die Konstruktion von Realität in den Nachrichtenmedien. Analyse der aktuellen Berichterstattung* [*The construction of reality in the news media. Analysis of ongoing news coverage*]. Freiburg and Munich: Alber.

Sherif, M. (1966). *The psychology of social norms*. New York: Harper and Row.

Shoemaker, P. J. (1996). Hardwired for news: Using biological and cultural evolution to explain the surveillance function. *Journal of Communication*, 46(3), 32–47.

Shoemaker, P. J., and Reese, S. D. (1991). *Mediating the message. Theories of influences on mass media content*. New York and London: Longman.

Staab, J. F. (1990). *Nachrichtenwert-Theorie. Formale Struktur und empirischer Gehalt* [*Theory of newsworthiness. Formal structure and empirical performance*]. Freiburg and Munich: Alber.

Stocking, S. H. and LaMarca, N. (1990). How journalists describe their stories: Hypotheses and assumptions in newsmaking. *Journalism Quarterly*, 67, 295–301.

Tuchman, G. (1978). *Making News*. New York: Free Press.

Vallone, R. P., Ross, L., and Lepper, M. R. (1985). The hostile media phenomenon: Biased perception and perceptions of media bias in coverage of the Beirut massacre. *Journal of Personality and Social Psychology*, 49, 577–85.

Weischenberg, S. (1992). *Journalistik, Vol. 1: Mediensysteme, Medienethik, Medieninstitutionen* [*Journalism studies: Media systems, media ethics, media institutions*]. Opladen: Westdeutscher Verlag.

Westerstahl, J., and Johansson, F. (1986). News ideologies as moulders of domestic news. *European Journal of Communication*, 1, 133–49.

Westley, B. H., and McLean, M. S. (1957). A conceptual model for communication research. *Journalism Quarterly*, 34, 31–8.

Zillmann, D., and Bryant, J. (eds.) (1985). *Selective exposure to communication*. Hillsdale, NJ: Lawrence Earlbaum Associates.

Chapter 7

Journalism as a Symbolic Practice
The Gender Approach in Journalism Research

Gertrude J. Robinson

Introduction

Throughout the past quarter of a century, journalism as a profession has been studied from three major perspectives. The first or political economy approach relates the outcome of the news process to the economic structure of the news organization. As such it focuses on the impact of advertisers on media institutions and their practices. Although this approach is crucial for understanding the relationship between media industries in a given country, it is unable to clarify why different capitalist countries have different media systems, or how their legal frameworks affect the functioning of public and private networks. Sociological theories, in contrast, have from the start focused on the production moment of the social communication process. They investigate such important issues as reporter–source relationships, occupational routines, and constraints on professional autonomy. They have also surveyed the ethnic and gender composition of the reportorial cadres in different countries, the nature of news work and its routines, as well as the strategic use of professional values to protect reportorial autonomy. The theory's limits lie in the assumption that news work is an individualistic undertaking and in its inability to explain what may be called the "para-ideological" values that journalists develop as members of their profession.

The much less familiar cultural approach is a recent newcomer to journalism research and has been used by only a few investigators. Among these are Michael Schudson (1992) and feminist scholars such as Liesbet van Zoonen (1994) and myself (Robinson, 2005). It investigates the constraining force of broad cultural symbol systems on organizational and occupational routines. These symbol systems comprise language, narrative conventions and underlying values, which are rarely brought to consciousness by the practitioner. Herbert Gans, for instance, discovered that such meta-values as ethnocentrism, altruistic democracy, responsible capitalism, small-town pastoralism, and individualism, guided and framed the reporting of US broadcast journalists in the 1970s (Gans, 1979). Tony Bennet elaborates that an important filter through which news is constructed is "the cultural air we breathe," the whole ideological atmosphere of our society, which tells us that some things can be said and that others best not be said (1982, p. 303).

The cultural approach thus overcomes the theoretical distinction between the system and the subject, both of which are unique moments in the media's cultural meaning production in modern society. Yet, even here, only a small group of researchers acknowledge that gender is an immanent category in meaning making.

The Gender Approach

It is very difficult to disentangle gender theory from cultural theories of communication, because these two designations cover such a large variety of different approaches. I am differentiating between the two, however, to draw attention to the theoretical similarities and differences between them (Franklin, Lurie, and Stacey, 1992). Although feminist thought is extremely diversified in its theoretical assumptions and its goals, there are certain common elements shared by all types of feminism. Among them are the fact that gender is viewed as a primary category of social organization, rather than a secondary add-on to such social categories as class, education, ethnicity, and religion. This implies that feminist researchers systematically focus on the complex relationships between women and men in everyday life (van Zoonen, 1994). The gender approach thus acknowledges that gender and identity are socially constructed, rather than merely biologically determined. It furthermore makes female experience a central focus of attention and creates new categories for codifying this experience, such as the recognition of emotions and subjectivity, as well as the reciprocity between the researcher and the subject (Melin-Higgins, 2002, p. 1). Finally, feminist thought is concerned with the practices of women as social actors and how their asymmetrical power situations to men have come about and affect their social existence. As such, most feminisms have had an activist agenda, namely: promoting equity and social change as well as encouraging self-actualization for all members of society.

Extensive gender research in the past thirty-five years has shown that gender operates on three levels: the individual, interpersonal, and group levels, and that it involves three communicational processes. In other words, gender informs the social and the symbolic work we do, to identify ourselves as women and men in social situations, as well as the meanings we attach to these behaviors. As a classifying system, gender divides people into two mutually exclusive categories: females and males. Because our society does not recognize hermaphrodites as a third possible classification, the biologically based dualism seems to refer to something fundamental and immutable in society. Yet, all people have within their social make-up, both female and male characteristics such as individualism, perseverance, honesty, and emotionalism. Yet, the values ascribed to these characteristics, differ from society to society and over time. Gender also works as a structuring structure, locating women and minorities into a dominant/subordinate caste within the social system, which requires females to constantly announce and act out their subordination. On the all-encompassing ideological level, finally, gender functions as a classifying system, which designates women, who constitute

52 percent of the total population, as a minority and thus as an "interest group." The effects of each of these classificatory processes are exemplified in the ways in which the journalistic profession is organized and the ways in which it operates as a social system.

Communicator scholarship has demonstrated that journalists develop a special worldview with unique sets of ideals, values, and rules. Among these are the ideal of objectivity, the value of neutrality, and special rules pertaining to how reporting activities are to be carried out. Consequently, scholars such as Barbie Zelizer (1993) argue that journalism is practiced by what she calls an "interpretive community" which has developed an identifiable "culture." Margareta Melin-Higgins and Monika Djerf-Pierre define this culture as "what a body of journalists at a particular point in history feels, thinks . . . (en)acts and is" (1998, p. 6). As a living set of practices, journalism varies from country to country and from one epoch to another. Viewing journalism as having a unique "culture" enables me to make the connection between the profession's social structure and the ways in which females and males *within* the profession develop different professional practices and outlooks. These differences are constructed over time and as a function of the prevailing power structure in the newsroom, where dominant (male) and subordinate (female and ethnic) professionals encounter very different work environments (Valdivia, 1995, p. 9).

Most sociological descriptions of the professions fail to mention that women's work is systematically structured by gender and that these gender biases are imported into the organizational structure. They also fail to note that this importation is not innocent, but that gender biases negatively affect the ways in which females are able to wield power in the organizational setting. Juliet Webster comments that the gendering of jobs cannot be reduced to a discussion of women's role in the domestic sphere, or their reserve army status in the labor force, but must also be seen as arising out of the interplay of socially ascribed and therefore shifting roles within organizations (1996, p. 8). Cynthia Fuchs Epstein, who has extensively studied such professions as law, medicine, and engineering, clarifies that the cultural biases against women are imported into the organizational setting through what she calls structural and informal processes (1988, p. 145). Broadly, cultural biases manifest themselves in interpretive processes that sex-type certain positions and work assignments, and thus in turn affect such structural processes as access, promotion, and remuneration. On the informal level, sex labeling of statuses functions like a filter through which only some can pass (Epstein, 1988, p. 153). Together, these processes indicate that professions function not only like a social system, whose networks of power are structured by gender, but also develop expectations about how females and males ought to behave in the working situation. A country's general "culture" thus sets the stage and when individuals act according to its norms, their behavior reinforces the current gender patterns.

According to the gender approach, an individual's involvement in a profession needs to be analyzed from both a structural (organizational) and a hermeneutic (meaning) perspective, which traces how social structure affects interpretation and behavior. Gender theories combined with cultural theories of power create a new way of investigating journalism as a symbolic practice. Through these four previously unexplained professional issues can be clarified. They are: (1) how professional access is skewed; (2) how female promotion is delayed through assignment to "soft news" beats; (3) how female pay scales still differ from those of males; and (4) how the male dominated newsroom devises strategies for isolating female staff, thus creating a unique "climate" at work.

This chapter demonstrates the power of my version of cultural gender theory to analyze some of the systemic biases inherent in the social reproduction of the journalistic profession in North America and Europe. The evidence is drawn from two representative samples of Canadian daily print and broadcast personnel undertaken in 1995. Out of the large amounts of evidence contained in my *Gender, journalism and equity: Canadian, US and European experiences* (Robinson, 2005), I focus on only one issue: the "glass ceiling phenomenon" in female promotion and what it reveals about the role of women in the profession.

The "glass ceiling": myths and reality

In the early 1990s, females comprised 61 percent of the staff, but only 4.6 percent of corporate officers in the US Fortune 500 industries. Similar figures were found in Canada, where they comprised only 6.2 percent of directors in these companies and 9 percent in Crown corporations such as the Canadian Broadcasting Corporation (CBC), the banks and the public service (Morgan 1988). What has kept females out of the boardrooms? A frequent response to this query has been: the "glass ceiling." But what does this mean? The US Department of Labor defines the term as: "those artificial barriers based on attitudinal and organizational bias, that prevent qualified individuals from advancing upward in their organization into management level positions." Such a definition is too broad to be useful. What is needed instead is a theory that can elucidate the specific behaviors, practices, and attitudes that females encounter in their attempts to reach the top. Beyond that, it is important to determine at what point a minority is able to influence the existing power structure. Sociological investigations have placed this boundary at one third of a given group, suggesting that at this point a minority can change the operating rules by making strategic deals with the majority. This means that one can use a figure of less than 30 percent in a particular management position as a rough indicator of the existence of the "glass ceiling."

Cynthia Fuchs Epstein explains the "glass ceiling" as a "boundary maintenance" mechanism, which involves both physical as well as symbolic processes which are imported into organizations through recruitment (1992, pp. 236–7). What this means for understanding this mechanism is that cultural designations (such as gender and ethnicity) are not necessarily more powerful than organizational- or socio-psychological designations, but rather that there is an *interaction* between all three, which tends to reinforce their combined effects.

The Canadian and US Managerial Situation
in Print and Broadcasting

Comparing the positions of Canadian and US newspaper managers, my evidence shows that Canadian females are ahead of their US sisters in managerial clout, even though they too continue to be excluded from the top or publisher position. There are an average of 10 percent female editors-in-chief in Canada in all circulation types, versus a minuscule 0.8 percent in the United States. The same discrepancies are faced on all of the other management levels and demonstrate that circulation affects promotion differently in the two countries. In Canada, large circulation papers are females' best bet, while in the United States it is exactly the opposite, small circulation dailies offer the best managerial chances for female staff. On the second and third managerial levels, US figures are about half of those in Canada. At the editor and assistant/associate editor level, Canadian females hold an average of one-third (27 percent) of these positions, while their US sisters register only 14 percent in small circulation dailies, with proportions of less than 1 percent in the other two circulation categories. On the third management level, that of managing editors, Canada's female proportion is between 10 percent and 45 percent depending on circulation, whereas it ranges from 13 percent to 16 percent in the United States (Marzolf, 1993, p. 11).

A comparison of North American and European management statistics demonstrate that the "glass ceiling" is manifest in Europe, just as it is in North America. This is a very important discovery, because it has been argued that countries with socially liberal policies and strong unionization, such as Denmark and Sweden, would favor female managerial progress. The comparative evidence demonstrates that this is not true. There are 10 percent editor/publishers in Canada, and 6 percent in the United States, but none in the European countries, which means that females have not even reached the "token" status at the higher management levels that they enjoy in North America. Only one German alternative newspaper, the *taz*, had a female editor-in-chief, at the turn of the century, according to Giesela Brackert (1992, p. 90). Second, European figures demonstrate that their "glass ceilings" are located at the *bottom* of the managerial hierarchy in comparison to North America. This means that females have only reached what we have called editorial chiefs (city editors, news editors, etc.) At this level, Germany and Spain register 20 percent females, Denmark 18 percent, and Italy 15 percent and Canada (14 percent). In Canada the glass ceiling is located two levels above this, at the managing editor (24 percent) and the editorial group (25 percent) level, where one-quarter of the personnel are now women.

Why these variations in figures? As Epstein suggested, there is an *interplay* between gender, organizational, and socio-psychological factors in the recruitment to top management that differs from country to country. Margaret Lünenborg's (1997) interviews elicited heavily gendered responses to the lack of females in management. Enlightened Danish and German male managers cited "a lack of qualified female candidates," which turns out to be a typical male-gendered preconception based on *presumption* rather than *evidence*. German and Danish female respondents were closer to the mark. They opined that only childless and unmarried female journalists could accept managerial positions which required ten-hour long working days.

My Canadian data indicate further that females have done even better in television management than in the print media. In Canada, almost one-fifth (18 percent) of all top executive producer positions are today female, with fully one-third (30 percent) of the next two levels of positions: news directors and desk heads, also occupied by women. The figures for the United States are 12 percent, 27 percent and 22 percent respectively (Stone, 2001, p. 2). Together, these comparisons indicate that Canadian females in television management have reached the one-third level at which they can begin to strategize and influence the majority, and thus play an effective managerial role.

The Canadian and international evidence on the "glass ceiling" phenomenon suggest that there are two very general sets of social factors which inhibit career development. The first is the difficulty of combining professional with family responsibilities. Clearly the solutions to this problem depend partially on a given country's social legislation, including rules about maternity/paternity leave; the availability and cost of day care and society's options for the care of elders. Interviews with media personnel have revealed an additional set of social factors inhibiting female career development. These may be called *systemic* and are inherent in the ways in which female managerial staff is treated by their mostly superior male colleagues. Two of these practices have aroused attention in Europe, but have rarely been mentioned in North America. They are associated with the *interpretations* of "availability" and the notion of "writing skill." Margaret Lünenborg (1997, p. 155) is the first to demonstrate the linkage between time spent on the job with the professional self-understanding of "journalistic competence." She also discovered that the unique interpretation of "writing ability" as an unteachable gift grows out of the "craft" origins of the profession. In both print and broadcasting this conception has inhibited the *rationalization* of reporting practices, as well as a movement toward collective time management in the newsroom. With new technologies such as computers, data bases, cell phones, and instant video recording capabilities, the newsroom's collective time requirements for news production can surely be compressed into an ordinary 7–8 hour working day, providing more time for both gender's "parenting" needs.

Feeling the "Glass Ceiling": "Interpretive" Barriers and "Token" Statuses

Catalyst (1995) mail survey of 1,251 US female vice presidents and 1,000 male CEOs identifies six barriers to female advancement into corporate leadership, which graphically illustrate how gender interpretations affect managerial progress. The most important barrier, according to female executives, is *interpretive* and consists of gender stereotyping of female managerial capabilities. Fully

52 percent of females, but only a quarter (25 percent) of the males consider this barrier most important. It is followed by female exclusion from informal networks and their lack of "line" experience. The final three barriers which were mentioned are: the inhospitable corporate climate, lack of mentoring, and the narrow definition of "experience," which is measured in terms of years worked for a company, rather than by more objective criteria. All of these criticisms are familiar to media managers in supervisory positions.

O'Leary and Ickovics (1992) point out that gender stereotyping is grounded in two attitudinal processes: gender stereotyping of work and social role preconceptions. Gender stereotyping of work refers to male managers' sets of beliefs that females, as a result of their gender, are incapable of carrying out managerial functions (1992, p. 9), while social role preconceptions relegate females into the "private sphere" of the home and thus underrate their commitment to careers. When these role-related expectations conflict, as in the selection for top management positions, they become particularly salient and are difficult to eradicate.

What exactly is going on here? It is important to remember that performance standards for managerial positions are often vague and there is little supervision. Consequently, trust becomes one of the major preoccupations in managerial recruitment (Agocs, 1989, p. 5). Overcoming role-related expectations, O'Leary and Ickovics found, requires abandoning the stereotype that women's "natural place" is in the home. Female manager's chances continue to be undermined by beliefs that they will drop out to have children and/or to marry and that they are therefore not wedded to their careers, together adding up to the belief that females are not "career primary" workers (1992, pp. 10–11).

In addition there is the reluctance that female managers evidence when they are offered a promotion into top positions. Why do their male colleagues show none of this reticence? Researchers such as Elisabeth Klaus (1998) and Susanne Keil (2001) have documented two reasons for this reluctance. They are: first, the "isolation" a female encounters at the top, because she lacks a network of relationships in the new organization. And the second is her "token" status, which means that she is unable to marshal the resources of time and money to make her ideas happen (Kanter, 1980, p. 311). My own research has found a third negative effect: "sexual harassment" which is, in all of its forms, more prevalent among female than male professionals.

Rosabeth Kanter's organizational research discovered that there are two types of tokenism, rather than just one and that they are related to the *group situation* in which a woman or minority find themselves at the top. The experience of "token" status is thus not uniform, as was initially assumed, but is encountered in different degrees in two types of group situations. Kanter calls the first the "skewed" (less than 30 percent minority) situation and the second the "tilted," less than 15 percent minority position (Kanter, 1976, p. 240). Since most Canadian print and broadcast personnel are located in the "skewed" management situation, in which they constitute about 30 percent of the group and therefore can bargain with the majority, they do not consider themselves discriminated against. Only their sisters at the top of the power hierarchy, where there are less than 15 percent female personnel, feel the full brunt of being viewed as a "token." At the top, the deviant individual is not only excluded from the informal power networks, but also sidelined from getting her ideas accepted and has to bear the brunt of never being assessed on her own merit.

There is only one study, by the German media scholar Susanne Keil, that explores what it *means* to adapt to a "tilted" management environment. Her interviews with female broadcast managers reveal that they are aware of their inability to change their newsrooms' formal structure, although they believe they have informal power to influence the organizational *culture* (2001, pp. 157–9). Female managers attempt to do this through informal networking *across* organizational divisions, as well as modifying their own managerial behavior. Their strategies include being more democratic in decision situations, introducing an "issue" focus in editorial meetings in order to undermine the competitive power rituals and consciously trying to restructure the gendered beat structure by encouraging staff to cover different issue domains.

Another way in which isolation at the top manifests itself for female managers is through sex-segregated work assignments, which are manifested in all countries and professions. Even though managerial positions are today considered gender neutral, my organizational media data reveal that there is segregation *within* management ranks. As a result of ongoing gender barriers, female and male managers have different median ages and social characteristics and are drawn from different professional specializations. Because female managers have worked for fewer years in their company than their male compatriots, female managers tend to be recruited from *outside* of the organization, whereas males have come up through the ranks. This means that when male managers reach the top, their *informal networks* are intact, while female incumbents have to recreate these networks from scratch.

The final manifestation of isolation at the top, I found, is sexual harassment, which has not been systematically studied before. My representative sample of female and male professionals confirms that more females than males have encountered harassment practices. Nearly one-half (49 percent) of all female staff, but only 39 percent of males answered "maybe" to the question: "Is sexual harassment a problem for female journalists?" To clarify harassment activities, feminist scholarship suggests it be divided into three categories: verbal, physical, and psychological. The responses indicate that female practitioners are most prone to verbal harassment: almost two-thirds (60 percent) of female staff have encountered it at least once. Psychological harassment comes in second place with almost one-half (43 percent) of female media personnel having experienced it at least once, while physical harassment has been experienced as well, by an astounding one-fifth (20 percent) of females at least once. As expected, percentages are much lower for male staff: only 13 percent have experienced verbal harassment at least once, 9 percent have experienced psychological harassment, and a mere 1 percent have experienced physical harassment on the job. The proportions of female and male respondents who have *witnessed* harassment, in contrast, are extremely close. About one-half of all staff have witnessed verbal harassment, a quarter have witnessed psychological harassment, while a full quarter (26 percent) of female staff, but only 11 percent of males have witnessed at least one case of physical harassment. All these findings are significant at the p < 0.05 level and indicate that harassment is another means by which a majority keeps a minority in check.

The Gender Approach: An Evaluation

Barbie Zelizer (1993) has shown that the journalistic profession does not function as an integrated social system, because females and other minorities have very different professional experiences than their white male counterparts. There are thus *systemic biases*, which utilize gender and/or ethnicity to construct a system of social stratification. This affects the type of work (beats) to which females are assigned, their promotion and position in the hierarchy, as well as their differential remuneration for work of equal value. Alhough this gender stratification has been reduced for the younger group of professionals in the past thirty years, it has not yet been totally eliminated in the 21st century.

In the promotional process, gender theory has been able to elucidate the "attitudinal" and "interpretive" preconceptions of male managers. Attitudinally, it has been shown that male managers tend to choose to recruit people for top positions on the basis of their own self-interest, rather than the qualifications of the candidate. O'Leary and Ickovics call this the "rational choice" (1992, p. 14) theory. Among the interpretive preconceptions that work against the female managerial candidates, as we have seen, are the ideas that they are not "work primary" and that they will therefore be less committed. Both of these preconceptions have been disproved by the Canadian evidence, but they nevertheless continue to inhibit the progress and effectiveness of female and ethnic staff in the heterosexual media workplace.

The gender approach has also explained why females and minorities are reluctant to move into the journalistic management ranks at the present time. It has demonstrated that this reluctance is a "rational response" to female managers' lack of personal networks in the new firm and their exclusion from informal networks. There is furthermore the stressfulness of playing the "token" role, in a situation where personal qualifications become invisible.

The gender approach has furthermore discovered that "sexual harassment" is an additional strategy, which is practiced at all organizational levels for keeping female colleagues in check and that is linked it to their "token" status. The more "skewed" (less than 15 percent) the group situation in which the female manager finds herself, the more likely that sexual harassment will occur, even at the managerial top. And frequently there are no means for redress.

Despite the gender approach's ability to pin point *systemic biases* in the journalism profession, Margrit Eichler alerts us to an important theoretical *caveat* concerning this approach. In her *Double standard* (1980), she notes that gender is both the most useful and the most dangerous explanation imaginable and must therefore be applied dialectically. This means that all gender analyses have to be in two stages. First, descriptive, charting the presence of gender differences and similarities in all kinds of journalistic situations. As such gender combined with supervisory responsibility and organization size can explain differences in salary levels between female and male professionals. However, she warns, this explanation is only probabilistic. Gender by itself, though *necessary*, is not a *sufficient* prerequisite for making *causal* inferences.

Female journalists' reluctance to accept promotion into management positions is a case in point. Here we have an observed difference between female and male incumbents, yet no explanations have been offered why this happens. As Epstein and others have pointed out, the reluctance has something to do with the "token" status one occupies (defined as the inability to command the time and material to carry out one's ideas), as well as the lack of a support network, for females recruited from outside of the firm. Both of these outcomes could also be experienced by black or ethnic journalists, because they too are different from the overwhelmingly white male management elites.

This shows that gender theory must be combined with organization and actor analysis, as well as a hermeneutic approach, which is able to explore the meanings people attach to their experiences. Here, linguists have shown that language functions not only as a descriptive medium, but also as an *expressive* medium. Because of this duality, survey methodologies have to be complemented with participant observation techniques and interviews, which probe the meanings that social actors attach to their behaviors.

References

Agocs, C. (1989). *Walking on the glass ceiling: Tokenism in senior management*. 20 pp. Paper presented at the Canadian Sociology and Anthropology Association conference. Quebec City.

Bennett, T. (1982). Media, "reality", signification. In: M. Gurevitch, T. Bennett, J. Curran, and J. Wollacott (eds.), *Culture, society, and the media* (pp. 287–398). London: Methuen.

Brackert, G. (1992). Reflections on women and media. In G. J. Robinson and D. Sixt (eds.), *Women and power: Canadian and German experiences*. 2nd edition (pp. 90–7). Montreal: McGill Studies in Communications and Goethe Institut.

Catalyst. (1995). *Women in corporate leadership: Progress and prospects*. New York.

Eichler, M. (1980). *The double standard: A feminist critique of the social sciences*. Guilford: New York: St Martin's Press.

Epstein, C. F. (1992). Tinkerbells and pinups: the construction and reconstruction of gender. In M. Lamont and M. Fournier (eds.), *Cultivating differences: Symbolic boundaries and the making of inequality* (pp. 232–56). Chicago, IL: University of Chicago Press.

Epstein, C. F. (1988). *Deceptive distinctions: Sex, gender and the social order*. New Haven, CT: Yale University Press and New York: Russell Sage Foundation.

Franklin, S., Lurie, C., and Stacey, J. (1992). Feminism and cultural studies. In P. Scannel, P. Schlesigner, and C. Sparkes (eds.), *Culture and power* (pp. 90–111). Newbury Park, CA: Sage.

Gans, H. (1979). *Deciding what's news*. New York: Vintage Books.

Kanter, R. M. (1976). The impact of organization structures on work behavior of women and men. *Social Problems*, 23(3), 415–30.

Kanter, R. M. (1980). The impact of organization structure: Models and methods for change. In R. Ratner (ed.), *Equal employment policy for women* (pp. 311–27). Philadelphia, PA: Temple University Press.

Keil, S. (2001). *Einsame Spitze? Frauen in Führungspositionen im öffentlich-rechtlichen Rundfunk* [*Lonely top: Women in leadership positions in public broadcasting*]. Münster: Lit Verlag.

Klaus, E. (1998). *Kommunikationswissenschaftliche Geschlechterforschung: Zur Bedeutung der Frauen in den Massenmedien und im Journalismus* [*Communicational gender studies: Women in journalism*]. Opladen: Westdeutscher Verlag.

Lünenborg, M. (1997). *Journalistinnen in Europa: Eine international vergleichende Analyse zum gendering im sozialen System Journalismus* [*Female journalists in Europe: An international comparison on gendering in journalism*]. Opladen: Westdeutscher Verlag.

Marzolf, M. T. (1993). *Women making a difference in the newsroom*. (August). 16pp. Paper prepared for the Commission on the Status of Women, AEJMC. Kansas City.

Melin-Higgins, M. (2002). *Opportunities and problems in feminist methodology*. Paper presented to the Gender and Communication Group at the IAMCR meeting, Barcelona.

Melin-Higgins, M., and Djerf-Pierre, M. (1998). *Networking in newsrooms: Journalist and gender cultures*. Paper presented to the Gender and Communication Group at the International Association for Media and Communication Research (IAMCR) meeting, Glasgow.

Morgan, N. (1988). *The equality game: Women in the federal public service (1908–1987)*. Ottawa: Advisory Council on the Status of Women.

O'Leary, V., and Ickovics, J. (1992). Cracking the glass ceiling: Overcoming isolation and alienation. In U. Sekaran and F. Leang (eds.), *Womanpower: Managing in times of demographic turbulence* (pp. 7–30). Newbury Park, CA: Sage.

Robinson, G. J. (2005). *Gender, journalism and equity: Canadian, US and European experiences*. Creskill, NJ: Hampton Press.

Schudson, M. (1992). The sociology of news production revisited. In J. Curran and M. Gurevitch (eds.), *Mass media and society* (pp. 141–60). London: Arnold.

Stone, V. (2001). Race, gender and TV news careers. Retrieved September 15, 2001, from www.missouri.edu/~jours/tvers/html

Valdivia, A. (1995). Feminist media studies in a global setting: Beyond binary contradictions and into multicultural spectrums. In A. Valdivia (ed.), *Feminism, multiculturalism and the media: Global diversities* (pp. 7–29). Thousand Oaks, CA: Sage.

van Zoonen, L. (1994). *Feminist media studies*. Thousand Oaks, CA: Sage.

Webster, J. (1996). *Shaping women's work: Gender, employment and information technologies*. London: Longman.

Zelizer, B. (1993). Journalists as interpretive communities. *Critical Studies in Mass Communication*, 10(2), 219–37.

Part III

Methodology and Methods of Journalism Research

Chapter 8

Comparing Journalism across Cultural Boundaries
State of the Art, Strategies, Problems, and Solutions

Thomas Hanitzsch

Introduction

Comparative research on journalism has, in recent years, gained increased attention. The end of the cold war and the onward march of globalization increasingly created opportunities for researchers to meet at international conferences. At the same time, new communication technologies triggered the rise of global networks of scientists, and funding agencies become increasingly aware of the merits of cross-national research. Academic journalism education has responded to this trend by offering highly specialized degree programs, a process that particularly takes place in Europe.[1] However, this has not always been the case. When, at the beginning of the 1990s, Blumler, McLeod, and Rosengren (1992) called comparative research the communication field's "extended and extendable frontier" (pp. 3–4), cross-cultural work was characterized as probing and preliminary. This has been especially true for the study of journalism. Now, at the dawn of the third millennium, researchers in the field of media and communication studies are increasingly adopting a comparative strategy.

The rising significance of cross-cultural research notwithstanding, comparative methodology is rather little discussed, and research reports often lack in theory and conceptualization (Chang et al., 2001; Livingstone, 2003). While new technologies have made it possible to conduct extensive surveys, process enormous quantities of data and then make these data available to researchers working in various countries, a sophisticated discussion about theories, concepts, designs, and methods in comparative communication research has just begun (Hantrais and Mangen, 1996; Wirth and Kolb, 2004).

Still, most comparative work in journalism research is not based on tailor-made cross-cultural studies but on a secondhand analysis of data from single-nation studies. Because these studies often use different conceptualizations and methodologies, any attempt to extract meaning from these data may become a highly hazardous endeavor. Genuinely comparative research on journalism is rare, in particular if it involves more than two or three cultures. The study of Patterson and Donsbach (1996), who probed into the political roles of journalists in Germany, Great Britain, Italy, Sweden, and the United States, may serve as an excellent example of conceptually deliberate cross-national research. As comparative research is an essential, if not the most important strategy to understand the nature of journalism and how it works across cultural boundaries, journalism studies certainly needs more cross-cultural researches of this kind; and the "setting is ripe for studies that incorporate more than one country in a single analysis" (Berkowitz, Limor, and Singer, 2004, p. 161).

What Is Comparative Research?

The roots of cross-cultural research can be traced to the English scholar Edward Tylor, whose book *Primitive culture* (1871) became a milestone in English-speaking anthropology. The first major internationally comparative study was probably Émile Durkheim's (1897/1973) research on suicide and social anomy. Half a century later, after World War II, cross-cultural research became increasingly influential in the social sciences and humanities and rapidly permeated psychology (e.g. Triandis and Lambert, 1980), sociology (e.g. Kohn, 1989b), comparative politics (e.g. Larson, 1980), as well as organizational/management research and the sociology of work (e.g. Hofstede, 1980). The growing interest in comparative studies can be seen in the rising number of academic journals devoted to cross-cultural research. Among these one can find the *International and Comparative Law Quarterly* (founded in 1952), *Comparative Studies in Society and History* (1958), *Comparative Politics* (1968), *Journal of Cross-Cultural Psychology* (1970) and *Journal of Intercultural Communication Research* (2006), to name only a few.

Despite this long tradition of institutionalization, the terminology in comparative research is often ambiguous and confusing. Consider concepts such as cross-country, cross-national, cross-societal, cross-cultural, and cross-systemic comparisons, with the prefix "inter" and "trans" sometimes substituting for "cross" (Øyen, 1990). At least until the 1980s, most comparative research in the social sciences was cross-national and, as such, mostly limited to a comparison of two nationally defined populations to which the researchers happened to have access. This holds true for journalism studies as well, in which comparative research took off with the pioneering work of Jack M. McLeod and Searle E. Hawley (1964), who developed a professionalism index for journalists, and its subsequent application in a number of countries. Nevertheless, it was not before the 1990s that cross-cultural comparison became a popular strategy in journalism research.

The comparison of national journalism systems – still the dominant approach in the field (Reese, 2001) – is well documented in the literature. One should mention the five-nations study of Patterson and Donsbach (1996), the 22-nations survey of Splichal and Sparks (1994), studies that compare news content across European countries (Blumler, 1983; Gurevitch, Levy, and Roeh 1993), the Global Monitoring Project (Spears and Seydegart, 2000), as well as the comparisons of Germany with Great Britain (Köcher, 1986; Esser, 1998) and the United States with Germany (Quandt, 2006), Russia (Wu, Weaver, and Johnson 1996), China and Taiwan (Zhu et al., 1997), and Israel (Berkowitz, Limor, and Singer 2004). Most recognized is arguably the UNESCO-inspired "Foreign Images" study involving 29 countries (Sreberny-Mohammadi, Nordenstreng, and Stevenson, 1984), which was replicated in the 1990s by Annabelle Sreberny-Mohammadi and Robert L. Stevenson on a sample of 38 countries (Wu, 2000).

Other studies compared language areas within countries (Canada: Pritchard and Souvageau, 1998; Switzerland: Marr et al., 2001), (former) states within a particular nation (East and West Germany: Schoenbach, Stuerzebecher, and Schneider, 1998), or ethnic groups within a country (Hanitzsch, 2006a). In addition to these, one could compare cross-border regions (e.g. the European Union, ASEAN, and Latin America), functionally equivalent institutions and organizations (e.g. press councils and ethics codes) as well as populations of journalists according to gender, race, ethnicity, social class, age, education, religion, and other cultural characteristics.

Given the often confusing terminology and different interpretations of key concepts, the term "comparative" should accommodate a considerable degree of abstraction in order to capture the variety of comparative research. Perhaps, the term "comparative" works best when boiled down to concepts of culture (van de Vijver and Leung, 1997). We may call a study comparative if *two or more a priori defined cultural populations are compared according to at least one functionally equivalent concept*. One could, of course, argue that *all* social research is comparative (Beniger, 1992), but cross-cultural studies pose specific conceptual and methodological challenges to the researcher, and some of these are discussed with respect to the concept of equivalence (see below).

Benefits and Challenges of Comparative Research

What makes comparative research desirable? Most scholars argue that cross-cultural research is indispensable for establishing the generalizability of theories and the validity of interpretations derived from single-nation studies. Another important aspect of comparative studies is that they force us to test our interpretations against cross-cultural differences and inconsistencies (Kohn, 1989a; van de Vijver and Leung, 1997). In journalism studies, the advantages of comparative research are obvious. While the empirical inquiry into newsmaking has generated a vast quantity of data, some of the more fundamental questions in journalism research remain largely unresolved. What shapes the news and the structures of journalism most? Is it politics, economy or culture? How do the conventional Western values of objective journalism fit with non-Western cultures? Does the increasing dissociation of journalism from the political system in all cultures lead to reliance on economic rationalities? These and other highly pertinent research questions notwithstanding, explanatory studies are virtually nonexistent (Donsbach and Patterson, 2004), and conceptually deliberate comparative research projects such as those carried out by Patterson and Donsbach (1996) and Hallin and Mancini (2004) are still the exception rather than the rule.

Comparative studies also pose many challenges. First, when very different systems or time periods are being analyzed, the extent of the differences may overwhelm meaningful comparison (Blumler, McLeod, and Rosengren, 1992). These differences may not only be large and multidimensional, but also vary by domain (Kohn, 1989a). What we treat as a similarity at one level of analysis may reveal myriad differences at more detailed levels of analysis. Second, researchers often understate heterogeneities within the cultures being compared when focusing on differences between the units of analysis (Blumler, McLeod, and Rosengren, 1992), but sometimes variances within cultures may be greater than variations across cultural boundaries (Øyen, 1990). This, above all, may be the case in modern news production, as diverse journalistic cultures coexist in any given society. Third, the so-called "Galton's Problem" may arise because differences and similarities, for instance between Great Britain and the United States in terms of message content or professional values, can be thought as "caused" by the respective national cultures or as the result of diffusion across cultures (Scheuch, 1990). Diffusion is particularly likely when nations share a common cultural origin, and is even more so with the onward march of globalized media production and consumption. The professional ideology of objectivity, for example, has spread from the United States to most parts of the world, contributing to what Reese (2001) calls an emerging class of "cosmopolite" (p. 178) journalists who share a common standard and understanding of journalism.

Comparative research also faces significant epistemological challenges. One problem which arises in many cross-cultural studies is that they produce "measurement out of the context" (Livingstone, 2003, p. 482) by assuming methodological and theoretical universalism. Furthermore, cultures are often evaluated through the lens of the researchers' different cultural value systems. The only way to overcome ethnocentrism is through collaborative research, but this strategy often requires enormous resources in terms of time, funding, infrastructure, and, most importantly, willingness to compromise. This may be the reason why collaborative research is sometimes described as "exhausting," "a nightmare," and "frustrating" (Livingstone, 2003, p. 481). Therefore, given all the pros and cons of cross-cultural comparison, researchers need to develop a clear idea of why a comparative strategy serves the purpose of their research better than a non-comparative design (Chang et al., 2001).

Strategies of Comparative Research

Once a researcher or a team of researchers decides to engage in comparative research, it becomes necessary to explicate and justify which strategy to adopt. In theory, the decision for a particular research strategy has to be functional for the purpose and focus of the study. Different strategies of comparative research can be identified by (1) the proximity of the cultural populations studied; (2) the function of cases in the research design; and (3) the way concepts and operationalizations are constructed and applied in diverse cultural contexts. In journalism studies, however, only a few scholars have explained and justified their choice of comparative strategy (e.g. Patterson and Donsbach, 1996; Zhu et al., 1997).

1 A "classic" taxonomy of comparative research strategies has been proposed by Przeworski and Teune (1970, pp. 31–46). The two political scientists distinguished *most similar systems designs* (MSSD) from *most different systems designs* (MDSD). The former aims to identify key features that are different among similar cultures. Examples are comparisons of Western nations that share some substantial political, economic, social, and cultural similarities. This method, used by Donsbach and Patterson (2004) and Hallin and Mancini (2004), keeps the number of experimental variables relatively small by neutralizing some differences and accentuating others, thus making it easier to determine the factors that account for the observed outcome (Landman, 2000). The most different systems design, however, aims at similar outcomes among very diverse cultures. It is assumed that if similar relationships between dependent and independent variables are found in all cultures, then the cultural differences between the units in comparison must be of little or no relevance. This strategy has rarely been used in comparative journalism research, and although not explicitly stated, the comparisons of the United States with Brazil (Herscovitz and Cardoso, 1998) and Uganda (Mwesige, 2004) may fall in this category.

2 The sociologist Melvin Kohn (1989b, pp. 20–4) suggested a fourfold typology of comparative studies according to the function of cultural populations in the research design. The first type looks at different nations as the *objects of study*; the researchers' primary interest is to understand the particular countries for their own sakes (e.g. Wilke, 1998). In the second type, where nations are the *context of study*, the investigators are primarily interested in testing the generality of findings and interpretations (e.g. Herscovitz and Cardoso, 1998; Mwesige, 2004). When nations are the *units of analysis*, the researchers are mainly concerned with the way certain phenomena are systematically related to variations in national characteristics, which often leads to classifications of nations along one or more context dimensions (e.g. Weaver, 1998a; Deuze, 2002). In the fourth type of comparative research, *transnational research*, nations are treated as components of larger international systems, taking into account the fact that nations are not isolated entities, but rather are systematically interrelated (e.g. Sreberny-Mohammadi, Nordenstreng, and Stevenson, 1984; Wu, 2000).

3 In the most general sense, comparative studies can be classified according to the way concepts and operationalizations are constructed and applied in diverse cultural contexts. In the *safari* approach to comparative research, investigators conduct their study at least partly in a cultural context different from their own, and in most cases researchers compare their own countries to other nations (e.g. Köcher, 1986; Wu, Weaver, and Johnson, 1996; Esser, 1998). It is also not uncommon for research to be entirely conducted in a foreign context (e.g. Hanitzsch, 2006a). By using the *application* approach, researchers replicate a study originally designed for another culture and apply it to their own

context (e.g. Herscovitz and Cardoso, 1998; McMane, 1998). In other words, researchers "borrow" their concepts, research designs, and operationalizations from other studies, drawing on their own work or that of others, and apply it to different cultural contexts, perhaps after doing some adjustments to the original research tools. Most of the time, however, investigators use only parts of the original instruments, such as Weaver and Wilhoit's (1991, 1996) measurement of the journalists' role perceptions. Lastly, the *assembly* approach stands for the truly collaborative development, application, evaluation and publication of research (e.g. Patterson and Donsbach, 1996; Berkowitz, Limor, and Singer, 2004).[2]

Methodological Issues

Selection of cultures

Although the question of which cultures should be included in a comparative study is essential and requires careful deliberation, much cross-cultural research on journalism has failed to justify the selection of cultural units. This seems to be a common problem in communication and media studies, where the selection of cultures is mostly made in consideration of convenience: justified by availability, personal preferences and existing research networks, language skills, priorities of funding bodies, resources allocated for research, and so forth (Chang et al., 2001). One excellent example of a theory-driven selection of countries is the comparison of China, Taiwan, and the United States by Zhu et al. (1997).

If the cultures in comparison are not deliberately selected, researchers may find it difficult to identify causal relationships and single out the determinants of cultural variance. Still, the best way to make an optimal use of the potential of comparative research is to work with a quasi-experimental design (Wirth and Kolb, 2004). Cultures could be selected according to their scores on theoretically identified context dimensions on the ecological level (e.g. degree of press freedom and level of democratization) so that the variance in the target variables can be attributed to the impact of particular *a priori* specified context factors.[3] Whatever considerations serve as rationale for the sampling, the selection of cases essentially needs to be theoretically justified; it should be by design, not by accident (Chang et al., 2001).

The problem of equivalence

Equivalence should be seen as the major problem in comparative research (Wirth and Kolb, 2004), and when the problem of equivalence is ignored, investigators expose their studies to the danger of bias. In this respect, van de Vijver and Leung (1997) distinguish three kinds of bias in cross-cultural research: construct bias, method bias, and item bias. Considering this distinction, we briefly discuss equivalence in terms of concepts, methods, and administration as well as language and meaning.

Equivalence of concepts: The constructs used – those which define the unit of analysis and those which are measured – must be identical across all cultures included in a comparative study, but in cross-cultural journalism studies this premise is often disregarded. The concepts of "autonomy" or "editor," for instance, are far from self-evident, as they often have different meanings in different contexts and at different levels of analysis. Who exactly is a journalist is defined in many ways, and often a definition that serves one culture does not apply to another. Journalism may have different normative functions and serve different interests in different societies, while the role of the journalist may vary from one culture to another.

What the concept of "journalism" captures is highly contingent on the socio-historical backgrounds in which journalism operates. A look at Weaver's (1998b) *The global journalist*, a valuable international source book containing a collection of 25 surveys of journalists, is revealing: Although many researchers borrowed from the original definitions of Weaver and Wilhoit (1991), one will find a chaotic coexistence of competing and often conflicting conceptual definitions. While some researchers, for instance, limited their survey to traditional news journalists, others excluded journalists working for popular or special-interest publications. Most studies included full-time editors but excluded freelancers, whereas the question of whether photographers and camera operators are actually journalists has been treated in many ways.

In order to deal with the problem of equivalence on the conceptual level, investigators have essentially three choices: First, if the researchers did not pay attention to the equivalence problem prior to and during the development of concepts, they could determine the extent to which they actually achieved equivalence of concepts *post hoc*, perhaps by means of advanced statistical analysis (e.g. factor or reliability analysis). Second, the researchers could control conceptual equivalence prior to data collection and then determine the level of achievement *post hoc*. Both solutions are most suitable for the *safari* and *application* strategies. Third and finally, investigators could develop their concepts jointly, involving colleagues who have profound knowledge of all cultures included in the study. The reward of this *assembly* strategy could be concepts that are, to the largest possible extent, "culture-free," showing a maximum overlap across all participating cultures.

Equivalence of methods and administration: In international research endeavors, methodological and procedural habits often turn out to show large, country-specific differences, leading to frustration among participating investigators. Not only do the preferred modes of data collection vary, but also differences occur in sampling methods, "acceptable" response rates, uses of visual cues, and methods of training interviewers, among others (Jowell, 1998). Convenience sampling should be generally avoided in comparative research, because it provides no way to ensure equivalence. Researchers not only have to make sure their units of analysis are selected in an equivalent manner, but also they need to guarantee that the method of sampling (e.g. random or quota sampling) is the same across all cultures. Splichal and Sparks (1994), for instance, who administered a survey of 1855 first-year journalism students in 22 countries, left the decision over sampling methods entirely to the individual collaborating researchers. In the landmark study of Donsbach and Patterson (2004), journalists were selected from organizational rosters or by news editors, but in the case of Italy the sample was drawn from the membership list of the National Union of Journalists.

Concepts need to be measured in the same way (indicators, scales, etc.) in all participating cultural populations by using the same set of scientific methods. In many cases it makes a substantial difference when investigators use face-to-face interviews, telephone surveys, online surveys, or self-administered questionnaires, especially when it comes to culturally sensitive questions. Social desirability with respect to the acceptance of freebies in journalism (Hanitzsch, 2006b), for instance, is more likely to occur in face-to-face interviews than in surveys using self-administered questionnaires. However, even the same method of data collection may still produce different behaviors among respondents of different cultural backgrounds. People from certain cultures may not be comfortable or motivated in their role as subjects of research; and their responses may be affected by particular cultural values (Johnson and Tuttle, 1989). In cultural contexts that are considered to be highly collectivistic, the level of social desirability may be higher than in predominantly individualistic cultures. The same is true for the level of generalized acquiescence. Respondents from certain cultures tend to answer more positively than others, regardless of the actual questionnaire content. This problem even appears in single-nation studies, in which, for instance, journalists from different ethnic groups are being compared (e.g. Hanitzsch, 2006a).

Finally, administration bias can occur when the culture-specific attitudes, behaviors and/or characteristics of the interviewers produce methodological artifacts (Wirth and Kolb, 2004). In many Asian cultures it matters whether professional journalists are interviewed by professors, staff researchers or students, as status plays an essential role in interpersonal communication. Therefore, interviewers should be carefully selected and trained. They should be familiar with the cultural environment, have a high level of education and command of the local language. Ideally, they should come from the same racial or ethnic group and be of equivalent social status to their respondents (Johnson and Tuttle, 1989).

Equivalence of language and meaning: Bias in comparative research is often caused because definitions and categories or, in the case of survey research, the verbalization of items, have different meanings due to language-specific connotations. Therefore, questions and coding instructions should have a broadly equivalent meaning in all included cultural populations, and items that are intended to measure a particular construct should be designed to ensure valid and equivalent measurement in all studied cultures. For evaluating the journalists' perception of media roles, for instance, many researchers replicated the original scale developed by Weaver and Wilhoit (1991), but cultural differences may lead to different interpretation. The items that were originally designed to measure an "adversarial" understanding of journalism may conflict with a preference for consensus and harmony in many Asian cultures. Consequently, low support for these items does not necessarily mean that the interviewed journalists are less critical and independent. Rather, Asian journalists might perceive the attitudes these items represent as overly aggressive and culturally inadequate, but they still could report from an adversarial stance.

A widely applied method to control for the peculiarities of language cultures is the *translation–backtranslation* procedure, in which a translated version of the questionnaire or coding instructions is first produced and then is backtranslated into the original language. The result from the backtranslation will be compared with the original version to evaluate the quality of the translation. Ideally, this procedure is iterated until a reliable match of the two versions is achieved (Wirth and Kolb, 2004). Another method is *cultural decentering*, which removes culture-specific words, phrases and concepts that are difficult to translate from the original version of the instrument. Van de Vijver and Leung (1997) suggest a *committee approach*, in which an interdisciplinary and multicultural team of individuals who have expert knowledge of the cultures, languages and research field in question jointly develop the research tools.

A Short Guide to Systematic Comparative Research

Journalism scholars who intend to engage in comparative research do not have to reinvent the wheel, they are well-advised to take advantage of conceptual and methodological progresses made in other disciplines which have a long tradition in comparative research, such as political science, sociology or psychology (Kohn, 1989b; van de Vijver and Leung, 1997; Landman, 2000).

First, journalism researchers should always ask themselves whether a cross-cultural comparison will *extend the scope* of their interpretations sufficiently to make the venture worthwhile (Kohn, 1989a). The purposes and expectations of comparative research are not self-evident; they should be explicated and not taken for granted (Gurevitch and Blumler, 2004).

Second, the research should be situated in a *theoretical or conceptual perspective*. In journalism studies, a large part of comparative researches are not based on sound theory, leaving unclear ideas as to what constitutes the common reference that allows for comparison. If an empirical research is not related to some sort of theoretical perspective, its explanatory power remains limited.

Third, when a theoretical framework is absent, the formulation of research questions or hypotheses becomes a game of guess work. Gurevitch and Blumler maintain that initial conceptualizations should include a *prior statement of expectations* about what might emerge from the comparison, as this will provide useful guidance through both the research design and analysis of the findings.

Fourth, it goes without saying that researchers should not try to interpret data relating to a culture of which they know little or nothing (Jowell, 1998). *Expert knowledge of all cultures* included in the research is essential.

Fifth, "equivalence should be established and cannot be assumed" (van de Vijver and Leung, 1997, p. 144). The *problem of equivalence* in terms of constructs, methods and administration, language and meaning as well as means to their solution have to be addressed in every publication of cross-cultural comparative studies.

Notes

1 Five European universities (the Universities of Aarhus, Amsterdam, Wales and Hamburg together with the City University) introduced a jointly operated MA program in International Journalism. Master programs in International Journalism are also offered by the University of Cardiff, Liverpool John Moores University and University of Central Lancashire. An MA in Comparative Journalism has been designed by the University of Wales, in Comparative International Journalism by Goldsmiths, University of London, and in International Media Journalism by the University of Coventry.

2 This taxonomy simplifies and integrates earlier attempts to classify types of comparative research. The term "safari approach" is borrowed from Hantrais and Mangen (1996, p. 4), while "assembly" is used by van de Vijver and Leung (1997, p. 36) in a different context.

3 International organizations increasingly provide detailed indicators which make the selection of countries much easier than ever before (e.g. Freedom House, ITU, NUA, UN, and World Bank).

References

Beniger, J. R. (1992). Comparison, yes, but: the case of technological and cultural change. In J. G. Blumler, J. M. McLeod, and K. E. Rosengren (eds.), *Comparatively speaking: Communication and culture across space and time* (pp. 35–50). Newbury Park, CA: Sage.

Berkowitz, D., Limor, Y., and Singer, J. (2004). A cross-cultural look at serving the public interest: American and Israeli journalists consider ethical scenarios. *Journalism*, 5(2), 159–81.

Blumler, J. G. (ed.) (1983). *Communicating to voters: Television in the first European parliamentary elections*. London: Sage.

Blumler, J. G., McLeod, J. M., and Rosengren, K. E. (1992). An introduction to comparative communication research. In J. G. Blumler, J. M. McLeod, and K. E. Rosengren (eds.), *Comparatively speaking: Communication and culture across space and time* (pp. 3–18). Newbury Park, CA: Sage.

Chang, T.-K., Berg, P., Ying-Him Fung, A., Kedl, K. D., Luther, C. A., and Szuba, J. (2001). Comparing nations in mass communication research, 1970–97: a critical assesment of how we know what we know. *Gazette*, 63(5), 415–34.

Deuze, M. (2002). National news cultures: a comparison of Dutch, German, British, Australian and US journalists. *Journalism & Mass Communication Quarterly*, 79(1), 134–49.

Donsbach, W., and Patterson, T. E. (2004). Political news journalists: partisanship, professionalism, and political roles in five countries. In F. Esser and B. Pfetsch (eds.), *Comparing political communication: Theories, cases, and challenges* (pp. 251–70). New York: Cambridge University Press.

Durkheim, E. (1897/1973). *Der Selbstmord [Suicide]*. Neuwied: Luchterhand.

Esser, F. (1998). Editorial structures and work principles in British and German newsrooms. *European Journal of Communication*, 13(3), 375–405.

Gurevitch, M., and Blumler, J. G. (2004). State of the art of comparative political communication research: poised for maturity? In F. Esser and B. Pfetsch (eds.), *Compar-*

ing political communication: Theories, cases, and challenges (pp. 325–43). New York: Cambridge University Press.

Gurevich, M., Levy M. R., and Roeh, I. (1993). The global newsroom: convergences and diversities in the globalization of television news. In P. Dahlgren and C. Sparks (eds.), *Communication and citizenship: Journalism and the public sphere* (pp. 195–216). London: Routledge.

Hallin, D. C., and Mancini, P. (2004). *Comparing media systems: three models of media and politics*. New York: Cambridge University Press.

Hanitzsch, T. (2006a). Mapping journalism culture: a theoretical taxonomy and case studies from Indonesia. *Asian Journal of Communication*, 16(2), 169–86.

Hanitzsch, T. (2006b). Selling the autonomy of journalism: the malpractice of corruption among Indonesian journalists. In H. Xiaoming and S. K. Datta-Ray (eds.), *Issues and challenges in Asian journalism* (pp. 169–88). Singapore: Marshall Cavendish Academic.

Hantrais, L., and Mangen, S. (1996). Method and management of cross-national social research. In L. Hantrais and S. Mangen (eds.), *Cross-national research methods in the social sciences* (pp. 1–12). London: Pinter.

Herscovitz, H. G., and Cardoso, A. M. (1998). The Brazilian journalist. In D. H. Weaver (ed.), *The global journalist: News people around the world* (pp. 417–32). Cresskill, NJ: Hampton Press.

Hofstede, G. (1980). *Culture's consequences: International differences in work-related values*. Beverley Hills, CA: Sage.

Johnson, J. D., and Tuttle, F. (1989). Problems in intercultural research. In M. K. Asante and W. B. Gudykunst (eds.), *Handbook of international and intercultural communication* (pp. 461–83). Newbury Park, CA: Sage.

Jowell, R. (1998). How comparative is comparative research? *American Behavioral Scientist*, 42(2), 168–77.

Köcher, R. (1986). Bloodhounds or missionaries: role definitions of German and British journalists. *European Journal of Communication*, 1(1), 43–64.

Kohn, M. L. (1989a). Cross-national research as an analytic strategy. In M. L. Kohn (ed.), *Cross-national research in sociology* (pp. 77–102). Newbury Park, CA: Sage.

Kohn, M. L. (1989b). Introduction. In M. L. Kohn (ed.), *Cross-national research in sociology* (pp. 17–31). Newbury Park, CA: Sage.

Landman, T. (2000). *Issues and methods in comparative politics: An introduction*. London: Routledge.

Larson, A. L. (1980). *Comparative political analysis*. Chicago, IL: Nelson-Hall.

Livingstone, S. (2003). On the challenges of cross-national comparative media research. *European Journal of Communication*, 18(4), 477–500.

Marr, M., Wyss, V., Blum, R., and Bonfadelli, H. (2001). *Journalisten in der Schweiz. Eigenschaften, Einstellungen, Einflüsse* [Journalists in Switzerland: Characteristics, attitudes, influences]. Konstanz: UVK.

McLeod, J. M., and Hawley, S. E. (1964). Professionalization among newsmen. *Journalism Quarterly*, 41(4), 529–39.

McMane, A. A. (1998). The French journalist. In D. H. Weaver (ed.), *The global journalist: News people around the world* (pp. 191–212). Cresskill, NJ: Hampton Press.

Mwesige, P. G. (2004). Disseminators, advocates and watchdogs: A profile of Ugandan journalists in the new millennium. *Journalism*, 5(1), 69–96.

Øyen, E. (1990). The imperfection of comparisons. In E. Øyen (ed.), *Comparative methodology: Theory and practice in international social research* (pp. 1–18). London: Sage.

Patterson, T. E., and Donsbach, W. (1996). News decisions: journalists as partisan actors. *Political Communication*, 13(4), 455–68.

Pritchard, D., and Souvageau, F. (1998). The journalists and journalisms of Canada. In D. H. Weaver (ed.), *The global journalist: News people around the world* (pp. 373–93). Cresskill, NJ: Hampton Press.

Przeworski, A., and Teune, H. (1970). *The logic of comparative inquiry*. New York: Wiley.

Quandt, T., Löffelholz, M., Weaver, D. H., Hanitzsch, T., and Altmeppen, K.-D. (2006). American and German online journalists at the beginning of the 21st century: A binational survey. *Journalism Studies*, 7(2), 171–86.

Reese, S. D. (2001). Understanding the global journalist: A hierarchy-of-influences approach. *Journalism Studies*, 2(2), 173–87.

Scheuch, E. K. (1990). The development of comparative research: Towards causal explanations. In E. Øyen (ed.), *Comparative methodology: Theory and practice in international social research* (pp. 19–37). London: Sage.

Schoenbach, K., Stuerzebecher, D., and Schneider, B. (1998). German journalists in the early 1990s: East and West. In D. H. Weaver (ed.), *The global journalist: News people around the world* (pp. 213–27). Cresskill, NJ: Hampton Press.

Spears, G., and Seydegart, K. (2000). Women's participation in the news. In G. Spears and K. Seydegart (eds.), *Who makes the news? Global media monitoring project* (pp. 10–45). London: WACC.

Splichal, S., and Sparks, C. (1994). *Journalists for the 21st century: Tendencies of professionalization among first-year students in 22 countries*. Norwood, NJ: Ablex.

Sreberny-Mohammadi, A., Nordenstreng, K., and Stevenson, R. L. (1984). The world of the news study. *Journal of Communication*, 34(1), 134–8.

Triandis, H. C., and Lambert, W. W. (1980). *Handbook of cross-cultural psychology*. Vol. 1: *Perspectives*. Boston, MA: Allyn and Bacon.

Tylor, E. B. (1871). *Primitive culture: Researches into the development of mythology, philosophy, religion, art, and custom*. London: J. Murray.

van de Vijver, F. J. R., and Leung, K. (1997). *Methods and data analysis for cross-cultural research*. Thousand Oaks, CA: Sage.

Weaver, D. H. (1998a). Journalist around the world: commonalities and differences. In D. H. Weaver (ed.), *The global journalist: News people around the world* (pp. 455–80). Cresskill, NJ: Hampton.

Weaver, D. H. (ed.) (1998b). *The global journalist: News people around the world*. Cresskill, NJ: Hampton.

Weaver, D. H., and Wilhoit, G. C. (1991). *The American journalist*. 2nd edition. Bloomington, IN: Indiana University Press.

Weaver, D. H., and Wilhoit, G. C. (1996). *The American journalists in the 1990s: US news people at the end of an era*. Mahwah, NJ: Lawrence Erlbaum Associates.

Wilke, J. (1998). Journalist in Chile, Ecuador and Mexico. In D. H. Weaver (ed.), *The global journalist: News people around the world* (pp. 433–52). Cresskill, NJ: Hampton.

Wirth, W., and Kolb, S. (2004). Designs and methods of comparative political communication research. In F. Esser and B. Pfetsch (eds.), *Comparing political communication: Theories, cases, and challenges* (pp. 87–111). New York: Cambridge University Press.

Wu, H. D. (2000). Systemic determinants of international news coverage: A comparison of 38 countries. *Journal of Communication*, 50(1), 110–30.

Wu, W., Weaver, D. H., and Johnson, O. V. (1996). Professional roles of Russian and US journalists: A comparative study. *Journalism & Mass Communication Quarterly*, 73(3), 534–48.

Zhu, J.-H., Weaver, D. H., Lo, V., Chen, C., and Wu, W. (1997). Individual, organizational, and societal influences on media role perceptions: A comparative study of journalists in China, Taiwan, and the United States. *Journalism & Mass Communication Quarterly*, 74(1), 84–96.

Chapter 9

Methods of Journalism Research – Survey

David Weaver

Surveying journalists is both similar and dissimilar to surveying the general public. Many of the same caveats and rules for survey research apply equally to both groups. For example, careful attention must be given to wording questions that are as free as possible from obvious biases, to ordering questions so as not to prejudice answers to subsequent questions, to limiting the length of the interviews, to carefully defining one's population and randomly sampling it (if sampling is necessary), to deciding which mode of interviewing (face to face, mail, Internet, telephone) is most appropriate, to determining which design (cross-sectional, trend, or panel) to use, and to employing the most revealing methods for analyzing the data.

But there are differences between surveying journalists and the general public. These include a recognition that many journalists are in the habit of asking questions rather than answering them, that many are under severe deadline pressures that do not allow for lengthy (or even brief) interviews while at work, that many are quite skeptical or critical of surveys in general, and that many are suspicious of survey researchers' guarantees of anonymity and underlying motivations for conducting surveys.

This chapter discusses some of these differences and also the strengths and weaknesses of the survey method for studying journalists as compared with other methods such as observation, in-depth interviews and content analysis based on the author's experiences with three large national telephone surveys of US journalists (Weaver and Wilhoit, 1986, 1996; Weaver et al., 2007), a mail survey of foreign correspondents in New York and Washington, DC (Willnat and Weaver, 2003), and the editing of a book containing reports of surveys of 20,280 journalists working in 21 different countries and territories (Weaver, 1998).

Strengths of Surveys

As compared with other methods of studying journalists, such as newsroom observations or in-depth interviews, surveys have several advantages. The most often mentioned of these is representativeness or generalizability, sometimes referred to by researchers as external validity. If care is taken to draw a random sample from a well-defined population of journalists (or the public), then it is possible to generalize to a much larger population within known limits of sampling error.

Thus, if the goal of a study is to estimate the characteristics or attitudes of a large group of journalists, such as various demographics (age, gender, education, income), and or political leanings or attitudes about various issues, then the carefully conducted sample survey should be the method of choice.

Another advantage of surveys is that they permit the gathering of information about a large number of variables in a relatively short time for reasonable cost, and they also produce quantitative data that can be analyzed using a variety of statistics. Still another advantage is that most surveys are "not constrained by geographical boundaries" (Wimmer and Dominick, 2006, p. 180), especially if they are conducted by telephone, mail or via the Internet. There are also archives of survey data that can be compared across time and space to get a better idea of larger trends and patterns in journalists' characteristics and attitudes, as in the national studies of US journalists in which many of the same questions have been asked from 1971 to 2002 (Weaver et al., 2007). Increasing globalization has resulted in more cross-national surveys being done now, especially by survey researchers using the same questions translated into different languages (see, e.g. Inoguchi et al. (2005) on findings from the AsiaBarometer surveys carried out in ten Asian countries, and Arcenaux (2006) on findings from the EuroBarometer surveys done in nine European countries).

Weaknesses of Surveys

Surveys also have several disadvantages when compared with other methods for studying journalists. One of the most important is the measurement of actual journalistic behavior. Observations and content analyses are better (more valid) methods of studying what journalists actually do than are surveys that ask journalists what they do. This is true not only for journalists but also for people in general, who tend to answer questions about behavior in socially desirable ways or who cannot accurately perceive or remember the details of their own behavior. Surveys are stronger for assessing basic characteristics and opinions or attitudes than for measuring behavior.

Another weakness of surveys is that they often do not answer "why" or "how" questions very well because most of the questions force respondents to choose among fixed response categories. Although the measures, or variables, in a survey can be correlated with each other to determine the strongest and weakest correlates of various attitudes or opinions, often the researchers cannot anticipate in advance all the possible reasons for, or predictors of, these attitudes. Unless a number of open-ended questions are included that allow respondents to say in their own words why they hold certain views or how they developed, surveys will be weaker than in-depth interviews for answering "why" and "how" questions. And large-scale surveys usually cannot afford to include very many open-ended questions because of the time-consuming job of recording and analyzing the texts of the answers.

Surveys are also not strong for determining causal relationships, especially the more common one-shot or one-time surveys. Because all of the questions are asked at about the same time, it is often difficult to know the time ordering of the relationships between the variables measured in a survey. For example, if a researcher finds a correlation between levels of job satisfaction and perceived performance of the news organization in influencing the public, does this mean that journalists are more likely to be dissatisfied because they perceive that their organization is doing a poor job of informing the public, or that they perceive poor performance of their news organization because they are more dissatisfied? Unless panel surveys are done, where the same journalists are interviewed over time, it is often not possible to determine the time ordering of various correlations empirically, and thus not possible to tell which is the cause and which the effect, one of the necessary conditions for determining causality (Stempel et al., 2003, pp. 161–2, 234–5).

Another problem in determining causal relationships is controlling for all other possible causes, either statistically (by measuring them) or physically (by randomly assigning subjects to different conditions and then seeing what the effects are, as in experimental studies). In general, surveys are not strong on this condition either, because as Shoemaker and McCombs (2003, p. 234) note,

> The use of statistical controls, however, is only as good as the researcher's ability to identify and measure possible alternative explanations. It is far easier to rule out alternative explanations in a randomized experiment, where the experimenter randomly assigns subjects to treatment groups, thereby controlling for a vast array of unidentified and unmeasured variables.

Finally, surveys are becoming more difficult to conduct because of the overuse of them, the attempts by some telemarketers to sell something under the pretense of conducting a survey, the increased emphasis on privacy in this age of identity theft, and the use of answering machines, caller-identification devices, cellular telephones and other technologies to screen telephone calls. Many news organizations and journalists are growing increasingly reluctant to participate in surveys because of increased pressures to do more in their jobs, the volume of email they receive, and suspicions about the purposes of many surveys. Still, surveys of journalists are generally easier to conduct than newsroom observation studies, where access to news organizations is often very difficult to obtain. But large-scale surveys, especially those using telephone or face-to-face interviews, can be quite expensive to conduct. The cost for a 50-minute telephone interview in our 2002 survey was about $70, and these costs keep rising.

We turn now to some considerations in actually conducting surveys of journalists as compared with surveys of the general public.

Questions and Questionnaires

Many survey textbooks emphasize the importance of carefully structured questionnaires and clear questions. As Fowler (1988, p. 74) puts it, "Good questionnaires maximize the relationship between the answers recorded and what the researcher is trying to measure." This is especially applicable to surveying journalists, who are likely to be more critical of questions asked and less willing to be forced into choosing mutually exclusive response categories, than are members of more general publics. This suggests that more open-ended questions should be used in surveying journalists than in most general public surveys, if at all possible.

In our own surveys of journalists, we have added more open-ended questions in each subsequent study, even though the answers take more time to analyze than those from closed-ended questions that can be quickly coded and tabulated. The open-ended questions allow journalists to respond in their own words and often help to answer "why" or "how" questions that cannot be answered well with closed-ended questions. The open-ended questions also provide rich direct quotations that can be used to elaborate or illustrate patterns produced by the answers to closed-ended questions.

One example of this from our surveys of US journalists is the use of a follow-up open-ended question to a closed-ended question about job satisfaction (Weaver et al., 2007, p. 264). After being asked a closed-ended question: "All things considered, how satisfied are you with your present job – would you say very satisfied, somewhat dissatisfied, or very dissatisfied?" the next question was open-ended: "What are the most important reasons you say you are (very satisfied, fairly satisfied, etc.) with your present job?" This open-ended question provided a number of reasons for job satisfaction or dissatisfaction that we as researchers could not have anticipated in advance, and it allowed us to do a content analysis of the answers to identify the most often (and least often) mentioned reasons, as well as providing many interesting and revealing direct quotes.

In general, open-ended questions on a certain subject should usually come before closed-ended, so as not to suggest answers to respondents, but this is not always the case if the open-ended question is one that asks "why" a certain answer was given, as in the job satisfaction example above, or asks for an elaboration of an answer to a closed-ended question. In our most recent survey of US journalists, for example, we asked a closed-ended question about where the journalist would most like to be working in five years – in the news media or somewhere else. For those who answered "somewhere else," we asked two open-ended questions about the field or occupation in which they would like to be working and why they wanted to leave the news media (Weaver et al., 2007, p. 263).

In asking about journalistic freedom or autonomy, however, we asked an open-ended question first before the closed-ended questions to avoid suggesting answers. We first asked, "On the whole, what do you consider to be the most significant limits on your freedom as a journalist?" Then we followed with two closed-ended questions about how much freedom the journalist usually had in selecting stories to work on and in deciding which aspects of a story should be emphasized (Weaver et al., 2007, p. 266).

Another problem with question wording in surveys is consistency (or lack of it) from one survey to another. As Asher (2001, p. 45) writes,

> even when the sponsor has no obvious ax to grind, question wording choices greatly influence the results obtained. In many instances highly reputable polling organizations have arrived at divergent conclusions simply because they employed different (although well-constructed) questions on a particular topic.

In studying US journalists from Johnstone et al.'s (1976) survey to our own in 2002 (Weaver et al., 2007), we have tried to keep most question wordings the same from one survey to another to be able to make comparisons over time that are not confounded by differences in question wording. A number of surveys of journalists in other countries have used the same wording to be able to make more controlled comparisons across national boundaries (Weaver, 1998). This is especially important in any comparative study of journalists to detect real differences and similarities in opinions, attitudes and behaviors. But as Thomas Hanitzsch has pointed out in his chapter on methods of comparative journalism research in this book, identical wording does not guarantee that journalists from different cultures understand and construct the meaning from these questions in the same way. A recent project that includes surveys of journalists in ten culturally diverse contexts is being led by Professor Hanitzsch under the name, "Worlds of Journalisms" (see www.worldsofjournalisms.org/ for more information about the methods being used to develop a survey questionnaire that can be used in these different settings).

Structuring the questionnaire is important in any kind of survey research, but especially in surveying journalists. The questionnaire should begin with questions that are not sensitive or difficult to answer, with the more sensitive or difficult questions near the end. Typically, demographic questions about age, income, marital status, number of children, etc. should be placed at the end of a questionnaire so as not to offend the respondent early in the interview or prompt an early refusal to continue the interview. In our studies, we begin by asking about the name of the news organization, the job title, the year that the journalist joined the news organization, how long the person has worked in journalism, and why he or she became a journalist. We ended with questions about ethnicity and race, religion, marital status, number of children, political party identification, the type of ownership of the news organization, income from the previous year, and whether the news organization has changed in size during the past few years (Weaver et al., 2007, pp. 262–7).

In between these beginning and ending questions, we have asked about the importance of different aspects of the job (such as pay, editorial policies, autonomy, etc.), satisfaction with the job, the ways that computers are used on the job, the frequency of feedback from superiors and others, supervisory responsibilities, amount of editing performed, freedom to select stories and emphasize different aspects of stories, frequency of doing reporting, membership in a journalists' union, views about audience members, beliefs about the media's impact on public

opinion, opinions about the use of various controversial reporting methods, influences on ideas about what's right and wrong in journalism, importance of various
news media roles and practices, evaluations of news organization's performance
in informing the public, views about the priorities of owners and senior managers
of news organization, influences on ideas of what is newsworthy, political leanings of self and news organization, views about laws concerning abortion and
firearms, descriptions of best work, readership of professional publications and
other news media, educational backgrounds and degrees, on the job training, and
amount of socializing with other people connected with journalism or communication (Weaver et al., 2007, pp. 262–9).

Sampling

In some countries, simple or systematic random sampling of journalists is a fairly
easy task because there are reasonably up-to-date and complete lists of journalists who are required to belong to a national union or other type of professional
organization, or to be licensed or certified in some manner. But in other settings,
where there are no fairly complete lists of journalists, such as in the United States
or Germany, sampling becomes more complicated and usually involves some kind
of multi-stage approach, where news organizations are first randomly sampled
and then journalists working for these news organizations are in turn randomly
sampled.

Most survey research books or chapters include descriptions of simple random,
systematic random, stratified random, and multi-stage random sampling techniques, as well as explanations of how to calculate sampling error (see, e.g.,
Wilhoit and Weaver, 1990; Asher, 2001; Stempel et al., 2003; Manheim et al.,
2006; Wimmer and Dominick, 2006). There is not space in this chapter to go into
much detail about these different sampling methods or the calculation of sampling
error, so the reader should consult one of the books mentioned above or another
research methods text for more details on these subjects.

The first step in sampling journalists (or anything else) is to define the population from which the sample is to be drawn. Is it all journalists working for daily
newspapers in a certain country, region, state or other geographical area? Is it
all journalists working for television stations in a certain area? Is it all journalists who belong to a certain professional association? Is it all full-time journalists
working for these various media or will part-timers, stringers and freelancers also
be included?

In our surveys of US journalists, we have had to use multi-stage random sampling to construct a representative sample because there is no list of journalists that
is even close to being complete. The largest journalism organization in the United
States is the Society of Professional Journalists (SPJ) with about 10,000 members,
but this is slightly less than one-tenth of all full-time US journalists working for
mainstream news media, so the membership list of SPJ cannot be used to represent
the population of all US journalists. There are many other journalistic organizations

in the United States but none of them can claim more than a small percentage of all journalists.

There are complete listings of various news media in the United States and many other countries, however, that include virtually all newspapers, radio and television stations, wire service bureaus or offices, and news magazines. These can be used to draw systematic random samples that are sometimes stratified by size of organization if the news organizations vary significantly in size, as is the case with daily newspapers in the United States where there are only a few with circulations above 500,000 that might be missed in simple or systematic random sampling.

In our US studies, we defined the population of journalists as all full-time editorial or news people responsible for the information content of English-language mainstream general interest news media in the United States. In other words, we were concerned in our studies only with journalists who worked for news media targeted at general audiences rather than special-interest or ethnic groups. These mainstream news media included daily and weekly newspapers, news magazines, radio and television stations, and general news or wire services (such as Associated Press and Reuters) based in the United States. We further defined journalists as those who had responsibility for the preparation or transmission of news stories or other timely information – all full-time reporters, writers, correspondents, editors, news announcers, columnists, photojournalists and other news people. We did not include librarians, camera operators, or audio or video technicians who assist in the creation and dissemination of news content, but who do not have direct responsibility for making decisions about what becomes news (Weaver et al., 2007, pp. 255–6).

This definition of journalist has been criticized as excluding many part-time and independent journalists who work for several different news organizations, and also many who work for non-news magazines, as well as numerous bloggers and others who have their own web sites. It seems likely that future studies of journalists will need to consider expanding the definition of who is a journalist, in light of all the new developments in newsgathering and dissemination, but this will make the task of defining and sampling the journalistic population even more difficult. For example, how does one define the population of news-related web sites and where does one find a fairly complete listing of such sites to sample? Are all bloggers journalists? If so, aren't all who communicate information on the web journalists? Is there no difference between someone who communicates online and a journalist? Is the distinction between communication and journalism becoming meaningless? These are questions with which future surveys of journalists will have to grapple.

In the United States, we have used a three-stage sampling plan in our 1982, 1992, and 2002 studies that consists of (1) compiling lists of the various news organizations (daily and weekly newspapers, radio and television stations, wire service bureaus and news magazines) and systematically sampling these lists; (2) obtaining lists (or at least total numbers) of journalists from the sampled news organizations; and (3) drawing a random sample of journalists from these lists. We have also supplemented this main random sample with separate samples from the membership lists of the four main minority journalist associations because of the scarcity of African-American, Asian-American, Hispanic and Native American journalists. In the 2002 study, we also included a separate sample from the membership list of the Online News Association to increase the number of web journalists (see Weaver et al., 2007, pp. 256–60, for more details). For comparisons over time, and for estimates of the demographics and other characteristics of US journalists, we used only the main random sample of US journalists.

As mentioned earlier, the definition and sampling of journalists will vary depending on the location and the goals of one's study. If the goal is to generalize the findings only to a certain group of journalists, such as members of an organization, the sample can be drawn in one step if one has access to the membership list. A systematic random sample can be drawn that includes every Nth (fourth or fifth, etc.) name from a random starting point between 1 and N. In the case of an organization that has 10,000 journalists on its list, one could draw every 20th name from a random starting point between 1 and 20 to obtain a sample of 500 journalists. The size of the sample will also vary according to the goals of a study, but generally one needs a sample of about 400 to obtain a sampling error of plus or minus 5 percentage points at the 95 percent level of confidence (Stempel et al., 2003, p. 241). A sample of 400 also provides enough cases to do some crosstabulations by type of medium, age, gender, etc. If the total population of journalists that one wants to generalize to is 500 or less, it is recommended that sampling not be done and that all members of the population be interviewed.

Interviewing

Most survey research books and chapters include discussions of the strengths and weaknesses of different kinds of interviewing, such as personal or face to face, telephone, mail, and in some cases e-mail or Internet surveys (see, e.g. Wimmer and Dominick, 2006, pp. 194–205). Even in this Internet age, it seems clear that most survey research of the public is done by telephone in those countries that have high telephone penetration. This is because telephone surveys offer higher response rates than mail or Internet surveys at a lower price than personal interviews, and they can be done quickly by a team of interviewers. Telephone surveys can also include more detailed questions, and interviewers can control the pace and order of the interview, as well as help clear up confusing questions or response categories.

There are some notable disadvantages to telephone interviewing, however, including the increasing use of caller ID devices for screening calls, cellular telephones that charge a fee to the recipient of a call by the minute, and the practice of "sugging" (selling something under the guise of doing a survey, which discourages participation). Other disadvantages of telephone interviewing include the inability to use visual illustrations (pictures, copies of newspapers or magazines, etc.).

In surveying US journalists, we have used telephone interviewing in all of our studies, but this is not the case in many countries. Of the 26 surveys of journalists conducted in 21 countries and territories that were reported in *The global journalist*, 13 were conducted by mail, five by personal (face-to-face) interviews, seven by telephone, and one by a combination of mail and personal interviews (Weaver, 1998, pp. 3–5). The telephone interviews were conducted in Australia, Great Britain (UK), Germany, Canada, and the United States and produced generally higher response rates than the surveys conducted by mail.

In the US studies, we sent letters explaining the study to all journalists in the sample two weeks before the interviewers called. In addition, the questionnaires were pretested on a small sample of local journalists who were not included in the samples for the studies. Telephone interviewers were instructed to ask each journalist for a convenient time for the interview and to reschedule if necessary. In the most recent 2002 survey, all journalists with confirmed valid telephone numbers were called up to 24 times, unless the journalist refused. Cases of unknown validity (persistent no answers or answering devices) were called a minimum of 14 times during the morning, afternoon, evening, late evening and weekend. Each refusal was attempted to be converted to a completed interview twice – at the first instance of refusal and again after a few days. Substitutions were allowed only if the original respondents had left journalism or could not be reached. If they had moved to another news organization, interviewers were instructed to track them. Substitutions were made with another person holding the same job title in the original news organization whenever possible. These efforts resulted in a response rate of 79 percent when those who were incapacitated, ill, deceased, never available, or no longer journalists were subtracted from the original sample and replacement names were chosen randomly from our original lists (Weaver et al., 2007, p. 261).

This very high response rate would not have been possible with mail or personal interviews, and probably not with Internet surveys either. We could not have afforded to do personal interviews with journalists in all 50 states, and we could not have followed up so often and so persistently with a mail survey. Also, we found journalists in the United States much more responsive to telephone calls than to letters or email messages, both for the lists of journalists working at a particular news organization and also for doing the actual interview, which took 50 minutes on average to complete.

Analyzing Survey Data

One of the advantages of doing computer assisted telephone interviewing (CATI) is that the interviewers enter the data directly into a computer file during the interview, so the fixed-response questions produce data that are ready to analyze using a spread sheet such as Excel or a statistical program such as SPSS (Statistical Package for the Social Sciences) as soon as the interviewing is completed. (See Riffe (2003) for more information about SPSS and data analysis.) There are also more programs available now for analyzing the text responses to open-ended questions, but this is a lengthier and more involved process than statistical analysis of closed-ended responses that are already coded into numbers at the end of a CATI survey.

The first step in analyzing quantitative data is obtaining the frequencies for each variable to examine the distributions of answers to make sure that all invalid values (no responses, refusals, don't knows) have been declared "missing" in the data file before attempting to compute any descriptive statistics (mean, median, mode, standard deviation, variance, etc.) or inferential statistics (various correlations or tests of differences between proportions or means) (Weaver, 2003).

The second step is to determine which measures are of most interest (the so-called "dependent" variables that one wishes to predict or explain) and which are likely to be predictors (or at least correlates) of these dependent variables (often called "independent" variables). Then one can use crosstabulations or correlations to check on the strength, direction, and statistical significance (if random sampling was employed) of these relationships. More complex statistical tests (often called multivariate) can be used to measure the relationships of several independent variables to one or more dependent variables (multiple regression, logistic regression, analysis of variance, etc.). (See Weaver, 2003, and Hayes, 2005, for more details on these statistics.)

A possible third step in analyzing survey data is to make comparisons with other surveys of journalists, from other time periods or other locations, that have asked similar questions. This was the approach taken in *The Global Journalist* book, where surveys of journalists from 21 different countries and territories were compared wherever possible (Weaver, 1998), and it was also the approach used in the series of surveys of US journalists done from 1971 to 2002 (Weaver and Wilhoit, 1986, 1996; Weaver et al., 2007). See the chapter on the methodology of comparative journalism research by Thomas Hanitzsch in this book for more information on the promises and pitfalls of comparing data about journalists and journalism across time and space.

Conclusions

This chapter has reviewed the major advantages and disadvantages of the survey as a method for studying journalists as compared with other methods such as observation, in-depth interviews, and content analysis. It has also discussed some of the major considerations and practices involved in constructing survey questions and questionnaires, in drawing samples of journalists for surveys, in conducting survey interviews with journalists, and in analyzing survey data. Where possible, comparisons between surveying journalists and the general public have been provided.

The survey remains one of the most common and most efficient ways of gathering representative information on the characteristics, opinions and attitudes of large groups of journalists. Surveys are less appropriate for collecting information on actual journalistic behavior than are observation studies and content analyses, and they are not as strong as in-depth interviews and observations for answering "why" and "how" questions. Ideally, surveys should include as many open-ended questions that allow journalists to speak in their own words as is practically possible, and they should be used in combination with other methods, such as content analysis and observation, to produce a more complete and nuanced picture of journalism and journalists around the world.

References

Arceneaux, K. (2006). Do campaigns help voters learn? A cross-national analysis. *British Journal of Political Science*, 36, 159–73.

Asher, H. (2001). *Polling and the public: What every citizen should know*. 5th edition. Washington, DC: CQ Press.

Fowler, F. J. Jr. (1988). *Survey research methods*. Revised edition. Thousand Oaks, CA: Sage.

Hayes, A. F. (2005). *Statistical methods for communication science*. Mahwah, NJ: Lawrence Erlbaum Associates.

Inoguchi, T., Basanez, M., Tanaka, A., and Dadavaev, T. (eds.) (2005). *Values and life styles in urban Asia. A cross-cultural analysis and sourcebook based on the AsiaBarometer survey of 2003*. Mexico City, Mexico: Siglo XXI Editores for University of Tokyo.

Johnstone, J. W. C., Slawski, E. J., and Bowman, W. W. (1976). *The news people: A sociological portrait of American journalists and their work*. Urbana, IL: University of Illinois Press.

Manheim, J. B., Rich, R. C., Willnat, L., and Brians, C. L. (2006). *Empirical political analysis: Research methods in political science*. New York: Pearson Longman.

Riffe, D. (2003). Data analysis and SPSS programs for basic statistics. In G. H. Stempel, D. H. Weaver, and G. C. Wilhoit (eds.), *Mass communication research and theory* (pp. 182–208). Boston, MA: Allyn and Bacon.

Shoemaker, P. J., and McCombs, M. E. (2003). Survey research. In G. H. Stempel, D. H. Weaver, and G. C. Wilhoit (eds.), *Mass communication research and theory* (pp. 231–51). Boston, MA: Allyn and Bacon.

Stempel, G. H., Weaver, D. H., and Wilhoit, G. C. (eds.) (2003). *Mass communication research and theory*. Boston, MA: Allyn and Bacon.

Weaver, D. H. (1998). *The global journalist: News people around the world*. Cresskill, NJ: Hampton Press.

Weaver, D. H. (2003). Basic statistical tools. In G. H. Stempel, D. H. Weaver, and G. C. Wilhoit (eds.), *Mass communication research and theory* (pp. 147–81). Boston, MA: Allyn and Bacon.

Weaver, D. H., and Wilhoit, G. C. (1986). *The American journalist: A portrait of US news people and their work*. Bloomington, IN: Indiana University Press.

Weaver, D. H. and Wilhoit, G. C. (1996). *The American journalist in the 1990s: US news people at the end of an era*. Mahwah, NJ: Lawrence Erlbaum Associates.

Weaver, D. H., Beam, R. A., Brownlee, B. J., Voakes, P. S., and Wilhoit, G. C. (2007). *The American journalist in the 21st century: US news people at the dawn of a new millennium*. Mahwah, NJ: Lawrence Erlbaum Associates.

Wilhoit, G. C., and Weaver, D. H. (1990). *Newsroom guide to polls and surveys*. Bloomington, IN: Indiana University Press.

Willnat, L., and Weaver, D. H. (2003). Through their eyes: The work of foreign correspondents in the United States. *Journalism*, 4, 403–22.

Wimmer, R. D., and Dominick, J. R. (2006). *Mass media research: An introduction*. 8th edition. Belmont, CA: Thomson/Wadsworth.

Chapter 10

Methods of Journalism Research – Content Analysis

Christian Kolmer

Motives and constraints of journalistic activity are linked to their impact on society through the journalistic product. Although a medium can have strong effects on a public simply by its existence (Donsbach, 1986), other forms of influence are related to the content, the information available to the public. Content analysis has become an important method of journalism research as a principal tool for analyzing the products of journalist activity. The relationship between the different environments in which journalists are working and their respective motivations and goals may vary from case to case, but an assessment of the qualities of journalistic work enables the scientist to gauge the relevance of the cultural, political and economic framework for production of media content. Thus in the several media systems that Hallin and Mancini (2004) identified, the role of journalists and media organizations differs notably. However, the ultimate relevance of these constraints for the daily work of journalists cannot be assessed without reference to the actual output of the journalistic production process.

As an example, the problem of bias cannot be discussed in a meaningful way without reference to content. Although many surveys among journalists have established the existence of certain political preferences (Donsbach, 1981), this will probably only become damaging to journalistic work that does not maintain the desired degree of objectivity when a slant one way or the other in the actual product can be demonstrated. Thus Groseclose and Milyo (2005) have examined political bias in US media sources by analyzing the quotation of political think tanks in news stories and comparing them to the quotation structures of political protagonists. Without any judgments of political orientations by themselves, they managed to compare actual media content with an extramedia baseline.

The use of content analysis as a methodology for communication research evolved notably after World War II. By 1952, Berelson had already published the first text book, paving the way for generations of media scientists. Nevertheless, the reception given to content analysis research outside of the scientific community has been rather reserved, especially in comparison to poll results. The relevance and validity of content analysis research has generally been impaired by the limits imposed on the studies by the restraints of the research economy.

Whereas sampling has been accepted for the investigation of great populations in medicine or social sciences, the approach to texts in literature or philosophy has mostly eschewed sampling. As far as the scope of a majority of studies has been limited to selected topics, media sources, periods of time, or even random samples of the coverage, the comparability of results to other research, based on interviews or observation has been restricted. Cross-national, or in a wider context, cross-cultural, comparisons are even more limited against this background.

The limiting factors have been addressed with methodological ingenuity, leading to a great variety of studies and subsequently to a much-improved understanding of the conditions, routines and procedures of journalistic activity. Nevertheless, in order to take into account the great variability of media content, in terms of chronological and media structures, the development of incessant and comprehensive studies becomes necessary; in other words continuous media monitoring. This long-term documentation of topic and protagonist structures over time does not only provide insights in the nature of journalistic activity but also establishes the basis and framework for more detailed studies on single topics, events, or media organizations. This way, continuous content analysis contributes to a better understanding of the impact of the media on society, insofar as observation of media content is a necessary condition for analysis of possible media effects. Brettschneider (2000) demonstrates the influence of television news on the perception of the state of the economy by the public. In his view "the comprehensive data are an indispensable source for studies on media effects relating to a variety of topics" (Brettschneider, 2004, p. 78).

Types of Content Analysis

Content-analytical methods have been classified in several ways, either by looking at the methodology or at the target of the analysis, linking media content either with the communicator, the recipient or the situation of the communication (Merten, 1995, pp. 119–278). Traditionally, hermeneutic or linguistic text analysis is confronted with the "classical" content analysis that has been developed to the most important methodological tool in communication science (Früh, 2001, pp. 47–66). Partly as a reaction to this dominance, alternative techniques have been developed in the past few decades.

Content analysis in the context of the present discussion "is a research technique for the objective, systematic, and quantitative description of the manifest content of communication" (Berelson, 1952, p. 18). This methodology has very often been defined as "quantitative-content analysis," whereas techniques developed in the hermeneutic or linguistic tradition are labeled as "qualitative." In contrast to these, other analysis methods that try to identify and analyze the characteristic and defining elements of media content, quantitative content analysis first of all establishes the numerical distribution of the variables and, second, makes inferences from these findings. Among communication scientists nowadays, there is agreement that content analysis can accomplish more than just a description of the subject matter of media products. From the results of content studies, conclusions about media organizations, their journalists, the social and political surroundings, and the probable media effects are possible and can be contrasted with other research. Insofar as every content analysis involves qualitative elements at least in the definition of the objectives of the study, the operationalization of the variables as well as in the interpretation of the results the confrontation of "quantitative" and "qualitative" analysis is misleading (Früh, 2001, pp. 67–74). In comparison with other techniques of content analysis, the classical methodology in the tradition of Berelson could be more appropriately labeled as standardized content analysis.

The whole range of content analysis techniques that relate to different research traditions can be classified according to Bonfadelli (2002) in Table 10.1.

The great majority of studies, in the United States as well as in Germany, draw on quantitative methods, in order to cope with the great amount of material typical for mass media content (Bonfadelli, 2002, p. 53).

Table 10.1 System of analysis instruments (Bonfadelli, 2002, p. 58 [translation by the author])

Counting and rating content – standardized quantifying instruments	
Descriptive	Topic, time, protagonist and stylistic structures
Explanatory	News values, clarity
Evaluating	Media bias research, reality check, media performance
Understanding text – qualitative perspectives of text analysis	
Communication science	Framing/schema theory
Ideology criticism	Rhetoric, discourse analysis, gender studies
Linguistics	Media language, dialogue analysis, conversation analysis, discourse analysi
Semiotics	Image analysis, advertising, gender studies
Cultural studies	Ritual, narrativity, reception analysis
Finding out reception and effects of media texts	
Communication science	Input–output analysis, media resonance, reception analysis

Limits and Benefits of Content Analysis in Journalism Research

The quantitative approach to content analysis has been criticized for several reasons. At purely emotional level, journalists in particular object to "bean-counting" as a misunderstanding of their creative work. The transfer from the analytical level of topic structures and tonality measures to the interpretative level of judgments, for instance of editorial quality, is not evident to practitioners engulfed by their daily work. Especially for such people, comparative analysis is instructive. The validity of inferences from quantities in the media content on the meaning and importance of this content has also been questioned from a scientific point of view. Quantifying media content entails the risk of underrating the importance of isolated cases and singular events that bring about effects out of proportion to their frequency. This distrust of mere figures masks the fact that non-standardized research techniques make inferences from structures and quantities too, but not in a similarly structured way (Früh, 2001, p. 68).

An even more basic objection to content analysis deals with the social context of the production and reception of media content that cannot be accounted for separately in the analysis (Ritsert, 1972). Insofar as this criticism applies to all types of empirical research, the solution relates not to the method of data collection, but to the basic design of the study. The application of comparative approaches in particular, both at national and international level, enables the researcher to allow for aspects of the social and political framework.

The classic definition of Bernard Berelson cited above, allows only for the analysis of "manifest" content that can be interpreted unequivocally according to the set of rules of the analysis. This definition therefore excludes all types of messages that cannot be interpreted without reference to other information – as, for instance, the literary means of expressing opinion "between the lines." Nevertheless, textual and visual information from mass media refers to the common understanding of the general public, because it is by definition produced for this unlimited public. A certain level of circumstantial knowledge is always necessary to understand a text correctly. This is assumed by the author of a text and can be expected from a trained media analyst that is living in the same environment as the target public of the analyzed medium. For instance, "the Chancellor" or the "boss of Daimler-Chrysler" are known by the majority of Germans and can therefore be identified in a text even when they are not mentioned by their names.

Nevertheless, identifying latent media content correctly is not trivial – even with exhaustive definitions and well-chosen examples, reliability of coding is limited. Therefore, researchers should try to base their hypotheses as far as possible on manifest characteristics that offer less difficulties for the analysis, for instance on the topics addressed instead of the frames alluded to, or to the persons and types of actions depicted in visuals instead of the favorability of the pictures. Measuring latent content is, however, still unavoidable when it comes to the tone of coverage. Reliable results can be obtained for these variables too, when the measurements of manifest and latent characteristics are separated.

Normally, academic research relies on sampling to deal with the great volume of mass media content; Bonfadelli (2002) states explicitly: "Only this method allows for *reliable* and *quantifying* statements about *great quantities of text*, which are typical for the mass media. Therefore representative samples are necessary . . ." (p. 53 [translation by the author]). From a critical perspective, the reliability of quantitative content analysis impairs the validity of the results. Critics especially take exception to these sampling procedures, because absences cannot be measured from text samples. As will be evident, these objections can at least be partly overcome by the introduction of continuous media monitoring. Despite this, a total analysis of the whole content of even single media outlets would be impractical.

Media Sample

Content analysis has to start with the definition of the basic population for the study. This decision includes several levels, ranging from the media outlets, over the relevant sections to the periods of the analysis. The first choice relates to the alternative case study versus long-time comparison. Whereas for a special study the selection of the media to be examined has to be derived from the guiding questions of investigation, a general analysis of journalistic output has to establish a frame of reference first, because the analysis of single media sources remains meaningless without reference to general standards. In the establishment of the time frame, the researcher should take into account the high volatility of media content that is characteristic of the ever-changing world of topics and trends in the media. The potential danger of small samples for the general validity of the results is obvious.

Transferring the concept of opinion leaders from individuals in their social environment to media sources in the public sphere leads to the identification of opinion-leading media. On the one hand, there is the definition of opinion-leading media sources that refers to their impact on other journalists. Media that are regularly used by journalists for personal information and as a source for the production of journalistic content act as inter-media agenda setters. Such media can be identified in several ways, for instance by polling journalists (Reinemann, 2003), by observation of journalistic activity, and by analyzing quotation structures in media content. These media constitute models that are perceived as successful and exemplary by journalist.

The continuous analysis of the quotations of other media in 37 German print and television media outlets shows the established lead of Spiegel and Bild-Zeitung as the most important media organizations in Germany (see Table 10.2).

This example illustrates patterns of opinion leadership within a national frame of reference. Among the ten most-quoted news organizations, there is no reference to international or foreign media. This pattern has changed recently with the emergence of the Al-Jazeera satellite channel as a competitor in the international television market, providing dramatic footage from the war and terrorism locations in the Middle East region (Hahn, 2005).

Table 10.2 Opinion leadership: quotations in German media January–June, 2004. Basis: 11,713 quotations in 37 German television and print media (Albrecht, 2004, p. 68)

Medium	No. of quotes
Spiegel	1,139
Bild-Zeitung	622
Focus	496
Welt am Sonntag	377
ZDF	349
ARD	335
Die Welt	321
Süddeutsche Zeitung	294
Berliner Zeitung	288

However, opinion-leading media can be defined as the media sources with the greatest impact on the general public. Besides circulation data and television ratings, the agenda-setting power of media types and single outlets can be established with the joint use of content analysis and polling. Examples from Germany show that television news has a relatively strong influence on the perception of problems by the population, although their capability to set the national agenda is restricted.

A striking example of the agenda-setting power of television is the mad cow disease (BSE) panic in Germany in 2000–1. Until fall 2000, German television reported about BSE as a problem of English farming without any relevance for Germany. After the discovery of the first infected cow, television reporting about BSE increased dramatically. This coverage not only influenced the perception of the most important problems by the public, but also the consumption of beef. Only nine months after the speedy decrease of media awareness of BSE, consumption behavior reached its former level (Communication from Central Market and Price Reporting Agengy for the Agricultural Sector, 2002, [Zentrale Markt- und Preisberichtstelle für Erzeugnisse der Land-, Forst- und Ernaerungswirtschaft, ZMP]).

These findings show that a sample of the respected national dailies, the main political weeklies and the television main evening news is suitable for establishing a frame of reference for content analysis studies. Depending on regional structures and the use of local media by the population, this sample has to be augmented by regional newspapers or television programs.

For reasons of comparison, therefore, television news should be analyzed entirely, whereas the evaluation of print media may be reduced to the news/politics and business sections if the objective of the study is an analysis of the media coverage of current affairs. Nevertheless, the selection of the material for analysis has to take into account the characteristics of the respective media systems. A distinction between the title page, the first page of the business section and the rest of the newspapers allows for the different constraints of the news selection in television and print media outlets. For topics that are addressed in special sections of print media (e.g. arts and technology), the limitation to the news and business sections shows how much these topics have grabbed the attention of the general public, whereas an exhaustive analysis has to incorporate the special sections.

The great variability in terms of topic structures and tonality of reporting is a defining element of journalism. Events and topics appear and disappear from the media agenda without an intelligible pattern. Therefore, only the continuous analysis of the whole content of a medium gives an accurate image of the media product. Although public opinion can be polled in a weekly or monthly cycle, an assessment of the impact of the media on public opinion is only possible with an uninterrupted analysis of the media content.

In many cases, content studies rely on media databases, such as Lexis-Nexis or Factiva, for their material. This is evidently not practical for continuous media monitoring, because these sources are not reproducing the media content in its entirety and structure, but even for a special topic analysis the use of databases is rather dangerous. Data retrieval and thus the quality of the material depend on the quality of the search string, the composition of which can suffer from gaps due to imperfect knowledge of the media content. It is quite probable that the researcher is not aware in advance of some aspects of his topics that have been raised in the media. Furthermore, database content can be proven to be incomplete and incongruent to the content published. However, e-papers are identical to the printed issues, but data retrieval is more complicated.

Analysis Levels

Media content can be analyzed on several levels, ranging from single information elements within a news story to a whole issue or news show. The levels and units of analysis are defined in respect to the research targets, they can relate to formal structures and the content of the material. Bonfadelli (2002) distinguishes between the syntactical, semantic and pragmatic levels of analysis in contrast to units of analysis, defined by formal or content criteria (see Table 10.3, overleaf).

On the one hand, the selection of the appropriate level of analysis has consequences for the results of a study. It is evident that the topic structure of the coverage can be analyzed in much more detail with a technique based on the examination of statements. On the other hand, analysis of the story level might render different results from an analysis at the statement level. This is especially important for the measurement of valuations (Reinemann and Engesser, 2001). Depending on the goals of an analysis and the definition of the tonality of a text, analysis at the story level might result in a more polarized characterization than

Table 10.3 Levels and units of analysis (Bonfadelli, 2002, p. 89 [translation by the author])

Levels of analysis

Syntactical level	Syllables per word: length of words
	Words per sentence: length of sentences
	Length of stories in cm per column, mm²
	Structure of sentences
	Clarity
	Title – lead – text – illustration
	Elements of design-like pictures, frames or coloring
Semantic level	Topics and topic structures
	Protagonists
	Valuations
	Arguments
Pragmatic level	Direct speech/quotations
	Instructions for action > intended effects

Units of analysis

Formal units	Whole issue: editorial content vs. advertisements
	Whole story: space in mm²
	Single sentences: number of words
	Single elements: lead (yes/no), illustrations (number)
Units of content	Topics per story
	Persons resp. groups of persons
	Arguments
	Valuations

---

the analysis at statement level. This results from the under-representation of neutral or ambivalent information that is ignored when a small surplus of positive or negative information is decisive for the evaluation of the whole story.

Such differences are confusing and at first sight undermine the validity of the respective results. But in fact, this example shows how content analysis functions as a tool for condensing information. The coarser the level of analysis gets, the stronger the pressure to subsume the information under a more extreme category, in order not to lose valuable data, in this case the positive or negative evaluations. Accordingly the codebook could expressly ask the analyst to code a report as "predominantly positive/negative," when it is overall neutral but contains a single piece of positive/negative information. To facilitate and document in respect of this decision, the codebook should provide a special code for these values. For the detailed analysis of the coverage of political and business protagonists, these findings suggest the superiority of coding on statement level, which additionally reproduces topic and source structures in a much richer data set.

Codebook: Categories and Definitions

In order to be objective, that is, independent from the personal characteristics of the researcher, and systematic, that is, designed with respect to the research questions and exhaustive in respect to the investigated communication, content analysis has to be based on rules. Characteristics of the media content that are evident, but not covered by these rules cannot be analyzed properly within the boundaries of the content analysis, and serve only as clues to the interpretation of the results.

For a comprehensive coding system, topic and protagonist categories are principally open, due to the incomplete knowledge of the researcher and ongoing changes in the real world. Nevertheless, the topic and protagonist categorical systems can provide a framework for the coding of all possible types of issues and protagonists, be they people or organizations. For the facilitation of the coding process, the coding system should consist of several levels of categorization providing residual categories for every sub-group. For topics and protagonists not covered by the system, the coder can be instructed to make a note in clear text. This allows for the continuous updating of the codebook.

Progress in information technology allows the use of a computer interface for data entry, dispensing with paper coding sheets. The use of the computer for the coding enhances coding speed and minimizes errors by the media analysts. These topics and analogous structured protagonist categories offer no serious problem for the training of media analysts. If only the main protagonist and the main topic are to be coded, rules for selecting these have to be formulated. With regard to the reliability of the coding, the volume of coverage – in lines or seconds for television news – is the decisive factor. In the case of two or more equally present topics or protagonists, the coder is not forced to make a decision and can choose the residual category "several protagonists" respectively "no main topic." The media analysts reproduce the media content faithfully, for instance coding criminal acts only as political crime, when a political motive or background is mentioned in the news story.

Much more difficult is the coding of valuations or tone of coverage. In order to stringently organize the coding of valuations, only valuations of protagonists, that is, of persons and organizations, are coded. The valuation only relates to the description of the protagonist, not to the event described. In the coding of valuations, the issue of "latent" content is encountered. Valuations can basically be expressed in two ways: by the use of terms with either clearly positive or negative connotations, such as "gangster" or "hero." This explicit rating can be contrasted with an implicit rating that embeds the description of the protagonist in positive or negative context. Media Tenor allows for the whole story as context unit – if the coder can relate ambiguous information to other unequivocal information in the same story, this context can be used to interpret the respective valuation. For instance "redundancies" are presented in a positive context, when the cost savings for the company are mentioned. However, the simple fact, that "redundancies" are reported in a business paper does not prejudice the information as per se positive.

A further version of implicit valuations refers to facts or issues that are perceived either positively or negatively in certain society. Rising jobless figures, for instance, are negative news, because these constitute negative information about the state of the economy, even when the journalist does not assess this development in explicit terms. In cases that cannot be decided unequivocally, the media analysts are required to code the valuation as "ambivalent." To distinguish between manifest and latent valuations, many studies measure them separately on scales with six values:

/0/ neutral
/1/ positive
/2/ quite positive
/3/ ambivalent
/4/ quite negative
/5/ negative

Whereas the rating of a protagonist can be analyzed with sufficient reliability, the assessment of the events described in the reporting is rather problematic. Besides clearly negative events, such as natural disasters, a big part of happenings in the real world cannot be evaluated without reference to basic values that cannot be imposed on the media analysts by the codebook in a sufficient way. As a substitute the concept of negativism can be traced back to the tonality of the reporting about protagonists.

Coder Training and Quality Control

Quality control comprises the whole range of measures taken in order to ensure that coding of materials takes place according to the rules. Quality control begins with the recruitment and training of the media analysts, but a continuous analysis coders' work also has to be checked in a regular and systematic way. Additionally, they have to be kept up to date with adaptations of the codebook and developments in both the real and media worlds.

For continuous analysis, the training of coders is of the utmost importance. Coders do not only need a thorough comprehension of the texts in terms of the facts described, but they also have to get used to working on the text in accordance with the coding rules. Training of coders for comprehensive content analysis can take up to 12 weeks. First, the capability of text comprehension has to be tested in order to avoid expensive training expenditure. For the analysis of business sections in particular, coders need to have more than a basic knowledge of economic terms and business life. With the use of glossaries, the required understanding and coding of business sections can be facilitated. Nevertheless, during the whole coding period, trained research personnel should be available for questions from the media analysts.

In contrast to analysis projects dealing with a defined period, a continuous content analysis has to deal with a changing media world; new topics, new protagonists and new terms get introduced into the media, whose existence very often cannot be anticipated. Therefore, systematic adaptations of the codebook are inevitable. These changes have to be communicated to the analysts immediately and their awareness and compliance has to be checked. Sections of the codebook in which subject matter is of comparatively little relevance to the analyzed material, have to be kept in mind by special training sessions.

Compliance with the coding rules is an indispensable condition for a reliable content analysis. Besides the reliability measurements that are normally applied by communication scientists and requested from the reviewed journals, a continuous monitoring of analysts, performance can enhance coding quality. The procedure comprises monthly standard tests with a pattern solution provided by the training department and checked by research personnel, as well as spot checks, drawn from the coded material and checked by staff from the training department. This ongoing quality control serves as a tool for establishing reliable results. As a guideline, Früh judges coder reliability between 0.75 and 0.85 for a topic variable of a special codebook focusing on the nuclear energy discussion as good to very good (Früh, 2001, p. 173), but Media Tenor aims at an average rate of correspondence of 90 percent, envisaging additional training sessions for analysts with a rate of correspondence below 85 percent. External validation of the coding system is improved by the discussion and presentation of results to editorial teams and journalists, as well as to clients with either a political or corporate background.

Special problems arise in the development of cross-national studies. Although the coding system in itself is neutral in terms of the national background, the wording of the respective categories is shaped in a national context. Translation of the codebook has to involve researchers and analysts from all countries involved in the project. If possible, standard tests should be conducted with identical texts in all countries, although the comprehension even of English texts is limited in other countries. However, translation into the respective languages may destroy or change latent content and thus prevent a correct reliability control. At least with regard to training staff, standard tests are indispensable for the establishment of cross-cultural reliability and validity of the analysis.

An international comparative analysis of topic structures in main evening television news exemplifies the differences caused by the different media environments, ranging from the media systems to the grade of involvement of the Iraq war of 2003. Arab satellite programs and television news from the Allied countries, the United Kingdom, and the United States focus much more on international politics than the news programs from Germany or South Africa. Table 10.4 (overleaf) shows in ways which content analysis can contribute to comparative international journalism research.

Over the past decade, continuous content analysis of leading media has evolved notably, although primarily as a tool for PR consulting and political media research.

Table 10.4 Topic structures of foreign television coverage in international television news. Basis: 155,889 news stories in 26 television news programs (Kolmer, 2006, p. 17)

	Germany	UK	USA	Arab satellite TV	South Africa	Total
Crime/domestic security	12.57	12.51	8.34	11.90	7.18	11.35
Domestic policy	10.58	14.31	13.46	22.09	13.47	14.63
International politics	22.97	32.61	49.17	44.51	18.71	32.61
Business/economy	9.92	6.42	1.96	8.50	3.64	7.58
Society/social policy	10.80	8.76	14.02	3.97	8.71	9.01
Environment/ transport/science	4.55	3.88	2.72	1.09	1.62	3.07
Sports	13.79	7.75	0.95	4.49	34.35	10.94
Accidents/natural disasters	9.40	6.66	5.35	2.20	6.90	6.47
Human interest/ history/other topics	5.41	7.10	4.02	1.25	5.42	4.33
Total	100	100	100	100	100	100

While political and economic actors have implemented "media monitoring" – continuous content analysis – as a tool for issue management, media organizations use the same data for quality control. Opinion leadership among news outlets can be measured by analyzing quotations and topic structures over time. The validity of professional norms, for instance the separation of news from opinion, can be checked by comparing different types of media in various countries with differing media systems. The availability of long-term timelines from different countries therefore poses new opportunities for journalism research. International comparisons of topic or protagonist structures will give new insights into the role of external factors in the shaping of journalistic procedures. In connection with other methods, content analysis offers new insights into the nature of journalism in changing world.

References

Albrecht, C. (2004). Der Wille zur Wirkung: Welche Themen die einflußreichsten Medien auf die Agenda setzten [The will to influence: Which topics influential media put on the agenda]. *Medien Tenor*, 146, 68–71.

Berelson, B. (1952). *Content analysis in communication research*. Glencoe, IL: Free Press.

Bonfadelli, H. (2002). *Medieninhaltsforschung: Grundlagen, Methoden, Anwendungen* [*Media content research: Basic principles, methods, and applications*]. Konstanz: UVK.

Brettschneider, F. (2000). Reality Bytes: Wie die Medienberichterstattung die Wahrnehmung der Wirtschaftslage beeinflußt (*How media coverage influences the perception of the state of the economy*]. In J. W. Falter, O. W. Gabriel, and H. Rattinger (eds.), *Wirklich ein Volk? Die politischen Orientierungen von Ost- und Westdeutschen im Vergleich* [*Really one people? Political orientations of East and West Germans in comparison*] (pp. 539–69). Opladen: Leske and Budrich.

Brettschneider, F. (2004). Medien tenor: Indispensable to a scientific analysis of media coverage. In *Medien Tenor. Agenda Setting Conference 2004: Conference Material*. Bonn.

Donsbach, W. (1981). *Gesellschaftliche Aufgaben der Massenmedien und berufliche Einstellungen von Journalisten. Ein Vergleich kommunikationspolitischer Konzepte über die Funktionen der Massenmedien mit empirischen Ergebnissen zum Selbstverständnis von Journalisten* [*Social function of mass media and professional self-conception of journalists. A comparison of communication-political concepts of the function of mass media with empirical results about the self-conception of journalists*]. Philosophy dissertation. Mainz.

Donsbach, W. (1986). *The impact of television on rural areas of tunesia. A panel field experiment on changes in social perception, attitudes and roles after the introduction of television*. Section sociology and social psychology of the International Association for Mass Communication Research. New Delhi.

Früh, W. (2001). *Inhaltsanalyse: Theorie und Praxis* [*Content analysis: Theory and practice*]. Konstanz: UVK.

Groseclose, T., and Milyo, J. (2005): A measure of media bias. *The Quarterly Journal of Economics*, CXX(4), 119–237.

Hahn, O. (2005). Arabisches Satelliten-Nachrichtenfernsehen. Entwicklungsgeschichte, Strukturen und Folgen für die Konfliktberichterstattung aus dem Nahen und Mittleren Osten [Arab satellite news TV. History of development, structures and consequences for conflict reporting from the near and Middle East]. In C. Eilders and L. Hagen (eds.), *Medien und Kommunikationswissenschaft, Themenheft "Medialisierte Kriege und Kriegsberichterstattung,"* 53, pp. 241–60.

Hallin, D. C., and Mancini (2004). *Comparing media systems. Three models of media and politics*. Cambridge, UK: Cambridge University Press.

Kolmer, C. (2006). *Worlds apart. Structures and tendencies in the foreign coverage of German, English, US, Arab and South African television news*. Paper presented to the ICA Preconference 2006, Messages from abroad – Foreign political news in a globalized media landscape. Munich, June 17, 2006.

Merten, K. (1995). *Inhaltsanalyse: Einführung in Theorie, Methode und Praxis* [*Content analysis. Introduction in theory, methodology and practice*]. Opladen: Westdeutscher Verlag.

Reinemann, C. (2003). *Medienmacher als Mediennutzer. Einfluß- und Kommunikationsstrukturen im politischen Journalismus der Gegenwart* [*Media producers as media users. Influence and communication structures in contemporary political journalism*]. Cologne, Vienna, Weimar: Böhlau.

Reinemann, C., and Engesser, E. (2001). Können sich Aussagen und Beiträge widersprechen? Die Relevanz sozialpsychologischer Erkenntnisse zur Personenwahrnehmung für die inhaltsanalytische Tendenzmessung [Can statements and stories contradict another? The relevance of social-psychological insights about the perception of personality for content-analytical measurements of tone]. In W. Wirth and E. Lauf (eds.), *Inhaltsanalyse: Perspektiven, Probleme, Potentiale* [*Content analysis: Perspectives, problems, potentials*] (pp. 218–33). Cologne: Herbert von Halem.

Ritsert, J. (1972). *Inhaltsanalyse und Ideologiekritik: Ein Versuch über die kritische Sozialforschung* [*Content analysis and criticism of ideology. An essay about critical social science*]. Frankfurt/Main: Athenäum Fischer.

Chapter 11

Methods of Journalism Research – Observation

Thorsten Quandt

Beyond Everyday Perception: Observation as a Method of Media and Journalism Research

Imagine you are sitting in a street café on a sunny afternoon. The streets are busy, and you can watch the people passing by. Maybe you can see a mother with a twin buggy – she is in a hurry and moves quickly toward a nearby lift to the subway. A young man, probably a student, is sitting at the table next to you. He is reading a newspaper with great interest, so the coffee in front of him is getting cold. Another guest is an elegant lady in her mid forties. She is talking to somebody on her cell phone. While you are watching this scenery, an ambulance is driving down the road at high speed with its siren blaring. The student looks up from his paper to see what is happening, and the lady starts to talk louder in order to drown the noise, then suddenly, she ends her call by quickly saying "I call you later." All this happens in just a few seconds, and it is most likely that you are perceiving many more details: The color of the lady's dress, the unusual size of the buggy, the stubble of the student, the pleasant smell of the coffee in front of you, and so on.

This was just one example of an everyday observation. Probably everybody could add many more situations where they are scrutinizing their surroundings and the actions of their fellow human beings. As Selltiz, Jahoda, Deutsch, and Cook put it in their classic book on "Research Methods in Social Relations": "We are all constantly observing – noticing what is going on around us . . .; as long as we are awake, we are almost constantly engaged in observation. It is our basic method of getting information about the world around us" (Selltiz et al., 1967, p. 200). However, in the social sciences, the term "observation" has a more specialized meaning. It refers to a certain method of data gathering, and it has some methodological implications that even go beyond the data gathering process. Several specifics separate a scientific approach from everyday observation (or "chance observation," as Selltiz et al. call it (1967, p. 200), as described here some forty years ago:

> Observation becomes a scientific technique to the extent that it (1) serves a formulated research purpose, (2) is planned systematically, (3) is recorded systematically

and related to more general propositions rather than being presented as a set of interesting curiosa, and (4) is subjected to checks and controls on validity and reliability.

(Selltiz et al., 1967, p. 200)

The first three points are certainly true for any type and use of the method, including tightly structured, automated observations or much more open, qualitative approaches; the latter, however, is still questioned by many, and especially by authors that favor a more "open," qualitative approach – they regard an observation as a more subjective thing, which is inherently an interpretation process that cannot be controlled in the same way as other types of data gathering. Actually, in communication and journalism studies, the observation is very often reduced to this special type of a qualitative, explorative method – by its critics as well as its followers. In effect, observation studies are still regarded as being a, "soft" approach by the large majority of journalism researchers – and as a mere addition to the other methods of data gathering. This is a very unfortunate reduction: Several breakthrough studies in communicator research relied on observations, and a lot of information about journalism in particular could not be gathered without such studies. Actually, the observation is the oldest and probably most direct way to gain information about journalism – early communication and journalism research did not rely so much on interview studies or content analysis, but mainly on observation.[1]

In the following section, we introduce several types of observation studies in order to show that there is much variation to the method that goes beyond "everyday perception" and "qualitative exploration". Then, we evaluate the pros and cons of some important approaches by discussing possibilities and uses of observations studies on the basis of "real life" scenarios and solutions to common research interests. Finally, we briefly outline paths for further development and future uses of observations in journalism studies.

Observation Studies: Typology

We started this chapter with the description of an "everyday" observation – which can also be described as an open, participant observation without a structured instrument. This is seen as the dominant role model of observation studies by many, because it is the "standard mode" of perception. However, this is just a small segment of what is available. Basically, there are three relevant dimensions that differentiate between the various types of observation studies. The first is the grade of standardization, the second is the involvement of the observer in the field, and the third is the obtrusiveness of the observation situation. There are several variations to each of these and not all combinations are practicable (for an overview see Gehrau, 2002).

The most prominent variation in data collection usually refers to the *grade of standardization*, that is, whether the observer uses a standardized codebook as opposed to open documentation, such as writing down his impressions in a diary.

There are also combinations and in-betweens, such as standardized codebooks with some open items (for instance, writing down "additional observations"). Besides this basic differentiation, there are numerous other variations. For example, one could also discern between automatic and traditional "manual" observation. Automatic observation includes data collection with computers, such as archiving log files or web site use (which can be seen as an automatic machine coding of human behavior). This also points to another differentiation criterion. Some observations are "direct" in the sense that the observation is synchronous to the observed behavior, whereas others use "behavior traces" (Wolling and Kuhlmann, 2003, p. 138) as their basis of analysis. These "traces" are the observable result of earlier behavior, mostly in the form of physical artifacts,[2] so the data collection is not taking place at the same time as the behavior itself.

The *involvement of the observer* (which is mostly defined by his or her level of participation) is another relevant dimension to discern between different types of observation studies. In many situations, an observation is only possible if the observer becomes part of the observed reality: "The participant observer gathers data by participating in the daily life of the group or organization he studies" (Becker, 1958, p. 652). However, participant observation can cause ethical problems (when the observer remains incognito, therefore coding behavior of people that are unaware of the observation) as well as reactivity (when the observer alters the field due to his participation). Nevertheless, this is sometimes the method of choice in journalism studies, because it is the only way to get access to the field and the respective observation subjects – some professionals are only observable by other professionals. There is one misconception about the term "participant" observation, though: Very often, one can read that the observer was "participating" in the field, although obviously, he remained absolutely passive. This is the case with many newsroom observations, where the observer does not work as a journalist, but only observes what he sees without getting involved in the journalistic process. For the sake of clarity, one should add here whether the observer was actively participating or not because active participation and inclusion in the observed processes denotes a very special type of observation, whereas passive participation is basically a "standard" field study.

To remain passive or become active is a quality of the observer's involvement that is sometimes confused with the *"visibility" and obtrusiveness of the observation*. However, from the outside, even the presence of a passive observer can be known to everybody in the field (open observation), whereas an active observer can remain invisible because he is working as a journalist and taking notes in secret (hidden or undercover observation) – or vice versa. The obtrusiveness is a quality of the whole observation situation – it has something to do with the positioning of the observer and the knowledge of the observed subjects about being observed. In an open observation, this knowledge might affect the behavior of the subjects (reactivity); therefore many researchers prefer hidden observations. In contrast to an open observation, hidden or undercover observations are carried out without the knowledge – and usually without the approval – of the observed. It goes without saying that this can pose severe ethical problems, as mentioned above. However, field observations in journalism are very often just partially open. For example, if one observes the behavior of a specific journalist, it might be necessary to follow him, for instance, to a press conference. Out of practical considerations, it might be impossible to inform every individual that the journalists (and the observer) will meet during that conference. So the journalist knows about the observation, but other people in the field do not.

This is not the only variation of observation situations. Usually, one type of study is overlooked in journalism studies: Observations can also be used in experimental designs. In most cases, this results in a very specific "setting" as well – while non-experimental observations are nearly always carried out in the field, a lot of experimental observations are laboratory based. There are exceptions to the rule, and one could also set a controlled stimulus in the field as part of an experimental design; so the connection between experiment and laboratory is not necessary. However, experiments are an uncommon form of research, at least in journalism studies,[3] and experimental field observations are even more rare than laboratory experiments.

Besides the above-mentioned forms of differentiating observation studies, there are other, less prominent distinctions (such as self-observation/introspection versus outside observation) (Gehrau, 2002, p. 31). However, we believe that most types of observations in journalism studies can be described using the differentiation principles named here. The three main dimensions (standardization of the instrument, involvement of the observer in the field, obtrusiveness of the observation situation) open up a space where we can locate most studies. It must be noted that some areas of this space describe unlikely combinations, such as a fully standardized, actively participant, but hidden observation (but that does not mean that such combinations are impossible). However, some other combinations are used very often, because they are working very well in certain fields. Three of these combinations are described in more detail below, because we feel that these are probably the most interesting for journalism researchers.

Applications and Scenarios for Journalism Research

In this short section, we cannot offer a full methodological discussion on the merits and problems of observation studies – there are other, more specialized works on empirical research that do this (Berger, 2000; Stempel, Weaver and Wilhoit, 2003; Bryman, 2004). However, we would like to present some possible uses of the method in journalism studies by briefly describing common scenarios. This short overview might give a good impression of the possibilities as well as the restrictions of the method.

Newsroom observations

Newsroom observations are probably the "standard" of observations in journalism studies. In this type of research, an observer goes "into" the media organizations and tries to observe the work of journalists in an everyday setting. All kinds of newsrooms and journalists have been successfully observed by researchers world-wide (e.g. Berkowitz, 1992; Christensen, 2003; Clausen, 2004; Matthews, 2005; Quandt, 2005). The history of this type of study goes back to early gatekeeper research, and it includes some of the discipline's classic studies (see note 1).

Newsroom studies are comparably popular for several reasons. First, it is the method of choice when trying to get a first impression of the work routines and work conditions of journalists. Therefore, especially new and unknown types of journalistic work are the ideal companion for this kind of exploration study. Second, it allows for an "unfiltered" view on the social reality of journalistic work (as long as reactivity and other side effects of the observation are under control). We know from combined survey/observation studies that observation studies are better in getting "objective" data on what the journalists are doing and for how long (Altmeppen, Donges, and Engels, 1999), whereas interview studies give us a good impression of the opinions, attitudes, estimations and values of the journalists. Third, as mentioned above, newsroom studies have a long tradition. There are many studies that can serve as a role model, and to a certain extent, one can compare findings. Last but not least, newsroom studies can serve as a source for inspiration when doing research on a certain type of journalism. Very often, new ideas and questions arise from a newsroom study – which can be checked later on, using representative survey studies. In this sense, newsroom studies help to find the unexpected and surprising.

Naturally, the range of possible designs is wide, from highly structured observation by a passively participating observer whose role is known to everybody in the field (e.g. Quandt, 2005) to the undercover observation by an actively participating observer who primarily takes notes (Wallraff, 1977, as a non-scientific[4] example). One can observe individuals as well as whole newsrooms (Rühl, 1969), focusing every type of behavior or just selected actions (such as decision and writing processes). The choice of method depends very much on the research aim and practical considerations, which goes without saying, but also on the knowledge of the field – structured observations are only an option if the observer can develop categories for a codebook based on earlier studies. If there is insufficient knowledge of the expected phenomena, the researcher has to use open instruments such as observation diaries.[5]

Input(-throughput)-output analyses

Journalism researchers have always been interested in the selection processes that take place in newsrooms, but also in other stages of the news production process, for example in news agencies, in PR departments, in the political sphere and elsewhere. The biggest part of the related research took place in newsrooms – actually, that was the main interest of the early gatekeeper studies: focusing on the selection processes of the editors. However, input-throughput-output analysis is a special form of observation that is not necessarily bound to the newsroom, and it is somewhat different from the standard newsroom studies as described above.

The input-throughput-output study is not focusing on the journalist's work routines per se, but on the flow of the news items and what happens to these items during the editorial processing.

As the name indicates, this type of study checks for information input into the news system (or parts of it), looks what happens in this system, and compares it with the output. Therefore, its observation object is not the journalist or a group of journalists, but a particular selection stage (horizontal perspective) or the news item on its way through the different stages (vertical perspective). In the early gatekeeper studies, one can find the roots of this type of research design: David Manning White asked a wire editor to collect all the news items he had to process during the day. After the work day, the editor had to explain for each collected news item why he kept it – or not (White, 1950). While this study did include some kind of self-observation by the journalist, it predominantly relied on a combination of content analysis (or interpretation) and interviews. Actually, one could completely ignore the throughput by just analyzing what goes into the "black box" of the newsroom and what leaves the system, thus excluding any observation part. Usually, this is described as an input-output study. While mere input-output studies are much more popular, a full input-throughput-output study can offer a deeper understanding of the selection processes in the newsroom, because it is not based on assumptions of what might have happened there. This comes at a price, though. Observing the path of the various selection processes in newsrooms is a very complicated task. Usually, there are many stages that a given news item will pass, even in one newsroom. In the highly team-oriented working environments of modern news media, it can be extremely difficult to follow a news item that is affected by various decision and selection processes in a network of subject relations. Basically, news processing is not always linear, so tracing the way of the news can be like finding a path in a labyrinth. It becomes even more complicated when doing an analysis on several stages of the process and trying to analyze what exactly happens to the news items in these stages. Here, it would be sensible to concentrate on individual news items or a small section of the news input, even more since the amount of information that has to be processed in news media is huge. For example, news agencies usually produce hundreds or thousands of individual news items every day (Quandt, 2005), and most news media use this material extensively.

So depending on the researcher's interest, there are several options for input-throughput-output studies: case studies might focus on individual news items during the whole selection process, other studies will try to control all the news that pass one selection stage. The latter will probably be relying on a standardized code scheme, whereas the first will use a full case description. In both instances, the observation does not necessarily depend on an observer in the field: Observing input, throughput and output could be automated or be done by the journalists themselves (if organized intelligently, this will not affect the actual selection process during the work hours). However, such a study will require more than that. If the researcher is interested in the reasons for the selection processes, he has to ask the respective editors for their views and their explanations. Therefore, the researcher must combine several methods here.

Usability studies

Our first two research scenarios were somewhat "traditional," at least from the perspective of a journalism researcher. Both were focusing on newsroom – or at least production – processes. This is the "classic" perspective of journalism research, which is largely "journalists" research. However, journalism researchers should be interested in other elements of the information process – for example the news content and the audience.

Observation studies can be used with success for analyzing the reception of news items in various ways. In the past ten years, many studies have focused on the "usability" of online media (most of them being "practical" market research, rather than scientific "pure research"). Here, the researchers are interested in optimizing news media by observing their use and finding problems in the reception process. Nevertheless, there are also other aspects to this type of study – for example, it can be used to develop user typologies and analyze the logics of news reception directly in the situation of a given media use. It does not come as a surprise that this type of study has been applied to "new" (online) media. Here, the knowledge about the actual use of the media is rather limited.

Methodologically, usability studies can come in various forms, but all of these include the presentation of some (news) media material to an audience or individuals. The use of the presented material will be observed and subsequently analyzed. Therefore, this type of study can be aimed at the content and/or the reception process, thus offering a lot of variation possibilities in both directions. For example, one can manipulate the stimulus material and present it to various groups of users in order to find causal connections between the changes in certain variables and the users' reactions (experimental setting). Usually, this kind of usability study takes place in a laboratory with a maximum amount of control over the observation's setting. It depends on the study's aims whether the observer and the data gathering tools such as cameras or microphones/recording devices are visible or not – but in any case, lab settings are regarded as being artificial. There has been criticism that the findings are not easily transferable to real-life situations (which is not necessarily the aim of experimental studies, though).

It must be noted that usability studies are not limited to experimental observations in laboratory settings. One could conceive usability studies under real-life conditions as well, and they do not have to be experimental. It is also possible to combine the observation with additional methods, such as asking the user for explanations of his actions during the use situation – and there are many possibilities that have not even been tried in journalism studies so far.

The Future of Observation Studies in Journalism Research

Observation is a very powerful research method. As pointed out in the last section, it offers many possibilities for journalism research, and it can be used in many different situations. It is not limited to unstructured, open participant observation, which is very often regarded as the "role model" for observations.

Nevertheless, one cannot deny some problematic sides of observation studies. Some are obvious from our previous descriptions, and some are very well documented in the literature (e.g. Selltiz et al., 1967; Becker, 1958; Berger, 2000; Gehrau, 2002). The most prominent criticism can be summed up as follows:

- In most cases, drawing random samples is nearly impossible. Therefore "representativeness" (in the sense of conclusions based on inferential statistics) cannot be achieved.
- Field access can be difficult and rather complicated. In some cases, direct access will not be possible at all.
- Under field conditions, potential sources of trouble cannot be fully controlled. One cannot foresee all events that might threaten the success of the study.
- In addition to unforeseen events, there are other sources of problems – for example, the interaction of the observer with the field can lead to unwanted effects and reactivity.
- Field observations are largely regarded as having a low reliability. Obviously, "inter-observer" checks (as an analogy to inter-coder reliability checks) will not be possible in most cases due to practical reasons. It might not be pipossible to send two or more observers into the field.
- When doing undercover or hidden observations, one has to carefully consider ethical – and legal – consequences. Serious social research has to care for the observed individuals as well, so there are some paths that cannot be used.

Nonetheless, there are also a lot of positive and rather unique qualities of the method (see the references above; most of these points are discussed in the same literature).

- It allows for direct insights into the observed phenomena. The data are not filtered by the estimations and self assessments of the actors, at least when directly observing their actions. So, this is very much "what you see is what you get." Therefore, observations are usually regarded as ranking high in (external) validity.
- Observations can be used to explore unknown fields and lead to rather unexpected findings. Non-standardized observations are great tools for finding new research questions based on surprising insights.
- Some types of observations produce in-depth information that can be helpful to get an idea of the complex interrelations of the observed phenomena under real-life conditions.
- For some research questions, observation studies are simply the only solution. There are quite a few situations where you cannot get valid information through interviews or content analyses, for various reasons. For example, not all kinds of human behavior can be actively reflected by the actors themselves and therefore

interviews will only result in "plausible" reconstructions – that might be systematically wrong.

Most likely, there are many more pros and cons to the method, but this should be sufficient to give a hint of the restrictions and possibilities for research. However, even when taking the downsides into account, we firmly believe that especially in journalism research, observation studies can lead to unique findings, and that they are dearly needed – with good reason.

In recent decades, researchers have primarily used interviews and content analysis. On the one hand, these standard methods of communication studies have been developed to an astonishing level of sophistication. However, one had to witness, as Nord puts it: "evermore narrow studies that proclaim more and more about less and less" (Nord, 1985, p. 1; quoted in Weaver, 1988, p. 38). And Weaver adds: "Many journalists charge that such research is too theoretical, too abstract, too quantitative, and not written in easily understandable language" (Weaver, 1988, p. 22). Here, observation studies – with their "down to earth" approach and an open eye for the field – can be a helpful remedy. This does not mean that they should serve as a substitute for the other methods. We believe that they are a much more helpful addition with a special place and function in the research process. They allow for alternative views on social reality, and they can be successfully combined with other methods (as described above).

However, the biggest task for the near future will be the further development of the method and a professionalization of its use. There are still many methodological gaps to be filled. This requires researchers who are willing to give up old prejudices and get involved with a "new" (and yet old) method. As always, following a new avenue is risky – however, we believe that its direction is promising.

Notes

1 This is especially true for the early phase of journalism research: In the beginning, a lot of scholars were practitioners, using their own everyday observations as the starting point of their teaching and reasoning. However, this early phase (before the 1930s) was more about teaching journalistic "techniques" (such as writing) and not so much about social research (cf. Weaver and Gray, 1980, 124ff.). But even after the advance of social scientific methods in journalism and communication studies, observations still played an important role (this time as a research method). For example, one of the most prominent "founding fathers" of modern communication studies, Paul Lazarsfeld, did use observations – among other methods. He was not alone: Observation studies were a respected tool of the social sciences in the 1940s and '50s. Journalism research did follow this trend: Some seminal gatekeeper studies from the '50s and '60s were relying on (self) observation (like White, 1950 and Gieber, 1956).

2 This is the case with log files. One could go even further and argue that every content analysis is nothing else than an "asynchronous" observation of behavior traces in the form of media texts. It is questionable, though, whether media content can

be directly linked to earlier behavior of one particular individual. A lot of media content is produced in a team (this is even true for most newspaper articles that are largely based on agency material) in organizational structures, so a direct conclusion from the result to an earlier action is not possible.

3 The situation is different in other disciplines. In psychology, for example, observation studies in experimental settings play a very important role. Beginning with the first half of the 20th century, "behaviorists" such as B. F. Skinner and J. B. Watson were analyzing animal (and later on: human) activities through observation. In contrast to the anthropologist and sociological approach, their observations took place in controlled experimental settings (cf. Watson, 1913; Skinner, 1938). Furthermore, some of the most spectacular psychological experiments of the 20th century (such as Bandura, Ross, and Ross 1961; Milgram 1963, 1974; Zimbardo 1971) were basically observation studies as well.

4 Undercover and insider observations (cf. Soloski, 1979, as an example where the observer worked as a journalist) are not used very often as a scientific method in journalism studies. Most of these observations emanate from a non-scientific context.

5 A diary can be used in addition to a standardized observation in order to explain problematic codings or peripheral observations. There are also combinations of both open and standardized elements: A semi-standardized observation instrument can contain elements like empty space for ad hoc codings that are assigned to unexpected elements in the field.

References

Altmeppen, K.-D., Donges, P., and Engels, K. (1999). *Transformation im Journalismus. Journalistische Qualifikationen im privaten Rundfunk am Beispiel norddeutscher Sender* [*Transformation in journalism. Journalistic qualifications in private broadcasting – the example of North German stations*]. Berlin: Vistas.

Bandura, A., Ross, D., and Ross, S. A. (1961). Transmission of aggression through imitation of aggressive models. *Journal of Abnormal and Social Psychology*, 63, 575–82.

Becker, H. S. (1958). Problems of inference and proof in participant observation. *American Sociological Review*, 23, 652–60.

Berger, A. A. (2000): *Media and communication research methods: An introduction to qualitative and quantitative approaches*. Thousand Oaks, CA: Sage.

Berkowitz, D. (1992). Non-routine news and newswork: Exploring a what-a-story. *Journal of Communication*, 42(2), 82–95.

Bryman, A. (2004). *Social research methods*. 2nd edition. New York: Oxford University Press.

Christensen, C. (2003). *Lack of resources or love of infotainment? Factors affecting story selection in local and regional television news in Sweden*. Conference paper. 23 pages. Annual Conference of the International Communication Association, San Diego.

Clausen, L. (2004). Localizing the global: "Domestication" processes in international news production. *Media, Culture and Society*, 26(1), 25–44.

Gehrau, V. (2002). *Die Beobachtung in der Kommunikationswissenschaft* [*The observation in communication studies*]. Konstanz: UVK.

Gieber, W. (1956): Across the desk. A study of 16 telegraph editors. *Journalism Quarterly*, 33, 423–32.

Matthews, J. (2005). "Out of the mouths of babes and experts": Children's news and what it can teach us about news access and professional mediation. *Journalism Studies*, 6(4), 509–19.

Milgram, S. (1963). Behavioral study of obedience. *Journal of Abnormal and Social Psychology*, 67, 371–8.

Milgram, S. (1974). *Obedience to authority: An experimental view.* New York: Harper and Row.

Nord, D. P. (1985, September 30). Career narrative. Unpublished memorandum, 1.

Quandt, T. (2005). *Journalisten im Netz. Eine Untersuchung journalistischen Handelns in Online-Redaktionen [Journalists in the net. A study on journalistic action in online newsrooms].* Wiesbaden: Verlag für Sozialwissenschaften.

Rühl, M. (1969). *Die Zeitungsredaktion als organisiertes soziales System [The newspaper editorship as an organized social system].* Bielefeld: Bertelsmann Universitätsverlag.

Selltiz, C., Jahoda, M., Deutsch, M., and Cook, S. W. (1967 [1951]). *Research methods in social relations.* Revised one-volume edition. New York: Holt, Rinehart, and Winston.

Skinner, B. F. (1938). *The behavior of organisms: An experimental analysis.* New York: Appleton-Century.

Soloski, J. (1979). Economics and management: The real influence of newspaper groups. *Newspaper Research Journal*, 1(1), 19–28.

Stempel, G., III, Weaver, D. H., and Wilhoit, G. C. (eds.) (2003). *Mass communication research and theory.* Boston, MA: Allyn and Bacon.

Wallraff, G. (1977). *Der Aufmacher. Der Mann, der bei "Bild" Hans Esser war [The lead. The man who was Hans Esser at "Bild"].* Cologne: Kiepenheuer and Witsch.

Watson, J. B. (1913). Psychology as the behaviorist views it. *Psychological Review*, 20, 158–77.

Weaver, D. H. (1988). Mass communication research. Problems and promises. In N. W. Sharp, (ed.), *Communications research: The challenge of the information age* (pp. 21–38). Syracuse, NY: Syracuse University Press.

Weaver, D. H., and Gray, R. G. (1980). Journalism and mass communication research in the United States: Paste, present and future. In G. C. Wilhoit and H. de Boek (eds.), *Mass communication review yearbook.* Vol. 1 (pp. 124–51). Beverly Hills, CA: Sage.

White, D. M. (1950). The "gatekeeper": A case study in the selection of news. *Journalism Quarterly*, 27, 383–90.

Wolling, J., and Kuhlmann, C. (2003). Das Internet als Gegenstand und Instrument der empirischen Kommunikationsforschung [The Internet as an object and instrument of empirical communication research]. In M. Löffelholz and T. Quandt (eds.), *Die neue Kommunikationswissenschaft. Theorien, Themen und Berufsfelder im Internet-Zeitalter. Eine Einführung [The new communication studies. Theories, topics and occupational fields in the Internet age. An introduction].* (pp. 131–61). Wiesbaden: Westdeutscher Verlag.

Zimbardo, P. G. (1971). *The power and pathology of imprisonment.* Congressional Record. (Serial no. 15, October 25, 1971). Hearings before subcommittee no. 3, of the Committee on the Judiciary, House of Representatives, 92nd Congress, First session on corrections, Part II, Prisons, Prison reform and Prisoner's rights, California. Washington, DC: US Government Printing Office.

Part IV

Selected Paradigms and Findings of Journalism Research

Chapter 12

Journalism Research in the United States

Paradigm Shift in a Networked World

Jane B. Singer

In March 1924, the first issue of *Journalism Bulletin* was published by the American Association of Teachers of Journalism. It contained, among other items:

- A consideration of whether journalism is a profession. The author, a law professor, felt no hesitation in making such a classification (Miller, 1924).
- An essay, based on a survey of 14 heads of US journalism programs, on the value of a doctor of philosophy degree for teaching students to do newspaper work. Newsroom experience was shown to be of "undoubtedly greater value" (Higginbotham, 1924, p. 10), though a response two issues later pointed out that as only two people with PhDs were included in the study, and those degrees were not in journalism because no doctorate in the field was available yet, the generalization was perhaps unfounded (Scott, 1924).
- A suggestion from "Daddy" Bleyer (1924) for approaches to conducting newspaper research that grouped potential topics into categories such as the papers' form, content, and effects.

Eight decades later, *Journalism Bulletin* has become *Journalism & Mass Communication Quarterly* and been joined by more than 125 other English-language communication journals. United States journalism and mass communication programs award more than 500 doctorates annually (Coffey, Becker, and Vlad, 2004), and the overwhelming majority of university employers seek applicants with PhDs (Downes and Jirari, 2002). Not too shabby for a field declared to be "withering away" before most of those newly minted scholars were born (Berelson, 1959, p. 1).

Yet the paradigms that emerged for studying journalism in the 1920s, '30s, and '40s remain dominant in the United States today. Methodological and theoretical approaches borrowed from the social science and humanities fields that initially shaped communication studies continue to inform the conceptualization and categorization of research-worthy problems in ways this chapter suggests have become restrictive. As old explanatory devices are challenged by societal changes and by new media that erode boundaries of form and function, journalism studies' first real paradigm shift may be under way.

Intellectual Roots and Contemporary Paradigms

Although the study of journalism in the United States originated in the 19th and the early 20th centuries within humanities departments, largely as a subset of writing and rhetoric, it shifted toward the social sciences as it developed. At Wisconsin in the 1930s, Bleyer created a PhD minor in journalism within existing doctoral programs in political science and sociology; other American universities soon began hiring people with such doctorates to teach and conduct journalism research guided by social science methods and perspectives (Weaver and McCombs, 1980). Social science themes shaped the problems that interested these new scholars, notably the influence of political institutions (and associated propaganda), the role of communication in social life, and social-psychological implications of communication (Delia, 1987). Communication was defined as having a function and observable, measurable effects that could be evaluated by developing testable theories with explanatory power (Berger and Chaffee, 1987).

These scholars studied "mass communication," a term coined in the late 1930s that has generated argument ever since (Chaffee and Metzger, 2001). The word "mass" is value-laden, outdated, and unflattering. The word "communication" has been interpreted mainly in terms of linear message transmission, stemming from Shannon and Weaver's mathematical conception of the process (1949) and subsequent refinements of their model, rather than the interactive experience of sharing and responding to such messages. Despite periodic calls to break free of the limiting connotations of "mass communication" to accommodate changes in both society and the media (Darnell, 1971; Rogers and Chaffee, 1983; Turow, 1992), the problematic phrase has stuck.

"Journalism" might seem a less troublesome term, tied as it is to a specific practices and products. Yet as a scholarly field, journalism has struggled to distinguish itself from the broader "mass communication." Within the academy, journalism programs also have struggled politically to be seen as more than trade schools. That sore subject raised in the debut issue of *Journalism Bulletin*, the value of scholars in preparing practitioners, has never gone away. Campus politics, along with demands of institutional accreditation and individual promotion and tenure, have meant that the intellectual study of journalism in the United States has ridden the coat tails of the study of communication – itself derivative of the study of other aspects of society – rather than developing significant conceptual paradigms of its own (Medsger, 1996). Moreover, most of the borrowed paradigms date to the 1980s or earlier, with few major new theoretical contributions since (DeFleur, 1998; Bryant and Miron, 2004) and few if any adaptations to a 21st-century media environment.

That said, an enormous amount of journalism-related research is conducted in the United States every year. Most of it is empirical; between 1980 and 1999, only a quarter of the articles published in major US mass communication journals were based on qualitative research, a category that encompassed legal and historical work (Kamhawi and Weaver, 2003).

Most journalism research in the United States also has an underlying normative view of a desirable society – one that is democratic, secular, individualistic, orderly, and pluralistic (McQuail, 1994). That the national social ideal informs the scholarly ideal is neither surprising nor unusual. But it is particularly helpful in explaining academic inquiry into journalism because US journalism is itself a paradigmatic American institution. Those adjectives characterize journalism as it is idealized by the profession – and by former professionals who become academics. United States journalists tend to adhere to what Gans (2003) calls the journalistic theory of democracy: They see their role as providing information that enables citizens to make wise choices for self-government. Much journalism research has been concerned with the degree to which they succeed.

The fact that many scholars are former journalists also helps account for the fact that much journalism scholarship in the United States is descriptive, containing little or no theoretical component (Kamhawi and Weaver, 2003; Bryant and Miron, 2004). These researchers were socialized to locate, observe, investigate, and document occurrences, then to convey that information within a framework of accepted news conventions. Many do much the same thing when they make the transition to accepted academic conventions, documenting "facts" more easily than generating broad conceptualizations. Moreover, they tend to rely on methods that are extended versions of either interviewing or interpreting documents; surveys and content analyses account for nearly two-thirds of recent work published in major US research journals (Kamhawi and Weaver, 2003).

When they incorporate a theoretical component, their options are either closely linked to mass communication concepts, as described above, or frame journalism as merely an object of study. Information processing approaches derive from psychology, as do cultivation and schema theories. Agenda-setting and framing studies are forms of media effects research. Uses and gratifications theory, which examines motives for attending to mass communication, developed largely as a response to the effects tradition by positing active audiences who choose to use media in particular ways for particular purposes. Theories involving media hegemony trace their lineage to political and economic concepts. And the sociology of news work tradition, which dates to the 1950s, applies longstanding sociological concepts to the newsroom. For example, the notion of gatekeeping, which derives from sociology and is the forerunner of much media sociology work (Reese and Ballinger, 2001), gives journalists a pivotal role in determining what information the public receives. It continues to be widely applied, especially in studies of political coverage.

Journalism scholars also have borrowed and applied paradigms from fields outside the social sciences. For example, journalism ethics scholarship combines philosophical principles with norms common to all professions; legal and historical research draws on other humanistic disciplines. But for legal, historical, and ethical scholars, journalism is simply the topic to which existing theoretical and methodological frameworks are applied. The enriched context they provide is valuable, but the approaches themselves are derivative.

This is not to say that tracing roots to multiple disciplines is a bad thing. On the contrary, journalism scholarship must draw on its interdisciplinary genealogy in order to address today's complex issues. The problem is that the various rich branches rarely intermingle, and there has been little cross-fertilization to create original or novel species. Rather, each approach has evolved largely on its own and has tended to be self-referential and reiterative; as such, it has been stunted from evolving to meet the integrated needs of a changing media environment.

Research Categories

To what topics, or objects of study, have these paradigms been applied by US scholars? Although there are many ways to categorize journalism research, these four may be useful in highlighting the need for conceptual adaptation: form, function, finances, and fiduciaries.

Form

Form includes the study of journalistic content and the vehicles that carry it. In the last two decades of the 20th century, more than 70 percent of the studies published in leading US journals dealt with either broadcast or print media, and another 10 percent with these two forms combined. Fewer than 10 percent considered the media in general (Kamhawi and Weaver, 2003). Content analysis has been the workhorse in this area, with 486 content analyses appearing from 1971 through the mid-1990s in *Journalism & Mass Communication Quarterly* alone. Much of this work was atheoretical; only about a quarter of the studies contained an explicit theoretical framework, and more than half lacked hypotheses or research questions (Riffe and Freitag, 1997).

Function

Function encompasses study of the effects of journalistic content and the ways media audiences use that content. The functionalist approach to journalism scholarship in the United States dates to Lasswell in the 1940s and Wright in the 1960s. They identified key mass communication functions as surveillance (informing and providing news), correlation (monitoring public opinion and enforcing social norms), transmission (teaching and increasing social cohesion) and, Wright's addition, entertainment (Lasswell, 1960; Wright, 1960). Despite intellectual difficulties with functionalism, the definition of media function as an explicit task, purpose, or motive serves as a well-understood common ground (McQuail, 1994). It provides a foundation for a range of other concepts, from agenda-setting (McCombs and Shaw, 1972) to cultivation theory (Gerbner et al., 1980) to the "knowledge gap" hypothesis (Tichenor, Donohue, and Olien, 1970) and more.

The corollary to studying media function is studying audience needs and uses of those media. More than thirty years ago, Katz and his colleagues (1973, 1974) grouped needs into categories such as cognitive (acquiring information, knowledge, and understanding) and affective (gaining an emotional, pleasurable, or aesthetic experience), and "uses and gratifications" theory remains widely used by

US scholars (Kamhawi and Weaver, 2003; Bryant and Miron, 2004). Much of the research into journalism audiences and their interaction with journalistic products traces its conceptual lineage to work on media functions and effects, audience uses and gratifications, or both.

Finances

Finances include the connections among and impacts of economic structures, policy-making institutions, and media companies. There has always been a tension in the United States between the constitutionally protected public service role of the press and the economic forces driving and driven by media industries. Ongoing media deregulation and "conglomeratization" have launched numerous explorations into possible connections between economic theory and media reality. Relationships among media ownership, company size, commercial ties, and news content have never been clear, but the professional normative construct of autonomy leads both journalists and academics to view with grave suspicion any potential encroachment on independent judgment (Larson, 1977).

The most significant break with traditional US paradigms of journalism research can be seen in research by critical and cultural scholars, much of which draws on a political economy perspective with European origins. In addition to examining media hegemony and other power relationships, this work encompasses everything from policy critiques to post-structural analyses of media institutions. Nor do these scholars tend to use paradigmatic quantitative methods, preferring textual or discourse analyses to content analyses, ethnographies to surveys – and often a critical essay format that is not data-based at all. Despite criticism that they are "preoccupied with critical perspectives rather than research" (DeFleur, 1998, p. 85), their work is valuable precisely because it searches for alternative understandings of contemporary journalism.

Fiduciaries

Fiduciaries, or those entrusted with "doing journalism" – the journalists themselves – constitute a fourth category. In addition to sociological studies of news work and workers, much legal and ethical scholarship exploring the rights and responsibilities of journalists falls into this area, as does exploration of the media's role in the social construction of reality (Berger and Luckmann, 1967). Although there is some overlap with economic concerns, particularly organizational constraints, here the focus is on the practitioner and his or her situated practices. Primary methods of analysis in this area include surveys and case studies.

This body of work incorporates several themes. One considers the journalist as a member of a community, such as a profession (McLeod and Hawley, 1964; Johnstone, Slawski, and Bowman, 1976), an interpretive community (Zelizer, 1993), or a news organization (Bantz, 1990; Beam, 1990). Another looks at the ways in which journalists "make news" (Tuchman, 1978), including the creation of work routines and structures. Examinations of journalists' social roles are foundational to the field, dating at least to the Lippmann–Dewey debate of the 1920s. Recently, newsroom convergence, which calls for journalists who can produce content across media forms, has been the impetus for fresh studies of work roles and relationships.

Paradigm Shift

In summary, journalism scholarship in the United States, stretching over eight decades, has deepened understanding within existing paradigms derived primarily from other social science and humanities disciplines. Approaches encompassed in a framework established generations ago have contributed to a cumulative, collaborative enterprise that has extended the scope and precision of knowledge about American journalistic products and practices. Yet few, if any, new journalism or mass communication theories have emerged in the past quarter-century. All stem from a media environment that lacked widespread use of multi-channel cable television or the Internet, media that challenge functional perspectives. Scientific paradigms are not infinitely useful. Eventually, old explanations become inadequate for the phenomenon of interest, and changes in both the definitions of relevant problems and the techniques for analyzing them become necessary (Kuhn, 1970).

Such is the situation for journalism scholars in the United States today. Widespread social forces, including globalization, are creating an impetus for change. With notable exceptions, such as the cross-cultural work culminating in *The Global Journalist* (Weaver, 1998), most US scholarship has focused on journalism within the country, yet neither media institutions nor audiences remain geographically bounded. Changes in media consumption patterns make it increasingly hard to measure media effects. Declining levels of civic engagement challenge the notion of what constitutes a "good" society and journalism's role within it. Demographic shifts mean fewer English speakers able to consume mainstream journalistic products; in 2000, 47 million US residents spoke a language other than English at home, a nearly 50 percent jump from 1990 (Shin and Bruno, 2003).

But of particular interest to many journalism scholars is the shifting nature of the media themselves, including ongoing technological change within multifaceted social, cultural, and historical contexts (Boczkowski, 2004). Concepts related to journalistic forms, functions, finances, and fiduciaries all mutate and overlap in today's media environment and demand news ways of thinking about them. Fluidity across various borders is a key characteristic in each area, contributing to the difficulty of applying existing paradigms.

Forms

Most US journalism scholarship has considered specific media forms, such as the newspaper, and early descriptive scholarship related to the Internet took a similar approach. There have been many content analyses of web sites over the past decade, despite problems in applying a method designed to explore a finite and stable product to a medium that is neither (McMillan, 2000). Scholars looking at online journalism have done a lot of categorizing and counting of elements such as links or multimedia attachments.

But the initial utility of such counting diminishes fast as the new medium expands and becomes commonplace. More important, counting components of an individual site overlooks the nature of a networked medium in which the whole is significantly more than the sum of its parts. Examining any one component in isolation tells us little; significance lies in the combination of contributions and the limitless nature of the aggregated whole.

Network analysis and associated paradigms of interconnectivity hold great promise for journalism studies. The approach has been used to examine convergence among media industries (Chon et al., 2003) and the use of hyperlinks in online journalism (Tremayne, 2004), as well as connections among online producers and users (Schneider and Foot, 2004). There are tremendous additional opportunities, including those Howard (2002) proposes as part of a synergistic research design he calls "network ethnography." In general terms, examining ways in which online content and production elements are interwoven can take us beyond paradigms grounded in finite, concrete media forms that essentially date to Bleyer's (1924) suggestions for studying the newspaper.

Similarly, the forms of news itself are fluid and flexible online. Traditional journalism uses a limited number of formats, such as text or video, to fill a finite news hole with perishable content. Online, the environment for journalism offers a rich variety of storytelling formats, presenting an ever-changing mix of old and new information to users who access it through a multiplying variety of digital devices. Efforts to apply paradigms designed to measure stable content within concrete media forms are coming to resemble throwing darts at a constantly morphing dartboard.

Functions

It is not news that distinctions between interpersonal and mass communication functions are dubious at best. Schramm (1958) said as much half a century ago – at the same time stressing the need to study mass communication as a distinct social institution. Many others have pleaded for a broader conceptualization of function over the years; contemporary media underscore the need. Mass and interpersonal communication are inextricably linked online, where anyone with a web site is able to reach, instantly and globally, into an enormous range of social and institutional settings (Lievrouw et al., 2001). Definitions that allowed mass communication to develop its own identity separate from other forms now hinder understanding of how today's communication vehicles – and the journalism they contain – work.

The idea of "mass" itself also has become increasingly problematic. The notion of a mass audience, shaken over the past 25 years as cable fragmented the television audience, dissolves entirely online. Although mainstream media sites continue to attract large audiences, aggregator services such as Yahoo! News, with little connection to traditional journalism, are overtaking them in popularity (Online/Ownership, 2007). User-generated news services are another step removed from traditional mass media; RSS readers, which deliver news tailored to a particular individual, may finally fragment us into media universes of one. Of course, an opposite assessment also is possible: Any single story uploaded to the web can be read by one billion people around the world, a "massive" audience indeed.

At the same time, blogs, wikis, and other forms of "citizen journalism" enable millions of people to produce continuously updated, timely, and (at least to someone) "newsworthy" content. Are bloggers producing "mass" communication or "interpersonal" communication or a hybrid? Does it matter? What is evident is that the traditional one-to-many linear and hierarchical model of mass communication, even with all its feedback loops built in (Westley and MacLean, 1957), is of little use in a world in which the media producer and media consumer are interchangeable – in which he or she is, in fact, the same person.

In some ways, this incessantly active audience fits into a uses and gratifications framework (Chaffee and Metzger, 2001). Certainly, online users are actively selecting content to fit a range of desires or needs – they must do so unless they want to stare at a single screen forever. But the melding of various communication forms online – not only mass and interpersonal but also human-machine interaction, as well as new sites of identity construction and articulation – suggests the need for significant expansion of what now is a relatively simple concept. Uses and gratifications theory might be reconceptualized to include needs to create and disseminate content, as well as to engage in an iterative process with and about that content. Interactions between online and offline communicative activities and goals also should be considered.

Finances

Media economic structure also is fluid, as transnational companies merge and partner with one another, and media products flow across porous geopolitical borders. Financial concerns highlight the need for scholars to adjust their thinking to accommodate the global nature of all communication activities. Currently, the most promising paradigm is that which historically has received shortest shrift among US journalism scholars. Holistic critical and cultural studies approaches, which draw heavily on perspectives originating outside of the United States for theoretical and political inspiration (McLuskie, Hegbloom, and Woodfin, 2004), are well suited to studying the nature of communication in a dynamic global context. They also are useful for considering power structures and hegemony issues called into question by a truly global medium.

At a more micro level, there are plenty of "financial" issues related to new media to keep journalism scholars busy. One example is economic support for online journalism. Although online news is beginning to make money, no economic model has emerged that seems likely to make new media as profitable as old media were, meaning the "economic base supporting the most difficult and expensive journalistic undertakings is eroding" (Online/Intro, 2005). In addition to the relationship between resource allocation and content, research-worthy issues include shifts away from the old advertising-supported media model and the separation (or lack of it) between commercial, entertainment and editorial information online.

Fiduciaries

Scholarship that examines who is responsible for journalism is similarly vital at a time when the definition of a journalist is increasingly a normative one. When everyone can publish information instantly and disseminate it globally, everyone is a publisher – but not necessarily a journalist. Professional journalists will be defined by the degree to which they try to adhere to ethical guidelines of their professional culture; in the United States, these include commitment to truth, independence, and accountability.

For researchers studying news practitioners and their work, the first step of identifying the study subject has become much harder. The networked, participatory online medium can be a hall of mirrors: Who is a journalist, who is a source, and who is an audience member in an open, endlessly iterative news environment? The definition of what constitutes news also has become broader. News dissemination no longer need be connected with a recognized media outlet. So-called "amateur journalism" is likely to grow exponentially as digital devices become smaller, cheaper, more ubiquitous, and easier to connect to a network.

The challenge is also an opportunity for journalism scholars to develop theories uniquely their own. The previous discussion suggested that one of the few conceptual approaches with a direct connection to journalism has been gatekeeping – precisely the least applicable today. In a media environment with unlimited sources of information, there are no discrete gates through which that information passes and thus no need for anyone to tend them (Williams and Delli Carpini, 2000). Journalists have recognized this paradigm shift and have responded partly by nudging the definition of gatekeeping away from story selection and toward news judgment, values, and professional practices (Singer, 1997). Journalists also are providing more options for personalization and other forms of audience control over content. It remains for researchers to develop paradigms that can accommodate the new reality of "news" and explore its implications within a broader social context.

Conclusions

The time is opportune for a look at what the paradigms of journalism scholarship might be and what questions they can profitably address in today's fluid and inextricably interconnected media environment. Conventions and categories that have served US scholars for eight decades are becoming restrictive as borders of all kinds disappear. This chapter has suggested that the impetus for a paradigm shift comes from a range of factors, including globalization, social transformations, and institutional change, but perhaps especially from the blurring of once-clear distinctions related to journalism forms, functions, finances, and fiduciaries.

It is through such changes in the criteria both for identifying problems and proposing solutions to them that progress, or advancement of knowledge and understanding, occurs (Kuhn, 1970). Journalism scholarship in the United States was born of the social sciences and humanities, whose researchers converged on mass communication as a topic that posed interesting new problems within existing frameworks. In subsequent decades, the field split into a variety of sub-sets, offering a smorgasbord of topics for scholarly scrutiny. The result has been a steady narrowing of analytic and interpretive focus, so that researchers have devoted themselves to examining different aspects of one particular form, for example, often through a single conceptual or methodological lens. There has been thorough exposition of individual theories and topics, particularly as applied to specific media forms and functions, but relatively little synthesis among them.

Paradigm shift involves a change of focus, a recognition that old approaches no longer adequately address important questions. For journalism scholars, those questions have little remaining relevance to "mass communication," a term that their predecessors used to carve a field out of multiple foundational disciplines but that has lost most of its conceptual value today. The underlying diversity of the intellectual tradition needs to be reclaimed and its strands united in order to study contemporary journalism in the rich and multifaceted context it demands. New paradigms are most likely to emerge from a combination of traditionally disparate approaches – for instance, a scientific method of gathering data combined with a more culturally informed and holistic analysis of those data.

Forms and functions of communication are converging, overlapping, and becoming indistinguishable as distinct areas of study. Media institutions and structures also are fluidly combining and recombining in ways that transcend previous boundaries of various kinds, including economic and geographic. The study of journalists and journalism – the emerging field of journalism studies – may serve as an ideal intellectual place for new explorations of these changes. Journalism, a self-consciously fiduciary enterprise within a networked global society, is inherently an interdisciplinary undertaking and increasingly a cross-cultural one. It waits for us to discover the paradigms that will address the questions raised by this 21st-century journalism.

References

Bantz, C. R. (1990). Organizational communication, media industries, and mass communication. *Communication Yearbook*, 13, 502–10.

Beam, R. A. (1990). Journalistic professionalism as an organizational-level concept. *Journalism Monographs* 121. Columbia, SC: Association for Education in Journalism and Mass Communication.

Berelson, B. (1959). The state of communication research. *Public Opinion Quarterly*, 23(1), 1–17.

Berger, C. R., and Chaffee, S. H. (1987). The study of communication as a science. In C. R. Berger and S. H. Chaffee (eds.), *Handbook of communication science* (pp. 15–19). Newbury Park, CA: Sage.

Berger, P. L., and Luckmann, T. (1967). *The social construction of reality.* Garden City, NY: Doubleday.

Bleyer, W. G. (1924). Research problems and newspaper analysis. *Journalism Bulletin,* 1(1), 17–22.

Boczkowski, P. J. (2004). *Digitizing the news: Innovation in online newspapers.* Cambridge, MA: MIT Press.

Bryant, J., and Miron, D. (2004). Theory and research in mass communication. *Journal of Communication,* 54(4), 662–704.

Chaffee, S., and Metzger, M. (2001). The end of mass communication? *Mass Communication and Society,* 4(4), 365–79.

Chon, B. S., Choi, J. H., Barnett, G. A., Danowski, J. A., and Joo, S.-H. (2003). A structural analysis of media convergence: Cross-industry mergers and acquisitions in the information industries. *Journal of Media Economics,* 16(3), 141–57.

Coffey, A. J., Becker, L. B., and Vlad, T. (2004, August). Survey of doctoral programs in communication: Updated report for 2002–3 graduates. Retrieved November 14, 2005, from: www.grady.uga.edu/annualsurveys/doctoralsurvey/doc03sum.htm

Darnell, D. K. (1971). Toward a reconceptualization of communication. *Journal of Communication,* 21(1), 5–16.

DeFleur, M. L. (1998). Where have all the milestones gone? *Mass Communication and Society,* 1(1/2), 85–98.

Delia, J. G. (1987). Communication research: A history. In C. R. Berger and S. H. Chaffee (eds.), *Handbook of communication science* (pp. 20–98). Newbury Park, CA: Sage.

Downes, E. J., and Jirari, J. (2002). Hiring trends in the communications disciplines. *Journalism & Mass Communication Educator,* 57(1), 49–58.

Gans, H. J. (2003). *Democracy and the news.* New York: Oxford University Press.

Gerbner, G., Gross, L., Morgan, M., and Signorielli, N. (1980). The "mainstreaming" of America: Violence profile no. 11. *Journal of Communication,* 30(3), 10–29.

Higginbotham, L. (1924). Practice vs. PhD. *Journalism Bulletin,* 1(1), 10–12.

Howard, P. N. (2002). Network ethnography and the hypermedia organization: New media, new organizations, new methods. *New Media & Society,* 4(4), 550–74.

Johnstone, J. W. C., Slawski, E. J., and Bowman, W. W. (1976). *The news people: A sociological portrait of American journalists and their work.* Urbana, IL: University of Illinois Press.

Kamhawi, R., and Weaver, D. H. (2003). Mass communication research trends from 1980 to 1999. *Journalism & Mass Communication Quarterly,* 80(1), 7–27.

Katz, E., Blumler, J. G., and Gurevitch, M. (1974). Utilization of mass communication by the individual. In J. G. Blumler and E. Katz (eds.), *The uses of mass communications: Current perspectives on gratifications research* (pp. 19–32). Beverly Hills, CA: Sage.

Katz, E., Gurevitch, M., and Haas, H. (1973). On the use of the mass media for important things. *American Sociological Review,* 38(2), 164–81.

Kuhn, T. S. (1970). *The structure of scientific revolutions.* 2nd edition. Chicago, IL: University of Chicago Press.

Larson, M. S. (1977). *The rise of professionalism: A sociological analysis.* Berkeley, CA: University of California Press.

Lasswell, H. D. (1960). The structure and function of communication in society. In

W. Schramm (ed.), *Mass communication* (pp. 117–30). Urbana, IL: University of Illinois Press.

Lievrouw, L. A., Bucy, E. P., Finn, A. T., Frindte, W., Gershon, R. A., Haythornthwaite, C., Kohler, T., Metz, J. M., and Sundar, S. S. (2001). Bridging the subdisciplines: An overview of communication and technology research. *Communication Yearbook*, 24, 271–95.

McCombs, M. E., and Shaw, D. L. (1972). The agenda-setting function of mass media. *Public Opinion Quarterly*, 36(2), 176–87.

McLeod, J. M., and Hawley, S. E., Jr. (1964). Professionalism among newsmen. *Journalism Quarterly*, 41(4), 529–38.

McLuskie, E., Hegbloom, M., and Woodfin, F. (2004). In the company of Hanno Hardt: A festschrift on the future of critical communication studies. *Journalism*, 5(2), 227–41.

McMillan, S. J. (2000). The microscope and the moving target: The challenge of applying content analysis to the world wide web. *Journalism & Mass Communication Quarterly*, 77(1), 80–98.

McQuail, D. (1994). *Mass communication theory*. 3rd edition. London: Sage.

Medsger, B. (1996). *Winds of change: Challenges confronting journalism education*. Arlington, VA: Freedom Forum.

Miller, R. J. (1924). The professional spirit. *Journalism Bulletin*, 1(1), 3–9.

Online/Intro. (2005). The state of the news media 2005: An annual report on American journalism. Washington, DC: The Project for Excellence in Journalism. Retrieved November 14, 2005 from: stateofthemedia.org/2005/narrative_online_ownership.asp?cat=5&media=3

Online/Ownership. (2007). The state of the news media 2007: An annual report on American journalism. Washington, DC: The Project for Excellence in Journalism. Retrieved August 17, 2007, from: stateofthemedia.com/2007/narrative_online_ownership.asp?cat=4&media+4

Reese, S. D., and Ballinger, J. (2001). The roots of a sociology of news: Remembering Mr Gates and social control in the newsroom. *Journalism & Mass Communication Quarterly*, 78(4), 641–58.

Riffe, D., and Freitag, A. (1997). A content analysis of content analyses: Twenty-five years of *Journalism Quarterly*. *Journalism & Mass Communication Quarterly*, 74(4), 873–82.

Rogers, E. M., and Chaffee, S. H. (1983). Communication as an academic discipline: A dialogue. *Journal of Communication*, 33(3), 18–30.

Schneider, S. M., and Foot, K. A. (2004). The web as an object of study. *New Media & Society*, 6(1), 114–22.

Schramm, W. (1958). The challenge to communication research. In R. O. Nafziger and D. M. White (eds.), *Introduction to mass communications research* (pp. 3–28). Baton Rouge, LA: Louisiana State University Press.

Scott, F. W. (1924). Significance of the PhD. *Journalism Bulletin*, 1(3), 88–90.

Shannon, C., and Weaver, W. (1949). *The mathematical theory of communication*. Urbana, IL: University of Illinois Press.

Shin, H. B., and Bruno, R. (2003, October). Language use and English-speaking ability: 2000. Retrieved November 14, 2005, from: www.census.gov/prod/2003pubs/c2kbr-29.pdf

Singer, J. B. (1997). Still guarding the gate? The newspaper journalist's role in an on-line world. *Convergence: The Journal of Research into New Media Technologies*, 3(1), 72–89.

Tichenor, P. J., Donohue, G. A., and Olien, C. N. (1970). Mass media flow and differential growth in knowledge. *Public Opinion Quarterly*, 34(2), 159–70.

Tremayne, M. (2004). The web of context: Applying network theory to the use of hyperlinks in journalism on the web. *Journalism & Mass Communication Quarterly*, 81(2), 237–53.

Tuchman, G. (1978). *Making news: A study in the construction of reality*. New York: Free Press.

Turow, J. (1992). On reconceptualizing "mass communication." *Journal of Broadcasting and Electronic Media*, 36(1), 105–10.

Weaver, D. H. (1998). *The global journalist: News people around the world*. Cresskill, NJ: Hampton Press.

Weaver, D. H., and McCombs, M. E. (1980). Journalism and social science: A new relationship? *Public Opinion Quarterly*, 44(4), 477–94.

Westley, B. H., and MacLean, M. (1957). A conceptual model for communication research. *Journalism Quarterly*, 34(1), 31–8.

Williams, B. A., and Delli Carpini, M. X. (2000). Unchained reaction: The collapse of media gatekeeping and the Clinton–Lewinsky scandal. *Journalism*, 1(1), 61–85.

Wright, C. R. (1960). Functional analysis and mass communication. *Public Opinion Quarterly*, 24, 605–20.

Zelizer, B. (1993). Journalists as interpretive communities. *Critical Studies in Mass Communication*, 10(3), 219–37.

Chapter 13

Journalism Research in Germany
Evolution and Central Research Interests

Siegfried Weischenberg and Maja Malik

The Beginnings: The "Publizistische Persönlichkeit" and Political Deformations

In Germany, the first scholarly attempts to analyze journalism in a systematic way are rooted in the middle of the 19th century, when Robert Prutz (1845) published his *Geschichte des Journalismus* [*History of journalism*]. But it was not until the beginning of the 20th century that the sociologist Max Weber (1911) first suggested a concept for an empirical study of journalism. On the "First German Sociologists Day" in 1910 in Frankfurt, he presented his idea of a "Soziologie des Zeitungswesens" ["Sociology of the press"], posing questions which are still central to journalism research today. However, his empirical pilot project could only partially be accomplished (Kutsch, 1988).

It took almost another 60 years until empirical journalism research was established as an independent field of study in Germany. Initially, the "Zeitungswissenschaft" ["Science of the Press"] in German-speaking countries developed as a historical rather than a socio-scientific discipline, focusing on individual journalists as "Publizistische Persönlichkeiten," that is, outstanding personalities in the journalistic profession. One of a few exceptions to this is a study by Dieter Paul Baumert (1928) which describes the "Entstehung des deutschen Journalismus" ["The evolution of German journalism"] with regard to the institutional constraints of journalistic work. However, most scholars were concerned normatively with extraordinary journalists and the nature of journalism (e.g. Spael, 1928). Thus, central research questions focused on individuals and their biographies, or on analyzing journalistic skills (e.g. Groth, 1928–30; Dovifat, 1931). As research concentrated on the abilities and the ethos of single journalists, theoretical complexity as well as the empirical output of this "normative individualism" (Löffelholz, 2003, p. 32) remained little.

This also applies for the period of National Socialism (1933–45). While reception studies and content analyses were increasingly based on empirical methods, particularly regarding broadcasting, research on newsmaking continued to use biographical and practical rather than systematic perspectives. Moreover, academic research after 1933 was increasingly determined by political impact regarding ideology, finances, topics and personnel. As an example, Emil Dovifat's *Zeitungswissenschaft* [*Science of the press*] (1931) was rewritten, and renamed *Zeitungslehre* [*Textbook of the press*] in 1937; thereby characterizing the press' function as a means of political leadership. However, while leading scholars of the subsequent West German communication science had already worked in the large journalism departments in Nazi Germany, the discipline itself came to terms with the role of journalism as well as the function of journalism research in the Nazi period rather late. In fact, this issue still provokes controversial debates (e.g. Hachmeister, 1987; Duchkowitsch, Hausjell, and Semrad, 2004).[1]

In East Germany, a Marxist-Leninist "Science of the Press" was established after 1945, later mainly performing under the title "Sektion Journalistik" ["Section Journalism"] (Budzislawski, 1962, p. 45; Traumann, 1971, p. 5) at the University of Leipzig. Here, much effort was made to derive a theory of "Socialistic Journalism" from the works of Marx, Engels, and Lenin. In 1975, the "Sektion Journalistik" published the German translation of a fundamental work by the Soviet scholar Gurjewitsch (1975) in which "the character of journalism" as well as "organizational principles of working in the newsroom" were related to key chapters of the classic communist works. However, as one of the scholars from the Leipzig journalism department argues, critical awareness had been increasing during the last years before the peaceful revolution in the former German Democratic Republic – leading to a decline of acceptance of journalism research and teaching (Grubitzsch, 1990, pp. 402).[2]

In Western Germany, journalism research continued to focus on individualistic and normative questions after 1945, thereby placing the "Publizistische Persönlichkeit" with their "hardships, requirements and intentions" (Böckelmann, 1993, p. 38) in the center of the debate. Journalism was conceived as the work of individuals, whose qualities and characteristics determined the news. Consequently, the discipline was concerned with the "proper journalist," who was expected to meet certain ethical demands in order to perform his duty. Likewise, leading German researchers with profound practical journalistic experiences conceptualized the newsroom as a "spiritual and intellectual production area" (Hagemann, 1950), or "spiritual enterprise," concerned with an "intellectual working process" (Dovifat, 1967). Thus, journalistic performance was reduced to the result of actions of seemingly autonomous individuals only – a perspective which obstructs the recognition of the social, political and economical constraints that determine the characteristics of journalism as well as its effects.

Take-Off: Empirical Studies on Journalists and Media Criticism

Since the end of the 1960s, various attempts have been made to shed light on the routines of newsmaking; particularly the factors influencing the journalists' news decisions were analyzed. In the light of general social changes, for example, the student movement and structural developments in the media, a noticeable interest in understanding the underlying mechanisms of newsmaking had emerged. Thereby, the drawbacks of the discipline, that should have had provided knowledge of this matter, became apparent. So far journalism research in Germany had had only little interest in empirical analyses of news production, but had been focusing on assessing idealistic norms for the journalistic profession.

It was time to discard the idea of the journalist as an autonomous individual, particularly since sufficient funding was now available for empirical projects aiming at political consulting. In response to the empirical research in the United States, numerous German studies now explored the journalistic profession and analyzed "what journalists think and how they do their work" (Kepplinger, 1979). Yet, partly due to methodological reasons, analyses of the "subjective dimension" of news production dominated most of the research, that is, the focus was on the journalists' attitudes and on their role perceptions. In detail, the journalists' professional consciousness, their attitudes toward the audience, and their professional self-concepts were analyzed; journalistic autonomy and socialization within media organizations were explored; and particular roles, such as sports reporter, local editor, or chief editor, were investigated (Weischenberg, 1995).

The increase of research activities about the characteristics and attitudes of German journalists was also triggered by an extensive criticism of journalism, which was voiced by academics after the 1976 general elections, and provided a significant basis for subsequent communication policies of Federal Germany. Central to this media criticism was the allegation that West German journalists represented a homogeneous, curious, and idiosyncratic population group. They were criticized for being geared more to their colleagues than to their audience (Donsbach, 1982); their political attitudes seemed to diverge from the rest of the population (Kepplinger, 1979). Moreover, they were said to have extensive autonomy in decision-making within the process of news production, so that journalists' attitudes and characteristics as well as the development of the media caused consistent news in most of the media. Thus, confined choices for the audience and restricted communication possibilities were suspected. From that followed *Legitimationsprobleme des Journalismus* [*Legitimation problems of journalism*] (Donsbach, 1982), due to the comparatively small group of journalists whose left-wing party-political preferences were seen to exercise great social power without legal basis. On the grounds of these arguments, conclusions about media content were drawn from survey data, and suggestions about journalists' attitudes were based on findings of content analyses.

Within the scope of this media criticism, journalists were described as an "Entfremdete Elite" ["Alienated Elite"] (Rust, 1986), strongly differing from the rest of the German population in terms of their attitudes and indifferent to the public's wants and needs. Thus, scholars assumed that journalists were able to impose their attitudes on media content. Likewise, it was claimed that the attitudes of German journalists differed from those of their colleagues in other countries. In contrast to Anglo-American journalists, who perceived themselves as non-partisan "bloodhounds," German journalists saw themselves supposedly as "missionaries," particularly concerned with expressing their own views (Köcher, 1985).

Assumptions such as these were mostly based on findings regarding the journalistic image of the audience and the journalists' reference groups, as well as the comparison of demographic characteristics of journalists with those of the audience (Noelle-Neumann, 1979, p. 141; Donsbach, 1982, p. 195). However, methodologically such conclusions are poorly validated; partly they are even drawn from speculations and idiosyncratic interpretations of results (Weischenberg, 1989). Yet, these studies had strong impact on the discussions about journalism in Germany, for example in the debate about the implementation of private broadcasting in West Germany in the mid-1980s. A synopsis of the studies on journalists by the time can be found in a secondary analysis by Hans-Jürgen Weiß and his associates (Weiß, 1978).

Gaining Complexity: The Newsroom as a Social System and Theoretical Foundations

While empirical studies on journalists were developing, a paradigm shift in German journalism research was introduced by Manfred Rühl in 1969. His case study about "Die Zeitungsredaktion als organisiertes soziales System" ['The Newspaper Newsroom as Organized Social System'] provided new insights into communication processes in newsrooms. Thus, Rühl's study not only stimulated studies of news organizations, it also encouraged the combination of theoretical and empirical research. Moreover, it inspired the adoption of systems theory for analyses of journalism in Germany (Rühl, 1980).

This branch of research on news organizations grounded in systems theory and committed to the approaches of institutional and industrial sociology, comprised analyses of news production within formalized social structures. Thus, it opposed the practical and normative "ideal of personality journalism, independent from any institution" (Rühl, 1989, p. 260), as well as the reduction of journalism to a "mix of roles" (p. 254). By contrast, particular attention was paid to the consequences of journalistic actions which are determined by their constant interaction with their social environments.

Since the end of the 1960s, this theory-based empirical research on newsrooms provided various case studies that followed different aims and objectives. These studies contributed significantly to a theoretical conception of the newsroom as a social system, particularly by including ideas of cybernetics and structuration theory. Ulrich Hienzsch, for example, drew on both Rühl's work and the criticism of it to develop his hypothesis of "Die Zeitungsredaktion als kybernetisches System" ["The newspaper newsroom as a cybernetic system"] (1990). In his case study on the new electronic production methods of a large West German regional newspaper, he analyzed the information processes which underlie news production under changing technological circumstances.

Referring to Anthony Giddens' structuration theory, Klaus-Dieter Altmeppen (1999) recently explored the relationship of system and structure in the newsroom, thus laying the predominant focus on systemic decision premises. He showed that the routines of newsmaking are not entirely controlled by what systems theory calls "decision programs." Instead, journalists use coordinated action to independently combine single work steps to editorial working processes which relate to the situational context. According to this, coordination such as conferences, informal arrangements and chats are considerable components of the journalistic work and serve to handle risks.

In addition to interviews, participant observation was repeatedly applied as a method for research on newsrooms based on systems theory. Yet, individual case studies in this field of study clearly exceed the number of comparative analyses. Central research questions were concerned with organizational structures and working conditions in particular media, the development of inner press freedom, the analysis of decision structures, or changes in news production due to new technical achievements (Weischenberg, 1995). A more recent branch of research on newsrooms provides rather applied studies; suggesting trendsetting management and marketing strategies for newsrooms by drawing on practical experience and observation (e.g. Rager, Schäfer-Dieterle, and Weber, 1994; Möllmann, 1998; Meckel, 1999).

To summarize, research on newsrooms based on systems theory has contributed much to a better comprehension of editorial decision-making processes. It has become apparent that in news organizations, challenges and interactions emerge that remain undetectable by looking at individuals only.

Expansion: Macro Theories of Journalism and First Representative Surveys

After 1990, journalism studies in Germany were particularly influenced by two major developments. First, several broadly designed theoretical works endeavored to apply Niklas Luhmann's theory of social systems to journalism. Second, the two first representative studies about the journalistic profession were conducted, finally realizing Max Weber's suggestion of a systematic survey of journalists in Germany.

The increased engagement with journalism on a macro-theoretical level emerged from criticism of the empirical research focusing on individuals. As an individual-centered definition of journalism reduces the function and performance of journalism to the activities of single individuals, it cannot recognize the structural factors shaping journalistic communication. Those factors have to be evaluated in consideration of the specific conditions within a particular society. Thus, in order to systemize parameters of news production, the following questions need to be addressed:

- Which preconditions of news production are provided by the media system?
- How do media organizations constrain journalistic work?
- Which performances and effects emerge from media content?
- Which characteristics and attitudes of media actors are significant for news production? (Weischenberg, 1992, p. 67)

Thus, the norms, structures, functions and roles that determine journalism are addressed. Journalism is conceptualized as a social system, as a social entity showing a complex structure and being closely interwoven with other social systems in various ways. In terms of the way journalism describes reality, this is not seen as the work of individuals but as the result of various communication processes within systemic conditions.

Those concepts of journalism based on systems theory are rooted in Rühl's suggestion to abstract journalists as individuals from journalism as a social system (Rühl, 1980). By using the difference between system and environment as a theoretical tool, they rather focus on relevant functions and structures of journalism than concentration on the individuals involved. The underlying theory of functional systems considers individuals involved in journalism not as a part of journalism, but as a part of the system's environment; thus placing the focus of research on decision structures (independent from the individual) and theoretically embedding journalism in a society with specific characteristics. Such systems-theoretical concepts are based on particular empirical and epistemic premises. These are:

- Modern society with differentiated structures needs an entity for its constant and contemporary introspection.
- This, again, needs professional observers who create "media reality" due to their own observations and accounts.
- These observations show specific communication mechanisms which differentiate journalism from other areas of public communication (e.g. literature, advertising or public relations).

The diverse theoretical concepts define journalism in different ways – either seeing journalism as a self-contained social system or considering it part of a larger system, such as "mass media," "pubic sphere" or "published communication" (Scholl and Weischenberg, 1998, p. 63). Thus, it is still discussed today to what extent journalism actually fulfills an exclusive function in society (either on its own or in connection with other areas of public communication). However, in the course of these considerations, it became widely accepted to regard journalism as a social construction that possesses specific attributes in a particular society at a certain time; and thus, is able to render specific required services.

However, critics of these systems theory-based concepts primarily questioned the view that the function and performance of journalism was not linked to individuals' thinking and actions. Hence, several macro-theoretical considerations reflected on the shortcomings of both the theory of social systems as well as the individual-centered approaches. They tried to overcome these by linking systems theory with constructivism, action theoretical approaches, structuration theoretical enhancements, or recently, cultural studies. Since then, the theoretical debate in German journalism research is particularly concerned with the question to what extent the thoughts and actions of individuals can (also) be attributed to the function and performance of journalism (Löffelholz, 2000). Certainly, this does not only apply to journalism research in particular but represents a relevant question for social sciences in general.

Empirical research also advanced considerably in the 1990s – after the German Reunification and the establishment of private broadcasting next to public service stations. For the first time, representative studies of German journalists were conducted. Although many previous studies had referred to journalism as a whole, their explanatory power was always limited to particular groups of journalists only, for they mostly aimed at analyzing or comparing single occupational fields. This is demonstrated in Frank Böckelmann's bibliography (1993) which describes more than 700 communicator studies conducted between 1945 and 1990 in the Federal Republic of Germany, the German Democratic Republic, Austria, and Switzerland.

At the beginning of the 1990s, almost simultaneously, two representative surveys were giving information about German journalists' occupational composition as well as their characteristics and attitudes. However, these surveys drew on different definitions of journalism and used different sampling methods.

- For the Hanover study "Sozialenquête über die Journalisten in der Bundesrepublik Deutschland" ["Social survey of journalists in the Federal Republik of Germany"] (Schneider, Schönbach, and Stürzebecher, 1993, 1994), a quota-sample of 1,568 journalists in salaried positions, working for newspapers, magazines, broadcasting stations and news agencies, were interviewed by phone. The study's aim was to explore historical and system-related differences in West German and East German journalism.
- In contrast to this, the Münster study "Journalismus in Deutschland" ["Journalism in Germany"] (Weischenberg, Löffelholz, and Scholl, 1993, 1994, 1998) was based on a more comprehensive, theory-governed definition of journalism. The study's aim was to describe and explain the functional mechanisms of journalism as a social system. The random sample comprised 1,498 journalists in salaried positions as well as freelance journalists, who worked not only for the "traditional media," but also for "marginal media" such as media services, classified advertisement papers, and city magazines. Thus, the variety of the journalistic profession could be taken into account. The selected journalists were interviewed personally; the survey questions were designed according to those used for the "American journalist" studies by David H. Weaver and G. Cleveland Wilhoit (1986/1991), in order to provide a basis for international comparisons. With the attempt to describe "Journalismus in der Gesellschaft" ["Journalism in society"] (Scholl and Weischenberg, 1998), the empirical findings were then discussed in relation to the preliminary systems-theoretical considerations. In doing so, the function of journalism for society could be analyzed in connection with the relevant actors, their characteristics and attitudes.

In spite of their different theoretical and methodological approaches, these two studies yielded similar results in many respects. Particularly, their findings earmarked a change of perspective regarding the degree to which journalists' professional role perceptions were considered significant to their professional actions and news decisions. In contrast to the findings and interpretations of previous studies that had drawn conclusions about media content from the journalists' characteristics, attitudes and role perceptions, both of the new studies presented more differentiated propositions. Those can be explained by theoretical, methodological and empirical changes. In terms of the theoretical approach, organizational constraints of the newsroom were considered; methodologically, new items were included in the surveys; and empirically, journalists' attitudes and role perceptions might have had changed, because the findings showed that journalists now tended to see themselves as objective news providers rather than as missionaries or controllers.[3]

Furthermore, detailed comparative journalism studies were conducted in Germany since the beginning of the 1990s. The project "Media and Democracy" (e.g. Patterson and Donsbach, 1996) collected data concerning professional attitudes, editorial structures and news decisions in five countries; Frank Esser (1998) sought to find influencing factors shaping the national and cultural identity of journalism in Great Britain and Germany; and Holger Sievert (1998) considered further the question to what extent journalism in Europe has aligned and synchronized. Besides these studies focusing on the system of journalism as a whole, numerous other studies engaged with comparing single aspects, for example, ethics, research strategies, working conditions and so on.

Moreover, the interrelations of journalism with its social environment were theoretically and empirically analyzed as more and more differentiated in the 1990s. Barbara Baerns' "Determination Hypothesis" (1985) was long regarded as the route to follow in terms of the relationship between journalism and public relations. According to Baerns, public relations are determining the topics and timing of reporting. However, this perspective has broadened since the mid-1990s, when research considerations moved from public relations' effects on journalism to the analysis of interrelating influences, interdependencies and alignments of both fields. Likewise, the importance of theoretical reflections on the relationship between journalism and public relations increased, using both action-theoretical approaches on a micro level and systems-theoretical concepts on a macro level (Altmeppen, Röttger, and Bentele, 2004).

Status Quo: New Challenges and Theoretical Clearing Up

Recently, German journalism research has faced up to the theoretical and empirical challenges that arise with the change of the object of investigation originating from the possibilities of new communication technologies. Relevant research questions now concern the borders between journalism and advertising, information and entertainment, observation and performing, facts and fiction, mass communication and individual communication (e.g. Altmeppen and Quandt, 2002; Neuberger, 2004). Likewise, professional and editorial structures of online journalism are analyzed, thereby investigating new segments of journalism and comparing them to those of the "traditional" media (e.g. Neuberger, 2000; Löffel-holz et al., 2003; Quandt, 2005).

Furthermore, a new representative survey of journalists in Germany was conducted in 2005. The replication of the study "Journalism in Germany" updates the findings of the 1993 survey. It aims at investigating the organizations and actors providing news and exploring their characteristics, attitudes and working conditions (Weischenberg, Malik, and Scholl, 2006). The comparison of the two surveys' findings shows that journalism in Germany is a rather sound social system in terms of its function. For example, this becomes evident by looking at the journalists' professional role perceptions, which do not differ much between 1993 and 2005. Most German journalists still feel committed to the standards of objective news journalism. Likewise, communicative intentions such as controlling are still of subsidiary relevance, whereas the aim to represent "reality" is still widespread among German journalists. Consequently, journalists in Germany largely hold on to the traditional values of their profession, although the general conditions of journalism are changing, due to changing economic, technological and organizational circumstances.

After several decades of empirical research and recent theoretical efforts, journalism studies in Germany are now due for clearing up. The efforts focus on systematization, struggles with the definition of journalism, attempts to define clearly the borders between journalism and, for example, public relations, and profile of the inevitably interdisciplinary character of relevant research which is oscillating between sociology, science of history, linguistics, political science and cultural studies. Furthermore, journalism researchers try to work out supposed or actual differences between the various theoretical approaches to journalism using systems theory, action theory or constructivism, or suggest adopting a new perspective on journalism research as part of cultural studies. These proposals demonstrate the attempt to develop a "super theory" – an attempt that already led to disappointment in research on media effects. But although the current theoretical debate emanates from journalism concepts on the macro level, many empirical studies still draw on an individualistic definition of journalism.

In terms of internationality, journalism research in Germany is still at a development stage – although noticeable advances have been made in recent years. For a long time, international cooperation and references were initiated mainly by single institutions and persons. Regarding the recognition of foreign research, particularly Anglo-American literature is perceived, while studies from non-English countries – including other European countries – are considered less. Exceptions are Austria and Switzerland, because the absence of language boundaries facilitates cooperation. Likewise, only few German studies attract international attention, because the most important journals of journalism research in Germany are published in the German language. Thus, theoretical developments and empirical output of German research have been recognized abroad only sporadically. However, today the researchers' efforts on expanding international relationships between researchers, institutes and their work are evident.

As this outline demonstrates, German journalism research is a quite differentiated, albeit patchy field of study. It embraces a large variety of questions, provides various empirical findings and engages with a plurality of theoretical perspectives.

Notes

1 In fact it was the science of history that provided the first significant contributions to the role of journalism in Nazi Germany (e.g. Frei and Schmitz, 1989).

2 From a West German point of view, journalism research in the German Democratic Republic was analyzed by Blaum (1980).

3 However, the notion of journalists' professional role perceptions and how they influence their decision-making remains controversial among journalism researchers in Germany – which might be due to the issue's relevance for media policy (Löffelholz, 2000, p. 45).

References

Altmeppen, K.-D. (1999). *Redaktionen als Koordinationszentren: Beobachtungen journalistischen Handelns* [*Newsrooms as centers of coordination: Observing journalistic actions*]. Opladen and Wiesbaden: Westdeutscher Verlag.

Altmeppen, K.-D., and Quandt, T. (2002). Wer informiert uns, wer unterhält uns? Die Organisation öffentlicher Kommunikation und die Folgen für Kommunikations- und Medienberufe [*Who informs, who entertains? The organization of public communication and its consequences for media and communications professionals*]. Medien- und Kommunikationswissenschaft, 1, 45–62.

Altmeppen, K.-D., Röttger, U., and Bentele, G. (eds.) (2004). *Schwierige Verhältnisse: Interdependenzen zwischen Journalismus und PR* [*Challenging circumstances. Interdependencies of journalism and public relations*]. Wiesbaden: Verlag für Sozialwissenschaften.

Baerns, B. (1995). *Öffentlichkeitsarbeit oder Journalismus? Zum Einfluß im Mediensystem* [*Public relations or journalism? Effects on the media system*]. 2nd edition. Cologne: Verlag für Wissenschaft und Politik.

Blaum, V. (1980). *Marxismus-Leninismus, Massenkommunikation und Journalismus: zum Gegenstand der Journalistikwissenschaft in der DDR* [*Marxism and Leninism, mass communication and journalism. Journalism studies in the German Democratic Republic*]. Munich: Minerva.

Böckelmann, F. (1993). *Journalismus als Beruf: Bilanz der Kommunikatorforschung im deutschsprachigen Raum von 1945 bis 1990* [*Journalism as a profession. Review of communicator research in German-speaking countries, 1945–1990*]. Konstanz: Universitätsverlag.

Budzislawski, H. (1962). Über die Journalistik als Wissenschaft [Journalism studies as a science]. *Zeitschrift für Journalistik*, 2, 43–9.

Baumert, D. P. (1928). *Die Entstehung des deutschen Journalismus. Eine sozialgeschichtliche Studie* [*The Evolution of German Journalism. A socio-historical study*]. Munich, Leipzig: Duncker & Humblot.

Donsbach, W. (1982). *Legitimationsprobleme des Journalismus: Gesellschaftliche Rolle der*

Massenmedien und berufliche Einstellungen von Journalisten [*Legitimation problems of journalism. The mass media's role in society and journalist's professional attitudes*]. Freiburg, Breisgau, Munich: Alber.

Dovifat, E. (1931). *Zeitungswissenschaft* [*Science of the press*]. Berlin: Walter de Gruyter.

Dovifat, E. (1937). *Zeitungslehre* [*Textbook of the press*]. Berlin: Walter de Gruyter.

Dovifat, E. (1967). *Zeitungslehre* [*Textbook of the press*]. 5th edition. Berlin: Walter de Gruyter.

Duchkowitsch, W., Hausjell, F., and Semrad, B. (eds.) (2004). *Die Spirale des Schweigens: Zum Umgang mit der nationalsozialistischen Zeitungswissenschaft* [*The spiral of silence. Coping with national socialist science of the press*]. Münster: LIT Verlag.

Esser, F. (1998). *Die Kräfte hinter den Schlagzeilen: Englischer und deutscher Journalismus im Vergleich* [*The powers behind the headlines. A cross-cultural comparison of English and German journalism*]. Freiburg: Alber.

Frei, N., and Schmitz, J. (1989). *Journalismus im Dritten Reich* [*Journalism in the Third Reich*]. Munich: Beck.

Groth, O. (1928–30). *Die Zeitung: Ein System der Zeitungskunde* [*The newspaper. A system of press studies*] Mannheim, Berlin, and Leipzig: Bensheimer.

Grubitzsch, J. (1990). Traditionen, Altlasten und Neuansätze der Leipziger Journalistenausbildung [Traditions, legacies and new approaches of journalists' education in Leipzig]. *Rundfunk und Fernsehen*, 3, 400–6.

Gurjewitsch, S. M. (1975). *Karl Marx und Friedrich Engels als Theoretiker des kommunistischen Journalismus* [*Karl Marx and Friedrich Engels. The theorists of communist journalism*]. Leipzig: Karl-Marx-Universität, Sektion Journalistik.

Hachmeister, L. (1987). *Theoretische Publizistik: Studien zur Geschichte der Kommunikationswissenschaft in Deutschland* [*Theoretical journalism studies. Studies on the history of communication science in Germany*]. Berlin: Spiess.

Hagemann, W. (1950). *Die Zeitung als Organismus* [*The newspaper as an organism*]. Heidelberg: Vowinckel.

Hienzsch, U. (1990). *Journalismus als Restgröße. Redaktionelle Rationalisierung und publizistischer Leistungsverlust* [*Journalism as residual. Editorial rationalization and loss of journalistic performance*]. Wiesbaden: Deutscher Universitäts-Verlag.

Kepplinger, H. M. (ed.) (1979). *Angepaßte Außenseiter: Was Journalisten denken und wie sie arbeiten* [Aligned outsiders. What journalists think and how they do their job]. Freiburg and Munich: Alber.

Köcher, R. (1985). *Spürhund und Missionar: Eine vergleichende Untersuchung über Berufsethik und Aufgabenverständnis britischer und deutscher Journalisten* [Bloodhounds and missionaries. A comparative study about professional ethics and role perceptions of journalists in Great Britain and Germany]. Dissertation. Munich.

Kutsch, A. (1988). Max Webers Anregung zur empirischen Journalismusforschung: Die Zeitungs-Enquête und eine Redakteurs-Umfrage [Max Weber's contribution to empirical journalism research. The newspaper survey and a journalists' poll]. *Publizistik*, 1, 5–31.

Löffelholz, M. (2000). *Theorien des Journalismus: Ein diskursives Handbuch* [*Theories of journalism. A discursive handbook*]. 2nd edition 2004. Wiesbaden: Westdeutscher Verlag.

Löffelholz, M. (2003). Kommunikatorforschung: Journalistik [*Communicator research: Journalism studies*]. In G. Bentele, H.-B. Brosius, and O. Jarren (eds.), *Öffentliche Kommunikation. Handbuch Kommunikations- und Medienwissenschaft* [*Public commu-*

nication. Handbook of communication and media studies] (pp. 28–53). Wiesbaden: Westdeutscher Verlag.

Löffelholz, M., Quandt, T., Hanitzsch, T., and Altmeppen, K.-D. (2003). Online-Journalisten in Deutschland: Forschungsdesign und Befunde der ersten Repräsentativbefragung deutscher Online-Journalisten [Online journalists in Germany. Research design and results of the first representative survey of German online journalists]. *Media Perspektiven*, 10, 477–86.

Meckel, M. (1999). *Reaktionsmanagement: Ansätze aus Theorie und Praxis [Newsroom management. Theoretical and practical approaches]*. Opladen and Wiesbaden: Westdeutscher Verlag.

Möllmann, B. (1998). *Redaktionelles Marketing bei Tageszeitungen [Newsroom marketing in daily newspapers]*. Munich: Fischer.

Neuberger, C. (2000). Journalismus im Internet: Auf dem Weg zur Eigenständigkeit? Ergebnisse einer Redaktionsbefragung bei Presse, Rundfunk und Nur-Onlineanbietern [Journalism on the Internet: On its way to autonomy? Results of a newsroom survey of print, broadcasting and online-only providers]. *Media Perspektiven*, 7, 310–18.

Neuberger, C. (2004). Lösen sich die Grenzen des Journalismus auf? Dimensionen und Defizite der Entgrenzungsthese [Are the borders of journalism disappearing? Dimensions and shortcomings of the delimitation hypothesis]. In G. Roters, W. Klingler, and M. Gerhards (eds.), *Medienzukunft – Zukunft der Medien [Media future – future of the media]* (pp. 95–112). Baden-Baden: Nomos.

Noelle-Neumann, E. (1979). Kumulation, Konsonanz und Öffentlichkeit. Ein neuer Ansatz zur Analyse der Wirkung der Massenmedien [Cumulation, consonance, and the public. A new proposal for the analysis of mass media effects]. In E. Noelle-Neumann (ed.), *Öffentlichkeit als Bedrohung: Beiträge zur empirischen Kommunikationsforschung [The public as a threat. Contributions to empirical communicator research]* (pp. 127–68). Freiburg and Munich: Alber.

Patterson, T. E., and Donsbach, W. (1996). News decisions: Journalists as partisan actors. *Political Communication*, 13, 455–68.

Prutz, R. E. (1845). *Geschichte des deutschen Journalismus: Erster Teil [History of journalism. First part]* Göttingen: Vandenhoeck and Ruprecht. (Autotyp of the 1st edition. Göttingen 1971)

Quandt, T. (2005). *Journalisten im Netz: Eine Untersuchung journalistischen Handelns in Online-Redaktionen [Journalists on the Internet. Observing journalists' actions in online newsrooms. A study]*. Wiesbaden: Verlag für Sozialwissenschaften.

Rager, G., Schäfer-Dieterle, S., and Weber, B. (1994). *Redaktionelles Marketing. Wie Zeitungen die Zukunft meistern [Newsroom marketing. How newspapers cope with the future]*. Bonn: Zeitungsverlag-Service.

Rühl, M. (1969). *Die Zeitungsredaktion als organisiertes soziales System [The newspaper newsroom as organized social system]*. 2nd edition 1979. Freiburg: Bertelsmann.

Rühl, M. (1980). *Journalismus und Gesellschaft [Journalism and society]*. Mainz: Von Hase and Köhler Verlag.

Rühl, M. (1989). Organisatorischer Journalismus: Tendenzen in der Redaktionsforschung [Organizational journalism. Trends in newsroom research]. In M. Kaase and W. Schulz (eds.), *Massenkommunikation: Theorien, Methoden, Befunde [Mass communication. Theory, methods, results]* (pp. 253–69). Opladen: Westdeutscher Verlag.

Rust, H. (1986). *Entfremdete Elite? Journalisten im Kreuzfeuer der Kritik [Alienated elite? Journalists in critics' cross fire]*. Vienna: Literas.

Schneider, B., Schönbach, K., and Stürzebecher, D. (1993). Journalisten im vereinigten

Deutschland: Strukturen, Arbeitsweisen und Einstellungen im Ost-West-Vergleich [Journalists in reunified Germany. Comparing structures, work modes, and attitudes in east and west]. *Publizistik*, 3, 353–82.

Schneider, B., Schönbach, K., and Stürzebecher, D. (1994). Ergebnisse einer Repräsentativbefragung zur Struktur, sozialen Lage und zu den Einstellungen von Journalisten in den neuen Bundesländern [Results of a represantative survey about structure, social position and attitudes of journalists in the new German federal states]. In F. Böckelmann, C. Mast, and B. Schneider (eds.), *Journalismus in den neuen Ländern: Ein Berufsstand zwischen Aufbruch und Abwicklung* [*Journalism in the new German states. A profession between boost and liquidation*] (pp. 145–90). Konstanz: Universitätsverlag.

Scholl, A., and Weischenberg, S. (1998). *Journalismus in der Gesellschaft: Theorie, Methodologie und Empirie* [*Journalismus in society. Theory, methodology and empirical research*]. Opladen and Wiesbaden: Westdeutscher Verlag.

Sievert, H. (1998). *Europäischer Journalismus: Theorie und Empirie aktueller Medienkommunikation in der Europäischen Union* [*European journalism. Theory and empirical research on contemporary media communication in the European Union*]. Opladen: Westdeutscher Verlag.

Spael, W. (1928). *Publizistik und Journalistik und ihre Erscheinungsformen bei Joseph Görres (1798–1814): Ein Beitrag zur Methode der publizistischen Wissenschaft* [*Journalism and its manifestations in Joseph Görres' work (1798–1814). A contribution to the methodologies of journalism studies*]. Cologne: Gilde-Verlag.

Traumann, G. (1971). *Journalistik in der DDR* [*Journalism studies in the German Democratic Republic*]. Munich and Pullach, Berlin: Saur.

Weaver, D. H., and Wilhoit, G. C. (1986/1991). *The American journalist: A portrait of US news people and their work*. Bloomington, IN: Indiana University Press.

Weber, M. (1911). Geschäftsbericht: Soziologie des Zeitungswesens [Business report. Sociology of the press]. In *Schriften der Deutschen Gesellschaft für Soziologie. Serie 1, Band 1* [*Scripts of the German Sociology Association. Series 1, Volume 1*] (pp. 39–62). Tübingen: Mohr.

Weischenberg, S. (1989). Der enttarnte Elefant: Journalismus in der Bundesrepublik – und die Forschung, die sich ihm widmet [The exposed elephant. Journalism in Germany and the research dedicated to it]. *Media Perspektiven*, 4, 227–39.

Weischenberg, S. (1992). *Journalistik: Band 1: Mediensysteme, Medienethik, Medieninstitutionen* [*Journalism studies. Vol. 1: Media systems, media ethics, media institutions*]. Opladen: Westdeutscher Verlag.

Weischenberg, S. (1995): *Journalistik: Band 2: Medientechnik, Medienfunktionen, Medienakteure* [*Journalism studies. Vol. 2: Media technology, media functions, media actors*]. Opladen: Westdeutscher Verlag.

Weischenberg, S., Löffelholz, M., and Scholl, A. (1993): Journalismus in Deutschland: Design und erste Befunde der Kommunikatorstudie [Journalism in Germany. Design and first results of the communicator study]. *Media Perspektiven*, 1, 21–33.

Weischenberg, S., Löffelholz, M., and Scholl, A. (1994). Merkmale und Einstellungen von Journalisten: "Journalismus in Deutschland II" [Journalists' attitudes and characteristics. "Journalism in Germany II"]. *Media Perspektiven*, 4, 154–67.

Weischenberg, S., Löffelholz, M., and Scholl, A. (1998). Journalism in Germany. In Weaver, D. H. (ed.), *The global journalist. Studies of news people around the world* (pp. 229–56). Creskill, NJ: Hampton Press.

Weischenberg, S., Malik, M., and Scholl, A. (2006). *Die Souffleure der Mediengesellschaft:*

Report über die deutschen Journalisten [*Prompters of media society. Report about journalists in Germany*] Konstanz: UVK.

Weiß, H.-J. (1978). Journalismus als Beruf: Forschungssynopse [Journalism as profession. Synopsis of research]. In Presse- und Informationsamt der Bundesregierung. *Kommunikationspolitische und kommunikationswissenschaftliche Forschungsprojekte der Bundesregierung (1974–1978)* [*Communication Policy and Communication Research Projects in Germany (1974–1978)*] (pp. 109–39). Bonn: Presse- und Informationsamt.

Chapter 14

Journalism Research in the UK
From Isolated Efforts to an Established Discipline

Karin Wahl-Jorgensen and Bob Franklin

A Paradox: The Gap between Practice and Research

The United Kingdom boasts one of the most well-established and prestigious traditions of journalism in the world, but research *about* journalism has been slow to develop, scant in quantity, and scattered across a variety of fields, few of them centrally concerned with news media. This chapter explores the reasons for this dissonance between journalism practice and research. We argue that a research tradition for journalism in the UK is emerging, rather than well established. The culprit for this tardy scholastic development is the institutional location of journalism education, until very recently, outside the university, as journalists are trained "in house" by news organizations that emphasize professional skills (Delano, 2000; Purdey, 2000).

Two consequences follow. First, much of the academic and scholarly literature about journalism in the UK derives from social science disciplines, particularly sociology. By contrast, industry-related training has focused on imparting practical skills to journalists. What is lacking, then, is a sustained home-grown disciplinary tradition. Second, our thesis suggests a case for UK exceptionalism. The location of journalism training outside of the university sector reflects organizational and structural factors which have meant that UK journalism research is not only late in developing, but also relatively isolated from the global context.

A Century Behind: The Development of Journalism in Higher Education

The understanding of journalism as a basic craft that relies more readily on "rat-like cunning, a plausible manner and a little literary ability" than on rigorous training and reflection remains deeply rooted in British newsrooms (Tomalin, 1969).

The first daily newspaper in the English-speaking world, the *Daily Courant*, was published in London in 1702. The professionalization of journalism in Britain occurred in the late 19th century, in response to developments including increased literacy, the spread of urbanization, a revolution in printing technologies, the invention of the typewriter, and the consolidation of journalistic work within newsrooms (Høyer, 2003). The professionalization of journalism was also evidenced in the creation of the National Association of Journalists in the late 19th century, while a trade organization, the National Union of Journalists, emerged in 1907 (Bromley, 1997).

The organizational efforts of journalists illustrated their self-perception as an occupational group with its own needs and concerns – albeit a not especially cohesive group. It was also an occupation, however, that eschewed university training. An attempt to establish a journalism training course at the University of London in 1937 failed after only two years, dismissed by the newspaper industry as overly theoretical and out of touch with the daily realities of journalism (Bromley, 1997, p. 334). For their part, universities argued that the technical skills of journalism lacked sufficient academic rigor to warrant inclusion in the curriculum. The early history of British journalism education demonstrates Zelizer's maxim that journalists and academics inhabit "parallel universes" (Zelizer, 2004). Formal training within the academy was discarded in favor of learning on the job, with journalists honing their "craft" through practical experience.

The National Council for the Training of Journalists (NCTJ) was founded in 1951 to formalize this training. Initially, trainee journalists completed a three-year program, during which they studied English, central and local government, and shorthand at local colleges of further education, and followed the NCTJ's correspondence course in newspaper law. By contrast, skills-based vocational training took place in the newsroom. Literature on journalism relevant to such training was available, with Sir Isaac Pitman's series of books teaching journalism skills (Bull, 1926) being an essential companion to the budding journalist of the day. The critical approach typical of academic work, however, was absent from journalism studies for the greater part of the 20th century. As Rod Allen (2005) reflected:

> Until about thirty years ago . . . practically the only way into newspaper journalism was to sit at the feet of (or more likely, to sit at a desk near) an older journalist. If you were lucky, he (it was invariably a "he") would teach you the rudiments of the job, take you on an assignment or two and help you learn to pay for your round in the local pub.
>
> (p. 318)

It was not until 1970 that a university-based full-time vocational training program was established which won accreditation from the NCTJ. This postgraduate course, founded by *Picture Post* publisher Tom Hopkinson at the University of Cardiff, stressed the skills-based orientation that embodied the philosophy of the NCTJ. This late arrival of academic training in journalism contrasts sharply with the US experience, in which journalism education that foregrounds a strong liberal arts training has been around for the better part of a century (Bromley, 1997; Allen, 2005).

The major development since the 1970s has been the transition to an essentially graduate occupation (Tunstall, 1977, pp. 334–5). Across the 1990s, there has been a remarkable growth in journalism training within universities (Delano, 2000). In 1994, the University of Sheffield became the first of the Russell Group (the top 15 research universities) to offer an undergraduate course in journalism, which combined practical training with a more conventional liberal arts education. Just over ten years on, there are more than 600 undergraduate courses with journalism in their title (Allen, 2005, p. 319), although only nine university-based centers offer NCTJ-accredited postgraduate diplomas. Today, 98 percent of journalists hold undergraduate degrees, and 58 percent have a qualification in journalism, while a substantial minority (42 percent) have completed a postgraduate diploma or MA-level education (Hargreaves, 2002).

This swift expansion since the 1990s, however, has meant that practical training has run ahead of research in universities, reflecting in part the fact that much of the growth in journalism training programs has occurred in the "new universities" created by the higher education reforms of 1992. These institutions are generally (1) less well-resourced, (2) less research-oriented, and more teaching oriented, and (3) have stronger commitment to vocational training rather than academic knowledge. Consequently, they express a keener commitment to the skills-based learning emphasized by NCTJ. But while they have generated well-trained practitioners, they have proved less effective in producing reflective research.

The Research Assessment Exercise (the national review of academic research which allocates funding to universities and departments every five years on the basis of research achievements) further challenges the development of home-grown research in journalism studies by concentrating funding in research-oriented universities, while most institutions that conduct journalism training receive little, if any, funding to promote research.

Research in journalism studies

One consequence of this brief history is that home-grown journalism studies research is a recent arrival in the UK. It is difficult to identify a research-based book with the words "journalist" or "journalism" in the title published between Tunstall's (1971) *Journalists at work* and McNair's (1994) *News and journalism in the UK*. The great majority of "classics" in the field originated from sociology, and to a lesser extent political science and media studies, rather than journalism departments. The origin of journalism research in sociology departments has had profound consequences for the preoccupations and tenor of the work. In particular, British work in journalism studies has rarely viewed the profession in isolation, but has always considered the relationship between journalism and the social world.

Production Studies

The rise of work on journalism corresponded with the consolidation of sociology as a discipline in the early 1960s (Halsey, 2004). Early scholarship in the sociology of journalism was often interested in understanding processes of news production. Elite media organizations, and their newsgathering and reporting practices and routines, came under scrutiny in studies conducted in the early 1970s. Jeremy Tunstall's book, *Journalists at work* (1971; see also Tunstall, 1970a), is among the earliest research-based studies in journalism, and exemplifies the approach of pioneering studies in the sociology of journalism. Tunstall's study examined the work of specialist correspondents in national news organizations, using survey research and interviews. His ambition was to understand journalists' professional roles, goals and careers, the organizations in which they worked, and the relations they give rise to. His purpose was primarily to describe professional practices, rather than assume the more critical stance that characterized later work in the field.

Following Tunstall's approach, researchers in the late 1970s began to broadly describe the news production process. Philip Schlesinger's 1978 study, *Putting reality together*, for example, focused on radio and television journalists at the BBC. Schlesinger identified a culture of conformity in the revered public service institution. He characterized journalists there as slaves to the clock, suggesting that the emphasis on speed in news delivery is a defining feature of newsroom culture. He described newsmaking as a heavily routinized activity, in which control over the production process is key to successful operation. Golding and Elliott (1979) similarly characterized the news production process as a "highly regulated and routine process of manufacturing a cultural product on an electronic production line" (cited in Golding and Elliott, 1999, p. 119). Some of this early news production research has been criticized for its overly mechanistic depiction of the news production process, which is unnecessarily pessimistic about the agency of journalists, but these pioneer studies also delivered enduring insights into the routines of news production, the self-understandings of journalists, and the hierarchies which operate in the newsroom.

Scholars who contributed to the field of journalism studies during this formative period included individuals such as James Curran, Jeremy Tunstall, James Halloran, Jay Blumler, Denis McQuail, Phillip Elliott, and Oliver Boyd-Barrett (Tunstall, 1970b). Many continue to shape the field to this day, but none were actively engaged in training journalists and consequently journalism research made only a modest contribution to the creation of reflective practitioners. But the ethnographic and sociological approach to the study of news production is now a sustained tradition, refined over the intervening decades, and producing a good deal of research focusing on the work of large, national news organizations such as the BBC (Cottle and Ashton, 1998; Harrison, 2000; Born, 2005).

While early journalism research investigated the general structure of news production, some scholars took an interest in specialists, such as crime reporters (Chibnall, 1977) and political journalists (Seymour-Ure 1968, 1974; Tracey, 1977). Michael Tracey's 1977 book, *The production of political television*, for example, used interviews with and ethnographic observation of newsworkers at ITV and the BBC to understand the making of programs involved in the policy-making process, focusing on how government and commercial organizations attempt to influence coverage. Developing this early work, scholars with backgrounds or interests in political science have continued to contribute to the academic literature about journalism. Studies of political journalism and public relations have grown stronger in recent years, testifying to the growth of political communications research and its links with journalism studies. Jay G. Blumler's studies serve as the foundation stones for subsequent political journalism scholarship focusing on the "crisis in public communication" (Blumler and McQuail, 1968; Blumler, 1981; Blumler and Gurevitch, 1995). Barnett and Gaber's (2001) book on Westminster correspondents and how they deal with the "spin machine" of Tony Blair's New Labour government, is just one of a series of books on the reporting of politics. The authors suggest that the management of information has led to a crisis of political journalism, which has caused the failure of the media's critical watchdog role. As such, the problem of "packaging politics" (Franklin, 2004) and its consequences for journalism and, more broadly, democracy, have been central to the field across the past decade. During this time, other researchers have turned their attention to the relationships between journalists and their sources, exploring how public relations practitioners, interest groups and social movements struggle for media access (e.g. Davis, 2002).

Cultural Studies, Political Economy and Journalism

In contrast to the frequently descriptive intent of production studies, some strands of early journalism research adopted an explicitly critical agenda, from a tradition informed by Marxist theory. Such work challenged prevalent contemporary understandings of how journalists conduct their work and how journalistic texts circulate and operate in society. The Glasgow University Media Group's study *Bad news* (1976), and the companion volumes *More bad news* (1980) and *Really bad news* (1982), attempted to "reveal the structures of the cultural framework which underpins the production of apparently neutral news" (1976, p. 1). Based primarily on content analysis of news from 1975, and focusing on how the public service broadcasters, the BBC and ITN, reported industrial disputes, these books demonstrated that television news – despite making claims to impartiality – ultimately reproduces the viewpoints of the most powerful social groups. The Glasgow Group argued that news stories privileged management interpretations of these disputes, while offering only scant attention and credibility to trade union viewpoints. These volumes received a hostile reception by the media, especially the BBC (Eldridge, 2000), but were widely read among journalism practitioners and scholars. The critical work of the Glasgow Media Group continues to this day, engaging with social issues ranging from the coverage of HIV/AIDS to the Israel/Palestine conflict, although the focus in more recent work has shifted from the production to the reception of news stories (e.g. Eldridge, 2000; Philo and Berry, 2004). Other early critical work highlighted different aspects of news media's structural bias. One study revealed, for example, that the interpretive framework of violence dominated coverage of Anti-Vietnam demonstrations, limiting a substantive discussion of the issues raised by the protesters (Halloran, Elliott, and Murdock, 1970).

Media scholars Graham Murdock and Peter Golding developed the political economy approach, studying not only media production processes, but also the ways in which they relate to the competitive market relationships of capitalism. As early as 1974, they articulated the defining ideas of a political economy critique of news media, which has a continuing relevance for contemporary analyses:

> For us the mass media are first and foremost industrial and commercial organizations which produce and distribute commodities within a late capitalist order. Consequently we would argue, the production of ideology cannot be separated from or adequately understood without grasping the general economic dynamics of media production and the determinations they exert.
>
> (Murdock and Golding, 1974, p. 206)

Concurrently, the Centre for Contemporary Cultural Studies (CCCS) at the University of Birmingham conducted seminal research on journalism and media studies. Their 1978 book, *Policing the Crisis*, studied the social construction of a moral panic around mugging, through coverage in news media (Hall et al., 1978). Their analysis identified "news" as the "end product of a complex process which begins with a systematic sorting and selection of events and topics according to a socially constructed set of categories" (p. 55). This work signaled the need to study news production in terms of ideological processes and social control. Stuart Hall and his colleagues suggested that news media "effectively but "objectively" (p. 60) contribute to constructing "consensual" views of society, and that the consensus coincides with, and is defined by, the ideas of the most powerful. This – essentially Marxist – position is elaborated in their influential description of primary and secondary definers. Primary definers – the accredited representatives of major social institutions that are seen to have access to accurate or specialized information on particular topics – come to establish the primary interpretation of the topic, whether it be race, the war in Iraq, or industrial disputes. Arguments against this primary interpretation put forward by secondary definers (including media professionals themselves) are then obliged to contest this already established framework (p. 58).

This critical tradition of journalism studies, together with the insights of the detailed early production studies, exercised a profound influence on later scholars in the field. The work of the CCCS not only questioned the utility of the "strategic rituals" of objectivity, but also illustrated that media representations can have profound ideological consequences. This insight has informed and spawned subsequent studies of representation, especially those focused on marginalized groups such as ethnic minorities, asylum seekers, and women. Cultural-studies approaches have also shaped our understanding of the media's ability to create "moral panics," in which particular events (such as mugging, child abuse or paedophile attacks) are connected to a perceived larger malaise, ultimately justifying increased social control.

The Demographics of Journalism

Another approach to understanding the relationship between journalism and the social world has examined what might be termed the social demography of the profession. This approach, which has generated a flurry of published work in the past few decades, connects with industry concerns, and has often been supported by news organizations (e.g. Delano and Henningham, 1995; Henningham and Delano, 1998; Delano, 2000). This research shows that although many budding journalists dream of glamorous careers at national newspapers or at the BBC, the vast majority of British reporters – 65 percent – begin their careers in regional and local papers (Henningham and Delano, 1998). The industry is male-dominated – (75 percent of journalists are male) and there is a continuing discrepancy between the salaries of male and female journalists, with women earning on average 83 percent of men's salaries (Henningham and Delano, 1998). Women are less likely to work in news and current affairs, while men dominate the higher echelons of the newsroom hierarchy (Ross, 2005, p. 291).

Ainley (1998) revealed that British journalism constitutes an apartheid-style system in which the majority of black and Asian journalists are employed on black newspapers and periodicals, while white journalists effectively colonize mainstream media. Broadcasters employed the highest number of ethnic minority journalists across the news media, while Ainley found less than 20 black journalists at all the national newspapers, out of 3,000 employees. Even more alarmingly, there were only 15 black/Asian journalists working in the provincial press out of a workforce of approximately 8,000. Other work on the demographics of the profession has detected a "glass ceiling" in journalism, as well as problems of institutional discrimination. It has also cautioned that the culture of the newsroom remains distinctly white and male. These studies reflect a growing awareness in news organizations about the need for a more diverse workforce. Some researchers have suggested that women journalists will report the news differently from their male colleagues (Ross, 2001). As Linda Christmas (1997) argued, women journalists "tend to put readers' needs above those of policy makers" and tend to be more people-oriented than issue-oriented (p. 3). Other scholars have criticized such statements, suggesting that the gendered nature of newsmaking – as when women journalists are assigned to cover "lifestyle" stories, while male journalists are assigned as political correspondents – is the result of discriminatory practices that perpetuate existing inequalities (e.g. Allan, 2004, p. 120).

History of Journalism

The place of journalism in society has been contextualized in a long-standing tradition of scholarship on the history of the press and broadcasting. Raymond Williams, in a series of books published in the 1960s, laid the groundwork for cultural studies, as well as for understanding journalistic writing as key cultural texts. In *The long revolution*, he argued that the extension of literacy created a revolution in communications, allowing for emancipation through open discussion, the extension of human relationships, and public influence on the direction of institutions (Williams, 1961, p. 383). Williams described the history of the popular press in Britain and, on the basis of his historical analysis, advised presciently against the increasing concentration of ownership in media industries, arguing it posed a threat to the democratic potential of the communications revolution. Williams' interest in the relationship between media of the public sphere and cultural formations became a lasting preoccupation. It shaped the direction of later cultural studies work toward an interest in mass media.

Another influential work, James Curran and Jean Seaton's historical account of the British press and broadcasting in the 19th and the 20th centuries, *Power without responsibility*, was first published in 1991. It questioned a Whig or progressive interpretation of history, and demonstrated that although British journalism has been seen as an independent force for liberty, the press and broadcast institutions should also be understood as political actors in their own right. Work in the history of journalism thus contributed not only to an understanding of the rich tradition of newsmaking in Britain, but also allowed for an appreciation of the limits of objectivity, impartiality and independence, and – more fundamentally – of our models of historical interpretation (Seymour-Ure, 1991).

The Language of Journalism

Studies of the language of journalism have been slower to emerge. In *Bad news* (1976), the Glasgow Media Group observed that "the almost complete lack of convergence between the discipline of linguistics, the literary and stylistic criticism of texts and the rag-bag of sociological content analysis provides an unfavourable climate for analysing news language" (p. 21). They sought to rectify some of these shortfalls by studying linguistic features of journalism, including the visual codes of television news and the organization of mediated conversation. They suggested that news talk creates "preferential hearings which invite the competent listener to hear the talk as neutral" (p. 25). Subsequent British scholars in sociolinguistics have contributed to a technically refined understanding of how journalists' language is not purely denotative or "objective," but carries a heavy ideological baggage. This is not the result of conscious "bias," but an inherent feature of language. Scholars including Allan Bell (1991), Roger Fowler (1991), Norman Fairclough (1995), and Sonia Livingstone and Peter Lunt (1994) have anlayzed a range of formal features of journalism, including patterns of talk in genres such as interviews, radio DJ shows, television talk shows, and the use of sources in news reporting. They have looked at how journalists create membership categorization, distinguishing between "us" and "them" when discussing groups including asylum seekers, criminals and Muslims (Richardson, 2004).

Studies of Local and Regional Journalism

Departing from the majority of the scholarship, which focuses on the production and texts of national-level journalism, a small but distinctive body of work on local and regional journalism reflects the strength, diversity and challenges of news media in Britain. This work has typically been critical of the object of study. David Murphy's book, *The silent watchdog* (1976), for example, questioned the assumption that the press is a "bastion of freedom," suggesting that "at the local level . . . where governments cover up except on rare occasions, the press does not uncover, cannot uncover and has no inclination to uncover" (p. 11). Based on ethnographic observation and interviews, Murphy's book examined the role of journalists in local communities. He proposed that local newspapers are inextricably entwined in local power relations. Other work on regional and local papers has examined the reporting of race, suggesting that they, as much as their national counterparts, contribute to perpetuating "negative perceptions of blacks and to define the situation as one of intergroup conflict" (Critcher, Parker, and Sondhi, 1975, p. 194).

Scholars' awareness of the local press' importance is also evident in the scope of some large-scale studies of media coverage, which have included local news. When David Deacon and Peter Golding (1994) studied mediated debates over Thatcher's controversial poll tax, they examined coverage in local, regional and national media, suggesting that it is necessary to take all types of news into consideration to understand the complexities of political communications. Scholarship that pays attention to the central role of local journalism in the British news world has been sustained to the present (e.g. Hetherington, 1989; Franklin and Murphy 1991, 1998; Franklin, 2006), tracing the consequences of technological, economic and social changes for local newsmaking. This focus on local journalism represents one of the few developing and continuing bodies of work in the broader field of journalism studies, contributing to an understanding of the vital and important local press, in a place that is home to some of the most prestigious *national* news organizations in the world.

Support for journalism research

Much of the research described here could not have been completed without the financial support of governmental, non-governmental and news organizations. While such support sometimes militates against a critical orientation, it has rarely prevented rigorous scrutiny and, subsequently, institutional soul-searching. The BBC, for example, has funded research on a range of topics, including the operation of 24-hour television news channels (Lewis, Thomas, and Cushion, 2005), and the role of embedded journalists in the Iraq conflict (Lewis, Thomas, and Cushion, 2005), but undoubtedly the most outstanding work has been Lord Asa Briggs continuing study (with five volumes currently completed) of *The history of broadcasting in the United Kingdom* (e.g. Briggs, 1961). The commercial sector of television has financed the "companion" five-volume history of independent television, *Independent television in Britain*, (e.g. Sendall, 1983). Independent Television News has funded studies to critique the Glasgow Media Group's work (Harrison, 1985), the newspaper industry has supported research on the demographics of journalism (e.g. Hargreaves, 2002), the Society of Editors financed studies of diversity in the newsroom (Cole, 2004), while various governments have commissioned studies on how new policies affect media coverage. The introduction of television cameras into the House of Commons in 1989, for example, was studied by researchers funded by Parliament (Franklin, 1992), as well as by the Hansard Society (Hetherington, Ryle, and Weaver, 1990). In Britain, such research has demonstrated the existence of a dialog between universities, industry and government, and has contributed in vital ways to public debate and scholarly knowledge.

The themes identified here have persisted over the past three decades, even if the research itself has been episodic. What has emerged is a body of empirical work and theory which is critical and interdisciplinary, and engages with problems including the political economy, production, professional cultures, texts, and reception of journalism.

The future of British journalism research

We have argued that the brief history of British journalism studies has been shaped profoundly by the location of journalism education outside of the university. Overall, there has been a lack of critical, home-grown research creating reflexive practitioners. At the same time, Britain is home to some of the most detailed ethnographic studies of news production, emerging out of the discipline of sociology.

There is room, nevertheless, for a more optimistic appraisal of the state of journalism studies as a discipline. In the UK, journalism is an expansive profession. Industry forecasts suggest that there will be an additional 20,000 journalists in the United Kingdom by 2010 (Hargreaves, 2002). As detailed above, there has been a corresponding growth in departments of journalism, students of journalism and journalism teaching and research staff in UK higher education. This growth has been reflected in the interests of major publishers, for whom an expansion of their journalism lists is an increasing priority. Sage, for example, has recently launched a new book series, "Journalism Studies: Key texts," while the Open University Press continues to publish successful journalism titles in the "Issues in Cultural and Media Studies" series. Two new journals, *Journalism Studies* and *Journalism; Theory, Practice, Criticism*, were launched in 2000 and the former title, with a UK-based editor, moved to six issues a year from February 2006. Also in the UK but with a global reach, *Journalism Practice* was launched in February 2007.

There are hopeful trends in the development of professional and academic associations. From 2006, the main British association of academic media and communication researchers, MeCCSa, was merged with the Association of Media Practice Educators (AMPE). Similarly, the Association of Journalism Education, which began as a promotional interest group for journalism teachers, is becoming increasingly research-orientated. Even if, as outlined above, the

Research Assessment Exercise fails to support the work of vocational training programs at "new" universities, the last exercise in 2001 emphasized practice-based research. This bureaucratic incentive now encourages practitioners to reflect on their "craft," boosting the relationship between journalists and the academy.

As a result of all these trends, we are seeing a slow, but steady move away from a conservative, skills-based curriculum, toward a more reflective curriculum, taught by research-active academics. This move has also been fueled by the increasingly international context of journalism studies. Throughout this chapter, we have advanced a thesis of UK exceptionalism. The unique trajectory of journalism studies here has meant that the field has taken shape in relative isolation from scholarship in other countries. Nevertheless, scholars here have always drawn centrally, if critically, on a bedrock of US literature. At the same time, scholars trained in the UK have moved elsewhere, and their work has been informed by, and diffused, the sensibilities of British journalism studies. With the foundation of ICA's journalism studies division, the field is becoming increasingly internationalized, and scholars in the UK have enthusiastically taken part in these developments.

Ultimately, the view that "journalism can be taught as, and should be regarded as, a serious academic discipline and not simply a vocational training" (DeBurgh, 2003, p. 95) is gaining ground. The history of journalism research in the United Kingdom may be brief, but its future is bright.

References

Ainley, B. (1998). *Black journalists, white media*. Stoke-on-Trent, UK: Trentham.

Allan, S. (2004). *News culture* (2nd edition). Maidenhead: Open University Press.

Allen, R. (2005). Preparing reflective practitioners. In R. Keeble (ed.), *Print journalism: a critical introduction* (pp. 317–28). London: Routledge.

Barnett, S., and Gaber, I. (2001). *Westminster tales: The twenty-first-century crisis in British journalism*. London: Continuum.

Bell, A. (1991). *The language of news media*. Oxford: Blackwell Publishing.

Blumler, J. G., and McQuail, D. (1968). *Television in politics*. London: Faber and Faber.

Blumler, J. G. (1981). Political communication: democratic theory and broadcast practice. *University of Leeds Review*, 24, 43–63.

Blumler, J. G., and Gurevitch, M. (1995). *The crisis in public communications*. London: Routledge.

Born, G. (2005). *Uncertain vision: Birt, Dyke, and the reinvention of the BBC*. London: Vintage.

Briggs, A. (1961). *The birth of broadcasting 1896–1927*. Oxford: Oxford University Press.

Bromley, M. (1997). The end of journalism? Changes in workplace practices in the press and broadcasting in the 1990s. In M. Bromley and T. O'Malley (eds.), *A journalism reader* (pp. 330–50). London: Routledge.

Bull, A. E. (1926). *Authorship and journalism: How to earn a living by the pen*. London: Pitman.

Chibnall, S. (1977). Law-and-order news: An analysis of crime reporting in the British press. London: Tavistock.

Christmas, L. (1997). *Chaps of both sexes? Women decision-markers in newspapers: Do they make a difference?* London: BT Forum/Women in Journalism.

Critcher, C., Parker, M., and Sondhi, R. (1975). *Race in the provincial press.* University of Birmingham: Centre for Contemporary Cultural Studies.

Cole, P. (2004). *Diversity in the Newsroom: Employment of minority ethnic journalists in newspapers* Cambridge, UK: Society of Editors.

Cottle, S., and Ashton, M. (1998). *From BBC newsroom to BBC newscentre: On changing technology and journalist practices.* Bath: Bath Spa University College.

Curran, J., and Seaton, J. (1991). *Power without responsibility.* 4th edition. London: Routledge.

Davis, A. (2002). *Public relations democracy: Politics, public relations and the mass media in Britain.* Manchester, UK: Manchester University Press.

Deacon, D., and Golding, P. (1994). *Taxation and representation: the media, political communication and the poll tax.* London: John Libbey.

DeBurgh, H. (2003). Skills are not enough: The case for journalism as an academic discipline. *Journalism,* 4(1), 95–112.

Delano, A. (2000). No sign of a better job: 100 years of British journalism. *Journalism Studies,* 1(2), 261–72.

Delano, A., and Henningham, J. (1995). *The news breed: British journalists in the 1990s.* London: London Institute.

Eldridge, J. (2000). The contribution of the Glasgow Media Group to the study of television and print journalism. *Journalism Studies,* 1(1), 113–27.

Fairclough, N. (1995). *Media discourse.* London: Edward Arnold.

Fowler, R. (1991). *Language in the news: Discourse and ideology in the press.* London: Routledge.

Franklin, B. (ed.) (1992). *Televising democracies.* London: Routledge.

Franklin, B. (2004). *Packaging politics: Political communications in Britain's media democracy.* 2nd edition. London: Edward Arnold.

Franklin, B. (ed.) (2006). *Local journalism, local media: The local news in context.* London: Routledge.

Franklin, B., and Murphy, D. (1991). *Making the local news: The market, politics and the local press.* London: Routledge

Glasgow University Media Group (1976). *Bad news.* London: Routledge and Kegan Paul.

Glasgow University Media Group (1980). *More bad news.* London: Routledge and Kegan Paul.

Glasgow Media Group (1982). *Really bad news.* London: Routledge and Kegan Paul.

Golding, P., and Elliott, P. (1979). *Making the news.* London: Longman.

Golding, P., and Elliott, P. (1999). Making the news (excerpt). In H. Tumber (ed.), *News: A reader* (pp. 112–20). Oxford: Oxford University Press.

Hall, S., Critcher, C., Jefferson, T., Clarke, J., and Roberts, B. (1978). *Policing the crisis: Mugging, the state, and law and order.* Basingstoke: Macmillan.

Halloran, J. D., Elliott, P., and Murdock, G. (1970). *Demonstrations and communication: A case study.* Harmondsworth: Penguin.

Halsey, A. H. (2004). *A history of sociology in Britain.* Oxford: Oxford University Press.

Hargreaves, I. (2002). *Journalists at work.* London: Publishing NTO/Skillset.

Harrison, M. (1985). *Whose bias?* Berkshire: Policy Journals.

Harrison, J. (2000). *Terrestrial TV news in Britain: The culture of production.* Manchester: Manchester University Press.

Henningham, J. P., and Delano, A. (1998). British journalists. In D. H. Weaver (ed.), *The global journalists: News people around the world* (pp. 143–60). Creskill, NJ: Hampton Press.

Hetherington, A. (1989). *News in the regions*. London: Macmillan.

Hetherington, A., Ryle, M., and Weaver, K. (1990). *Cameras in the Commons*. London: Hansard Society.

Høyer, S. (2003). Newspapers without journalists. *Journalism Studies*, 4(4), 451–63.

Lewis, J., Thomas, J., and Cushion, S. (2005). Immediacy, convenience or engagement? An analysis of 24 hour news channels in the UK. *Journalism Studies*, 6(4), 461–79.

Livingstone, S., and Lunt, P. (1994). *Talk on television: Audience participation and public debate*. London: Sage.

McNair, B. (1994). *News and journalism in the UK*. London: Routledge.

Murdock, G., and Golding, P. (1974). For a political economy of mass communications. In R. Miliband and J. Saville (eds.), *The socialist register 1973* (pp. 205–34). London: Merlin Press.

Murphy, D. (1976). *The silent watchdog: The press in local politics*. London: Constable.

Philo, G., and Berry, M. (2004). *Bad news from Israel*. London: Pluto Press.

Purdey, H. (2000). Radio journalism training and the future of radio news in the UK. *Journalism*, 1(3), 329–52.

Richardson, J. E. (2004). *(Mis)representing Islam: The racism and rhetoric of British broadsheet newspapers*. Amsterdam: John Benjamins.

Ross, K. (2001). Women at work: Journalism as en-gendered practice. *Journalism Studies*, 2(4), 531–44.

Ross, K. (2005). Women in the boyzone: Gender, news and *her*story. In S. Allan (ed.), *Journalism: Critical issues* (pp. 287–298). Maidenhead, UK: Open University Press.

Schlesinger, P. (1978). *Putting reality together*. London: Constable.

Sendall, B. (1983). *Independent television in Britain – origins and foundation 1946–1980*. London: Macmillan.

Seymour-Ure, C. (1968). *The press, politics and the public*. London: Methuen.

Seymour-Ure, C. (1974). *The political impact of mass media*. London: Constable.

Seymour-Ure, C. (1991). *The British press and broadcasting since 1945*. Oxford: Blackwell.

Tomalin, N. (1969). Stop the press I want to get on. *Sunday Times Magazine*, October 26.

Tracey, M. (1977). *The production of political television*. London: Routledge and Kegan Paul.

Tunstall, J. (1970a). *The Westminster Lobby correspondents: A sociological study of national political journalism*. London: Routledge and Kegan Paul.

Tunstall, J. (ed.) (1970b). *Media sociology*. London: Constable.

Tunstall, J. (1971). *Journalists at work. Specialist correspondents: their news organizations, news sources, and competitor-colleagues*. London: Constable.

Tunstall, J. (1977). Editorial sovereignty in the British press. In O. Boyd-Barrett, C. Seymour-Ure, and J. Tunstall, *Studies on the press* (pp. 249–341). London: HMSO.

Williams, R. (1961). *The long revolution*. London: Penguin.

Zelizer, B. (2004). *Taking journalism seriously: News and the academy*. New York: Sage.

Chapter 15

South African Journalism Research

Challenging Paradigmatic Schisms and Finding a Foothold in an Era of Globalization

Arnold S. de Beer

Introduction

Journalism research in 21st-century South Africa is perhaps not very different from that of any other Western democracy with a successful media system (de Beer and Tomaselli, 2000). However, in the early 2000s it has, to a certain extent, become complacent. Media owners are by and large satisfied about the *bottom-line* fueling more and more profit. Contented audiences lap up the entertainment fare and the soft digestible infotainment/info-education showered on them in the form of globalized, mostly American-made, words and images. Potential academic journalism researchers have, largely, turned their attention to the more profitable domain of public relations, marketing and other forms of corporate communication in a market-driven media environment. There are several reasons for this state of affairs.

During the apartheid years, serious journalism research in a coherent and nationwide front was severely lacking (de Beer and Tomaselli, 2000). On the one hand, academic researchers who did not want to get themselves embroiled in the political mayhem of the time, concentrated on the "safe" world of empirical positivism and "objective" studies. Researchers in the critical mould directed their studies to be part of the larger struggle against apartheid. This has led to a paradigmatic schism in the field that lasted well into the first decade after the democratic elections in 1994. The route to some kind of normalization was tedious. A general swell in journalism research to embrace new-found freedoms and possibilities in the post-apartheid era was found lacking. Trust among researchers in the academic community had to be fostered; new challenges had to be identified, and a new generation of researchers had to come to the fore to help invigorate journalism research, not only in a post-apartheid society, but also in a new globalizing world bringing a wide array of challenging issues to be addressed. It would be a fallacy, however, to ascribe the difference in research approaches only to apartheid.

Just as in the United States and Western Europe, there were clear schools of thought regarding "objective, non-involved, scientific" (e.g. functionalist) research *vis-à-vis* "subjective and immersed" (e.g. critical, neo-Marxist) research. A post-modernist, if not globalizing academic and research world, has wiped away much of the stern ontological and epistemological demarcations. Now, the idea of research in a triangular mode has even become fashionable among senior South African critical media studies scholars (Tomaselli, 2004a, 2004b; Williams, 2004).

When confronted with the daunting task of deconstructing the role played by the media in the apartheid era, Keyan Tomaselli (an arch-anti-positivist, and arguably the leading South African media and journalism research scholar), offers the advice that media content researchers, discourse scholars, and quantitative analysts should, for instance, have joined forces to come to grips with the South African Human Rights Commission's (SAHRC) inquiry into racism in the South African media in 1999 (Tomaselli, 2000). Such an effort would have been an important stepping stone in forging a new post-apartheid context for journalism research. Instead, the SAHRC's inquiry, as was the case with the media hearings of the Truth and Reconciliation Commission (TRC), became a battleground for journalism research and praxis debates and arguments (de Beer, 2000). These long-standing "ideological schisms" made it very difficult to achieve a coherent journalism research platform.

Racism as a Context for Journalism Research Paradigms

Whichever way one looks at it, South African journalism research entered the age of globalization with a legacy of media reporting reminiscent of that of the American media and larger societal experience, not the least of which is that of racism. While it is perhaps opportune, if not opportunistic, to leave the past behind and to focus future journalism research on the challenges of globalization, the influence of the past cannot be swept away under the academic carpet without having a strenuous effect on the future of journalism research in the country (Williams, 2004).

This is especially clear when one considers and compares the phases of journalism research and the larger South African society with that which transpired in the United States, a country playing not only an overwhelming role in the process of political, economic and cultural globalization, but also in terms of setting a framework for journalism education and research.

In their groundbreaking work on media and racism, Wilson and Gutiérrez (1995) argued that certain historical stages in news reporting could be discerned in societies experiencing conflict, especially racial conflict, and the media's reporting thereof, namely exclusionary, fear, confrontational, stereotypical and multiracial reporting.

At the beginning of the 21st century, and while trying to find a journalism research foothold in a globalizing world, the present media and journalism research situation in South Africa still seems to reflect all five of the historical stages experienced in the United States as identified by Wilson and Gutiérrez (1995). One could argue that these phases have become the manifest, or at least latent, agenda for journalism research in a South Africa confronted with globalizing issues.

The history of apartheid news reporting is to a large extent that of racial *exclu-*

sion (Williams, 2000). Even some liberal-minded newspapers treated black people as part of the "native question" during the first half of the 20th century, while the Afrikaans media strongly promoted the idea of "separate development" till the late 1960s. Black journalists, researchers and other media spokespeople argue that the legacy of racial reporting and journalism research are still vividly present in South African society (Krabill, 2004; Williams, 2004). Media owners and editors argue in typical self-reference style that though the contents of newspapers (such as the new highly "successful," low-prized tabloids *Sun/Son*) might not be in everyone's taste, it at least avail the opportunity to half a million (black) new newspaper buyers, and seemingly more and more new readers, previously excluded from the market, to find "their voice." Respected journalist Joe Thloloe and other senior black media editors, consider this development as a new kind of apartheid or racism, but now in the disguise of globalization and a new market-centered media expansion. Present-day journalism researchers and former anti-apartheid editors Berger (2004) and Harber (2004) find themselves on different sides of this debate: Berger argues that these tabloids cannot seriously be considered to be part of journalism, at least not in the way the press has a role to play in strengthening a fledgling democracy, while Harber avers that the *Sun*, with its run-away circulation, might yet prove to be the single most important newspaper in up-coming elections.

During apartheid, *fear* was an important mobilizing force (Giliomee, 2003), which did not disappear in 1994. Crime, and more specifically news about crime, instilled a new kind of apprehension among especially the white section of the population. But, the globalized movement of masses of people finding new places to make a living (e.g. the "southward movement of Africa" to the tip of the continent due to, among other reasons, international neo-liberal economic politics) also changed the demographics of South Africa to such an extent, that more journalism research is needed on how this process is affecting minorities being portrayed in the media: either as whites feeling threatened by a possible "copy-cat-Zimbabwean" experience or by new forms of xenophobic reporting of black people in the media (e.g. Wasserman, 2003).

Though the South African media might not have the manifest meaning to do so, some strains of news coverage and consequent journalism research are still perceived in a *confrontational* sense as "us versus them" (Williams, 2000; Wasserman, 2003). It will need a paradigm shift for the media and researchers to raise to the challenge of not only posing domestic news coverage in a less confrontational style, but also to deal with globalization issues such as Kyoto, the GATT, the IMF, the World Bank, and other globalized transnational agreements and institutions in a manner that does not pit white against black.

South African media and journalism research has for decades been caught not only in *stereotypical* race selection in media news coverage, but also in the way research had structurally distinguish between races (for instance, audience research grouped the population into white, Indian, colored and black). Through its policy of affirmative action and black empowerment, the ANC government had since 1994 in a sense brought racism back by its classsification of black (meaning black

Africans, Indians and coloreds – in that order) and white people. This stereotypical classification influences journalism research in a number of ways, for instance in the way media is perceived to be either black or white; or in the prioritizing of national research fields with an emphasis on development, and in the allocation of research grants to "previously disadvantaged" groups or individuals (see www. nrf.ac.za/). New post-9/11 international stereotypes have at the same time also been formed in the South African media, e.g. the "ugly American" in Iraq; and the "terrorist inclined" Muslim world (see de Beer, Wasserman, and Botha, 2004), which now also need original and creative journalism research

According to Wilson and Gutiérrez (1995), *multiracial* news coverage is the antithesis of exclusion. The reality, however, remains that the South African media is still very much divided, for example Afrikaans newspapers, such as *Beeld* and *Die Burger*, emphasizing news important to their reader base (the latter also to the Afrikaans-speaking colored community), and black English-language newspapers, such as *Sowetan* and *New Nation*, almost exclusively covering news related to the black community. On a national scale, the South African Broadcasting Corporation was structurally changed to reflect the demographic profile of the country (read black majority), while a high ranking former ANC political official was appointed as head of news in a drive to change news content toward "nation building." Whether it is just an assumption, or a reality that the SABC as "his master's voice" has changed owners from the National Party to the ANC is still for journalism research to tell (e.g. Wasserman, 2003).

Journalism Research: The Legacy

Ten years after the end of apartheid, and looking ahead to what the next twenty-five years could hold, Krabill (2004) argues that the greatest challenge for building a praxis of equal parts practitioner, theorist and researcher, would be to find at the outset a clearly prescribed journalism research path. This would not mean that every media individual must be "equal parts practitioner, theorist and researcher; it does mean that the extent to which we define ourselves as one *over and against* the others, is the extent to which we fail to integrate the three" (Krabill, 2004, p. 357). According to Krabill (2004), journalism research and theory in "the next quarter century need to consider more seriously the people – taken as both individuals, and as various kinds of groups – involved in all aspects of media as a social process of making meaning."

An approach to primarily focus on the role all individuals and groups can play was obviously absent during the previous quarter of the century under apartheid rule. The impact of the divide-and-rule policy of the National Party from 1948 to 1994 in journalism research is described by de Beer and Tomaselli (2000) as an effort to negotiate ideological and paradigmatic schisms, and which was clear to see in the work of journalism/communication departments.

The first faltering steps in journalism research at university level (see de Beer and Tomaselli, 2000, for a broad-ranging overview) were in the mid-20th century when the department of journalism was founded at the Afrikaans language Potchefstroom University (PU – now the Potchefstroom campus of the University of North West – UNW). At the time paradigmatic schemes were very far away on the horizon. Potchefstroom decided to follow the Dutch and German routes of *perswetensc- hap* and *zeitungwisschenschaft*, but without the research rigor that these traditions would bring to their countries of origin. A decade later (in the 1970s), the depart- ments of communication at the Afrikaans universities of Orange Free State (UOFS – now the University of the Free State) and Rand Afrikaans University (now the Johannesburg University) followed. At the same time, communication departments were founded at the traditionally black universities of Fort Hare, Zululand, and Bophuthatswana (now part of the UNW). All of these departments, together with the department of communication at the University of South Africa (also founded in the 1970s), offered journalism as part of their communication programs.

In the 1980s, a graduate journalism department, based on the Columbia Uni- versity model was set up at (at that time, an Afrikaans-speaking) Stellenbosch University (SU). Journalism departments were also established at the technikons (since 2005, Universities of Technology) at Pretoria, Durban, Cape Peninsula, and Cape Town.

Due to perhaps a "snobbish" academic view of journalism as something "the study and research of which do not belong at universities," English-language institutions for higher learning were very slow to start programs for educat- ing and training journalists. The exception to the rule was Rhodes University, which became a foremost center for journalism education and training, and the University of KwaZulu-Natal, where a graduate program in cultural and media studies was founded in 1985. Through the work of Keyan G. Tomaselli, Ruth Teer-Tomaselli, and their colleagues, this research center gained international rep- utation in the last part of the 20th century, moving journalism research into the next era. At these two English language universities (Rhodes and Natal), jour- nalism research was geared toward a neo-Marxist or critical paradigm, and later based on models such as those of the Birmingham Centre for Cultural Studies.

The next important step in journalism education and research was when the Uni- versity of the Witwatersrand (Wits) belatedly started its journalism program in the early 2000s with Anton Harber, the renowned co-founder and former editor of the *Weekly Mail* (now the *Mail&Guardian*) as first professor and head of department.

Eric Louw (2000), a former member of the South African journalism research fraternity, and now an Australian research scholar, made the following helpful distinction (adjusted for the purpose of this chapter) regarding different paradig- matic approaches and some of their proponents during the first four decades of journalism research leading up to the year 2000:

- The mainstream liberal school, as well as liberal administrative researchers (mostly English speaking) kept a very critical stance from the state and its com- munication agencies, and were very much orientated toward the English liberal press and the role it could play in the dismantling of apartheid, for example Tony Giffard at Rhodes, now at the University of Washington, Seattle, USA.

- Media studies academics and the neo-Marxist/critical school (especially at Rhodes and Natal) were highly critical of the conventional media and did research developing praxis relationships between working class and/or black and non-racial organizations to contest hegemonic structures, for example, Les Switzer at Rhodes, later at the University of Houston; Keyan Tomaselli and Ruth Teer-Tomaselli; Eric Louw at Rhodes/RAU, now at the University of Queensland, Roy Williams, now in the UK and Graeme Addison, now a free-lance journalist, both formerly from the University of Bobputhatswana, now University of Northwest.
- The alternative-left practical school: Guy Berger at Rhodes; Clive Emdon, Chris Vick, Mansoor Jaffer, Franz Krüger (now at Wits), and others working at NGOs and other organizations.
- The Unisa interpretative school: Marthinus van Schoor, Pieter J. Fourie, and Koos Roelofse, and following from there, Gary Mersham at the University of Zululand.
- The American/European functional/eclectical school: Arnold de Beer at RAU/UOFS/PU-UNW/Stellenbosch, and Ena Jansen at Unisa. Within a kind of ivory-tower idealism, some researchers on Afrikaans campuses took refuge in "distanced" and "objective" or "uninvolved" research, often under the guise of being *wetenskaplik* (scientific).
- Conservative administrative researchers (mainly Afrikaans speaking) assisted the state by doing the research, especially content analysis, showing for instance in an "objective" way how the English-language press, was "biased," "unpatriotic," and "untruthful," for example, Pieter Mulder at PU-UNW, also T. L. (Tom) de Koning at RAU.

Journalism Research: The New Dispensation

The 1990s and the 21st century would usher in a new dispensation. Journalism research in South Africa found a new voice in researchers who could cross language, race and in some instances, also paradigmatic borders, but mainly working within the context of postcolonial/postmodern approaches. These journalism and media studies researchers include: Anton Harber and Tawana Kupe at Witwatersrand; Herman Wasserman at Stellenbosch University, now Newcastle in the UK; Guy Berger, Lynette Steenveld and Anthea Garman at Rhodes; Johannes Froneman at UNW (Potchefstroom); Johann de Wet at Free State; Sean Jacobs (now at Michigan-Ann Arbor); John J. Williams at the University of the Western Cape (UWC); Ron Krabill at the University of Washington (Bothell)/University of KwaZulu-Natal; Suren Pillay at UWC; and Gibson Mashilo Boloka at the Media Development and Diversity Agency, and Pedro Diederichs at the Tshwane University of Technology. Their work built to a certain degree, and is now supplemented by pre-1990s researchers, such as Keyan Tomaselli; Ruth Teer-Tomaselli at KwaZulu-Natal; Pieter J. Fourie at the University of South Africa; and Arnold S. de Beer at Stellenbosch University and the University of the Western Cape.

It is rather difficult to gauge the impact of these researchers on the national and international scene. Berger for instance, is very active at the crossroads of academe and the media and the journalism school he heads is arguably the foremost in Africa. In the more traditional sense of journalism research, only four of the researchers mentioned above have been acknowledged by the South African National Research Foundation as researchers: Tomaselli as a researcher of international standing; Fourie and de Beer as "established" researchers, while Wasserman has been rated in 2006 as a young researcher with the potential to become a leader in the field. All of these researchers now have to find their way in new developing journalism research paradigms. How the new and old paradigms interlink, was set out as follows by Wasserman (2004a).

> [The debate on journalism research paradigms] is by now [2004] not new, and similar discussions have marked the South African journalism and media studies landscape, at least since the 1970s and 1980s. While today the research being done at South African universities still reflects the different traditions [from that era], the respective schools of thought are much less influenced by the ideological divides of the past. Furthermore, a process of cross-fertilization between the different approaches to media and journalism taught at the various tertiary institutions in the country has also to an extent taken place. While this has in some cases resulted in a fruitful dialogue between research traditions, criticism has also been directed against the narrowing of paradigms in order to fit a politically correct curriculum – e.g. what Keyan Tomaselli has referred to as a "cut-and-paste Marxism" – that is not informed by a thorough theoretical grounding.
>
> (Wasserman, 2004a, pp. 180–1)

In the 25th special issue of *Ecquid Novi* of which he was guest editor, Wasserman (2004a) refers to an article in the same edition in which Keyan Tomaselli (2004a) relates how he and Arnold de Beer often locked horns in the past as a result of them representing schools of thought that at certain stages in the history of South African journalism and media scholarship occupied conflicting ideological positions. Tomaselli outlines some of these conflicts, as well as the productive results that flowed from these paradigmatic engagements. By positioning himself in his argument Tomaselli provides an example of the culturalist approach that often came into conflict with exponents of the communication science paradigm, and attempts to open up a space for theoretical approaches that have in the past often been considered unconventional or "unscientific" (p. 182).

One of the consequences of the new approach to journalism research is the way in which researchers from different universities for the first time on a national basis engaged each other in discourse about research paradigms. Or as Wasserman (2004a) calls it, "the emerging debate and critical self-reflection about research paradigms of the pas that have often been absent" (p. 181). In this regard Tomaselli played an important role as president of the South African Communication Association (Sacomm) by opening debate in an academic and collegial atmosphere. The increasing participation of journalism researchers on an international globalizing media platform, led by Tomaselli and others, also fueled this debate.

Present-Day Theoretical Research Approaches

No challenge is perhaps greater for journalism research in South Africa than finding its foothold within the world of often conflicting paradigmatic research approaches. Modernism still has its vestige in a structural functionalist approach in the country, while postmodernist approaches, such as critical theory and cultural studies, have also been carried over from the previous century to mark the main research approaches found in South Africa.

A characteristic of journalism research in South Africa, unlike research found in English-speaking countries, is the trend to focus on fewer topics. Developments in the 21st century, not the least since 9/11, and the continued development of e-media, as well as international issues such as globalization, call for a wider view, not only as far as particular issues of praxis are concerned, but also in terms of research approaches.

Neofunctionalism as a journalism research approach

As was indicated earlier, structural functionalist approaches dominated much of the research undertaken at predominantly Afrikaans university departments of communication, and carried over since 2003 to the department of journalism at Stellenbosch University (de Beer), where it now resides amazingly comfortably next to postcolonial (Wasserman), as well as feminist approaches (Lizette Rabe).

Because functionalism never had a large following in South Africa, the limited capacity of researchers working within this paradigm did not fully keep track with developments, such as the neofunctionalism of Jeffrey C. Alexander (1997), or of Niklas Luhmann (2000).

Neofunctionalism has been described as one of very few new theoretical approaches that could be applied to journalism and mass media study. To a large extend, South African researchers have missed this boat, as one of its main proponents, Alexander (2003), moved this approach out of the modernity frame by, *inter alia*, embracing the term "civil society" (in stead of "societal community"). Such a development could make neofunctionalism more approachable for those scholars working from a postcolonial point of view in South Africa. Alexander, together with Luhmann (2000) in his approach to mass media, opened the way for European (mainly German) and American scholars to displace the modernity sociological binary positions such as structure versus agency, and conflict versus order (Alexander, 1997). The time is perhaps ripe for this to happen in South Africa as well.

Mediatization and self-reference

What also seems to be lacking in both journalism research and the media, is to come to an understanding that the *mediatization* of society requires much more research on *media competence*. According to the European Centre for Media Competence, this cultural technique and key skill could be defined as the "ability to move about the world of the media in a critical, reflective and independent way, and with the sense of responsibility, using the media as a means of independent and creative expression" (Reichmayr, 2001). One way of doing this, would be to challenge the media in its present habit of self-reference (see, for instance, the way national media companies refer in a positive light to themselves regarding their new sensationalist tabloids – Harber, 2004). Taking its origins from semiotics, systems theory and postmodern culture, this is a research approach not yet seen developed to its full potential in South Africa.

Research Topics

There are a disparate number of journalism topics that urgently needs research. Some are more salient than others.

Journalism education

One of the issues that has been glaringly missing from South African journalism research agenda, is that of the education of training of journalists, not least to foster a new generation of journalism researchers.

It took more than four decades since the founding of the first journalism school at Potchefstroom for the South African media to involve itself on a national basis with journalism research when the first South African National Editors' Forum (Sanef) Skills Audit was undertaken. This audit resulted from serious discussions between the ANC government of president Thabo Mbeki, senior editors and academics (the so-called Sun City Indaba) about the apparent lack of journalism skills found in the South African media (de Beer and Steyn, 2002). This project was followed by the second Sanef audit in (Steyn, de Beer and Steyn, 2005) on media frontline managers' competencies. On a smaller scale, a number of university-industry projects have been executed by journalism researchers at, for instance, Rhodes University (e.g. Steenveld, 2002).

South Africa as part of Africa

International scholars are often amazed about how little journalism research is undertaken in Africa, including South Africa, on Africa itself. Unlike North American and European contexts, where theoretical and methodological frameworks for research in this field have been well developed, it is not the case with Africa. The South African journalism researcher Kupe (2004, pp. 353–6) argues, for instance, that new paradigms and issues suited for the African continent should be developed. He identifies several areas:

- The institutional role of journalism in especially Sub-Saharan Africa should be revisited. After four decades of democratic struggles and a slow return to political pluralism and media liberalization, a critical rethinking is important. One of the main issues is the way in which especially governments, but also society, view the role of journalists and their media (e.g. Wasserman and de Beer, 2004).

- From both a functionalist and postmodern point of view, there would be agreement that Africa faces major socioeconomic challenges. The modern Westernized media system of South Africa is often taken as a yardstick for the rest of Sub-Saharan Africa, while basic elements of infrastructure are not available and the most basic informational needs are not served.

- Africa is in dire need of new theoretical and research frameworks about the role of especially journalists and their media as far as organizational analysis, production and journalistic practices are concerned. For instance, theories of media production are well developed for European and North American media, but are not always applicable to their African context. This is especially the case where globalizing media companies own media in Africa, and just apparently take it for granted that they should be managed in the same way (Steyn et al., 2005).

- Pressured for having to serve democratizing watchdog roles, African journalists have a developmental role to play in a globalizing world. As Kupe (2004) argues: "It is time that we begin to make sense of such institutional and organizational contexts and dynamics in a much more intelligent way by linking them to the content/media text they produce and the audiences they seek to address" (p. 355) (also see Steyn et al., 2005).

- In a world where English has become the lingua franca of the global village, one cannot assume that countries in the developing world are all unilingual in their use and study of the media. The problematic methodological issue of the large number of languages and narrative traditions in Africa is not simplified by the use of a single language such as English. More often than not, an "English-only" policy makes a complex situation even more complex.

- The nature of African audiences also poses problems of theory and method for the researcher, given the multiple identities of African elites who often are multilingual and occupying shifting social positions that are "modern," as well as "traditional" (Boafo and George, 1992; Louw, 2000).

- Kupe (2004) argues that theory and research should also take cognizance of broader journalistic media and communication policies (stated and unstated) and the regulatory frameworks that play a role in shaping the media and communication landscape, dealing with questions such as: Who are the policy makers and "regulators" in a "democratising" and "developing" context in a "globalizing world" (p. 355)?

Some other research topics

Plagiarism that hit the American media with the turn of the century (Ekstrand, 2002), and which came full force down on the South African media in 2003, is a rather unfortunate, but clear case in point (e.g. Krüger, 2004). But, so are the ongoing issues surrounding race, language, culture, gender, and HIV/AIDS (e.g.

Wasserman and de Beer, 2004). The list is almost endless – the research process has a wide open field to sow the seeds of well-thought input – even be it from different paradigms.

Journalism Research Publications

The main peer-reviewed South African publishing outlets for journalism research with an international standing are *Ecquid Novi: African Journalism Studies*, and *Communicatio*, the South African journal for communication theory and research, and for media studies, *Critical Arts*. *Rhodes Journalism Review* offers a venue for opinion articles. Few South African journalism researchers have published in first league international journalism journals such as *Journalism Quarterly* and *Journalism Studies*. The impact on the international book forum has also been scant, with a relatively few journalism research monographs being published locally.

Conclusion

Finding a set of heuristic paradigms for South African journalism research in an age of globalization is a matter for serious academic debate. As was argued, the chances are there that such a paradigm(s) will be heavily influenced by the country's racial past and its present struggle to get rid of it, but it will also depend on how much researchers will be able to move across paradigmatic borders in order to find better solutions for a country in need of a more comprehensive and in-depth journalism research process.

References

Alexander, J. C. (ed.) (1997). *Neofunctionalism and after*. Oxford: Blackwell Publishing.

Alexander, J. C. (2003). *Contradictions in the societal community: The promise and disappointment of Parson's concept*. Yale University: Working paper, Center for Cultural Sociology.

Berger, G. (2004). Headline-grabbing tabloids: Are they journalism? Retrieved May 31, 2005 from Mail&Guardian Online, December 8, 2004: www.mg.co.za/articlePage.aspx?articleid=193128&area=/insight/insight_converse/

Boafo, S. T., and George, N. A. (1992). *Communication research in Africa: Issues and perspectives*. Nairobi: ACCE.

de Beer, A. S. (ed.) (2000). Focus on media and racism. Special edition of *Ecquid Novi*, 21(2).

de Beer, A. S., and Steyn, E. (eds.) (2002). Focus on journalism skills. Special edition of *Ecquid Novi*, 22(2).

de Beer, A. S., and Tomaselli, K. G. (2000). South African journalism and mass communication scholarship: negotiating ideological schisms. *Journalism Studies*, 1(1), 9–35.

de Beer, A. S., Wasserman, H., and Botha, N. (2004). South Africa and Iraq: The battle for media reality. In Y. R. Kamalipour, and N. Snow. *War, media and propaganda: A global perspective.* (pp. 179–88). Oxford: Rowman and Littlefield.

Ekstrand, V. S. (2002). The 21st century plagiarist: An old problem meets a new age. *Review of Communication,* 2(2), 160–3.

Giliomee, H. (2003). *The Afrikaners: Biography of a people.* Charlottesville, VA: Virginia University Press.

Harber, A. (2004). The *Daily Sun* shines in gore and glory over a changing land. *Ecquid Novi,* 25(2), 156–8.

Krabill, R. (2004). Reclaiming praxis. *Ecquid Novi,* 25(2), 356–9.

Krüger, F. (2004). *Black, white and grey: Ethics in South African journalism.* Cape Town: Double Storey.

Kupe, T. (2004). An agenda for researching African media and communication contexts. *Ecquid Novi,* 25(2), 353–6.

Louw, E. (2000). The death of Parks Mankahlana and the question of universal news values. *Ecquid Novi,* 21(2), 243–9.

Luhmann, N. (2000). *The reality of the mass media.* Cambridge, UK: Polity Press.

Reichmayr, I.-L. (2001). An essay: A case for media education. *Southeast European Media Journal.* Retrieved May 30, 2001 from www.mediaonline.ba/en/?ID=114

Steenveld, L. (2002). Training for media information and democracy. The South African National Editors' Forum and the Independent Newspapers' Chair of Media Information, Rhodes University, Grahamstown.

Steyn, E., de Beer, A. S., and Steyn, T. F. J. (2005). Managerial competencies among first-line news managers in South Africa's mainstream media newsrooms. *Ecquid Novi,* 26(2), 212–27.

Tomaselli, K. G. (2000). Faulting "Faultlines": racism in the South African media. In de Beer, A. S. (ed.). Focus on media and racism. Special edition of *Ecquid Novi,* 21(2), 157–74.

Tomaselli, K. G. (2004a). First and third and person encounters: *Ecquid Novi,* theoretical lances and research methodology. *Ecquid Novi,* 25(1), 210–34.

Tomaselli, K. G. (2004b). On research distractions and illusions. *Ecquid Novi,* 25(2), 365–72.

Wasserman, H. (2003). Post-apartheid media debates and the discourse of identity. *Ecquid Novi,* 24(2), 218–24.

Wasserman, H. (2004a). Reflecting on journalism research: A quarter century of *Ecquid Novi.* Editorial, *Ecquid Novi,* 25(2), 179–84.

Wasserman, H. (ed.) (2004b). *Ecquid Novi:* 25 years of journalism research. Special 25th anniversary edition, 25(1).

Wasserman, H., and de Beer, A. S. (2004). Covering HIV/AIDS: Towards a heuristic comparison between communitarian and utilitarian ethics. *Communicatio,* 30(2), 84–97.

Williams, J. J. (2000). Truth and reconciliation: Beyond the TRC process and findings. *Ecquid Novi,* 21(2), 207–19.

Williams, J. J. (2004). Towards a critical research methodology in journalism: Interrogating methodological assumptions. *Ecquid Novi,* 25(2), 257–74.

Wilson, C. C., II, and Gutiérrez, F. (1995). *Race, multiculturalism, and the media. From mass to class communication.* London: Sage.

Chapter 16

Journalism Research
in Greater China

Its Communities, Approaches, and Themes

Zhongdang Pan, Joseph M. Chan, and Ven-hwei Lo

Like any discursive system, journalism research articulates with the social setting where it is conducted, drawing from it inspirations, resources, and insights, and reflecting, speaking to, as well as shaping the setting in specific ways. In other words, journalism research addresses and frames the key issues in journalism of each society; it reflects the ideological contestation around and about these issues and informs journalists' everyday practices. Informed by this perspective, in this chapter, we seek to sketch the major themes and characteristics of journalism research in what is called Greater China.

All three members of Greater China – the Mainland, Taiwan, and Hong Kong – have undergone major social transformation in the past two decades. During this time, China accelerated its Communist Party-led reforms to transform itself from a socialist state economy to a significant participant of the global market. As part of this overall change, China's media is becoming increasingly commercialized. Meanwhile, Taiwan stabilized its democratic institutions with the second direct presidential election won by the pro-independence Democratic Progressive Party. The traditional political elite's grip on media was being rapidly eroded by the rise of alternative news outlets that spoke with a nativistic accent.[1] Hong Kong, during this time, ended the uncertainties and contentious period of waiting for the transfer of sovereignty from the UK to China and endured the post-transition setbacks such as economic depression, the SARS epidemic, and the political crisis culminating in street protests of half a million people in July 2003. All of these upheavals took place as market-driven journalism was thriving and the once lively and diverse press was increasingly shadowed by the political power in Beijing. These changes conditioned journalism research in the three Chinese societies in many ways. They have ignited scholarly inquiries on a wide range of issues related to journalism.

Journalism research in these three Chinese societies is also an integral part of media globalization and internationalization of journalism research. The movements of researchers and the adoption of digital technologies enabled the global diffusion of social science epistemology. One indication is that there have been increasing uses of similar theoretical concepts and social science methods as well as an increasing frequency of research collaborations and scholarly interactions both across the three Chinese societies and between scholars in these societies and those in other parts of the world. Another indication is that issues related to media globalization have risen to be among key concerns of journalism research, especially in China. A third indication is that research on journalism in the three societies often appears in monographs by publishers with a global reach and in journals that are considered "mainstream" in the West-centered field of journalism and mass communication research.

However, journalism research is inevitably constrained by both the composition of each scholarly community and its political economic environment. Journalism research in each of the three societies remains distinct in its theoretical concerns, conceptual emphases, and discursive styles. The broader social changes in the three Chinese societies and global infusion of journalism research form a larger context for us to examine these distinct characteristics.

Defining the Boundaries

To offer a critical review of the scholarly writings on journalism in the three societies, we have to draw the boundaries of inclusion. The issue has both textual and demographic aspects. Textually, we include only the scholarly writings on journalism in these Chinese societies, excluding writings on media in general or on other societies. Demographically, we include mainly the scholars who reside in one of these societies as they are the primary producers of related knowledge. We also include, however, the works by outside researchers whenever such works are found to have informed journalism research in the Chinese societies.

The application of these rules finds that a substantial majority of journalism researchers in Hong Kong and Taiwan received their PhDs in communication-related programs from research universities in the United States and the UK. The more active among them are concentrated in a few public-funded institutions that offer graduate programs at both the Master's and doctoral levels. In comparison, journalism researchers in China are more numerous and thinly spread over some 600 institutions. Most were once veteran journalists and received their advanced education in domestic institutions, majoring in Chinese literature or other humanities disciplines. The few who received advanced degrees from foreign countries also had undergraduate backgrounds in humanities. Similar to Taiwan and Hong Kong, however, the most visible researchers are concentrated in a handful of major institutions.

The literature so identified also reveals differences in conventions of academic activities in the three societies. In general, the community of journalism scholars in Taiwan is highly homogeneous and its members engage one another through its own journals. Its discursive interaction with the English literature is achieved through their academic training in the West and the practice of weaving extensive literature reviews in their publications. The fact that Hong Kong researchers often publish in refereed journals in the West clearly shows the same intellectual affinity with Western scholarly discourses.

The China case is different. Ten years ago, one scholar characterized China's communication research as having followed a "closed-off model." This characterization remains valid on the whole, but it needs a major revision. The infusion of Western theories and concepts in the past two decades has exerted major influences on journalism research in China, making it increasingly part of the global discourses on journalism. Such influence is stepped up as the Chinese book market is covered by an avalanche of translated academic works in the past decade. The process is precipitated by the Internet technology. In the past decade, many web sites dedicated to journalism research have been created. Many papers and even books published in the West, Taiwan and Hong Kong are posted on such web sites and read by students and faculty members across the country. As a result, the closing-off model of journalism research is increasingly untenable.[2]

This analysis shows that defining the domain for inclusion is also a substantive matter. It involves painting a sociological portrait of the research communities. These are what Wuthnow (1989) calls "communities of discourse" who engage in constructing the research discourses on journalism through activities of knowledge production. In addition to clear differences in political and media systems, the three societies differ in the composition of journalism researchers, in conventions for doing scholarly work, and in the methods of knowledge dissemination. These are among the factors mediating between systemic differences and the different but interacting research discourses in the three societies. It is against this sociological backdrop that we proceed to systematically analyze the research literature.

Understanding Journalism: Topics and Themes

A careful reading of the research literature in the three societies reveals three broad theoretical perspectives: political economic, socio-organizational, and cultural. While they seem to parallel the categories that Schudson (1991) used to characterize the journalism research in the United States, the specifics show clear distinctions. In addition, these perspectives often are blended in empirical studies. As a result, our review is organized by topical domains rather than by perspectives.[3]

On journalists

Researchers in all three societies have paid attention to studying journalists. The research in this domain follows closely the seminal surveys of American journalists (Johnstone, Slawski, and Bowman, 1976; Weaver and Wilhoit, 1996). Although the first ever attempt at surveying Hong Kong journalists took place in 1981, a fully developed survey with a probability sample was not possible until 1990 (Chan, Lee, and Lee, 1996). This survey provides crucial data on Hong Kong journalists, as Hong Kong was half way through its transition toward changing sovereignty. Meanwhile, similar surveys of journalists were conducted in Taiwan and in China respectively. Lo (1998) developed the 1994 survey of Taiwan journalists. A national survey of Chinese journalists was conducted to collect data on women journalists for the pending World Conference on Women in Beijing (Chen, Zhu, and Wu, 1998).

In 1996, the chapter authors spearheaded a comparative survey of journalists in the three Chinese societies. We developed the questionnaire in consultation with those used in surveys of American journalists. With a pooled sample of 3,014 respondents, the project was the first genuine comparative surveys of journalists across all three regions (Lo and Chan, 2004).

These surveys have yielded considerable information on journalists in the three societies. In general, Hong Kong journalists are much younger and less experienced than their counterparts in the other two societies. In all three societies, most journalists have some college education. Journalists in China and Taiwan appear to be more satisfied with their jobs than their Hong Kong counterparts. In all three societies, journalists are more satisfied with the intrinsic rather than the material aspects of their job. Across the three societies, journalists' sense of job autonomy has a strong positive correlation with their satisfaction with the intrinsic aspects of their jobs.

There are significant differences in journalists' perceptions of media roles. While in all three societies, journalists value the role of media disseminating factual information accurately and rapidly, more Chinese journalists value the roles of journalism in explaining government policies to the public, in helping the public to understand such policies, and in "guiding" public opinion. They also value less the investigative role. On beliefs about journalism ethics, while journalists in all three societies overwhelmingly reject accepting monetary rewards from potential news sources, they differ widely in their receptiveness of other ethically problematic practices such as accepting free gifts and trips from sources, moonlighting for other organizations, and toning down negative reports on government agencies or big advertisers (Lo, Chan, and Pan, 2005).

These findings are supplemented by other smaller surveys. For example, in China, a team of researchers conducted a survey of journalists of "influential outlets" across the nation in 2003 and found similar divergence among them in professional ethic beliefs. In Taiwan, a survey found that journalists reported having a significant degree of autonomy in making editorial decisions at the story level but not at the level of editorial policies of their organizations, and they felt their job autonomy was significantly lower than their expectations.

In China, journalist surveys were often initiated and designed by "outsiders" but carried out by "insiders," showing a peculiar practice in the internationalization of journalism research. This is the case with another major survey in 2002 where the first two authors of this chapter sought to survey journalists in Shanghai and Hangzhou. The results show that there is evidence of coexistence of two journalistic paradigms, the Party-press and the professional journalism, among Chinese journalists (Pan and Chan, 2003). The two belief systems lead journalists to emphasize different factors when evaluating their own profession and deriving job satisfaction (Chan, Pan, and Lee, 2004). The findings lead to the conclusion that professionalism has become a lens for China's journalists to view their craft.

On journalism craft

Researchers also take the socio-organizational perspective to examine journalism craft. Using methods such as field observations, case studies, and in-depth interviews, and at times, combining them with survey data, Taiwan researchers have explored a wide range of issues. Differentiating novices and experts, some researchers demonstrate that as journalists accumulate their experiences, they increase their cognitive sophistication to see the multifaceted nature of a news event, and to produce more in-depth and nuanced reporting. Researchers also show that sources in news are distributed in a way that favors the more powerful in society and reflects the historically formed ideological lineage of different newspapers. Within media organizations, journalists are found subject to the constraints emanating from the hierarchical line of authority and the media proprietor's controlling power embedded in the organizational structure and policies. Women journalists, while insisting that gender played no role in their adherence to the principle of objectivity, admitted that they were more likely to view politicians they were covering from a feminine perspective.

Hong Kong researchers frequently make use of their observations of newsmaking and journalists' comments on their work in their research. Most empirical references to newsmaking are made in connection to discussions of macro-level issues such as shifting power structures, self-censorship, and the rising tide of completely market-driven journalism (e.g. Chan and Lee, 1991; Lee and Chu, 1998). A central concern that cuts across studies of journalism craft is self-censorship, which is found to involve media professionals downplaying the coverage of sensitive topics, information, or opinions because of the perceived risks of covering them (Lee, 1998). Hong Kong researchers also often analyze news content to infer patterns in newsmaking practices, especially those associated with the impact of political ideology, dependency on political power, and organizational control. While operating mainly in the political economy perspective, these researchers also draw theoretical resources from the socio-organizational literature.

In China, examining various facets of journalism craft has been a mainstay in journalism research. Most of the writings in this category are based on impressionistic observations and atheoretical in nature. Things began to change due to involvement of overseas researchers, cross-border collaborations,[4] and new orientations of younger researchers. To this extent, the internationalization of journalism research not only is more visible but also has a more clearly traceable impact in China than in other two Chinese societies.

Judy Polumbaum (1990), an American scholar, carried out the first in-depth study of China's journalists and journalism craft. Others with similar US training have continued this line of research. For instance, in a field study of a newspaper, Zhou He shows that the party paper developed a schizophrenic personality of being both a party organ and a profit-seeking enterprise. Tensions between these identities are reflected in the organizational culture, daily operations, and journalistic practices. Zhongdang Pan takes a similar approach by making multiple field visits to selected media outlets and conducting in-depth interviews. Such efforts by overseas researchers have ignited cross-border collaborations and similar field studies by researchers inside China. This line of research shows that China's journalists operate in very uncertain terrains that involve forces of political controls, market pressure, and journalistic ideals. To cope with such uncertainties, journalists are compelled to "improvise" non-routine practices to avoid political landmines while achieving immediate, short-term, and tangible results. They also appropriate the official stipulation of journalism and media roles to coat their innovative practices in dealing with multiple and contradictory sources of pressure (Pan, 2005). The research in this area often blends theoretical resources from all three perspectives.

On macro contexts

In all three Chinese societies, journalism researchers have been wrestling with macro-level issues related to political power and market forces. This is particularly the case in China and Hong Kong. To a large extent, the political-economic perspective is an overarching theoretical framework in all three research communities, reflecting common concerns that have arisen from the rapid social changes and media globalization in the three societies. At the same time, there are important differences.

In Hong Kong, a major concern has been how the political transition of changing sovereignty would affect journalism as a profession and press freedom (So and Chan, 1999). These are closely related issues with multiple aspects. Some scholars have written about the inherent power dependency of the press and thus expected repositioning of the press to fit the shifting power structure after the 1997 handover. Others examined how Beijing's measures of exerting political pressure induced self-censorship, including prohibiting China-controlled corporations from advertising on media outlets deemed unfriendly to Beijing and creating a general sense of fear by jailing Hong Kong reporters in China. Some researchers reported that some news outlets started recruiting journalists from China (Lee and Chu, 1998). Such a measure was an extension of these outlets' general practice of recruiting journalists with congruent ideological orientations. Some scholars also showed that journalists in the party and commercial papers revealed different "journalistic paradigms" in responding to the changing political regimes (Chan and Lee, 1991).

Commercialization is seen a force that erodes the professional underpinning of journalism in Hong Kong. It is also viewed a response of the market-based media to the growing political influence of Beijing. Some researchers thus argue that press freedom can only be approached as part of a general struggle for democracy in Hong Kong. In the highly limited democracy of Hong Kong, the news media are found to play an important "surrogate democracy function" (Chan and So, 2005).

In China, research attention to macro-level issues is as intense as that in Hong Kong, but it takes on a very different perspective. Instead of adopting a critical stand rooted in the liberal democracy tradition found in the research of Hong

Kong scholars, Chinese scholars are overwhelmingly "administrative" in orientation. There are tactically formulated critical analyses[5] on issues such as press freedom, public's right to know, legal framework for press operations and press freedom, self-regulation in journalism, the need for news media to be oriented toward audiences and their life-worlds, the role of the press in investigating official corruption, and so on. All of these topics are framed and examined at the nexus of the political and the economic axes. At times, these issues may also be discussed in terms of news as a text and narrative that expresses and shapes cultural values. To the extent that these issues are outside the traditional realm of the official party-press ideology, the very discussion of them indicates a critical vantage point of the researchers.

However, a much larger volume of research writings has been on offering and justifying advice on how to reconfigure the media industries to strengthen the party's control over media content and to protect the national media in the midst of globalization, how media organizations and journalism practices need to do in order to ride the tide of commercialization, how journalists should improve media performance to meet both political and market demands, and how media organizations should adapt to the Internet and digital age. The basic methods employed remain policy annotations and analytical arguments. Only a few scholars residing outside China (e.g. Zhao, 1998) write critically about patterns of media changes in China's reforms, structural shifts with the decline of the party press and the rise of market-appeal newspapers, institutional impact of new technologies on the party-press system, and other macro-level topics.

With an exception such as Lee's study of the alternative press and democratization (Lee, 1993), macro-level analyses are, largely, missing in the Taiwan research literature. This is not to suggest that Taiwan researchers do not pay attention to systemic variables. Such variables are merely embedded in various studies on journalists and journalism craft. Although we can find discussions on macro-level issues such as press freedom, the impact of the 1987 lift of the press ban on media industries and on journalism practices, public interest and media policies, and labor relations in media industries, the macro-level issues have not fared as prominently as in Hong Kong or China.

Methodological and Discursive Characteristics

The above review shows that journalism research in the three societies has employed diverse social scientific methods. To see more clearly how and why the three discourses differ, however, we need to examine their methodological characteristics in comparative terms.

Methods utilized

As mentioned previously, survey method plays a significant role in all three communities. It represents a major infusion of Western journalism literature in three ways: (1) the conceptual framework of the sociology of professions adopted to study journalists and the key areas of measures from the classic studies in the United States; (2) the involvement of West-trained researchers with the methodological know-how in developing such projects, and (3) in the case of China, the research support from the outside. The use of survey method as a social scientific tool in China has been a relatively recent undertaking. Its growing popularity is a sign that journalism research in China has begun to move away from pure policy annotation toward empirical inquiry. It is also a sign that such research is being connected to the global scholarly discourse.

Content analysis is also widely used in all three societies. In Taiwan, much journalism research uses quantitative methods to examine news content. However, there is a clear trend toward more qualitative textual analysis, reflecting the linguistic turn of the social theories that has increasingly influenced Taiwan researchers' thinking about news as a cultural product and a form of representation. A recent systematic analysis of research funding proposals in Taiwan finds that researchers sometimes use various combinations of quantitative content analysis and interpretive textual analysis, reflecting also an increasingly strong leaning toward the cultural perspective. Using such methods, researchers content-analyzed style manuals from different media outlets to show that news styles are shaped on the basis of the cardinal principles of factuality and objectivity.

Researchers have also employed textual analysis of news discourse to examine news framing, conditions for experiencing reality, the agenda history that reflects the changing political culture from authoritarian rule starting at the end of 1940s to the present pluralistic democracy, the embeddedness of power and the dominant ideology in news texts, metaphors that undergird news texts, and even news as an aesthetic narrative. All of these topics are rooted in the cultural perspective.

In Hong Kong, quantitative content analysis is often used, but mainly for addressing sociological issues discussed in the previous section. Very rarely do we see Hong Kong researchers analyze news content as a form of representation in its own right. However, Hong Kong researchers make the most effective uses of archival (also called documentation) analysis and case study (or critical-event analysis). The former involves analyzing documents by government agencies and media organizations in combination with media texts, treating such texts as deposits of evidence for structural configurations and changes, and for the exercises of power and resistance.

Among China's scholars, similar documentation analysis is also conducted quite extensively. But only a very few utilized the method to address sociological questions of news production. At least in journalism research, Taiwan researchers do not use archival analysis as a major tool, although they do engage in case studies.

China's researchers also examine news texts extensively, but with only a few exceptions, such analyses are impressionistic and involve praising some specific type or style of reporting. Almost invariably, that which is praised depends on whether the researcher is arguing for the importance of the media's role in publicizing the party policies or in appealing to urban audiences.

Probably the most developed area of journalism research in China is that of journalism history. A large amount of research has been devoted to clarifying historical facts and offering a descriptive narrative on trajectories of some specific historical period or of a particularly influential media outlet in the past. Remaining underdeveloped is in offering theoretical interpretations of historical events and trajectories. In comparison, historical research is much less common in Hong Kong and in Taiwan.

Discursive characteristics

Differentiating two general categories of discursive characteristics will help us better appreciate differences in journalism research among the three societies. The first deals with the role of theories in research. For this, we differentiate research that focuses on problem-solving, theory-testing, or formalization as its primary goal. The second addresses broader meta-theoretical characteristics of epistemic independence and cross-discourse engagement.

Problem-solving and theory-testing are two distinguishable but related paths in scholarly research. In all three societies, problem-solving comes across as the most prominent feature of journalism research, indicating that researchers are deeply engaged in the actual changing journalism practices and media institutions. It also suggests that journalism research informs and is informed by journalistic practices. However, the three communities differ significantly in their uses of theories. While Hong Kong and Taiwan researchers generally formulate theoretical arguments, derive hypotheses for testing, and at least attempt to extend and develop theories, China's researchers reveal a much weaker inclination to do so. In Hong Kong and Taiwan, the shared formal training and the system of blind reviews for publications enable and require researchers to take theories seriously.

Formalization raises the bar for theory development and testing considerably. It refers to using formal logic to state a theory and to test a model. In all three societies, this is a less salient feature of journalism research. In China, it simply does not exist. To this extent, we can say that journalism research in all three Chinese societies is far from being a mature area of social scientific research. However, one may argue that the theory-driven problem-solving approach seen in Hong Kong and Taiwan is preferred and it serves as a supplement to, if not an alternative of, the formal approach.

We differentiate two meta-theoretical characteristics. By "epistemic independence," we refer to researchers taking a position in framing and addressing research questions that is compelled by scholarly concerns rather than conformity to the dictates of political authority or industrial interests. By "cross-discourse engagement," we refer to researchers' uses of theories and research literature from their colleagues in the "invisible college" (Crane, 1972) from both within and beyond their own societies.

Clearly, these two characteristics are closely related to each other. On both, journalism research in Taiwan and Hong Kong is very strong and the opposite is the case in China. The relative absence of cross-discourse engagement in China is partly a result of researchers' lack of formal research training in the West. Even though there has been a flood of Western scholarly works published in China, these works are much less likely to produce a paradigmatic impact when a majority of researchers do not have the corresponding overall worldview to integrate such intellectual resources into their research. Another contributory factor is the lack of commonly accepted conventions on research practices in China. For instance, the blind review process is often compromised in China because of the perceived need to balance representation of different institutions at a conference or in a particular issue of a journal.

The problem is even more serious with regard to epistemic independence. One major problem in China's journalism research is that systemically, there is no intellectual space free of the dominating influence of the party. Politics take ultimate command in the production of knowledge in social sciences. Years of living, learning, and using the official discourse by researchers in all social science disciplines have created a taken-for-granted mode of academic discoursing. It basically involves annotating party policies, offering actionable proposals to policy-makers or to industry leaders, and elaborating normative arguments to justify such policies or proposals. Such systemic configuration and constant reinforcement by the party-state in every facet of academic life help to explain why China's journalism research continues to be haunted by its particular brand of the "administrative" logic.

Moving Toward the Future

In this chapter, we examined journalism research in the three societies. Overall, we can conclude that journalism research in Hong Kong and Taiwan has covered a broad range of topics and has been genuinely interested in theory developing and testing. A distinct characteristic from Hong Kong that could be extremely valuable for journalism research in other parts of the world is researchers' effective uses of archival analysis and content analysis to address sociological questions. While sociologists have long recognized the importance of media content as a valuable source of sociological data, actually analyzing such data for broader theoretical issues has not been common in journalism research.

Taiwan researchers have been creative in analyzing news texts from the social and cultural linguistic perspective. Their studies on women journalists, on power structure inside a media organization, on discrepancies between perceived and expected job autonomy, on cognitive differences between novices and experts, and on aesthetics of news narrative all address theoretically important issues beyond Taiwan.

Taken as a whole, journalism research in Hong Kong and Taiwan helps to broaden the literature of journalism research that has been based largely in the West. It is done in transitional societies that were experiencing rapid structural and cultural changes. While echoing the core concerns and even findings from the West, the research in these two societies shows important contextualizing roles of systemic configuration and its changes unique to each society. It clearly constitutes valuable additions to the global scholarship on journalism, but it will take major internationalization efforts for such additions to be genuinely incorporated in the research literature. Toward this end, journalism researchers in these Chinese societies need to do more to make their work known to their Western colleagues. At the same time, such internationalization also demands greater willingness on the part of the Western scholars to care to explore.

In comparison, journalism research in China remains severely underdeveloped. This overall negative assessment must be qualified, however. First, we must place the current condition in a historical context. Only 25 years ago, there was no journalism research other than pure policy annotations. Modern social scientific methods only began to be introduced into China's journalism research in the 1980s and were not widely taught until about ten years ago. To the extent that the monolithic policy annotation has been replaced by research utilizing diverse methods and addressing a wide range of issues, journalism research has had a significant progress in a relatively short period of time. Second, despite heavily fortified political controls, the availability of the research literature via the Internet and research collaborations with scholars outside of China are beginning to change China's journalism research. Empirical research has begun to be valued and theories to be emphasized. The most visible changes are taking place among a new generation of researchers consisting of graduate students and young faculty members. They are also tied to infusion of intellectual influences from the West, through West-trained scholars who engage in collaborative research with Chinese scholars.

Globalization and internationalization are expected to have more noticeable impact in the years to come. Exchanges between Chinese journalists and journalists from outside are on the rise. More Chinese journalists aspire to learn from the professionalism as preached and practiced in the west. Alternative ways of doing journalism can creep into China through satellite television and web site services based outside China. The competition posed by the Hong Kong-based Phoenix TV is exerting pressure on Chinese television to be more responsive in its coverage of critical events around the world. As the impacts of TVBS and *Apple Daily*, a television broadcaster and a newspaper group from Hong Kong, on Taiwan demonstrate, competition posed by outside media players can result in pressures favoring the imitation of journalism culture from these challengers. Given the advancement of information technology and China's hunger for information, there is reason for us to expect such influence to grow.

Nonetheless, we expect a long and difficult path ahead before China's journalism research can reach a level of theoretical advancement and methodological sophistication comparable to that in Hong Kong and Taiwan. The reason is that journalism education remains in a condition of inadequately trained faculty, outdated curricula, insufficient resources, and handicapping political controls from the state.

In Hong Kong, due to the small size of the research community, journalism research does not have sufficient diversity in terms of range of topics covered, methods utilized, and theoretical perspectives taken. In Taiwan, the lack of sustained attention to macro systemic issues inevitably gives the research literature an "administrative research" flavor. The reluctance for researchers to publish in English also hampers the diffusion of their research findings.

A final point to note is that there has been a steady increase in opportunities and venues for interactions and collaborations among scholars in the three Chinese societies, making it a lively regional dynamic in the larger context of globalization. It is certain that journalism research in China will continue to benefit from well-trained scholars in Taiwan and Hong Kong, as has been the case in the past ten years. It is also possible that scholars in Hong Kong and Taiwan will continue to find changes in China fascinating and conduct research in and on China, as has been the case in recent years. Given these developments, as journalism research in China improves we could see emergence of a larger research community on Chinese journalism and more significant contributions that this community makes to the overall body of knowledge on journalism.

Notes

1 Whereas the former ruling party in Taiwan, the Nationalist Party, moved from the Mainland after its defeat by the Communist army in 1949, the Democratic Progressive Party represents the Taiwan residents who had populated the island before the arrival of the nationalist government. The "nativistic accent" here refers to the sentiment of treating "Taiwanese" as a category to contest that of "Chinese."

2 These analyses are derived from our observations that form the basis of what texts to include. Almost all scholars in China publish in Chinese on domestic outlets. The last decade witnessed the mushrooming of academic journals, trade journals, anthologies, and dedicated web sites. Although none of these venues has a formalized referee process, they are all included in this review. The situation is different in Hong Kong and Taiwan. Hong Kong scholars publish mostly in English in refereed journals in the United States and Europe. They also have books published in English by local and Western publishers. Taiwan scholars have their own refereed Chinese journals. Although most publish in Chinese, a few are bilingual. For our purpose, texts of both English and Chinese are included.

3 Due to space limit, except for a few representative publications in English, we will not list all individual pieces, especially those in Chinese, reviewed in this chapter. A complete reference list is available from the authors upon request.

4 Sample English publications discussed to here appear in the volumes edited by Chin-Chuan Lee (2000, 2003).

5 This characterization refers to journalism researchers adopting the official vocabulary to evaluate the performance of the party press in China. For example, such critical analyses may invoke the principle of press freedom, but expresses it in terms of "true" freedom of the press that serves the country, and by implication, the party's policies for the country. Such an expression tactically makes a differentiation from the conception of press freedom measured in universal standards.

References

Chan, J. M., and Lee, C. C. (1991). *Mass media and political* transition: *The Hong Kong press in China's orbit*. New York: The Guilford Press.

Chan, J. M., and So, C. Y. K. (2005). The surrogate democracy function of the media: Citizens' and journalists' evaluations of media performance. In A. Romano and M. Bromley (eds.), *Journalism and democracy in Asia* (pp. 66–80). London: Routledge.

Chan, J. M., Lee, P. S. N., and Lee, C. C. (1996). *Hong Kong journalists in transition*. Hong Kong: Hong Kong Institute of Asia-Pacific Studies at The Chinese University of Hong Kong.

Chan, J. M., Pan, Z., and Lee, F. L. F. (2004). Professional aspirations and job satisfaction: Chinese journalists at a time of change in the media. *Journalism & Mass Communication Quarterly*, 81, 254–73.

Chen, C. S., Zhu, J. H., and Wu, W. (1998). The Chinese journalist. In D. H. Weaver (ed.), *The Global journalist: News people around the world* (pp. 9–30). Cresskill, NJ: Hampton Press.

Crane, D. (1972). *Invisible colleges: Diffusion of knowledge in scientific communities*. Chicago, IL: University of Chicago Press.

Johnstone, J. W. C., Slawski, E. J., and Bowman, W. W. (1976). *The news people: A sociological portrait of American journalists and their work*. Urbana, IL: University of Illinois Press.

Lee, C. C. (1993). Sparking a fire: The press and the ferment of democratic change in Taiwan. *Journalism Monographs*, no. 128.

Lee, C. C. (1998). Press self-censorship and political transition in Hong Kong. *Harvard International Journal of Press/Politics*, 3, 55–73.

Lee, C. C. (ed.) (2000). *Power, money, and media: Communication patterns and bureaucratic control in cultural China*. Evanston, IL: Northwestern University Press.

Lee, C. C. (ed.) (2003). *Chinese media, global contexts*. London: Routledge.

Lee, P. S. N., and Chu, L. L. (1998). Inherent dependence on power: The Hong Kong press in political transition. *Media, Culture and Society*, 20(1), 59–77.

Lo, V. H. (1998). The new Taiwan journalist: A sociological profile. In D. H. Weaver (ed.), *The Global journalist: News people around the world* (pp. 71–88). Cresskill, NJ: Hampton Press.

Lo, V., and Chan, J. M. (eds.) (2004). *Changing journalists in mainland China, Hong Kong, and Taiwan*. Taipei: Chuliu Publication Corporation (in Chinese).

Lo, V., Chan, J. M., and Pan, Z. (2005). Ethical attitudes and perceived practice: A comparative study of journalists in China, Hong Kong and Taiwan. *Asian Journal of Communication*, 15(2), 175–93.

Pan, Z. (2005). Media change through bounded innovations: Journalism in China's media reforms. In A. Momano and M. Bromley (eds.), *Journalism and democracy in Asia* (pp. 96–107). London: Routledge.

Pan, Z., and Chan, J. M. (2003). Shifting journalistic paradigms: How China's journalists assess "media exemplars." *Communication Research*, 30, 649–82.

Polumbaum, J. (1990). The tribulations of China's journalists after a decade of reform. In Chin-Chuan Lee (ed.), *Voices of China: The interplay of politics and journalism* (pp. 33–68). New York: Guilford Press.

Schudson, M. (1991). The sociology of news production revisited (again). In J. Curran and M. Gurevitch (eds.), *Mass media and society*. 3rd edition (pp. 175–200). London: Edward Arnold.

So, C. Y. K., and Chan, J. M. (eds.) (1999). *Press and politics in Hong Kong: Case studies from 1967 to 1997*. Hong Kong: Hong Kong Institute of Asia-Pacific Studies at The Chinese University of Hong Kong.

Weaver, D. H., and Wilhoit, G. C. (1996). *The American journalist in the 1990s: US news people at the end of an era*. Mahwah, NJ: Lawrence Erlbaum Associates.

Wuthnow, R. (1989). *Communities of discourse: Ideology and social structure in the reformation, the Enlightenment, and European socialism*. Cambridge, MA: Harvard University Press.

Zhao, Y. (1998). *Media, market, and democracy in China: Between the party lines and the bottom line*. Urbana, IL: University of Illinois Press.

Chapter 17

Journalism Research in Mexico

Historical Development and Research Interests in the Latin American Context

María Elena Hernández Ramírez and Andreas Schwarz

Journalism Research in the Latin American Context

In Latin America, journalism studies as a specific sub-discipline started in the 1990s as the result of rather isolated efforts. Before that time, journalism was a subsidiary subject of communication research, a field at an early stage as well and considered to be marginal. Although a great deal of literature related to the press written before the 1950s has been found, most of it is of historical and cultural nature, or in some cases refers to legal-political approaches, and emerged within very specific contexts (Aguirre, 1996). This is an explainable tendency in the context of the continuous social crisis in the region.

Three main factors have contributed to the delay in the concrete definition of research programs for the study of journalistic phenomena:

1 the "precariousness and increasing dependence" of general scientific Latin American research (Fuentes, 1998, p. 37);
2 the direction followed by academic studies on journalism and communication (Herrera, 1998);
3 the very little interest in the production of scientific knowledge showed by the media industry (Marques, 1992, p. 94).

Despite the very heterogeneous conditions of Latin American countries, it can be stated that empiric investigation on communication and journalism in the launching period (the late 1960s and the early 1970s) was significantly influenced by the UNESCO developmental parameters. Through the Economic Commission for Latin America (CEPAL), UNESCO sought the commitment of the mass media to encourage economic growth by spreading values such as productivity, efficiency, competence, and innovation (Marques, 1992, p. 96).

With regard to the development of journalism studies in Latin America since the 1990s, Brazil, Argentina, Mexico, and Venezuela stand out. This fact is consistent with their leading participation in the general scientific production of their region, even though the overall figures are rather marginal.[1]

Second to Brazil, Mexico is the strongest Latin American contributor to the development of specific research on journalism. To understand the emergence of Mexican journalism research, which started as – and partially still is – a fragmented research field, and its status quo, one has to describe its historical development and the respective institutional and socio-political conditions that have often constrained further differentiation.

The Emergence of Journalism Research in Mexico – from Individual Efforts to a Specific Field of Study?

The pre-theoretical stage – historical groundwork and beginning politicization (the 1950s to the 1970s)

Journalism research in Mexico is intrinsically related to the broader field of communication studies. A brief description of the history of journalism education in the country may explain this assertion. The first recognized Mexican journalism school was the Carlos Septién García, founded in 1949 (www.septien.edu.mx/). It was followed by a bachelor's degree program in journalism at the Autonomous National University (UNAM) in 1951 and, three years later, by a journalism school at the University of Veracruz. Besides journalistic practice and tools, the curricula of the last two programs also included scientific theory and methodology from a broad range of social scientific disciplines. However, further differentiation was inhibited, because since the 1960s, the incipient journalism programs were replaced by broadly conceptualized degrees in communication studies. The educational goal shifted from the formation of mere "simple" journalists to that of "social communicators." This reorientation to more heterogeneous curricula was recommended by UNESCO and promoted through the International Center of Superior Communication Studies (CIESPAL) in Latin America, which intended to close the gap that the arising electronic media brought to the teaching of journalism in traditional schools.

According to Fuentes, who conducted extensive document analyses of all accessible contributions of Mexican communication studies, the pioneer period (1956–70) of these studies are characterized by three pivotal tendencies (1988, p. 27):

1 normative and historical studies of the press;
2 applications of diffusion research in the rural sector;
3 first reflections concerning the structure and social function of radio and television.

Research related to journalism focused on describing and categorizing the newspapers' history as well as the role of journalism during specific periods or in certain regions (Ruiz, Reed, and Cordero, 1974).

Mexican journalism research during the 1960s was shaped by the strong influence of theories and methodologies of US scholars, who conducted mostly quantitative empirical research in Mexico (Fuentes, 1988, p. 28). In the 1970s, Mexican scholars were focused on the description and analysis of structural aspects of the media in general (Del Río, 1972), on the concentration of the daily press (Granados Chapa, 1972), and on the ideological leaning, financing and forms of newspaper organization (Fernández, 1975). In concert with the advancement of electronic mass media, Mexican communication research began to establish its own paradigms. The increasing number of graduated communication researchers, specialized institutions, and academic journals accelerated this development. However, the growth in the number of communication programs at the university level in this period barely contributed to the improvement of research infrastructure.

Communication was regarded from the perspectives of functionalism, structuralism, and critical theories based on Marxism (Toussaint, 1975; Paoli, 1977). The latter were encouraged mainly by Latin American scholars who found political asylum in Mexico (e.g. Reyes Matta, 1978; Roncagliolo, 1978). Their research on international news flow, and the dominating news agencies of the industrialized Northern nations, is still considered to have a strong impact on the country's academic discourse on journalism (Fuentes, 1988, p. 33).

Further individual efforts concerning journalism in this pre-theoretical stage focused on aspects of professionalization and education (González Casanova, 1965),[2] on the constitutional regulation of print media (Castaño, 1967), and semiotic analyses of the press (Rivadeneyra, 1975). Others outlined basic concepts for investigating newspapers from a multidisciplinary perspective, including reflections about its societal functions and dysfunctions (Guajardo, 1967; Jiménez de Ottalengo, 1973).

However, the emerging research on journalism suffered from a lack of institutionalization, and was not able to explicitly define its objects of analysis. The field could not establish as a coherent discipline grounded on systematic approaches, clear tendencies, and comprehensive empirical data. The preferred and more affordable methods were content and discourse analyses.

Consolidation and academic crisis – the search for new orientations (late 1970s to late 1980s)

Since the late 1970s, various scholars increasingly tried to influence the national communication policy and processes of democratization by intervening in the political debates. However, in tandem with the country's economic situation, the inquiry of communication – including the still incoherent and fragmented field of journalism studies – found itself trapped in the middle of a *crisis* mainly because of curtailed governmental subsidies for research and the shutting of the academic labor market (Fuentes, 1997, p. 38).

The discussions regarding the need of democratizing communications encouraged by UNESCO intensified and led scholars to focus their efforts particularly on the reflection and research on media–government relationships and or dependencies. Many of the publications during this period had the character of political argument (Fuentes 1988, p. 35) discussing the need for a new informational law

(Solís, 1984) and the role of the press in democratization (Esteva, 1982). As the study of foreign images stimulated academic efforts in most of Latin America, Mexican scholars tried to examine as well how foreign news media shaped the nation's image (Luna, 1986) and drew attention to the obstacles that national communication policies set to a New World Information Order (NWIO) (Arrieta, 1980).

Most of the essayistic contributions and empirical studies during this period referred to ongoing political problems and controversies. The content analysis continued to be the dominating method and was mostly applied to examine ideological news biases (Delgado et al., 1981). Numerous studies on the news coverage of the 1985 devastating earthquake in Mexico City exemplify the impact of salient events on academic research (e.g. Ávalos, 1986).

Some scholars started to shift their attention to structural aspects and the societal impact of commercial and underground print media (Trejo, 1980). Others described roughly the characteristics of the Mexican press industry and suggested preferences of consumption (Olvera and Gómez, 1982). The state-owned paper industry (PIPSA) was analyzed as a structure of governmental control on the Mexican print media (Fuentes Fierro, 1983). Many scholars continued to approach journalism (mostly the press) from a historical perspective, but this approach slightly decreased by the end of this period. Still, little discussion and data were published about journalistic professionalization and ethics (e.g. Baldivia, 1981).

At the end of this phase, contributions started shifting their focus from print to broadcast media, principally referring to the growing power of Televisa, the major television consortium in Mexico. Scholars discussed the inherent organizational and political structures, which favored power abuse, and tried to demonstrate political biases within Televisa's news coverage (Trejo, 1985).

By this time, in the middle of the country's university crisis, researchers from Mexico City as well as Mexican graduates from the United States started to decentralize communication research by founding new academic programs in the western part of the country. The most notable were, and still are, the "Programa Cultura" (Culture Program) at the University of Colima and the "Centro de Estudios de la Información y la Comunicación" (Information and Communication Studies Center) at the University of Guadalajara, which quickly gained reputation and improved the productivity and institutionalization of the field (Fuentes, 1997, p. 39).

Professionalization and increasing sociological influences in Mexican journalism research (late 1980s to mid-1990s)

The 1980s university crisis brought Mexican scholars to look for alternative concepts and methodological approaches. Some began to adopt theoretical frameworks from the United States and Great Britain, because these countries were the main source of internationally distributed research literature, and had a wide range of accessible universities at their disposal. A number of Mexican researchers graduated abroad during this time (Cervantes, 2000, p. 170), among them Gabriel González Molina, who studied the organizational and structural conditions of news production in Televisa (1985) and introduced the concept of news values in Mexican journalism research (1986). His work has its roots in early British news production studies and cultural studies approaches (see the chapter of Wahl-Jorgensen and Franklin in this book). González Molina's strong impact on subsequent journalism research in Mexico is discernable through the efforts of various scholars who contributed to a new field termed "sociology of news production" (Hernández Ramírez, 1997), in which the pivotal focuses of research *are* the journalistic routines of news production, the processes of news gathering, the selection and edition of news, and relationships between reporters and their sources. The first empirical studies on news production conducted inside the newsrooms and on the impact of organizational routines on news as a product of social reconstruction were approached mostly by ethnographic methods (Hernández Ramírez, 1995; Cervantes, 1996; Lozano, 1996).[3] This branch of research represents the first established and comparatively steadily discussed framework of journalism research in Mexico.

At the same time, many studies focused on the presidential elections of 1988 (Arredondo, Fregoso, and Trejo, 1991) and 1994 (Acosta and Parra, 1995). Their predominant concern was the balanced representation of political parties and ideological bias in the news coverage of television programs and the press. Nonetheless, the main objects of analysis in those works were political communication processes instead of journalism. Similar research, guided by different interests, tried to explain how political journalism was legitimizing the power of the ruling regime (Trejo, 1995–6) and the impact of news media on political participation (de la Peña and Toledo, 1991). More than ever, the societal influence of Televisa and its strong ties with the government called the attention of the academia (Ortega and Gutiérrez, 1987).

Comparing this period of communication research in general with earlier periods, the disciplinary focus has shifted considerably to sociological approaches. During 1986–94, Fuentes identified 37.4 percent of 1,019 analyzed documents with a sociological focus (1996, p. 19). A similar trend could also be observed for journalism research. Although the quantitative output stayed comparatively low, the coherence and methodological approach makes it a research line of growing importance.

In addition to the growing influence of sociological approaches, a characterstic that may describe this phase is the increasing professionalization of both communication as well as journalism research. One indicator is the growing number of empirical studies (Fuentes, 1996, pp. 19–20), which in research on journalism, mostly means content analyses and ethnographic methods. Comprehensive surveys or observation designs are still embryonic, mainly due to the difficulties of getting access to media organizations. However, considerable progress at an observed at an institutional level because scientific associations (e.g. AMIC and CONEICC) arranged regular conferences and increased the number of specialized academic journals. Those publications have played a key role in the institutionalization of communication and journalism research as the lion's share of academic output was published in these journals between 1986 and 1994 (more than 50 percent of publications in communication studies). Most contributions were published in *Comunicación y Sociedad* (Information and Communication Studies Centre, CEIC) at the University of Guadalajara, *Estudios sobre las Culturas Contemporáneas* (Culture Program at the University of Colima), and *Revista Mexicana de Comunicación* (Manuel Buendía Foundation) (Fuentes, 1996, pp. 10–12).

The take-off of specific research on journalism and the influence of the socio-political milieu (mid-1990s to 2005)

One of the most rambling aspects of incipient Mexican democracy is the current legal system of social communication. This is the reason why it is not strange that 12 percent of all research done during 1995–2001 – a lively period in the process of the democratic transition – had focused on such aspect (Fuentes, 2003, p. 24).

The debate about the right to information, which started in 1977, became less important at the beginning of the 1980s. However, this debate remained latent in the academic agenda and regained strength in the second half of the 1990s, when certain political actors sought a deep legal reform to regulate the way the media operates (Esteinou, 1998). For the first time, the topic was analyzed from the perspective of comparative law approaches to information (Villanueva, 1998).

The new standpoint tries to go beyond the merely political arguments and tries to support the necessity for a modern and democratic legal frame, based on the identification of the legal causes that organically link the media with the Mexican post-revolutionary system (López Ayllón, 2000). Thus, the discussion centers on aspects such as the legitimate subsidies from the state to the press around the world, the right to the journalist's professional secrecy, journalism ethics and self-regulation of the media (Aznar and Villanueva, 2000), unionism or corporate association of journalism, and the lack of a right to reply and of legislation on the access to public information.

Ambiguity and obsolescence in legislation related to communication,[4] the collusion of interests between media owners and political power, and the embryonic culture of Mexican society on information transparency are facts that explain why after almost thirty years since the first debates over the right to information, there are still more works being produced of a rather argumentative than empirical nature. It also explains why the research done on journalism is still associated with socio-political factors.

With the progressive loss of hegemony of the PRI in the country, the mechanisms of the press–government relationships have been gradually revealed. This issue has always been the center of interest of researchers on journalism, but the context of the democratic transition and the increasing international watchfulness on this process have encouraged the publication of academic-political essays that have begun to develop theories about the historical structural model of the subordinated relationship of Mexican media to the public power (Carreño, 2000). Works on the local press having the same approach are, in fact, scarce (Sánchez, 1997).

The election process held in Mexico City in 1997, in which for the first time since the revolution a leftist government (PRD) attained power, caused acute academic observation of the media coverage. The reductions of self-censorship of radio news (Sosa, 1997) in contrast to the television news programs (Acosta and Vargas, 1998), were phenomena that became very noticeable. This political episode was the context for an incipient application of methodologies for the study on the reception and consumption of television news (Inestrosa, 1997), as well as for some isolated attempts to know the patterns of exposure of radio audiences to news programs as a means of political information (Aceves, 1997).

The victory of the PAN party in the federal election of July 2, 2000 – after 71 years of uninterrupted government by the PRI – generated expectations of change among all the social organized sectors. As to the field of communication and journalism, it opened the possibility to regain law projects to regulate social communication, to guarantee the people's access to public information, and to demand the public officials' accountability.

Through academic work and proselytism, a group of scholars and national newspaper publishers – the self-styled Grupo *Oaxaca* – advanced to Congress the discussion of the issue of access to public information. As a consequence, on June 12, 2003 the federal law for the access to public information came into effect. This event is of great significance because it takes part in the process of the transformation of the Mexican state and in the shaping of public opinion, and also because research connected to the making of effective legal norms will undoubtedly come as a result. In turn they will naturally widen the range of possibilities of journalistic practices (Villanueva and Luna, 2001).

It is during this period that the influence of the Anglo-Saxon knowledge of the sociology of news production – brought by Gabriel González Molina – increasingly spread at both theoretical and methodological levels (Hernández Ramírez, 1997; Cervantes, 2000). Several empirical works were developed, mostly postgraduate theses with modest but consistent contributions to the construction of the sociology of news production within a Mexican context. These studies deal with phenomena such as the news production of the local press (de León, 2003), the local television, photojournalism, news values in local crime news, source–reporter relationships, and reflection on news as a form of knowledge (Zacarías, 2001–2). Additionally the phenomena of technological convergence raises questions about transformations in the process of newspaper production (Zaragoza, 2002).

The reception of journalistic discourse in television news was first anlayzed by Vernik (1998) and Orozco (1998). Later, sponsored by the most important television consortium (Televisa), Lozano began – in a systematic cumulative manner – the development of a research trend on the "consumption of news programs in Mexico," including the negotiations of meaning of different types of audiences and their discourse perception regarding the credibility and objectivity of newscast programs (2001a).

Media treatment studies moved from the concern for news balance, toward the analysis of tabloidization of political news (Lozano, 2001b). The main focus was the presidential election within the process of political and social changes in the country (Trejo, 2001).

The discourse and content analyses prevail among the few methodologies used for empirical work, sometimes enriched by the perspectives of the agenda-setting approach (Aceves, 2003), socio-semiotics, pragmatics, and linguistics. International news flow in the Latin-American press was still studied (Lozano, 2000); and so was the coverage of Mexico in the American news system (Arredondo, 2002).

Some outstanding content analysis studies done during this period dealt with the media coverage and discourse strategies of the Zapatista rebellion in 1994 (Gómez Mont, 1999; Gutiérrez, 2004); the spectacular discourse of television news programs (de Gasperín and Torres, 1999); the fiction-making of reality (Aponte, 2000), and the press treatment of the alternation of the ruling party in 2000 (Santillán, 2004).

Although the Internet is currently the most studied of all media by Mexican researchers (second only to television), some of the specific analyses on the changes that the World Wide Web has brought to journalism focus on the transformation of the professional journalist profile (Crovi, 2002). But, in general, this research is still very scarce and only descriptive (Islas et al., 2002).

The gradual distancing between the press and political power evidenced the need to reflect upon the status or situation of journalism as a profession. Therefore, the difficulties to professionalize Mexican journalism (Torres, 1997), the working conditions, and union organization of news workers were described (Hernández López, 1999). A historical reconstruction of journalism education testified to the lack of appropriate Mexican teaching models (Hernández Ramírez, 2004). In this context the roots of the journalistic practices in Mexico were explored from the perspective of Bourdieu's "campus and habitus" concepts (García Hernández, 2000).

Although argumentative discussions around ethics of journalism were still common, work of a more theoretical nature as well as empirical surveys started to appear (Arroyo, 1998). One of these works systematizes the reflection of classical authors and intends to construct a model on the social responsibility of the mass media based on Norbert Elias' theoretical perspective (Fernández, 2002).

Historiographical studies moved from the descriptive level and tend then to evaluate and classify the work produced in the past one hundred years (Cruz, 2001). They seek to historically analyze journalism as a cultural product, based on its relationship with power and to document women's participation in the national press. Only exceptionally was the history of broadcasting journalism documented (Sosa, 2001).

Conclusions and Prospects

On the basis of this review, we can state that Mexican scholars seem to lack a strong interest in journalism as a clearly defined object of study, and have been strongly oriented toward current societal dynamics and the political transition in Mexico. Along with the dependency on the fluctuating and skimpy academic resources, several factors have impeded the consolidation of research traditions and formation of basic theoretical frameworks, and the methods to approach journalistic phenomena. Among those factors, we may count the lack of a consolidated journalistic profession, the ambiguous curricula in journalism education, the obsolescent legislation on communications, and the structure and ownership of Mexican mass media.

Mexican research on journalism continuously was influenced by concepts and approaches from foreign countries such as the critical perspectives of Latin American researchers (e.g. Fernando Reyes Matta), the empirical research tradition of the United States, or influences from the earlier British journalism studies – in Mexico mainly introduced by Gonzales Molina. In addition, the development and communication policy of UNESCO had considerable impact. It is true that these influences inspired a substantial amount of journalism-related research in the country, but they probably contributed to hinder the emergence of originally Mexican and consistently investigated theories or methodological approaches.

Contemporary journalism research in Mexico is still emergent. Global shifts on journalistic practices might influence institutional interests on this field. However, academic efforts to consolidate a specific trend of study will continue to be isolated for a long while, and the influence of socio-political milieu will undoubtedly prevail.

Notes

1 According to Fuentes (1998, p. 37), data from the Science Citation Index in 1978 indicate that only 1 percent from the recorded publications were produced in Latin America, and out of this figure "92 percent corresponds to Brazil, Argentina, Mexico, Chile and Venezuela," from which only a minor proportion stems from social science.
2 Empirical studies on professionalization of Latin American journalists were contributed by non-Mexican researchers: Day (1968) as well as McLeod and Rush (1969a, 1969b).
3 Authors such as Lippmann (1922), Tuchman (1978), and Schudson (2002), among others, are considered as the conceptual roots here.
4 The print law dates back to 1917, and the one on radio and television to 1960.

References

Aceves, F. (1997). La radio en Guadalajara [The radio in Guadalajara]. In *Anuario de Investigación de la Comunicación*, IV (pp. 24–5). Mexico: CONEICC.

Aceves, F. (2003). Problemas metodológicos en el estudio de la cobertura informativa de los medios en los procesos electorales [Methodological problems in the study of news coverage of elections]. In *Anuario de Investigación de la Comunicación*, X (pp. 353–68). Mexico: CONEICC.

Acosta, M., and Parra, L. P. (1995). *Los procesos electorales en los medios de comunicación. Guía para el análisis de contenido electoral en México* [*Electoral processes in the media. Guide for content analysis of election coverage in Mexico*]. Mexico, DF: Academia Mexicana de Derechos Humanos/UIA.

Acosta, M., and Vargas, N. (1998). Sinopsis global de las elecciones del '97 en cuatro noticieros [Global synopsis of the '97 elections in four television news programs]. *Revista Mexicana de Comuincación*, 10(53), 18–23.

Aguirre, J. M. (1996). *De la práctica periodística a la investigación comunicacional: Hitos del pensamiento venezolano sobre comunicación y cultura de masas* [From journalism practice to communication research: Mile stones of Venezuelan thought about communication and mass culture]. Caracas: Universidad Católica Andrés Bello.

Aponte, R. (2000, October). La oferta noticiosa: celebración de simulacros y cofradía de emociones por televisión. [News: celebration of illusions and falsehood of televised emotions]. *Versión, estudios de comunicación y política*, 10, UAM-X 127–48.

Arredondo, P. (2002). México en la prensa de Estados Unidos. Dos agendas informativas [Mexico in the US press. Two news agendas]. In Del Palacio (ed.), *Cultura, comunicación y política* [*Culture, communication and politics*] (pp. 201–12). Mexico: University of Guadalajara.

Arredondo, P., Fregoso, G., and Trejo, R. (eds.) (1991). *Así se calló el sistema. Comunicación y elecciones en 1988* [*How the system became quiet. Communication and elections in 1988*]. Guadalajara: University of Guadalajara.

Arrieta, M. (1980). *Obstáculos para un Nuevo Orden Informativo Internacional* [*Obstacles for a new world information order*]. Mexico: CEESTEM/Nueva Imagen.

Arroyo, A. (1998, May–August). Valores éticos en el periodismo escrito mexicano [Ethical values in Mexican print journalism]. *Revista Iberoamericana de Derecho a la Información*, no. 1, 95–143.

Ávalos, B. (1986). El vaivén de la palabra [The fluctuation of the words]. In A. Aguilar Zinser, C. Morales, and R. Peña (eds.), *Aún Tiembla* [*It is still quaking*] (pp. 209–30). Mexico: Grijalbo.

Aznar, H., and Villanueva, E. (eds.) (2000). *Deontología y autorregulación informativa. Ensayos desde una perspectiva comparada* [*Ethics and informational self regulation. Essays with a comparative perspective*]. Mexico: FMB/UNESCO/UIA.

Baldivia, J. (ed.) (1981). *La formación de los periodistas en América Latina: México, Chile, Costa Rica* [*The education of journalists in Latin America: Mexico, Chile, Costa Rica*]. Mexico: CEESTEM/Nueva Imagen.

Carreño, J. (2000). Cien años de subordinación entre prensa y poder en el siglo XX [100 years of subordination between the press and the power in the 20th century]. *Espacios de Comunicación UIA*, 4, 145–66.

Castaño, L. (1967). *La libertad de pensamiento y de imprenta* [*The freedom of opinion and the freedom of the press*]. Mexico: UNAM.

Cervantes, C. (1996, September–December). Construcción primaria del acontecer y planeación de la cobertura informativa. Propuesta metodológica para su estudio [A methodological proposal to study the first level of news building and the planning of news coverage]. *Comunicación y Sociedad*, 28, 49–82.

Cervantes, C. (2000). Para superar la ruta de los modelos, efectos y metáforas equívocas en la sociología del periodismo [Overcoming wrong models, effects and metaphors in the sociology of journalism]. In G. Orozco (ed.), *Lo viejo y lo nuevo. Investigar la comunicación en el siglo XXI* (pp. 169–83) [*The old and the new. Researching communication in the 21st century*]. Madrid: Ediciones de la Torre.

Crovi, D. (2002). Periodistas de un nuevo siglo [*Journalists of a new century*]. In Maldonado, P. (ed.): *Horizontes comunicativos en México. Estudios críticos* [*Communicative horizons in Mexico. Critical studies*] (pp. 229–46). Mexico: AMIC.

Cruz, R. (2001). La historia de la prensa en México durante el siglo XX [*The history of the Mexican press during the 20th century*]. In I. Lombardo (ed.): *La comunicación en la sociedad mexicana. Reflexiones temáticas* [*Communication in the Mexican society. Reflections*] (pp. 15–48). Mexico: AMIC.

Day, L. J. (1968). The Latin American journalist: A tentative profile. *Journalism Quarterly*, 45(3), 509–15.

de Gasperín, A., and Torres, A. (1999, June). Para una lectura crítica del discurso noticioso de la televisión mexicana [Aiming at a critical reading of the news discourse in Mexican television]. *Diá-logos de la Comunicación*, no. 55, 93–8.

de la Peña, R., and Toledo, R. (1991, May–August). Medios de comunicación y actitudes políticas de los ciudadanos del Distrito Federal [Media and political behavior of Mexico City's inhabitants]. *Comunicación y Sociedad*, 12, 115–38.

de León, S. (2003). *La construcción del acontecer. Análisis de las prácticas periodísticas* [*The (news) construction of reality. Analysis of journalistic practices*]. Mexico: UAA/UdeG/CONEICC.

Del Río, J. (1972). Anotaciones sobre los medios de información en México [Annotations about the news media in Mexico]. *Revista Mexicana de Ciencia Política*, 18(69), 5–45.

Delgado, M., Juárez, R. E., Suárez, J. D., Silva, S., and Villa, L. I. (1981, September). Análisis de la prensa en Guadalajara. La ideología en los editoriales de cuatro periódicos [Analysis of the press in Guadalajara. Ideology in the editorials of four newspapers]. ITESO *Ciencias de la Comunicación*, no. 4, 5–37.

Esteinou, J. (1998, September–December). El derecho a la información y la democratización del estado Mexicano [The right to information and the democratization of the Mexican state]. *Revista Iberoamericana de Derecho de la Información*, 2, 59–79.

Esteva, G. (1982). Prensa, derecho a la información y democratización de la sociedad mexicana [The press, the right to information and the democratization of Mexican society]. In El Día (ed.), *Foro Internacional de Comunicación Social* [International forum of social communication] (pp. 74–96). Mexico: El Día.

Fernández, F. (1975). Prensa y poder en México [The press and the power in Mexico]. *Estudios Políticos*, 2(2), 29–64.

Fernández, F. (2002). *La responsabilidad de los medios de comunicación* [*The responsibility of the media*]. Mexico: Croma/Paidós.

Fuentes Fierro, A. (1983). *Papel y medios impresos: desarrollo económico y derecho a la información* [*Paper and print media: Economic development and the right to information*]. Mexico: UAM Xochimilco.

Fuentes, R. (1988). *La Investigación de Comunicación en México. Sistematización documental 1956–1986* [*Communication research in Mexico. Systematic documentation 1956–1986*]. Mexico: Ediciones de Comunicación.

Fuentes, R. (1996). *La Investigación de la comunicación en México. Sistematización documental 1986–1994* [*Communication research in Mexico. Systematic documentation 1986–1994*]. Mexico, DF: University of Guadalajara/ITESO.

Fuentes, R. (1997, May–August). Consolidación y fragmentación de la investigación de la comunicación en México, 1987–1997 [Consolidation and fragmentation of communication research in Mexico, 1987–1997]. *Comunicación y Sociedad*, 30, 27–50.

Fuentes, R. (1998). *La emergencia de un campo académico: continuidad utópica y estructuración científica de la investigación de la comunicación en México* [*The emergence of an academic field: Utopian continuity and scientific structuration of communication research in Mexico*]. Guadalajara: ITESO/University of Guadalajara.

Fuentes, R. (2003). *La Investigación Académica sobre Comunicación en México. Sistematización Documental 1995–2001* [*Communication research in Mexico. Systematic documentation 1995–2001*]. Mexico: ITESO.

García Hernández, C. (2000). La práctica periodística: herencia de cambios históricos [The journalistic practice: The heritage of historical changes]. In C. Del Palacio (ed.), *Historia de la prensa en Iberoamérica* [*History of the press in Latin America*] (pp. 487–98). Mexico: University of Guadalajara/Altexto.

Gómez Mont, C. (1999). Médias et néo-zapatisme dans la crise mexicaine : la spirale du silence [The media and neo-zapatism during the Mexican crisis: The spiral of silence]. *Communication et Organisation*, 16, Université Michel Montaigne – Bordeaux, 165–84.

González Casanova, H. (1965). El futuro de los medios de información relacionado con la formación universitaria de los periodistas [The future of the news media related to the academic education of journalists]. *Revista de Ciencias Políticas y Sociales*, 11, 41–50.

González Molina, G. (1985). Mexican television news: the imperatives of corporate rationale. *Media, Culture and Society*, 8(2), 159–87.

González Molina, G. (1986). *Valores noticiosos: la distribución desigual del acceso periodístico* [*News values: The unequal distribution of journalistic access*]. Colima: University of Colima.

Granados Chapa, M. Á. (1972). Aproximaciones a la prensa mexicana. Notas sobre el periodismo diario [Approaches to the Mexican press. Notes on daily news]. *Revista Mexicana de Ciencia Política*, 18(69), 47–52.

Guajardo, H. (1967). *Elementos de periodismo* [*Elements of journalism*]. Mexico: Gernika.

Gutiérrez, G. (2004). *La rebelión zapatista en el diario El País (análisis del discurso)* [*The Zapatista rebellion in the newspaper El País (discourse analysis)*]. Mexico: University of Guadalajara.

Hernández López, R. (1999). *Sólo para periodistas. Manual de supervivencia en los medios mexicanos* [*Only for journalists. Manual of surviving in the Mexican media*]. Mexico: Grijalbo.

Hernández Ramírez, M. (1995). *La producción noticiosa* [*News production*]. Mexico: University of Guadalajara.

Hernández Ramírez, M. (1997, May–August). La sociología de la producción de noticias: hacia un nuevo campo de investigación en México [The sociology of news production: Towards a new research field in Mexico]. *Comunicación y Sociedad*, 30, 209–42.

Hernández Ramírez, M. (2004, January–June). La formación universitaria de periodistas en México [Academic education of journalists in Mexico]. *Comunicación y Sociedad*, 1, 109–38.

Herrera, E. (1998). Periplo de la investigación periodística y comunicacional en Venezuela [Overview on journalism and communication research in Venezuela] [Electronic version]. *Revista Latina de Comunicación Social*. Retrieved January 22, 2007 from www.ull.es/publicaciones/latina/a/80earle.htm

Inestrosa, S. (1997). Consideraciones generales en torno a las noticias por televisión en México [General considerations related to TV news in Mexico]. In S. Inestrosa (ed.), *Conferencia de las Américas. Diversidad tecnológica y comunicación* [*Conference of the Americas. Technological diversity and communication*] (pp. 67–77). Mexico: UIA/FELAFACS.

Islas, O., Gutiérrez, F., Albarrán, G., Camarena, E., and Fuentes-Beráin (2002). *Explorando el ciberperiodismo iberoamericano* [*Exploring Latin American cyber journalism*]. Mexico: ITESM/CECSA.

Jiménez de Ottalengo, R. (1973). El periódico como medio de comunicación colectiva y su estudio interdisciplinario [The newspaper as mass media and its interdisciplinary analysis]. *Revista Mexicana de Sociología*, 35(3), 615–29.

Lippmann, W. (1922). Public opinion. New York: Macmillan.

López Ayllón, S. (2000). El derecho a la información como derecho fundamental [The right to information as fundamental right]. In J. Carpizo and M. Carbonell (eds.), *Derecho a la información y derechos humanos* [*Right to information and human rights*] (pp. 147–81). Mexico: UNAM.

Lozano, J. C. (1996). *Teoría e investigación de la comunicación de masas* [*Theory and research of mass communication*]. Mexico: Alhambra Mexicana.

Lozano, J. C. (2000, March). La información internacional en la prensa latinoamericana [Foreign news in the Latin American press]. *Diá-logos de la Comunicación*, 57, FELAFACS, 49–60.

Lozano, J. C. (2001a). Consumo y lecturas negociadas de noticieros televisivos en Monterrey, Guadalajara y México DF [Consumption and negotiated reading of TV news programs in Monterrey, Guadalajara and Mexico City]. *Oficios Terrestres*, 9/10, 18–26.

Lozano, J. C. (2001b). Espectacularización en la cobertura informativa de las elecciones mexicanas a la Presidencia [Tabloidization of the news coverage of the presidential elections in Mexico]. *Comunicación y Sociedad* (Navarra), 14(1), 29–39.

Luna, L. (1986). México en la prensa extranjera [Mexico in the foreign press]. *Cuadernos del Centro de Estudios de la Comunicación*, 9, 15–24.

Marques, J. M. (1992). O divórcio entre a universidade e a indústria da comunicação na América Latina [Divorce of universities and the communication industry in Latin America]. In C. Luna (ed.), *Generación de conocimientos y formación de comunicadores* [Generation of knowledge and education of communicators] (pp. 91–112). Mexico: Opción/Felafacs.

McLeod, J. M., and Rush, R. (1969a). Professionalization of Latin American and US journalists, Part I. *Journalism Quarterly*, 46, 583–90.

McLeod, J. M., and Rush, R. (1969b). Professionalization of Latin American and US Journalists, Part II. *Journalism Quarterly*, 46, 784–9.

Olvera, O., and Gómez, P. (1982). Industria y consumo del mensaje impreso [Industry and consumption of print news]. *Connotaciones*, 3, 7–34.

Orozco, G. (1998). México. In K. Jensen (ed.). *News of the world. World cultures look at television news* (pp. 126–43). London: Routledge.

Ortega R., P., and Gutiérrez, J. L. (1987). *Imevisión y Televisa*: noticieros sin sociedad [*Imevisión* and *Televisa*: News programs without society]. In *Anuario CONEICC I: Crisis y Comunicación en México* [*Crisis and communication in Mexico*] (pp. 99–106). CONEICC/U. de Colima.

Paoli, J. A. (1977). *Comunicación e Información. Perspectivas teóricas* [*Communication and information. Theoretical perspectives*]. Mexico: Edicol, Trillas.

Reyes Matta, F. (ed.) (1978). *La noticia internacional* [*Foreign news*]. Mexico: ILET.

Rivadeneyra, R. (1975). *Periodismo. La teoría general de los sistemas y la ciencia de la comunicación* [*Journalism. General systems theory and communication studies*]. Mexico: Trillas.

Roncagliolo, R. (1978). Comunicación: cambio social y necesidad de un nuevo marco conceptual [Communication: Social change and the need for a new conceptual framework]. *Cuadernos de Comunicación*, 31(1), 12–21.

Ruiz Castañeda, M., Reed, L., and Cordero, E. (1974). *El periodismo en México. 450 años de historia* [*Journalism in Mexico. 450 years of history*]. Mexico: Tradición.

Sánchez, E. (1997). La prensa diaria de Guadalajara: desarrollo y perspectivas [The daily press in Guadalajara: Development and perspectives]. In J. Muriá (Ed): *Miscelánea Jalisciense* [*Miscellaneous of Jalisco*] (pp. 61–92). Mexico: Colegio de Jalisco.

Santillán, J. (2004). Los periódicos protagonistas del cambio político [Leading newspapers in the political change]. *Revista Iberoamericana de Comunicación*, 6, 41–72.

Schudson, M. (2002). *The sociology of news*. New York: Norton.

Solís, B. (1984). *Derecho a la Información* [*Right to information*]. Mexico: UAM Azcapotzalco.

Sosa, G. (1997). La elecciones de 1997 por el cuadrante radiofónico [The elections of 1997 on the radio]. *Revista Mexicana de Comunicación*, 9(50), 11–14.

Sosa, G. (2001). Repaso histórico al periodismo sobre radio en México [Historical review of radio journalism in Mexico]. *Revista Mexicana de Comunicación*, 13(69), 25–9.

Torres, F. (1997). *El Periodismo mexicano. Ardua lucha por su integridad* [*Mexican journalism. The hard struggle for its integrity*]. Mexico: Ediciones Coyoacán.

Toussaint, F. (1975). *Crítica de la información de masas* [*Criticism of the mass media news*]. Mexico: Anuies/Trillas.

Trejo, R. (1980). *La prensa marginal* [*The marginal press*]. Mexico: El Caballito.

Trejo, R. (ed.) (1985). *Televisa, el quinto poder* [*Television, the fifth power*]. Mexico: Claves Latinoamericanas.

Trejo, R. (1995–6, September–April). Prensa y gobierno: las relaciones perversas. Los medios, espacios y actores de la política en México [The press and the government: The perverted relationships. The media, arenas and actors of Mexican politics]. *Comunicación y Sociedad*, 25/26, 35–56.

Trejo, R. (2001). *Mediocracia sin mediaciones* [*"Mediacracy" without "mediations"*]. Mexico: Cal y arena.

Tuchman, G. (1978). *Making news: A study in the construction of reality*. New York: The Free Press.

Vernik, E. (1998). Comunidades cercadas: la exclusión urbana en la televisión y en la vida [Fenced communities: The urban exclusion in television and life]. In N. G. Canclini (ed.): *Cultura y comunicación en la ciudad de México II* [*Culture and communication in Mexico City*] (pp. 156–81). Mexico: UAM-I/Grijalbo.

Villanueva, E. (1998). *Derecho comparado de la información* [*The right to information from a comparative perspective*]. Mexico: RTC/Konrad/UIA.

Villanueva, E. (2000). *Derecho mexicano de la información* [*The Mexican right to information*]. Mexico: Oxford University Press.

Villanueva, E., and Luna, I. (eds.) (2001). *El derecho de acceso a la información* [*The right to information access*]. Mexico: UIA/FKA.

Zacarías, A. (2001–2). Las noticias, factores de percepción de la realidad: estructuras de conocimiento [The news, factors of reality perception: Knowledge structures]. *Revista Universidad de Guadalajara*, 22, Winter, 33–9.

Zaragoza, C. (2002). Periodismo en la convergencia tecnológica: el reportero [Journalism and technological convergence: The reporter]. *Revista Mexicana de Ciencias Políticas y Sociales*, 185, 151–64.

Part V

The Future of Journalism Research

Chapter 18

Reconsidering "Journalism" for Journalism Research

Ari Heinonen and Heikki Luostarinen

Introduction: Journalism by the Media and by the Public

Our purpose is to characterize the changing nature of journalism as an object of scholarly research. We suggest that while journalism as a common form of communication is still a vital element of democratic societies, its locus may be moving – at least partially – from the sphere of institutionalized profession and specialized organizations toward wider communication spheres that are not well established nor easily defined. This development results from changes both in society at large and within journalism itself, and is largely effected by the new enabling communication technologies. Two examples may illustrate our meaning.

After the terrorist strike in March 2004, Madrid experienced an extraordinarily sudden and strong upsurge of political activism. In a matter of hours, large numbers of people were organized to participate in rallies and demonstrations, and a campaign to promote voting activity was launched. Regardless of the actual effect on the election result of this rather impromptu political activism, it was a manifestation of two issues relevant for this treatise. First, political activism happened largely outside of the conventional political sphere (the major parties having ceased election campaigning due to the terrorist act). Second, the communication that enabled and supported this political activism also happened outside the traditional media and journalism. The main channel of communication was the mobile telephone, changed from a person-to-person device to a many-to-many medium, as was evidenced by local tele-operators registering sudden traffic peaks. Thus, to use Rheingold's (2002) term, "smart mobs" bypassed conventional spheres of political communication.

Another incident took place in Konginkangas, a rural area in central Finland, also in March 2004. On a dark, freezing night, a heavy truck collided with a bus full of sleeping young people on their way for a skiing holiday in Lapland. Twenty-three passengers were killed instantly. The following day the region was full of workplace discussions and e-mail and mobile telephone messages, as well as online discussion forum debates. Regarding the obvious and immediate question "why did this happen," it was interesting that, according to our personal observation, the media first evinced technical reasons, the citizen debate focused rapidly on more political questions, such as traffic policy, irresponsibility of the transportation business, the irrationality of domestic and EU directives, problems of logistics in modern production, etc. A rare occurrence received a generalized political interpretation which led to demands for policy changes. But rather than in the publicity of the media, this politicized debate happened more in many-to-many networks of citizens using modern communications technology.

These are some examples of how processes of politicization and action-oriented political communication can happen and in reality do happen outside of institutional mass communication including journalism. This suggests that the widely used term "mediation" needs clarification from the perspective of journalism research. In our view, it is important to distinguish between medialization and communicativeness. The former implies that the role of the mass media, and consequently journalism by the media, has increased in our societies. Various social actors from the political parties to citizens' organizations need to take into account the image of their actions in the media. Likewise, the citizens are more and more immersed in the overlapping fields of influence of various media that can reach much wider audiences than before. The consumption patterns of mass media have also become more varied as the assortment of media end-user devices has proliferated. In this sense, mediation is an apt term. But we argue that there is also the other side, which may be an even more important trend. This is the increased mediated communicativeness throughout many societies. It can be clearly seen that people exchange action-oriented messages ("come here!," "C U soon!," etc.), current information, experiences and feelings ("he was so ♥♥!") and other private and semi-public messages using a wide array of communication devices. This increased communicativeness typically takes place elsewhere than in the sphere of traditional media. This setting calls for an elaborated assessment of how to define the tasks for journalism research in our era.

Characterizing Journalism: Two Frames

In an attempt to characterize journalism as on object of scholarly research, we apply two frames of interpretation that seem to be prevailing approaches in journalism studies. Both have a common basis in that journalism is positioned into society in a normative way, that is, it is acknowledged that democracy and the public interest are legitimate sources of expectations toward journalism. The frames differ mostly in their emphases, which typically are demonstrated in research settings. While one frame investigates journalism more in the context of social change, the other interprets journalism more from internal changes in media and profession.[1] In real life, these approaches are naturally much intertwined, but for the analytical purposes of this chapter they are illustrative.

The media/profession-centric frame of understanding journalism entails at least an implicit view that journalism is distinct and relatively easily recognizable social activity. The basic characteristics of journalism include most notably (a) specialized agencies, media, which perform journalistic acts such as newsgathering and dissemination. What is important is that, as one result of the economic (and political) development commonly known as industrialization, the organizational models of journalism are based on entrepreneurship. Journalism is also characterized by (b) a distinct occupation – journalism has its doers, journalists. While the organizations of journalism are businesses, journalists are, respectively, paid laborers who make their living by doing journalism. In addition, (c) this workforce and also journalistic organizations, media, perform their journalistic acts following well-established behavioral patterns that have both practical and ethical dimensions. Important features in defining proper journalistic performance are, for instance, certain distancing positioning to the events reported, newsworthiness, objectivity, accuracy, etc. And last, (d) journalism is recognized by its products. Genres in journalism are different from those of other literary fields, and the compilations of journalistic products (newspapers, newscasts, even online news web sites) are easily distinguishable as such, largely regardless of the culture in which they are published (Groth, 1960; Chalaby, 1998; Heinonen, 1999; Schudson, 2003; Pietilä, 2004).

The particularity of journalism in this sense, as something that journalists and media do, lies in the historical evolution process of journalism, both as an institution and as a profession to a dominant form of public communication in democracies. This journalism by the media and by professionals is then the object of journalism research. Undoubtedly, and as has been proved, this approach offers a basis for most valuable studies – but it also has potential limitations from the perspective of journalism research. While noting the historical specificity of journalism (Chalaby, 1998), that is, that journalism was born in connection with certain developments of society (industrialization), it nevertheless often goes unnoticed in this frame, that exactly because journalism was not always there, it may not be eternal, not at least in its currently customary form with its presently recognizable features (Heinonen, 1999).

From another position, journalism can be defined so that its social functions are emphasized, either in the form of theories on modernity and functionalism, or more concretely on the level of the present Western political system. This *society-centric view of journalism* is based on theories of society or on normative theories, but in the efforts to explain journalism these premises are typically combined. In the society-centric view, one approach understands journalism as a public space, which synchronizes "great societies" of the modern era (such as the nation-state) into a common time zone, imparting a shared identity and a joint agenda. In this sense, journalism is a platform or forum of information exchange and interaction, which enables both democracy and enlightened citizenship as its characteristic features. Second, it is also possible to construct the functions of journalism from a more psychological point of view, because it takes place in the uses and gratifications research tradition. Still another dimension stresses the proactive functional role of journalism in society in the sense that journalism is seen to have certain social tasks to perform, such as maintaining social cohesion, and enhancing democratic processes by providing adequate information to citizens (McNair, 1998; Schudson, 2003; Pietilä, 2004).

To describe the society-centric research frame more generally, journalism is treated within it as something that is expected to serve the public interest. This social capability of journalism can naturally be evaluated in different ways, starting from the affirmative acceptance of current journalistic practices and institutions as the best possible, and ending with highly critical views according to which journalism is an agent of ideological control and subordination. But the common feature is that journalism is seen, in a way, from the outside, whereas in our opinion, the media-centric view of journalism is more inclined to study and explain journalism from the inside.

In conclusion, it seems evident to us that both frames are essential in journalism studies, and the task at hand is to avoid an either/or setting and find balanced research strategies. The media/profession-centric frame encourages us to enhance our understanding of how the agencies and doers of journalism operate, thus also allowing us to comment on the performance of journalism in the normative sense from the perspective of public interest. But adhering only to this frame may lead to a tunnel vision of journalism suggesting that public communication other than "proper" journalism is less significant. The perspective of the society-centric frame may sometimes be generalizing, but it allows us to contextualize journalism within the entity of public communication. Even more important is that the society-centric frame is perhaps more sensitive to the emerging modes of public communication which also affect the media journalism but are outside of the media/profession-centric research frame. We discuss these signs of change in journalism in the following sections.

Signs of Change in Journalism

After outlining journalism research as something which alternately applies a dual structure of interpretation frames consisting of media-centric and society-centric inclinations, we want to look into the signs of change affecting our research object both internally and externally. In order to enable the presentation of an at least somewhat coherent review of various trends in and around journalism, we introduce an analytical scheme of the reasons for changes in journalism. The overall context, of course, is society at large, but within that wider perspective it is possible to distinguish four principal clusters of agents that seem to explain the change in journalism. The scheme consists of sociocultural, business, professional-normative and technological reasons.

Sociocultural reasoning of change

This refers to a broad range of factors located in social, cultural, political and even demographic domains of society. For example, the expansion of informational content in present-day life emphasizes the role of media of all kinds both in people's occupational and leisure spheres ("mediation"). Connected to this is people's growing media literacy or media competency in the sense that they have become more fluent, not only in receiving but also in producing informational content ("communicativeness"). As information is flowing faster and more freely over and through national borders, the significance of the nationstate could be diminishing in comparison to transnational or even global communicational interaction.

At the same time, a certain contradictory trend is discernible. According to the ideal of journalism, society needs neutral, non-hierarchical, and open public spaces to which everybody is entitled, with an equal right to express his/her opinion. This ideal can be traced at least to John Milton's *Areopagitica* of 1644: Truth will prevail, but only if there is freedom of expression (Altschull, 1990, pp. 36–42). The question is whether this ideal is still shared by the audience of journalism. Life in a commercialized and promotional culture creates identities that are based on corporate cultures and brands, and not on ideals of equality and citizenship. Journalism will lose its legitimacy as a social space if people do not appreciate neutral communication promoting no special interest – or if they are even unable to make any distinction between marketing and journalism. In other words, journalism suffers in a society where no distinction is made between a private shopping mall and a public place, or between news and advertisement.

Business or economic reasoning

This is a pattern of explanations for change in journalism that embraces various elements such as conglomeratization. Media concentration is reaching new levels as part of the global economic system. Even very small local journalistic outlets tend to become parts of conglomerates which produce all kinds of media products – and, in some cases, much else as well. The effects of these connections are sometimes direct, for instance in the form of revenue expectations, unified journalistic style or controlled political opinion. But most often they are more indirect, stemming from the corporate culture in which journalism is typically seen to be devoid of any social function – or the social function is considered to be merely a part of the product's market value. Journalism is gradually losing its importance as a national arena of social information and discussion, which has also been the cornerstone of its profitability as a business. Political and economic elites use their own non-public networks for information and discussion, and for ordinary folk there are media formats and news entertainment in which centrally planned and globally distributed contents are published in national languages.

The commercialization of journalism has advanced more prominently in small and peripheral areas which have not until recently been commercially attractive. For instance, in a country such as Finland, the most significant trend in the newspaper business has been that it transformed in less than 20 years from a system based on locally owned independent papers to an industry characterized by the presence of affiliated companies of multinational media corporations. Of course, there are exceptions in this general picture, but the overall trend has been clear. At the same time, newspapers have been dissipating the heritage of their roots in political and educational educative movements, and adopted "shareholder value" as the guiding principle of their operations. This change has inevitably changed the contents of newspapers as well: "reader-friendly," entertaining, shocking, and amusing content with colorful visual layout is the goal of many papers. The traditional generic differences between news and entertainment, and journalism and marketing may be disappearing in the process of commercialization. This will obviously have a lasting effect on both the identity of the journalistic profession and the public image of journalism.

In critical discussions about journalism, Orwellian scenarios have been presented about its future: blurring of fictional and factual contents, infringements of privacy, scandals, and integration of political, economic and media power – as in today's Italy. The perils and sins of commercialization have been a prominent and popular theme – let us think, for instance, about what has been written by Postman (1986), Herman and Chomsky (1988), and Ramonet (1999). The popularity of this kind of criticism indicates important issues, whatever we think about its apocalyptic statements. Mistrust between journalism and its audience is a fact which has also been proved in opinion polls. This mistrust is not a new phenomenon, but it is clearly linked with the by-products of commercialization such as infotainment and infomercials.

Professional-normative

The third reasoning refers to a set of explanations in which the emphasis is on the inner developments of journalism, which are often inconsistent in nature. For instance, the rising educational level of the media workforce may have at least two different consequences. On the one hand, "proper" journalists may become more profession-conscious because education is one of the factors that foster the characteristics of professionalism, and transfers them over professional generations. The fact that an increasing number of practicing journalists have entered the field with formal professional education from journalism schools suggests that the features of professionalism have been consolidating among journalists. However, media in a broad sense has been a very attractive branch of education in many countries, and at least in Finland numerous new institutions and programs have been established to educate all sorts of "media professionals." Students often end up working in journalistic organizations, although they do not identify themselves as journalists and do not necessarily have any knowledge of the traditions and social role of the profession. On the basis of their education, they could work equally well in marketing, public relations, advertising, etc. – and that is what they are actually doing, moving freely from one media branch to another. In the long run, this development will make the profile of "a journalist" much more unclear both in the eyes of the audience and the profession itself.

In addition, often – though not exclusively – in relation to new media technology, journalistic work processes have changed so that previously relatively well-established job descriptions have been crumbling. Instead of having the professional identity of a press or television journalist, perhaps even on a certain dedicated beat, a journalist may have to work for multiple media, sometimes in a multi-professional team instead of being a "lone ranger." Convergence is admittedly an inadequate and often misused buzzword, but it actually accurately implies fundamental changes in the profession where the bases of identity have largely been formed according to publishing channel distinctions (Boczkowski, 2004; *Lessons in Convergence*, 2004).

Hence, doing professionally good work in journalism is becoming increasingly difficult. Journalists in the media are caught in the midst of growing pressures emanating from market forces, technology and the public. Not only are these expectations often contradictory in nature, but also the pace of expected change has increased rapidly. Professionals are torn between old virtues and changing working environment (Gardner et al., 2001). One strategy in this turmoil is to emphasize those features that most easily characterize a profession's distinctiveness among occupations and leave aside more complex dimensions. In Finland, the new ethical code of journalists is a case in point[2] In the former version of the code, journalists' role was derived not only from journalistic practices, but also from the profession's function in society with references to democracy, environment, and even peace. Instead, the new code ignores these aspects and concentrates on guarding journalist' rights in their practical work. Thus, journalists prefer to define themselves by what they do instead of what they are in relation to the public interest.

Technological reasoning

Finally, there is the technological reasoning of the changes in journalism. The development of journalism has always been affected by developments in technology, although it goes almost without saying that the effects of no technical innovation have been linear or deterministic in journalism. In particular, business considerations have always been important intervening factors in directing the nature of this relationship. It is noteworthy, that the journalism–technology relationship is also reciprocal. As technology molds journalism by setting limits or opening new avenues, journalism is both a customer and mediator of technology in society.

The latest new communications technology, digital network applications, has had important effects on the media. Since the journalistic media embraced and actually rather aimlessly rushed onto the Internet from the mid-1990s, new publications platforms have emerged, various new journalistic formats, even genres, have been introduced, and the relationship between producers and consumers of journalism have shown signs of changing. Technological change has also been one aspect in the change of working patterns and professional roles leading to the consequences mentioned earlier in the discussion of the professional-normative reasoning of change. Journalism research has widely covered these developments, but mostly in the media/profession interpretation frame (Hall, 2001; Pavlik, 2001; Boczkowski, 2004).

However, stepping outside of the realm of journalism by the media, it is possible to distinguish perhaps even more crucial developments, also regarding institutional media. Focusing on one of the most striking developments that today's new media technology has enabled, namely the rise of public's journalism (not be confused with public journalism), it is possible to describe not only new challenges to journalism, but also prospective areas of study for journalism research. Public's journalism refers here to the fact that new media, especially the Internet and related networks, combined with a multitude of mobile communication devices, are enabling both the audiences and sources of journalism to become active public communicators themselves. It is possible to distinguish at least four types of challenges to journalism that are arising as a result of new communication technology.

First, alternative media have found dramatically enhanced modes, especially in online publishing. A movement called the Independent Media Centre (IMC) is perhaps the most widely known example of this. It is a global network of grass-root movements' information centers criticizing the corporate-dominated globalization process. In their communication, the network makes efficient use of the Internet, offering abundant current information that regularly confronts the mainstream media news-feed. The IMC outlets also openly confront traditional values of professional journalism in that their contributors declare themselves to be activists *and* journalists, thus abandoning the assumed "innocent bystander" objectivity of journalism (see IMC web site at www.indymedia.org/).

Second, various examples of so-called do-it-yourself journalism either by individuals or more or less solid collectives have appeared, with weblogs being perhaps the most intriguing manifestation. Enabled by easily adoptable publishing software, weblogs of all kinds have mushroomed since the early 2000s (Gillmor, 2004). The majority of these are simply manifestations of people's desire for public self-expression, but many are relevant to journalism. There are weblogs that cover important social phenomena on a regular basis, offering eyewitness reports, opinions and comments. Sometimes these weblogs are maintained by professional journalists but outside formal journalistic organizations. In addition, weblogs have also entered the realm of the media industry, bringing new dimensions into journalistic storytelling and, at the same time, further blurring the distinction between journalism by the media and public's journalism.

Third, the number of both local and global community communication practices has increased, often combining new and old communications technology. Some of these communicating communities are virtual, that is, they exist only on the Internet, but real-life communities utilizing new communication options may be more relevant. Self-publishing communities may not deny the value of the media, but they are learning and experimenting with tools that allow them to communicate and inform about their important issues without depending on professional mediation.

Last, it is noteworthy that in the eternal struggle of news management, sources of journalism have found new communication channels that, at least in theory, also diminish the mediating role of media and its journalism. Especially in times of crisis, it is no longer sufficient to control mainstream media. In the election upheavals in late 2004, the Ukrainian mainstream media at first pretended that nothing special was taking place. Quite soon, however, it was established that the people in the streets had other channels of communication and were thus kept informed by the opposition. Another implication is that the sources can more effectively challenge the interpretations of the media by easily publishing original information.

We are not succumbing to technological determinism, but one has to admit that new communication technologies have been enabling forces in creating new modes of public communication outside journalism by the media. Some of these modes complement traditional media in that they acknowledge the importance of professional journalism, but serve some specific interests that the media are not serving well enough. Other types of new communication modes are in open confrontation with journalism by the media, accusing it of being the lackey of the establishment and failing in its duty of serving the public interest. This challenge goes beyond contents of journalism to the routines and values of professional journalism. And last, it is possible to distinguish parallel public communication which could not care less about journalism by the media. It is self-sufficient communication which serves well specific communities (such as isolated religious, subcultural or extreme lifestyle groups), being thus perhaps an extreme example of fragmenting audiences, but in this case turned into publishers.

The Changing Locus of Journalism

Assessing the state of journalism in the light of these signs of change, and keeping in mind our normative approach to journalism in democracy, it can be argued that although journalism by the established media still is an important factor in a democracy, it is becoming hollow in its purest form. Journalism by the established media may well look like journalism in its formal characteristics, but its relevance from the perspective of the ideals of participatory democracy may be minor. Despite of being formally correct, journalism by the media often remains on the level of rituals of publicity. However, communication that often is relevant for active citizenship and which sometimes even meets the formal characteristics of journalism is practiced (also) outside the realm of the media. Thus, journalism by the media seems to be eroding at the flanks (public's journalism) and putrefying from inside (increasing pressures from revenue logics). It is being bypassed, thus allowing room for new diversified publicities (often segmented), of which media publicity is just one. The situation is lamentable both for journalism and society.

Media and its journalism have of course launched some efforts to respond to these challenges using various renewal strategies. One of these is the so-called civic or public journalism, which has striven to change the practices of journalism by trying to tie the agenda-setting process closer to the citizens' everyday lives. In practical experiments, different channels have been created between journalists and their audiences, assuming that the performances of professionals will improve if they are more sensitive to the public's views. Second, media have invested in learning more about their audience. Various survey methods have been used with the aim of identifying the needs of the audiences – usually treated as consumers – even before they themselves are aware of these. Third, media have turned to certain kinds of confidence building measures, especially after traditional professionalism has proved to be an insufficient quality assurance method. When caught out for purveying false information, the media has typically publicly apologized, dismissed some key persons and launched internal inquiries.

These efforts by the media to maintain the status of journalism by the media have sometimes been successful, but their essential nature reflects the perpetual self-sufficiency of journalistic institutions. But taking into account not only the mediation of our societies but also increased communicativeness, it becomes quite clear that the changes in and around journalism outlined here deliver basically two messages regarding the relevance of journalism in the era of globalization and so-called information society.

The first is that the locus of journalism seems to be moving. While journalism as a recognizable activity has traditionally resided in dedicated domains of specific professional labor and organizational structures, the setting is becoming more complex. Internally, journalism is increasingly a product of a variety of occupational groups, of whom many have a professional identity other than journalistic as their professional frame of reference. Even those media workers whose self-identity reflects the ideals of professional journalism, need to adjust to the more indistinct and varying professional roles demanded by increasing cost-efficiency logics. Externally, journalism is facing the challenge of public's journalism, which shows that the media-centric view of journalism is defective because – excluding business-based organizational structures – journalism, or at least lookalike journalism that serves its target audiences well can be practiced outside the traditional sphere of journalism.

Second, the foci of journalism also need adjusting. That the locus of a social function is moving away from its original or traditional domain can be discerned elsewhere in society, too. For instance, political scientists have observed that both the forms and forums of politics have changed (Juppi, 2004). In other words, from the perspective of citizens, traditional political institutions, such as political parties, no longer have the function of sources of identity or platforms and channels of opinion building and expression. Different kinds of social movements, grassroots organizations and communities (real and virtual) have replaced parties as the basic units for social action. Similarly, conventional medical care has encountered various naturopathic and other alternatives. Neither politics nor medicine has by any means disappeared, but they are increasingly taking place elsewhere than in traditional institutions.

As result of these changes in political, cultural and other spheres in society, there are new social actors, agents and interfaces emerging that confront journalism with new expectations that may be remarkably different from those to which traditional journalistic routines are ready (or even willing) to respond. Therefore, although one can say that something like journalistic communication is still very much needed from the perspective of the public interest, this public interest is increasingly articulated in different and more varied ways than has been the underlying hypothesis of that journalism which was born in the industrial age. In addition, the public interest is often more difficult to define than before, and since it is articulated through new channels, it may be more difficult to observe in its nuances.

Implications for Journalism Research

Considering the tasks of journalism research, the setting that we have described here seems to demand more sensitivity to emerging new interfaces between journalism and social actions, and to developing communication practices beside and around professional journalism. At the same time, journalism research should, of course, pay attention to the developments inside media and in its journalism. Combining elements from both media and profession-centric and society-centric research frame, we propose a balanced three-dimensional perspective on journalism (Figure 18.1), which perhaps would enable us to reconstruct the object of journalism research so that the issues outside traditional journalism but relevant to democratic society could also be embraced.

Institutionalized media, having its economic and social basis in corporate culture and in economic and political elites, looks at its audience basically from above. At its worst, journalism by the media brings into the area of publicity only issues that can be sold as journalistic items and which can be seen as useful in the implementation of certain policies, decided in the domain of secrecy. This tendency seems to be taking over journalism and eroding its ideals of open discussion and information into a more ritualistic façade of publicity.

Public's journalism has its roots in the everyday experience and face-to-face

Figure 18.1 Field of journalism research

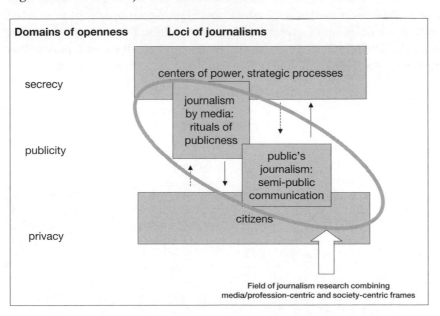

communication of citizens. This communication, traditionally taking place in the domain of privacy, can be brought by means of new technology into the domain of semi-public or public communication. In certain circumstances, public's journalism has challenged institutional journalism and its power-oriented system of sources in the interpretation of topical issues. It has tried, and to a certain extent succeeded, to influence strategic political and economic processes in some countries.

Journalism by the media and journalism by citizens have a lot of common issues to be reported and discussed, and they are in intense and rapid interaction. In practical situations, it is difficult to know who took the initiative and who is responding to it. And, naturally, it is a pure simplification to make a distinction between power elites and ordinary citizens and to assume that the latter would intrinsically be likely to advance democratic processes in society. But for analytic purposes it is important to see the different social basis of institutional journalism and its new challengers. This brings us to some conclusions.

First, journalism as practiced by the media is still a relevant and interesting research object. However, it would be useful to acknowledge, as the starting point, the prevailing discrepancy between industrially operating journalistic institutions and the ideals of journalism. Recognizing this obviousness would carry critical research beyond the limitations of repetitive studies confirming familiar results of deficiencies of journalism.

Second, more attention should be paid to journalism outside of institutional journalism, public's journalism. From the perspective of democracy and active citizenship, many new communication modes resemble journalism in its ideal typical form. By not dismissing out of hand these communication modes from the focus of journalism research, we would open up valuable avenues of research.

Third, in many instances, journalism by the media and public's journalism meet and have influence over each other. Many forms of public's journalism are in some relation to journalism, and conversely, institutional journalism cannot disregard its new rivals. The interfaces between different modes of journalism may tell us something important about the emerging forms of public communication.

Notes

1 These frames of interpretation are inspired by McQuail's (2000, pp. 6–7, 88–90) distinction of different approaches that can be distinguished in media theory, but adapted here very freely.

2 The ethical code of Finnish journalists is traditionally drafted and accepted by the Union of Journalists in Finland which covers practically all journalists in Finland. The code is also recognised by other relevant parties, such as employers' organizations, and is used as a basis for adjudications at the Finnish Press Council. The new code became effective in January 2005.

References

Altschull, J. H. (1990). *From Milton to McLuhan. The ideas behind American journalism.* New York: Longman.

Boczkowski, P. J. (2004). *Digitizing the news: Innovation in online newspapers.* Cambridge, MA: MIT Press.

Chalaby, J. K. (1998). *The invention of journalism.* Basingstoke: Macmillan.

Gardner, H., Csikszentmihalyi, M., and Damon, W. (2001). *Good work. When excellence and ethics meet.* New York: Basic Books.

Gillmor, D. (2004). *We the media. Grassroots journalism by the people, for the people.* Sebastopol, CA: O'Reilly.

Groth, O. (1960). *Die unerkannte Kulturmacht, 1. Band.* Berlin: Walter de Gruyter. Ref. in Pietilä (2004).

Heinonen, A. (1999). *Journalism in the age of the net. Changing society, changing journalism.* Tampere: Acta Universitatis Tamperensis.

Herman, E. S., and Chomsky, N. (1988). *Manufacturing consent. The political economy of mass media.* New York: Pantheon Books.

Juppi, P. (2004). *"Who are we? What do we want?" The animal rights movement as an object of discursive struggle, marginalization and moral panic in Finnish newspapers.* Jyväskylä: University of Jyväskylä.

Lessons in Convergence. (2004). Ifra Special Report 6.30. Darmstadt: Ifra.

McNair, B. (1998). *The sociology of journalism.* London: Edward Arnold.

McQuail, D. (2000). *McQuail's mass communication theory.* London: Sage.

Pietilä, V. (2004). *On the highway of mass communication studies.* Cresskill, NJ: Hampton Press.

Postman, N. (1986). *Amusing ourselves to death: Public discourse in the age of show business.* London: Heinemann.

Ramonet, I. (1999). *La tyrannie de la communication.* Paris: Galilée.

Rheingold, H. (2002). *Smart mobs: The next social revolution.* Cambridge, MA: Perseus.

Schudson, M. (2003). *The sociology of news.* New York: Norton.

Chapter 19

Theorizing a Globalized Journalism

Stephen D. Reese

Understanding journalism in an "era of globalization" means going beyond a general update of news systems and practices in various countries. As with other disciplines, journalism research must confront the phenomenon of globalization itself, and how it leads us to reconceptualize many of our measurements and questions. Until recently, the local, national, and international levels of analysis have been standard ways to organize our studies of journalists and journalism. But the "global" level is interpenetrating, spanning and connecting these other levels in important new ways. A deterritorialized journalism transcends national boundaries, and yet the "nation" has been a fundamental conceptual category in the social sciences, defining comparable units of analysis and fixing them as pre-defined containers for our phenomena of interest. As Wiley (2004) has suggested, it makes more sense to treat the nation not as a fixed taken-for-granted physical space but as a logic, one among many that help to organize social space and global flows (Sassen, 2003). Among the most important of these flows, of course, are media that provide new cultural spaces where national logics are articulated. Traditionally, journalism research has worked at the level of the nation-state or below. Much of the media sociology, for example, has been carried out in the United States or the UK, with the tendency to overgeneralize these findings within a specific national context to the rest of the world. Other countries may be included to round out the coverage of "world" journalism, or more ambitiously compared cross-nationally (e.g. Patterson, 1998; Weaver, 1998). These studies have been useful, but this national container still leaves crucial social space unaccounted for. Transnational ownership, non-national technological reach, extra-national diasporic communities, and supranational governmental forms have weakened the connection between journalism and its traditional nation-state base, leading to increasingly global logics within journalism. In this chapter, I consider how our theoretical work must change in accounting for such developments.

As a condition of modern life, globalization brings the growing apprehension by its residents of the world as a single place, a compression of social relationships, and acceleration of interaction within them. Two major views of cultural globalization capture a dark side of this process: a clash of civilizations view that pits the modern against the increasingly fragmented tribal (Barber, 1995) and a general homogenization, or McDonaldization, of world culture that erases national and regional differences – usually seen giving way to Western, US, capitalist influence (e.g. Herman and McChesney, 1997). News channels from Islamic fundamentalist sources beaming anti-Semitic content into European countries are an example of the former, while the spread of more corporate-friendly global news organizations such as CNN represents the latter. Neither scenario completely captures the broader questions for journalism research. Indeed, the more transparent framework of globalization as it relates to government and information yields a hopeful outlook for the future of journalism as a professional practice. We should look for a universalized global aspect of such a practice, but also consider how it is particularized in specific local contexts. Globalization mixes things up; our subjects, whether media or the professionals within them or citizens who rely on them are connected in ways not fully captured by their specific local setting. When I refer to global journalism I do not mean to suggest that it has replaced the local and national. In a broad sense, no media practice has escaped the transformations of globalization. Even the smallest Third World news agency with access to the Internet has changed the way it works (e.g. Aginam, 2005). So, we can see aspects of the global embedded in many settings, which makes theorizing more challenging. But we can find the global more clearly exemplified in certain emerging zones and practices, which I try to identify. Within this new social geography, I would particularly suggest three related propositions.

1 The reach, interconnectedness, and virtually real-time properties of a globalized media contribute to our experiencing the world as a whole, shaping the intensity and nature of that experience. This evolving media system creates what I describe as the global news arena.
2 Journalism, as a practice and interpretive community, is adapting to this emerging global news arena and increasingly must navigate between its traditional "vertical" orientation within whatever nation-state it is carried out and a "horizontal" perspective that transcends national frameworks.
3 A cultural identification is emerging among those involved with this new global dimension. A professional identification, more specifically, is emerging within journalism, which I argue increasingly shares common norms and values adapted to the needs of a more globalized system.

The Global News Arena

Globally transmitted media images and alignment of news norms encourage a conception of the "world" acting in a single community held together in time and space by the news gathering and distribution framework – with a synchronized and instantaneous quality that mobilizes and enables world citizens to engage each other in an emerging global news arena. This arena has both a spatial and temporal quality – beyond a presumed globally big audience size. The spatial aspect is based on journalism's connection with an audience that transcends national boundaries and geography; the temporal aspect refers to the simultaneity of its use. This synchronization and spatial reach of world communication is what makes a practical discursive space possible, with people regardless of location, brought more or less simultaneously into contact with a global agenda, which even if differing across national cultures is reinforced and aligned with respect to time and focus. So, the global audience's most crucial feature in this discussion is not its sheer "global" size – although it may often be large, but that it has been reconfigured in its denationalized spatial and synchronized temporal relationships.

By global journalism I mean a system of newsgathering, editing and distribution not based on national or regional boundaries – where it is not expected that shared national or community citizenship is the common reference uniting newsmakers, journalists, and audience. CNN International, the BBC, EuroNews, and other 24-hour satellite news networks are perhaps the most visible face of this phenomenon for many, at least English-speaking, people. The relatively small and elite audience for these news products leads some to dismiss their global role (e.g. Schlesinger, 2000; Curran, 2002), although at this stage they may nevertheless illustrate the shifting relationships among news gatherers, producers, and audiences. To this development we may add all the other many news organizations that have been affected by "globalizing" influence. Even ostensibly "non-global" media can now track almost instantly newsworthy developments around the world and must react knowing that their audience has had access to them via other media – making it more difficult to suppress stories. Concerning new Arab news networks underway, for example, Middle East Broadcasting Center head Ibrahim Hedeithy said that no one can afford the secrecy of the past when, for example, Saudi media delayed news of Iraq's invasion of Kuwait in 1990. "In this day and age, if you don't cover the news, if you try to hide things, you shoot yourself in the foot" (Shadid, 2003, p. 25).

The entire world need not be tuned into the same news broadcast, or news products need not become completely homogenized, for us to say that the media system has become more in tune with itself – with an increasingly well defined agenda of news and issues circulating around the globe. Shifts in the attention of the world press now take place at a rapid pace, with various national, regional, and local media reacting to and expanding on each other. Multiple perspectives and interpretations are in circulation at any given time, but still with a heightened mutual awareness, reflexiveness, and timeliness in their reaction to each other. Internet weblogs, discussion forums, emailing, and cellphone technology also channel this global flow of news, expanding its reach and contributing to it in ways never before imagined within traditional community-based news media.

This global news arena means that demands for transparency made of the state will increasingly be made of journalistic practice, as well. Discourses of media critique will be strengthened that appeal to global publics horizontally. The left-liberal critique, with its concerns for public access and challenges to corporate control, becomes more cross-nationally portable than the rightist perspective, given its concerns for national values and how media help uphold patriotism. Old criticism of news "bias" will be superseded by new issues brought about by the growth of global news, where a distributed access to events from multiple cross-referencing sources provides a new form of aggregate "objectivity." In the pooled results of this system, slanted or false reports are now more rapidly challenged or augmented – not only by other news organizations but also by thousands of readers and viewers who circulate, compare, and challenge reports via newsgroups and other online communities.

Perhaps dramatic reports of military conflict, including the war in Iraq begun in 2003, highlight most vividly this new dynamic of global journalism. For the first time, the world has relatively free access to information from the perspective of both the invading power and from the target population of that invasion. During the so-called television war in Vietnam, the world was shown images of battle, but largely from the US point of view. Today, with Arab satellite news organizations, images of American troops in action and civilian Iraqi casualties share attention in the world media. Officials must take rapidly shifting world opinion into account as a crucial factor in the success of any policy. Of course, some governments joined the US-led coalition in Iraq despite public opinion, but in the case of Spain, for example, the government was turned out a year later. Strong anti-war world opinion was not enough to prevent the Bush administration from proceeding to that conflict, but as casualties grew in the aftermath that opinion, both domestic and global, continued to weigh on decision-makers. Concerns remain for the traditional shortcomings of international news – including lack of context, sensationalism, and under-representation of key regions and perspectives – but these faults must now be understood within the context of a larger, realigned professional environment.

Shifting Orientations

As a social process, journalism increasingly must navigate between its "vertical" orientation aligned with its host nation-state and a "horizontal" perspective – a global outlook characterized by more cosmopolitan, pluralistic, and universal values that transcend narrow national frameworks. This fault line in the US context may be seen in the pulls toward a post-9/11 tribal patriotism, reflected in a unilateral preemptive national policy – set against a globalizing, multilateral and decentered world. This is a journalism caught between the globalization from above of new coordinating economic structures and military-based hegemony on the one hand, and the globalization from below of activists and the new inter-relationships of world public opinion on the other hand (Falk, 2003, 2004). We have entered an age, then, where our expectations of journalism in supporting democratic processes must be mapped onto a global platform. Studies of "world" news, for example, typically have adopted a nation-state basis for comparison, considering how the media in one country differ from another (e.g. Sreberny-Mohammadi, Stevenson, and Nordenstreng, 1984; Wu, 2004). The "national" perspective underlies other conventional analyses of "international" news, defined as the movement of media content from one country to another, the residents of which then deem that news as "foreign." Of course, news still is largely packaged and "domesticated" within national frameworks, but a journalism shaped by globalization, I would argue, has changed its alignment to become more denationalized – with relations among news producers, societal institutions, and audiences increasingly deterritorialized, no longer integrated along lines of common geography and governmental terrain.

In referring to this realignment, it is not to say that the global has now replaced the local – just that the nation-state, or even the local community, organizing principle no longer dominates. Nor do I mean that a homogenizing global force floats free from any specific place. Robertson (1995a), for example, advances the concept of glocalization to refer to this complementary interplay between the global and local. As a popular corporate marketing term during the last 20 years, "glocal" refers to the strategic adaptation of global brands to local markets. As an academic concept, glocalization reminds us that the global consists of interconnected localities, which in turn are formed with respect to global processes. An example in point, of course, is CNN, which calls itself the global news leader but which tailors news products for major world regions. Even this localization, however, is produced within an overall context of global standardization. Indeed, the very value of the global news brand, other than deep economic pockets, is that there is a style of newsgathering worth replicating across may particularistic locations. In the case of CNN, and other such media organizations, this overall logic must present the possibility of conveying a picture of the world in familiar formats, sources, and settings that will be familiar to its transnational, generally upscale, audience. Rather than explicitly national or local, this logic must necessarily be "on behalf of" a world community. In a critical view of CNN logic, Friedman (2002) argues that it semantically equates issues of diversity, democracy and (neo-liberal) globalization.

Cultural and Professional Identification

The globalized news system emerges from a network of interlocking relationships, made possible by shared ideas of news codes among the people within it. This leads to an important distinction. The emergence of global systems – whether economic, military, political, or media in this case – do not, as Friedman (1995) argues, necessarily produce a *cultural* globalization process. That requires a global awareness, a process of *identification* to be kept distinct from the existence themselves of global institutions and networks. As he notes, operating globally does not make one automatically cosmopolitan; transnational elites stick together – they may cross national borders but stay well within others: "Living in a small world can occur over vast expanses of territory" (Friedman, 2002, p. 22). Impressionistically, however, one can observe references to "world opinion" and the "international community" all on the rise because the entire world has access to more transparent reports about relevant events. Global elites – even if many operate more narrowly than their border crossing would indicate – are prompted to take on this new identification and must take into account this less parochial and more multilateral world opinion, driven by a more globalized media. The extent of this identification and the shape it takes on are emerging empirical questions.

As with other cultural forms and social practices, I argue that the profession of journalism is changing as it adapts reflexively to various forms around the world. These changes are not just transplanted from one country to another; they interact with local contexts, merge with other ideas, and reemerge to form new global hybrids. The United States is an important – some would say dominant – contributor to world culture in many areas, and it has been deeply involved in promoting American-style practices internationally, including journalism and an accompanying "free flow of information" ideology. Globalization, however, does not just mean Americanization. Thus, press practice cannot be understood solely as a product of missionary work – or even as an imposition of command and control by media owners. It emerges in an interactive process within a network of social relations and interests. Thus, this cultural shift in journalistic roles and norms is best understood within an evolving context of power relationships.

As journalists within these systems continue to engage the horizontal, denationalized dimension, it is important to ask the extent to which they (and their audiences) begin to take on any sense of a coherent "global" professional identification. Indeed, there is evidence of a stronger sense of identification with journalism than ever before as a global profession, which has enabled the spread of open reporting in Latin America, Asia, and the Middle East, regions where it was not typical before (e.g. El-Nawawy and Iskandar, 2002). I offer as an example a recent *New York Times* review of a documentary about Al Jazeera (Control Room). The reviewer said the journalists there cling to a journalistic ethic of objectivity and fairness, trying to navigate between their political allegiances and the code of their craft. More than that, many of them, forthright in their contempt for the American government, are equally candid in their embrace of the values of free expression and open debate that are in notably short supply in their countries of origin ("How Al-Jazeera," 2004, p. B19).

The participation in this arena of news organizations from diverse societies brings new importance to traditional journalism concepts such as objectivity. That is, given the mutual awareness of cultural and political difference brought about by a compressed global cultural arena, awareness of one's own bias increases the need and ability to pursue an "impartial" basis for communication. In addition, a leveling of news practice occurs toward this impartiality with increasing engagement particularly by television journalists in simultaneous and immediate reporting. In these settings, operating with the same equipment, access, and need for instantaneous transmission, technology has unified news routines even across organizations operating out of widely different national contexts.

News Types and Definitions

The global news arena is constituted by a wide range of media and new forms of journalism that operate and orient themselves beyond the confines of the nation-state. It is in part simply the recombination of news for different global consumption, a process that has changed how many news organizations are linked together. Stories, for example, in the *New York Times* and other US newspapers are reprinted in *Al Sharq Al Awsat*, edited in London and circulated in all Arab countries (Fakhreddine, 2003). France's *Le Monde* runs regular supplements reproducing original pages from the *New York Times*, giving English-speaking French a direct view of US policy debates (Hunter, 2003). In addition, a wide range of print, broadcast, and Internet on-line journalism is created and disseminated expressly for a diffused international audience, no longer based on specific geographic communities, which I may more specifically call "global journalism." Certainly, at the organizational level, global *media* may be the most easily defined and described, particularly in economic terms. Global media serve a global market, that is, transcending national boundaries. In this sense, global media are defined as such based on their control by transnational corporations (e.g. Herman and McChesney, 1997). These are real and tangible entities – firms that can be named and ranked by their financial assets. The resulting products of these media, such as films and entertainment television shows, fit easily into this global perspective, with Disney being a prime exemplar of a firm distributing culture in commodity form around the world. The news products of these firms, however, need some thinking through to determine how they best fit conceptually within a global system.

In general, then, I use "global journalism" to refer to that newsgathering practice that orients beyond national boundaries in a deterritorialized fashion. In this sense, it is a concept and not a category that embraces a variety of specific cases. With the term "globalizing journalism," I refer to the extent to which it is a process underway and not a fixed label, clearly distinct from the "national" and "local." For example, in his study of multinational corporations, Sklair (2001) determined them to be transnational, or "globalizing," if they are found to be self-consciously denationalizing and adopting a consciously global strategic view, as opposed to being primarily national companies with units abroad. In this sense, we may think of globalizing journalism as posing an empirical question as to how far along the process has unfolded. It is difficult to clearly identify a category of "global journalists," but clearly to the extent that they work for globally operating organizations they are subject to the same type of outlook, with many journalists explicitly said to need a "global" perspective (the philosophy, for example, of Newsworld, a trade association for international newsgathering professionals).

Hegemonic versus the Cultural

Understanding this global journalism means moving beyond the emphasis on the power of transnational corporate media. It is true that much of the news circulating globally is coordinated by a handful of large corporate organizations based in a few "global" cities, raising the logical concern that these firms operate with implicitly narrow and commercialized frames as to what constitutes appropriate news stories. But because global access to news means there are many "journalisms" available within any given country, originating both internally and externally, a focus only on giant global media firms fails to fully capture the evolving news process.

A "world culture" perspective on globalization suggests that change toward any uniform belief is not imposed but results from a more reflexive arena in which universal standards are taken into account (Robertson, 1995a, 1995b). While this approach might be criticized as overlooking real economic systemic influences, Jonathan Friedman (1995), for example, does not consider the two to be incompatible, arguing that cultural changes must be understood as a product of systemic change. What seems like a disorganized and disorderly postmodern pastiche of cultural forms and identities is the result of two processes: a fragmentation of the global system with its accompanying diversity of local projects and the "globalization of political institutions, class associations and common media of representation" (Friedman, 1995, p. 85). The seemingly disorderly cultural mix in the global arena is brought about by these conditions, which allow the easy generation and flow of ideas and practices, combined with the ability through new global social and institutional structures and media of communication to know about them the world over. A focus purely on corporate economic domination gives little attention to this interplay. Thus, it is simplistic to assume that globalization, only works to standardize and homogenize world culture or, on the other hand, that its main effect is to give local cultures and groups the power to contest perspectives imposed on them and proliferate their own. Rather, we need to understand the interplay between these forces.

While taking into account that much of journalism is produced by extensive and powerful global economic firms, other questions go beyond economic forces to ask what kind of cultural and social changes are taking place in the deterritorialized global news arena. Thus, we must consider the nature of people and social processes within these emerging global structures, decisions they make, and norms they develop.

Global Journalism

So, journalism occupies a crucial and shifting role in the changing institutions and citizenship alignments making up the emerging globalized public sphere. The global news arena has emerged from two major developments: globalization of media corporations in their transnational operation and the availability of technology that supports easy sharing of news and decision-making among news organizations. These developments yield two related research perspectives: political economic and organizational.

Global Ownership

From a political economic perspective the patterns of ownership connecting global media are crucial to their control, raising questions of the intrusion of commercial logic into the public sphere. Herman and McChesney (1997) define global media as a product of globally operating corporations, financing commercially oriented media content for the world's globally integrated market – at the expense of public-sector control, especially in broadcasting. Thus, in this view the globalization of news is defined in terms of the global reach of large media corporate organizations – the firms with the financial resources and internal coordination needed to function across great distance. Global coordination is achieved through centralized ownership by these enormous conglomerates. In addition to US-based companies such as AOL/Time-Warner (CNN owner), Disney (ABC News), and General Electric (NBC News), such dominant media corporations include Europe's largest broadcaster, Germany-based Bertelsman and Japan's Sony. The CNN brand and style of news, for example, becomes equivalent in that sense to the McDonald's arch, a globally standardized and recognized export.

This ownership effect may mean marketing the identical product worldwide and adapting it to local and regional markets. As mentioned earlier, many major media firms have moved to leverage their brand globally. Publications such as *Time*, *Newsweek*, and *USA Today* exploit their newsgathering resources by providing international editions of their product. The *Wall Street Journal* is also global in this respect, with Asian and European editions, including original content with local journalists. The *International Herald Tribune*, now owned by the *New York Times*, may aptly be considered a "global newspaper" printed simultaneously with editions for Europe, Asia, and the United States. Although these products may be adapted to regional interests, the appeal of the publication derives in large part from the presumed prestige (and financial resources) of its parent company, and some expectation of a global and not merely parochial perspective. (The *Christian Science Monitor* has functioned like this for many years; although controlled by a US-based church, as a news organization it has a reputation for non-partisan and non-national independence.) Like the predictable reliability of well-known franchise restaurants, the audience of expatriated North Americans for papers such as the *International Herald Tribune* no doubt appreciates having an English-language paper, but also one that takes a familiar Western-style journalistic perspective on world news. And European readers value it as a gatekeeper for the American view on world events. Emerging technologies in multimedia Internet and satellite television have led to further advances in a globally distributed journalism controlled by a single firm. Traditional print and broadcast news organizations alike have gone online with their work, making it available around the world. Broadcasting organizations such as the BBC, CNN, and ABC News have done the same.

Global Gatekeeping

Global inter-relationships are also forming among news organizations and the professionals working within them in ways not traced directly by ownership. The organizational level in particular draws attention to the practical needs of complex newsgathering and questions about relationships among journalists, editors, and owners – particularly concerning the extent to which emerging consensual norms allow journalistic organizations to function globally. The limited research in this area has focused on television (e.g. Paterson and Sreberny, 2004), which functions easily on a global level because of the universal appeal and accessibility of visual images. Indeed, this universal aspect of worldwide brands, such as CNN, raises concern over standardization against the heterogeneity of national cultures. CNN International has been joined by operations such as the BBC World Service Television in creating a worldwide system of news distribution. Other less visible organizational relationships provide the infrastructure for a globalized television, with wholesale distributors and cooperative exchanges of stories. Within these structures, the global emerges in two key ways: in the top-down control from powerful owners or other elites and in the emergent consensual growth of distributed decision-making among professional news producers.

The top-down control perspective focuses on how a common view may be imposed by powerful primary definers of news. The cultural imperialism approach is certainly alive in many discussions about global journalism, with concern that it will be dominated by Anglo-Western news priorities. Decision-makers in core countries (i.e. Western) still have significant influence over news distributed to the periphery, and much of the world's television images pass through newsrooms in a handful of key world cities. The expense of television newsgathering leads "retail" broadcasters worldwide to rely on image "wholesalers" for video, sound, and information – the most important being two London-based commercial agencies: Reuters Television (formerly VisNews) and APTN (the combination of World-wide Television News and Associated Press Television). In his research on these agencies, Patterson (2001) examined how World TV newsworkers established an agenda and their own frames of reference through the supply of visual images in story form, which strongly influenced the way news was selected and shaped by end-user organizations. Supporting the global homogenization thesis, he found that international news agency workers and broadcast journalists worldwide hold "the perception of a single, valid, and globally appropriate view of news" (Patterson, 2001, p. 350), minimizing concern for unequal flows and cultural relevance. Although this may be a highly functional outlook for news professionals from an organizational efficiency perspective, it is still a source for concern when judgments from afar override local realities. Patterson argues that this structure works to standardize the news agenda, by coordinating world television news through the news judgments of the London gatekeepers who then distribute images that dictate meanings resistant to alterations by the end users. His comparison of agencies shows a standardization of news product due in part to "a universal focus on standard frames of news coverage deemed acceptable to clients" (Patterson, 2001, p. 341).

Globalized journalism takes on a less-centralized, "emergent" quality when examined as a web of mutually beneficial relationships among news producers. The "global newsroom" metaphor helps describe the coordination that now increasingly takes place across national boundaries among cooperating broadcast organizations. In the largest such exchange, Geneva-based Eurovision, decision-making is not concentrated by virtue of common ownership but rather shared among "distributed" gatekeepers in a way that leads to consensus over a commonly available pan-national agenda of television stories. Cohen et al. (1996)

examined this coordination of the supply and demand for news in the form of requests and offers from member news organizations. Story lineups, largely event-driven, were marked by consensus on top stories, and diversity among the others. The authors found this "newsroom" a dynamic culture showing attempts to achieve consensus on appropriate news, while calling into question the particularistic news judgments of individual national news services. National news professionals offered and requested stories that they were socialized into perceiving as having universal interest, because they had to be agreed to by a group judgment.

At the individual journalist level we may ask how a globalized journalism affects standards and professional values of journalists themselves. Historically, journalism is so heavily defined with reference to its host culture (mostly US and Western European) and political context that we have little basis to understand how these "global journalists" will adapt in their view of news within this new system. Research so far has examined the values of journalists in specific countries as they compare across national settings (e.g. Weaver, 1998). From this comparative perspective, researchers have asked – with mixed results – whether journalists around the world are becoming more similar in their professional values and outlook. But this question of global professionalism has been asked with respect to these nations' journalists as a whole, not the subset of more "globalizing" news professionals. Putting professional values within a global context does not mean just comparing one nation's journalists to another, but rather a certain transnational type of journalist to other types. Beyond asking how journalists in country A differ from those in country B, we must now identify emerging standards of global press performance that transcend specific national cultures.

More broadly, an emergent professional model comes about in the gravitation toward consensual values and norms in a globalized world, an adaptation to the changing needs of newsgathering and distinct from any specific nation-based news culture. The global standardization of news through widely recognized name brands and formats would on the surface suggest that news is an unproblematically defined commodity, but the definitions of news at the global level are just as problematic as at the national level. By interacting with their colleagues journalists develop consensual professional values and outlook as to what news should look like – we need not call it standardization, but shared outlook serves a practical need in allowing this system to function. The disseminator role, for example, has become increasingly important to journalists, compared to the "adversarial" and "interpretive," according to Weaver and Wilhoit (1991). Not surprisingly, this role is most consistent with political neutrality and global applicability. As a value, speed conforms to the technological capabilities of news media that increasingly cut across national boundaries in delivering their products (Reese, 2001). Emphasizing speed of dissemination, over other interpretive and watchdog roles, equips journalists to avoid the value implications of news they produce within transnational organizations and to maneuver easily among media. More attention to these news values is needed to see how global journalism adapts in the balance of universal and parochial values.

Conclusion

Globalization has brought exciting developments to the practice of journalism and its potential contribution to a healthy global civil society. These changes also make theorizing and research more challenging as we attempt to clearly identify the units of analysis for precise investigation. One aspect of these changes that many of us would recognize is an emerging global social class of business executives, artists, celebrities, civil society workers, and activists, joined by a related class of media professionals. In many ways such groups as globetrotting sports stars, opera singers, and foreign correspondents have always worked on a worldwide basis. But we need to ask what degree of enhanced identification has emerged among such groups, which relate to each other more easily than they do to their neighbors in whatever their countries of origin. We further might ask what cosmopolitan values or other logic organizes them, and with what implications for the mission of journalism which increasingly is called upon to serve these non-national and non-local communities? Well-traveled academics, such as this author, intuitively sense the importance of these worldwide connections because we participate in them. But, of course, knowing these groups exist and systematically locating, defining, and measuring them is another matter – by definition they are often dispersed. This is just one example of the challenges we face in moving beyond the traditional levels of analysis. In any case, important dimensions of journalism are emerging that demand our attention. We need to be creative in identifying new case study sites, concepts, empirical strategies, and relationships that are appropriate to the global era.

References

Aginam, A. (2005). Media in "globalizing" Africa: What prospect for democratic communication? In R. Hackett and Y. Zhao (eds.), *Democratizing global media: One world, many struggles*. New York: Rowman and Littlefield.

Barber, B. (1995). *Jihad vs. McWorld: How globalism and tribalism are reshaping the world*. New York: Ballantine.

Cohen, A., Levy, M., Roeh, I., and Gurevitch, M. (1996). *Global newsroom, local audiences: A study of the Eurovision News Exchange*. London: John Libbey.

Curran, J. (2002). *Media and power*. New York: Routledge.

El-Nawawy, M., and Iskandar, A. (2002). *Al-Jazeera: how the free Arab News Network scooped the world and changed the Middle East*. Cambridge, MA: Westview.

Fakhreddine, J. (2003). News that travels well. *New York Times*, January 13, 2003, op-ed.

Falk, R. (2003). *The great terror war*. New York: Olive Branch Press.

Falk, R. (2004). *The declining world order: America's imperial geopolitics*. New York: Routledge.

Friedman, J. (1995). Global system, globalization and the parameters of modernity. In M. Featherstone, S. Lash, and R. Robertson (eds.), *Global modernities* (pp. 69–90). London: Sage.

Friedman, J. (2002). Globalisation and the making of a global imaginary. In G. Stald and

T. Tufte (eds.), *Global encounters: Media and cultural transformations* (pp. 13–32). Luton: University of Luton Press.

Herman, E., and McChesney, R. (1997). *The global media: The new missionaries of global capitalism*. Washington, DC: Cassell.

How Al Jazeera is squeezed by its politics and its craft, (2004). *New York Times*, May 21, 2004, B19.

Hunter, M. (2003). Is Paris seething? *Columbia Journalism Review*, January/February, 46–7.

Paterson, C., and Sreberny, A. (eds.) (2004). *International news in the twenty-first century*. Luton: University of Luton Press.

Patterson, C. (2001). The transference of frames in global television. In S. Reese, O. Gandy, and A. Grant (eds.), *Framing public life* (pp. 337–54). Mahwah, NJ: Lawrence Erlbaum Associates.

Patterson, T. (1998). Political roles of the journalist. In D. Graber, D. McQuail, and P. Norris (eds.), *The politics of news; the news of politics* (pp. 17–32). Washington, DC: Congressional Quarterly Press.

Reese, S. (2001). Understanding the global journalist: A hierarchy-of-influences approach. *Journalism studies*, 2(2), 173–87.

Robertson, R. (1995a). Glocalization: Time–space and homogeneity–heterogeneity. In M. Featherstone, S. Lash, and R. Robertson (eds.), *Global modernities* (pp. 25–44). London: Sage.

Robertson, R. (1995b). Theory, specificity, change: emulation, selective Incorporation and modernization. In B. Grancelli (ed.), *Social change and modernization: Lessons from Eastern Europe* (pp. 213–31).

Sassen, S. (2003). Globalization or denationalization? *Review of international political economy* 10(1), 1–22.

Schlesinger, P. (2000). The nation and communicative space, in H. Tumber (ed.). *Media power, professionals, and policies* (pp. 99–115). London: Routledge.

Shadid, A. (2003). Station's goal: the next al-Jazeera. *Austin American Statesman*, February 14, 2003, A25.

Sklair, L. (2001). *The transnational capitalist class*. Oxford: Blackwell.

Sreberny-Mohammadi, A., Stevenson, R., and Nordenstreng, K. (1984). The world of the news study. *Journal of Communication*, 34(1), 120–42.

Weaver, D. H. (ed.). (1998). *The global journalist: News people around the world*. Creskill, NJ: Hampton Press.

Weaver, D. H., and Wilhoit, C. (1991). *The American journalist: A portrait of US news people and their work*. 2nd edition. Bloomington, IN: Indiana University Press.

Wiley, S. (2004). Rethinking nationality in the context of globalization. *Communication Theory*, 14(1), 78–96.

Wu, H. D. (2004). The world's windows to the world: An overview of 44 nations' international news coverage. In C. Paterson and A. Sreberny (eds.), *International news in the twenty-first century* (pp. 95–110). Luton: University of Luton Press.

Chapter 20

Going beyond Disciplinary Boundaries in the Future of Journalism Research[1]

Barbie Zelizer

One thing certain about this era of globalization is that the future of journalism remains uncertain. Journalism faces a list of obstacles that are various and mighty. From its shrinking capacity to maintain economic viability to the unevenness of its intersection with the nation-state and global environment, journalism's role in covering distant events under strange and often inexplicable circumstances is as complicated as ever. Journalism faces a future dotted with as many question marks and unfilled parentheses as points of identifiable declaration.

It is no wonder, then, that the future of journalism research is as uncertain as journalism itself. As an area of inquiry, journalism's study has always been somewhat untenable. Negotiated across three populations – journalists, journalism educators, and journalism scholars – its centrality, necessity, and even viability have always been under some degree of attack: Journalists say journalism scholars and educators have no business airing their dirty laundry; journalism scholars say journalism educators are not theoretical enough; journalism educators say journalism scholars have their heads in the clouds. The heart of everyone's concern – what to do about journalism's future and how to understand it – is shunted to the side as everyone fixates on who will be best heard above the din of competing voices. Underlying the ability to speak about journalism, then, are tensions about who can mobilize the right to speak over others and who is best positioned to maintain that right.

This chapter draws from the premise that one of the biggest problems facing journalism research rests within the inability of journalists, journalism educators, and journalism scholars to hear each other on each other's terms. Resolution of this problem is exacerbated given the uncertainties that beset journalism in an age of globalization. The need to go beyond the tensions and negotiations separating journalists, journalism educators, and journalism scholars is important not only for journalism but for those impacted by its systematic constructions of how the world works. This chapter traces some of those tensions as they have come to shape journalism's study. And in so doing, it argues that the best, if not the only, way to consider journalism's future is by figuring out more fully what we know and how we know it. By tracking journalism's study across, not within, the many prisms through which it has been explored, it may still be possible to more completely account for all that journalism is and aspires to be in the public imagination.

The Role of Interpretive Communities in Disseminating Knowledge

The dissemination of knowledge follows a road that is uneven, potted, and widely unpredictable. Calling to mind a winding roadway on a dark, wintry night more than a fully-lit motorway, knowledge is shared and contested in ways that have as much to do with serendipity, circumstance, and people as with expertise. Adaptation to the novel and unknown is assumed to take place incrementally, alongside attentiveness to its surroundings and negotiation over its terms of reference. This is how Thomas Kuhn (1964) saw the growth of science, arguing that individuals and then collectives develop shared paradigms gradually by appealing repeatedly to those involved in their development. Problems and procedures are named and labeled in ways that can generate consensus, while battles ensue over competing insights that might alter existing classifications. Such battles linger in reduced form long after the new paradigms seem set in place.

All of this has less to do with knowledge itself and more to do with those who shape it, a point addressed by other scholars too – Émile Durkheim (1965 [1915]), Michel Foucault (1972), Nelson Goodman (1978), and Mary Douglas (1986). Coming from different vantage points, each independently argued that knowledge's development has as much to do with social forces – such as integration, power, solidarity, notions of suitability – as with cognitive ones.

Such a backdrop helps explain many of the tensions surrounding journalism and its study. Journalists, educators and scholars all exist within the boundaries – and confines – of separate interpretive communities (Zelizer, 1993b). Invoking the interpretive strategies of like-minded individuals, each group determines what counts as evidence and in which ways, making judgment calls about the journalistic practices worth thinking about and the kinds of journalism research that count. Journalism scholars, in particular, operate within communities that echo the broader disciplinary boundaries of the academy. Their disciplinary perspectives are critical, for they shape both how we look at journalism and how journalism positions itself in the public landscape.

It is no surprise, then, that journalism research has produced its own set of problems, its study developed in accordance with largely isolated pockets that reflect existing academic disciplines (Zelizer, 1998). Although a wealth of wide-ranging scholarship now addresses the practices, meanings, and effects of journalism, scholars have made little headway in sharing that knowledge beyond the boundaries of their own disciplinary frames, resulting in a body of knowledge about journalism that largely preaches to *the* converted but does little to create a shared frame of reference about how journalism works or what journalism is for. Moreover, much of this research is US by nature, standing in as a very limited but honorific gold standard for a wide range of journalistic practices implemented around the world. And most importantly, little of the existing research is ever shared with journalists themselves. In an era of globalization, when so many questions marks dot the horizon, we as scholars need to do better.

Journalism research has taken shape according to three premises:

1 The adoption of new conceptual frameworks has been dynamic and does not end with abstract concepts. Instead, those concepts extend into journalistic practice itself, where they require refinement and adaptation.
2 The forces behind the concepts we develop – whether they are individuals, organizations, professional lobbies, or informal groups – are critical to the knowledge that ensues. In most cases, such forces tend to be hierarchical, politicized, and reflect an enactment of cultural power, hindering and fermenting the development and dissemination of knowledge about journalism in certain ways and not others.
3 No single identified group, field or individual knows all that there is to know about journalism. It is to journalism's advantage to remain an evolving and porous area of inquiry, spread generously across craft, profession and academy, and within the latter across discipline, school of thought, and academic department.

Five Lines of Inquiry into Journalism

Five main lines of academic inquiry into journalism – sociology, history, language studies, political science, and cultural analysis – are under discussion here. Not the only modes of journalistic inquiry – missing, for instance, are economics and law – these alternative lines are proposed largely as a heuristic device that implies more mutual exclusivity than exists in real practice. But the perspectives they provide offer a glimpse of the range of alternatives through which journalism can be conceptualized.

While these lines of inquiry actively engage journalists and journalism educators to varying degree, they speak primarily to journalism scholars. Differences are slight but clear-cut, with each discipline tackling journalism by asking a slightly different version of the same question:

- Sociology asks how journalism matters.
- History asks how journalism used to matter.
- Language studies asks what are the verbal and visual tools by which journalism matters.
- Political science asks how journalism ought to matter.
- Cultural analysis asks how journalism matters differently.

Like all interpretive communities, scholars employing the different types of inquiry are driven by underlying assumptions imposed on each separate examination of the journalistic world.

Sociology

It is worthwhile considering sociology first, because it offers the default setting for thinking about how journalism works. Largely built upon a memorable body of work from the 1970s called the ethnographies of news or the newsroom studies (Tuchman, 1978; Gans 1979; Fishman 1980), sociological inquiry by and large has created a picture of journalism that focuses on people rather than documents, on the structures, functions and effects through which they work, and on the relationships, work routines, and other formulaic interactions involved in gathering and presenting news.

Situating individual journalists within a larger rubric that operates by its own priorities and rationale, sociology suggests that journalists function as sociological beings, coexisting with others through norms, practices and routines (White, 1950; Breed, 1955; Galtung and Ruge, 1965; Tunstall, 1970). Journalists are thought to exist in occupational, organizational and institutional settings that critically shape news production (Tunstall, 1971; Molotch and Lester, 1974). Journalists also invoke something akin to ideology in their newswork (Glasgow University Media Group, 1976, 1980; Gitlin, 1980; Curran and Gurevitch, 1991). In most cases, sociology has favored the study of dominant practices over deviant ones, often freezing moments within the newsmaking process for analysis rather than considering the whole phenomenon.

Sociology has thus created a picture of journalism from which much other inquiry proceeds. It emphasizes behavior and effect over meaning, looking too at news audiences as recipients of a larger mediated environment (McCombs and Shaw, 1972; Blumler and Katz, 1974; Robinson and Levy, 1986), and it sees journalists as professionals, albeit not very successful ones (Henningham, 1985; Katz, 1989; Zelizer, 1993a). While much of this work draws from scholarship published in the seventies and early eighties – and thus upholds somewhat dated notions like "the "newsroom" or "Fleet Street" long after they have run their practical course – of late certain central personalities in the sociology of news have revisited the terrain. Books from Herbert Gans (2003), Michael Schudson (2002), and Todd Gitlin (2002) – plus work coming from new voices in the field (Jacobs, 2000; Klinenberg, 2003) and from the political economy of news (Herman and Chomsky, 1988; Mosco, 1996) – suggest that sociology may now be better poised to address the contemporary trends of corporatization, standardization, and the multiple (often differently normative) nature of journalistic work in its more recent forms than it has till now. At the same time, recent work addressing journalism beyond the United States (Fox and Waisbord, 2002; Benson and Neveu, 2005) may help complicate the longstanding picture of primarily mainstream news organizations in the United States that have assumed a universal voice in standing in for our understanding of journalism as a sociological phenomenon.

History

The historical inquiry of news evolves largely from the earliest expansions of journalistic academic curricula. Central in establishing the longevity of journalistic practice, the history of news uses the past – its lessons, triumphs, and tragedies – to understand contemporary journalism. It locates problems in context, weaving events, issues and personalities across time into a narrative that renders journalism's past understandable. Within this frame, what has drawn academic attention has been that which has persisted. However, the picture has at times been narrowly drawn.

Largely dependent on documents rather than people, historical inquiry can be divided into three main kinds of documents that are organized by scale – history writ small, midway and large. Journalism history writ small refers to memoirs (Reith, 1949; Salisbury, 1983), biographies (Sperber, 1986; Cottrell, 1993), and organizational histories (Burnham, 1955; Tifft and Jones, 2000). Produced by "the first journalism historians" who "had their roots in the profession," these observers of journalism "were trained in neither history nor the social sciences; rather they had often left careers in journalism without ever telling their own stories" (Hardt, 1995, p. 5). Implicit here is the assumption that a detailed individual past can stand in for broad-based historical understanding, an emphasis that has helped set historical inquiry on the map of journalism's study.

History writ midway is work organized around temporal periods (Sloan, 1991; McGerr, 2001), themes (Knightley, 1975; Solomon and McChesney, 1993; Nord, 2001) and events (Bayley, 1981; Zelizer, 1992). Hinting at broader mechanisms by which to understand a specific historical instance, this work offers alternate ways to approach the past, as in codifying the mid-1800s as representative of "the penny press" (Mott, 1941/1962; Schudson, 1978; Schiller, 1981) or of technological progress more broadly (Boyd-Barrett, 1980; Stephens, 1988). In particular, the delivery of periodicized histories has been consonant with the provision of a professionalized curriculum in many US journalism schools.

History writ large primarily addresses the linkage between journalism and the nation state. While such scholarship has been both celebratory of the link (Briggs, 1961–95; Mayer, 1964; Emery and Emery, 1999) and critical (Curran and Seaton, 1985; Henningham, 1988; Kuhn, 1995), it draws detailed pictures of the institutional settings in which the national organs of journalism were established and maintained over time. Often concerned with journalism in democratic regimes, the work here in one view recounts "the heroic and passionate struggle of journalists for a free press, the creation of which ennobles both their own profession and the democracy it helps sustain" (Golding and Elliott, 1979, p. 20).

Missing here has been a more conscious complication of the role that history plays for the craft, profession and academy: The histories of journalistic practice published primarily in US journalism schools with the aim of legitimating journalism as a field of inquiry do not exactly fit the generalized, so-called objective histories that followed the model of German historicism, and insufficient effort has been directed at figuring out how these come together. Here too a focus on largely US history (and its progressive bias) has bypassed the extremely rich and varied evolution of journalistic practice elsewhere in the world (Bromley and O'Malley, 1997). Not surprisingly, much of this scholarship has had to wrestle with the question of who can lay claim to the past. The issue of "whose journalism history" remains to this day a challenge to those doing historical inquiry.

Language Studies

The study of journalism's languages assumes that journalists' messages are neither transparent nor simplistic but the result of constructed activity on the part of speakers. Language encodes larger messages about life beyond the sequencing of events that comprise a news event. Developed primarily only during the past thirty years or so, this work has been markedly European and Australian in development. The combination of formal features of language – such as grammar, syntax and word choice – with less formal ones – such as storytelling frames, textual patterns, and narratives – has grown to address verbal language, sound, still and moving visuals, and patterns of interactivity. In each case, language is seen as a socially contingent and negotiated process of meaning construction.

Three kinds of language study address journalism: informal, formal and pragmatic. Informal study uses language as a backdrop without examining extensively its formal features. Found in areas of inquiry such as content analysis (Lasswell and Jones, 1939; Schramm, 1959) and semiology (Fiske and Hartley, 1978; Hartley, 1982), this work has been sufficiently accessible to non-language scholars to force the question of language's relevance to the study of journalism. Over time it has sustained the recognition of language as a venue worthy of analytical attention.

The formal study of language – found in sociolinguistics, discourse analysis, and critical linguistics (van Dijk, 1987; Bell, 1991; Fowler, 1991) – focuses on the formalistic attributes of news language, such as word choice or sentence structure. These studies have helped set in place a comprehensive, complex and systematic portrait of journalists' patterned reliance on language in crafting the news.

The study of the pragmatics of language provides an emphasis on the patterns of language use in news as shaped by a range of pragmatic concerns. This research examines how journalists structure accounts of reality through stories, narratives, rhetoric, and frames, using language to affect a cause or service a specific aim. Scholarship includes work on narrative and storytelling conventions (Darnton, 1975; Schudson, 1982; Bird and Dardenne, 1988), rhetoric (Jamieson, 1988; Hariman and Lucaites, 2002), and framing (Entman, 1993; Reese, 2001). By drawing upon the broader functions of language, this work helps underscore the constructed nature of journalistic work even among those not interested in language per se.

This inquiry has gone in different directions, with framing largely focused on the political aspects of news language and narrative and storytelling targeting its cultural aspects and particularly alternative forms such as tabloids or newzines (Campbell, 1991; Bird, 1992). Not enough work has been done on the visual sides of news language, and this largely microanalytic work has suffered from a lack of interest among non-language scholars in applying its findings. At the same time, though, its basic premise that language is ideological challenges both traditional mainstream news scholarship as well as journalistic claims that the news is a reflection of the real.

Political science

Political scientists have long held a normative interest in journalism, querying how journalism "ought" to operate under optimum conditions. Interested in examining journalism through a vested interest in the political world and based on longstanding expectations about journalism acting in primarily capitalist democracies as government's fourth estate, this inquiry draws from an assumption of interdependency between politics and journalism. Questions about a so-called "mediated democracy" or "media politics" have driven scholars to ponder more stridently how journalism can better serve its publics.

Following loosely on the work of Walter Lippmann (1922/1960), political science inquiry implies that the crisis of modern democracy is a crisis of modern journalism. Organized by scale – small, middle, and large – this scholarship scopes out a largely normative and abstract view of journalistic practice and is concerned with transforming journalism's actual state into a more perfect enterprise. The tacit assumption is that "if we could get journalists to change how they go about doing their job, the news would be much improved" (Cook, 1998, p. 173).

Small-scale works focus on journalists' sourcing practices and on models of journalists' role perceptions and interactions with the political world (Sigal, 1973; Hess, 1984; Splichal and Sparks, 1994), translating broad concerns with journalism's political dimensions into a finite, identifiable setting or set of interactions. In particular, work on sourcing uses the link between journalists and sources to consider broad questions about journalistic power and autonomy through its intersection with the political world. Concretizing the linkage between journalism and politics, the recognition of sourcing as an exchange of media exposure for information reflects more broadly on the symbiotic nature of the journalism–politics relationship.

Mid-scale works examine journalism's impact on the political process, with particular attention paid to issues such as the strengths and limitations of freedom of expression or the role of journalism in the triumvirate of press, public, and polity (Graber, 1984; Entman, 1989). An extensive literature on public journalism has developed in this regard (i.e., Rosen, 1996), as has work on journalism's optimum role in the electoral process, which considers whether, to what extent and how journalists influence decision-making processes and policies (i.e., Patterson, 1993). Some of this work offers a combined normative-critical view of journalistic practice, appraising failings in news performance against the gaps in existent political theory (Hallin, 1986; Downing, 1996).

Large-scale typologies of interaction target the media's role in different types of political systems (Siebert, Peterson and Schramm, 1956; McQuail, 1987; Nordenstreng, 1997). Largely an outgrowth of post-World War II concerns in the United States over how journalists could best attend to the vagaries and power of fascist governments, these attempts to delineate the optimum linkage between different kinds of government and journalism continue to generate additional classification schemes that change with changing circumstances. The comparative dimension so prevalent here, though, simplifies the nuances and complexities evident in the linkages being examined.

Primarily US in focus and invested in an examination of the higher echelons of power, political science inquiry remains motivated by normative impulses. Often an abstract notion of the public takes the place of real people. This inquiry often concludes on notes of recuperation, emphasizing that journalism should be more in tune with more general political impulses in the society at large. In this regard, when considered from a political science perspective, journalism often does not deliver what it promises.

Cultural Analysis

The cultural analysis of journalism links the untidy and textured *materiel* of journalism – its symbols, rituals, conventions, and stories – with the larger world in which journalism takes shape. News is approached as a complex and multidimensional lattice of meanings for all those involved in journalism. Cultural analysis thus queries the givens behind journalism's own sense of self, seeking to examine what is important to journalists themselves and exploring the cultural symbol systems by which reporters make sense of their craft and profession.

Pronouncedly interdisciplinary and self-reflexive, this inquiry presumes a lack of unity within journalism – in newsgathering routines, norms, values, technologies, and assumptions about what is important, appropriate, and preferred – and in the available conceptual tools. It recognizes that journalists employ collective, often tacit knowledge in their work, yet assumes that what is explicit or articulated as that knowledge may not reflect the whole picture of what journalism is or tries to be.

Much of this inquiry has followed two strains, largely paralleling those evident in models of US and British cultural studies. The former, following on early work in the United States by John Dewey (1954/1927) and Robert Park (1940) and developed largely by James Carey (1969, 1986), focuses on problems of meaning, group identity and social change. The latter, following on the work of Stuart Hall (1973a, 1973b) and developed by a wide range of scholars (i.e. Cohen and Young, 1973; Brunsdon and Morley, 1978), attends to culture by way of its intersection with power and patterns of domination.

This work looks at much of what has not been addressed in other areas of inquiry. That includes journalistic worldviews (Manoff and Schudson, 1986), practices (Dahlgren and Sparks, 1992; Glasser and Ettema, 1998), breaches (Eason, 1986; Pauly, 1988), forms (Barnhurst and Nerone, 2001), representations (Ehrlich, 2004), and audiences (Bruhn Jensen, 1990; Bird, 2003). In each case, scholars target journalism with an eye to figuring out how it comes to mean. Inquiry thus assumes that journalism is relative to the assumptions of the cultural groups engaged in its production, and it focuses on the contextual factors that shape journalistic practice, necessitating some consideration of the blurred lines between different kinds of news work – tabloid and mainstream, reality television and broadcast network news. This inquiry also often stretches the boundaries of inclusion regarding what counts as journalism (i.e. Allan, 1999; Friedman, 2002).

Cultural analysis has tried to offset much of the disciplinary nearsightedness of journalism scholarship, particularly as it connects with new forms of journalism, new technologies, and altered expectations of what journalism is for. At the same time, the field's relativization of some of the originary terms for journalism and an ambivalence about what to do with journalism's reverence for facts, truth and reality, all of which are objects of negotiation when seen from a cultural lens, has limited the applicability of the cultural lens.

Sociology, history, language studies, political science, and cultural analysis – each of these disciplinary frames for studying journalism is singular and particular, creating a need for more explicit and comprehensive sharing across them. Not only would such sharing help generate an appreciation for journalism at the moment of its creation, with all of its problems, contradictions, limitations, and anomalies, but it would offset the nearsightedness with which much journalism scholarship has been set in place. How scholars tend to conceptualize news, news-making, journalism, journalists, and the news media, which explanatory frames they use to explore these issues, and from which lines of inquiry they borrow in shaping their assumptions about how journalism works could all shed light on these questions, which are all versions of what is the best way to think about journalism.

On the Future of Journalism Research

Tracking journalism's understanding across the different prisms mentioned in this chapter is critical, because failure to do so will further isolate journalism scholars from the complexity and singularity of the phenomenon they seek to examine. Understated till now has been the craft of journalism and its unspoken relevance for all kinds of journalism scholars. In talking to ourselves and often at cross-purposes, we may have begun to lose sight of why thinking about journalism is so critical. And while approaching the divergent understandings of journalism – as it takes on different shapes across national boundaries, media, interests, temporal periods, and localities – is difficult, adopting multiple views is necessary because existing journalism scholarship has not produced a body of scholarly material that reflects all of journalism. Nor has it produced a body of scholars who are familiar with what is being done across the board of scholarly inquiry.

This is in need of address, because numerous urgent questions remain unanswered. How can we maintain a reverence for the craft of journalism? How can journalism scholars establish better connections with journalists and journalism educators? Can we tweak existing journalistic models enough to incorporate indices of difference, such as gender, race, class, or ideological perspective, and to accommodate crisis not as an exception but as a rule? What is to be gained by comparing journalists across nation-states, or should we be trying to establish a model of the global journalist? None of these questions can be answered by the offerings of any one disciplinary frame. Rather, their address rests in the spaces between disciplinary frames and the interpretive communities that embody them.

Broadly, we need to examine not only what many of us know about journalism, but also how we have agreed on what we know. In tracking some of the interdisciplinary threads through which we examine the news, we may yet find a fuller way of reconsidering much of the existing scholarship. Doing so may point us in new directions in the future research of journalism, directions that resonate more broadly with the global concerns that face us. As the American Thomas Paine is rumored to have said long ago, journalism helps us "see with other eyes, hear with other ears, and think with other thoughts than those we formerly used." In thinking about the future of journalism research, we might do well to follow his lead.

Note

1   This article is adapted from Barbie Zelizer, *Taking journalism seriously: News and the academy* (Sage, 2004) and appears here with the permission of Sage Publications.

References

Allan, S. (1999). *News culture*. Buckingham: Open University Press.

Barnhurst, K., and Nerone, J. (2001). *The form of news*. New York: Guilford.

Bayley, E. R. (1981). *Joe McCarthy and the press*. Madison: University of Wisconsin Press.

Bell, A. (1991). *The language of news media*. Oxford: Blackwell.

Benson, R., and Neveu, E. (eds.) (2005). *Bourdieu and the sociology of journalism: A field theory approach*. Cambridge, UK: Polity Press.

Bird, S. E. (1992). *For enquiring minds*. Knoxville, TN: University of Tennessee Press.

Bird, S. E. (2003). *The audience in everyday life*. London: Routledge.

Bird, S. E., and Dardenne, R. (1988). Myth, chronicle and story: Exploring the narrative qualities of news. In J. W. Carey (ed.), *Media, myths and narrative* (pp. 67–87). Newbury Park, CA: Sage.

Blumler, J. G., and Katz, E. (1974). *The uses of mass communications: Current perspectives on gratifications research*. Beverly Hills, CA: Sage.

Boyd-Barrett, O. (1980). *The international news agencies*. London: Constable.

Breed, W. (1955). Social control in the newsroom: A functional analysis. *Social Forces*, 33, 326–35.

Briggs, A. (1961–95). *The history of broadcasting in the United Kingdom.* Vols 1–5. Oxford: Oxford University Press.

Bromley, M., and O'Malley, T. (eds.) (1997). *A journalism reader.* London: Routledge.

Bruhn Jensen, K. (1990). The politics of polysemy. *Media, Culture and Society,* 12(1), 55–77.

Brunsdon, C., and Morley, D. (1978). *Everyday television.* London: BFI.

Burnham, L. (1955). *Peterborough court: The story of The Daily Telegraph.* London: Cassell.

Campbell, R. (1991). *60 minutes and the news.* Urbana, IL: University of Illinois Press.

Carey, J. W. (1969). The communications revolution and the professional communicator. *Sociological Review Monographs,* 13, 23–38.

Carey, J. W. (1986). The dark continent of American journalism. In R. K. Manoff and M. Schudson (eds.), *Reading the news* (pp. 146–96). New York: Pantheon.

Cohen, S., and Young, J. (eds.) (1973). *The manufacture of news.* Beverly Hills, CA: Sage.

Cook, T. E. (1998). *Governing with the news.* Chicago, IL: University of Chicago Press.

Cottrell, R. C. (1993). *Izzy: A biography of I. F. Stone.* New Brunswick, NJ: Rutgers University Press.

Curran, J., and Gurevitch, M. (eds.) (1991). *Mass media and society.* London: Edward Arnold.

Curran, J., and Seaton, J. (1985). *Power without responsibility.* London: Fontana.

Dahlgren, P., and Sparks, C. (1992). *Journalism and popular culture.* London: Sage.

Darnton, R. (1975). Writing news and telling stories. *Daedalus,* 104(2), 175–92.

Dewey, J. (1954/1927). *The public and its problems.* Columbus, OH: Ohio State University Press.

Douglas, M. (1986). *How institutions think.* Syracuse, NY: Syracuse University Press.

Downing, J. (1996). *Internationalizing media theory: Transition, power, culture.* Thousand Oaks, CA: Sage.

Durkheim, E. (1965 [1915]). *The Elementary Forms of the Religious Life.* New York: Free Press.

Eason, D. (1986). On journalistic authority: The Janet Cooke scandal. *Critical Studies in Mass Communication,* 3, 429–47.

Ehrlich, M. (2004). *Journalism in the movies.* Urbana, IL: University of Illinois Press.

Emery, M., and Emery, E. (1999). *The Press and America.* 9th edition. Needham Heights, MA: Pearson, Allyn and Bacon.

Entman, R. (1989). *Democracy without citizens.* New York: Oxford University Press.

Entman, R. (1993). Framing: Towards clarification of a fractured paradigm. *Journal of Communication,* 43(4), 51–8.

Fishman, M. (1980). *Manufacturing the news.* Austin, TX: University of Texas Press.

Fiske, J., and Hartley, J. (1978). *Reading television.* London: Methuen.

Foucault, M. (1972). *The archaeology of knowledge.* London: Tavistock.

Fowler, R. (1991). *Language in the news.* London: Routledge.

Fox, E., and Waisbord, S. (eds.) (2002). *Latin politics, global media.* Austin, TX: University of Texas Press.

Friedman, J. (ed.) (2002). *Reality squared: Televisual discourse on the real.* New Brunswick, NJ: Rutgers University Press.

Galtung, J., and Ruge, M. (1965). The structure of foreign news: The presentation of the Congo, Cuba and Cyprus crises in four foreign newspapers. *Journal of Peace Research,* 2, 64–90.

Gans, H. (1979). *Deciding what's news*. New York: Pantheon.

Gans, H. (2003). *Democracy and the news*. New York: Oxford University Press.

Gitlin, T. (1980). *The whole world is watching*. Berkeley, CA: University of California Press.

Gitlin, T. (2002). *Media unlimited: How the torrent of images and sounds overwhelms our lives*. New York: Metropolitan.

Glasgow University Media Group (1976). *Bad news*. London: Routledge and Kegan Paul.

Glasgow University Media Group (1980). *More bad news*. London: Routledge and Kegan Paul.

Glasser, T., and Ettema, J. (1998). *Custodians of conscience*. New York: Columbia University Press.

Golding, P., and Elliott, P. (1979). *Making the news*. London: Longman.

Goodman, N. (1978). *Ways of Worldmaking*. Indianapolis, IN: Hackett.

Graber, D. (1984). *Processing the News*. New York: Longman.

Hall, S. (1973a). The determinations of news photographs. In S. Cohen and J. Young (eds.), *The manufacture of news* (pp. 176–90). London: Sage.

Hall, S. (1973b). *Encoding and decoding in the television discourse*. CCCS position paper. Birmingham, UK: Centre for Contemporary Cultural Studies, University of Birmingham.

Hallin, D. (1986). *The uncensored war: The media and Vietnam*. New York: Oxford University Press.

Hardt, H. (1995). Without the rank and file: Journalism history, media workers, and problems of representation. In H. Hanno and B. Brennen (eds.), *Newsworkers: Toward a History of the Rank and File* (pp. 1–29). Minneapolis, MN: University of Minnesota Press.

Hariman, R., and Lucaites, J. (2002). Performing civic identity: The iconic photograph of the flag raising on Iwo Jima. *Quarterly Journal of Speech*, 88, 363–92.

Hartley, J. (1982). *Understanding news*. London: Methuen.

Henningham, J. (1985). Journalism as a profession: A reexamination. *Australian Journal of Communication*, 8, 1–17.

Henningham, J. (1988). Two hundred years of Australian journalism. *Australian Cultural History*, 7, 49–63.

Herman, E., and Chomsky, N. (1988). *Manufacturing consent*. New York: Pantheon.

Hess, S. (1984). *The government–press connection*. Washington, DC: Brookings Institution.

Jacobs, R. (2000). *Race, media and the crisis of civil society: From the Watts riots to Rodney King*. Cambridge, UK: Cambridge University Press.

Jamieson, K. H. (1988). *Eloquence in an Electronic Age*. New York: Oxford University Press.

Katz, E. (1989). Journalists as scientists. *American Behavioral Scientist*, 33(2), 238–46.

Klinenberg, E. (2003). *Heat wave: A social autopsy of disaster in Chicago*. Chicago, IL: University of Chicago Press.

Knightley, P. (1975). *The first casualty: The war correspondent as hero, propagandist and myth-maker from the Crimea to Vietnam*. London: André Deutsch.

Kuhn, R. (1995). *The media in France*. London: Routledge.

Kuhn, T. (1964). *The structure of scientific revolutions*. Chicago, IL: University of Chicago Press.

Lasswell, H. D., and Jones, D. (1939). Communist propaganda in Chicago. *Public Opinion Quarterly*, 3(1), 63–78.

Lippmann, W. (1922/1960). *Public opinion*. New York: Harcourt Brace.

Manoff, R. K., and Schudson, M. (eds.) (1986). *Reading the news*. New York: Pantheon.

Mayer, H. (1964). *The press in Australia*. Melbourne: Landsdowne.

McCombs, M., and Shaw, D. (1972). The agenda setting function of the press. *Public Opinion Quarterly*, 36(2), 176–87.

McGerr, M. (2001). *The decline of popular politics: The American north, 1865–1928*. Bridgewater, NJ: Replica.

McQuail, D. (1987). *Mass communication theory*. London: Sage.

Molotch, H., and Lester, M. (1974). News as purposive behavior. *American Sociological Review*, 39(6), 101–12.

Mosco, V. (1996). *The political economy of communication*. London: Sage.

Mott, F. L. (1941/1962). *American journalism: A history of newspapers in the United States through 250 years: 1690–1940*. New York: Macmillan.

Nord, D. P. (2001). *Communities of journalism: A history of American newspapers and their readers*. Urbana, IL: University of Illinois Press.

Nordenstreng, K. (1997). Beyond the four theories of the press. In J. Servaes and R. Lie (eds.), *Media and politics in transition* (pp. 97–109). Leuven, Belgium: Acco.

Park, R. E. (1940). News as a form of knowledge. *American Journal of Sociology*, 45, 669–86.

Patterson, T. (1993). *Out of order*. New York: Alfred Knopf.

Pauly, J. J. (1988). Rupert Murdoch and the demonology of professional journalism. In James Carey (ed.), *Media, myths and narrative* (pp. 246–61). Newbury Park, CA: Sage.

Reese, S. D. (2001). Prologue: Framing public life. In S. D. Reese, O. Gandy and A. Grant (eds.), *Framing public life* (pp. 7–31). Mahwah, NJ: Lawrence Erlbaum Associates.

Reith, J. C. W. (1949). *Into the wind*. London: Hodder and Stoughton.

Robinson, M. J., and Levy, M. (1986). *The main source: Learning from television news*. Beverly Hills, CA: Sage.

Rosen, J. (1996). *Getting the connections right: Public journalism and the troubles in the press*. New York: Twentieth Century Fund.

Salisbury, H. (1983). *A journey for our times: A memoir*. New York: Harper and Row.

Schiller, D. (1981). *Objectivity and the news: The public and the rise of commercial journalism*. Philadelphia, PN: University of Pennsylvania Press.

Schramm, W. (1959). *One day in the world's press*. Stanford, CA: Stanford University Press.

Schudson, M. (1978). *Discovering the news*. New York: Basic Books.

Schudson, M. (1982). The politics of narrative form: The emergence of news conventions in print and television. *Daedalus*, 111(4), 97–112.

Schudson, M. (2002). *The sociology of news*. New York: Norton.

Siebert, F., Peterson, T., and Schramm, W. (1956). *Four theories of the press*. Urbana, IL: University of Illinois Press.

Sigal, L. (1973). *Reporters and officials*. Lexington, MA: DC-Heath.

Sloan, W. D. (1991). *Perspectives on mass communication history*. Hillsdale, NJ: Lawrence Erlbaum Associates.

Solomon, W., and McChesney, R. (eds.) (1993). *Ruthless criticism: New perspectives in US communication history*. Minneapolis, MN: University of Minnesota Press.

Sperber, A. M. (1986). *Murrow: His life and times*. New York: Freundlich.

Splichal, S., and Sparks, C. (1994). *Journalists for the 21st century*. Norwood, NJ: Ablex.

Stephens, M. (1988). *A history of news: From the drum to the satellite*. New York: Viking.

Tifft, S. E., and Jones, A. S. (2000). *The trust: The private and powerful family behind the New York Times*. Newport Beach, CA: Black Bay.

Tuchman, G. (1978). *Making news*. New York: Free Press.

Tunstall, J. (ed.) (1970). *Media sociology: A reader*. London: Constable.

Tunstall, J. (1971). *Journalists at Work*. London: Constable.

van Dijk, T. A. (1987). *News as discourse*. Hillsdale, NJ: Lawrence Erlbaum Associates.

White, D. M. (1950). The "gatekeeper": A case study in the selection of news. *Journalism Quarterly* 27(3), 383–90.

Zelizer, B. (1992). *Covering the body: The Kennedy assassination, the media and the shaping of collective memory*. Chicago, IL: University of Chicago Press.

Zelizer, B. (1993a). Has communication explained journalism? *Journal of Communication*, 43(4), 80–8.

Zelizer, B. (1993b). Journalists as interpretive communities. *Critical Studies in Mass Communication*, 10, 219–37.

Zelizer, B. (1998). The failed adoption of journalism study. *Harvard International Journal of Press/Politics*, 3(1), 118–21.

Zelizer, B. (2004). *Taking journalism seriously: News and the academy*. London: Sage.

Chapter 21

Journalism Education in an Era of Globalization

Mark Deuze

As journalism studies crystallizes into a more or less coherent field of study across the globe, one cannot but notice that the education and training of journalists is a subject much debated – but only rarely researched. Scholars have been calling for studies on schools of journalism, on the determinants of journalism education, and on the relationships between education, profession, and society (Cottle, 2000; Reese and Cohen, 2000; Altmeppen and Hömberg, 2002). As the education of journalists is primarily a matter of preparing people for the workplace, the rather singular ideological definition of journalism in most of the scholarly literature tends to get reproduced in its teachings. All too often "journalism" is presented in textbooks or debates as a rather monolithic entity serving certain purposes, providing certain services and working in certain ways in order to tell people what they need to know (Brennen, 2000). However, the professional and academic literature on journalism and its education is booming (see Löffelholz, 2004; Zelizer, 2004). Theoretically informed and empirically driven studies on journalism education are rare (Deuze, 2006). It is this blindness that I aim to address conceptually in this chapter, mapping the field on the basis of a synthesis of some of the key writings on journalism education in different parts of the world, basing this work on three key considerations:

1   Contemporary research on journalism is inherently global in nature, therefore studies on journalism education need to identify shared questions and challenges rather than focusing solely on essentialized institutional or national particularities (Holm, 1997, 2002; Fröhlich and Holtz-Bacha, 2003);
2   The variety of results, conclusions, and insights gained from journalism studies around the world suggests that journalists share a more or less consensual set of perceptions, values and ideas about who they are and why they (must) do what they do – generally referred to as journalism's occupational ideology (Deuze, 2005) – which is articulated and internalized through journalism education and newsroom socialization;
3   Thus, the structure, ongoing development and innovation, as well as the study of journalism education needs to be theoretically grounded in common problems and practices, allowing for practical differentiation and specification.

After briefly exploring these assumptions, I move on to identify some of the key critical debates in journalism education shared cross-culturally, indicating both the issues as well as the process of issue identification as core elements of a research project on journalism education.

Although globalization means different things to different people, in this chapter I primarily consider it in direct relationship to journalism in terms of its political economy (as in the increasingly international nature of media markets, ownership, and deregulation), and its social structure (referring to a convergence of ideas, values, and practices in contemporary journalisms around the world). Higher education is one of modernity's institutions – alongside with journalism – currently undergoing a process of change predominantly fueled by globalization. Fröhlich and Holtz-Bacha (2003, pp. 317–18) signal an international formalization of journalism education and an emerging consensus on homogeneous training standards as key trends in their recent comparison of journalism education in Europe and the United States. In recent decades, numerous examples of international collaborative projects in assessing the wants and needs of a changing journalism training and education environment have been undertaken by organizations such as the European Journalism Center in Maastricht, The Netherlands (Bierhoff and Schmidt, 1997; Bierhoff, Deuze, and de Vreese, 2000); the Southern Africa Media Training Trust and the Media Institute of Southern Africa (Lowe Morna and Khan, 2001); the South-American CIESPAL institute in Quito, Ecuador, and the UNESCO initiative Journet, a global network for professional education in journalism and the media. What becomes clear when considering these various projects is an amazing similarity of problems identified as topics of structural debate in most, if not all areas around the world regarding journalism education. Authors in their respective countries have also identified these problems, such as by Altmeppen and Hömberg (2002) in Germany, Dickson (2000) in the United States, and Morgan (2000) in Australia. As argued in the seminal work of Gaunt (1992) on international journalism training: "indeed, whatever the geographic area or sociopolitical context, journalism educators and media professionals have had to come to terms with the same problems" (p. 2).

A second shared challenge for research on journalism education is to find a critical answer to two distinct trends: first, a growing majority of newcomers in the journalism profession have some kind of formal degree or training in journalism; second, the demographic and occupational characteristics of journalists – including the plurality of their role perceptions and what Zelizer (2004) calls "the modernist bias of [their] official self-presentation" (p. 112) – are increasingly homogenous internationally. Comparing journalists from 21 countries, Weaver (1998, p. 456), for example, found support for claims that the characteristics of journalists are largely similar worldwide. A cross-national comparison of findings coming from surveys among journalists in different more or less similar countries yields results, which to some extent suggest similar processes of professionalization as expressed through the measured characteristics of media practitioner populations (Deuze, 2002). Several authors share this view, observing increasing homogeneity in news, news professionals, and training programs worldwide (Gaunt, 1992; Splichal and Sparks, 1994). What such overall findings and conclusions suggest, is that journalists in elective democracies share similar characteristics and speak of similar values in the context of their daily work, but apply these in different ways to give meaning to what they do (Shoemaker and Reese, 1996, p. 11). The question is, how journalism education in different parts of the world contributes to these significant trends, and how to come to terms with the opportunities and problems this generates for a profession "under the gun" worldwide in terms of declining audiences, credibility, and commercial viability, as well as facing pressures at work in an extremely competitive and deeply commercial industry, forced to adapt quickly to ever-changing market circumstances and an almost complete disconnect between mainstream journalism and younger audiences.

The third consideration underlying this chapter is the grounding of (research into) journalism education on common problems and practices. Education is one of liquid modern society's increasingly differentiated and internationalized institutions fulfilling a specific function that is essential to maintain order within society. As such, it contributes to the stabilization of the profession by producing graduates well versed in praxeomorphic knowledge, which mindset tends to be outdated the second they set foot in the "real" world. Journalism is changing rapidly – and not necessarily toward some new equilibrium sometime in the near future and from which perch it will continue to disseminate its multimedia news. The changes in journalism are reflective of wider transitions in contemporary "glocal" society, characterized by a growing interdependency of the local and the global. No one is outside any more, including journalism – which because of its traditional national bearings is increasingly losing touch with the everyday lived experiences of its intended audiences, who feel either swept away by seemingly uncontrollable global events (terrorism, global warming, worldwide migration, stock market crashes), or hopelessly tied up with narrow-minded and reactionary local affairs. In this context, we must investigate to what extent the education and training of journalists can be seen as a function of either the local, or global. Morgan (2000), for example, argues that ways of training and teaching journalists depend on culture, and should be seen as a function of a specific time and place. However, Reese and Cohen (2000) make a strong case for addressing issues in journalism education on a worldwide scale, claiming that particularly the US model of journalism education has been widely adopted in schools often staffed by graduates of American universities. Research and education are connected to the ongoing professionalization of journalism internationally, as the training of journalists evolves in formal and structural journalism education – a process that can be observed in widely differing stages of development across the globe (Deuze, 2006). It must be made clear, however, that journalism education indeed seems to be professionalizing on a worldwide scale, in which process Fröhlich and Holtz-Bacha (2003) have identified at least two common trends: a process of increasing formalization and (thus) standardization of training principles, as well as a proliferation of cross-national or even global programs, plans, and initiatives to "transnationalize" (Holm, 1997, p. 49) journalism education – as signaled earlier in this chapter. Propelled mainly by political and economical developments – the emergence of regional and global power blocs such as NAFTA, the Organization for African Unity, and the EU – educators everywhere seem to assume that tomorrow's journalist should be able to connect the local to the global – and this ambitious claim has obvious consequences for the way one teaches and contextualizes journalism. In a European context this for example translates to and increasing number of "Eurojournalism" projects (started as early as 1990 by schools in Denmark and The Netherlands), with discussions of issues regarding standardization and the effects of the transfer and integration of values across cultures and media systems this involves.

A worldwide comparison of contemporary approaches to, and programs of, journalism education also leads to a third conclusion: all over the world journalism education is proliferating and differentiating, schools are started, special programs and initiatives deployed, new institutions or foundations erected. The world of journalism education is becoming increasingly complex. At the same time – not in the least because of the trends as outlined above – journalism education everywhere is increasingly facing the same issues. Using the cross-national comparative work of Gaunt (1992) and Fröhlich and Holtz-Bacha (2003), one can define five distinct types of journalism education worldwide:

1 Training at schools and institutes generally located at universities (see for example Finland, Spain, United States, Canada, South Korea, Kenya, Argentina, the Gulf States, and Australia; this is becoming the dominant mode of training journalists-to-be worldwide; some educators, particularly in Africa and Latin America, resist this model on the grounds that it has neo-colonial features, making local programs increasingly dependent on global Western ideas and economies);
2 Mixed systems of stand-alone and university level training (France, Germany, India, Indonesia, China, Brazil, Nigeria, Turkey, South Africa);
3 Journalism education at stand-alone schools (Netherlands, Denmark, Italy);
4 Primarily on-the-job training by the media industry, for example through apprenticeship systems (Great Britain, Austria, Japan; Australia started this way, as this is a typical feature of the Anglo-Saxon model);
5 All of the above, and particularly including commercial programs at universities as well as in-house training by media companies, publishers, trade unions, and other private or government institutions (Eastern Europe, Cuba, North Africa, and the Middle East).

Although I do not want to reduce regional and local complexities too much, the literature does suggest most if not all systems of journalism education are moving toward the first or second model, indicating increasing levels of professionalization, formalization, and standardization worldwide. This is neither an inevitable nor necessarily linear development. Yet this trend is not unique to journalism education, as systems of higher education worldwide are expanding rapidly, innovating and differentiating existing programs, and adding all kinds of new courses, curricula, or even disciplines (Daun, 2002).

Whatever its shape or size, journalism education everywhere traditionally covers practical skills training, on the one hand, and general contextual education and liberal arts courses, on the other. Although the specific needs and demands of the media system differ from region to region and are largely determined by (and are a reflection of) the particular culture and foundation in law and history, the delicate balance between practical and contextual knowledge has always been the main area of attention within journalism programs worldwide. So it is within this context one can locate the program of journalism education research: shared concerns, issues, and debates; comparable developments in professionalization; inter- or transnationalization of education practices; and a heightened concern about the future of journalism education. In the second part of this chapter, I therefore focus on mapping an agenda of global journalism education research, identifying the key debates facing programs around the world when structuring, rethinking, and building institutions, schools, or departments of journalism where a combination of practical and contextual training is the prime focus.[1] I have organized the literature – consisting of scholarly research publications, trade journals, national and regional audits and reports – into ten categories, starting with philosophical notions of motivation and mission, ending with more "down-to-earth" concepts such as curriculum and pedagogy. This organization is based on the assumption that each step or debate flows from the previous step, whereas decisions made on every level function to enable or limit options in the next phase of structuring a program on journalism studies and education. It comes as no surprise that my main conclusion on all of the issues mentioned will consist of a call to arms for more intensive, rigorous, and cross-cultural research on journalism education using the considerations and steps as outlined here as a guide. The identified analytical categories can be conceptualized as ten fundamental questions:

1 *Motivation*: why journalism education?
2 *Paradigm*: what (set of) ideas guides journalism education?
3 *Mission*: what is the position of journalism education *vis-à-vis* the profession and its publics?
4 *Orientation*: on what aspect (or aspects) of journalism is the education based (such as: the media, genres, or functions of journalism in society)?
5 *Direction*: what are the ideal characteristics of those graduating?
6 *Contextualization*: in what social context is journalism education grounded?
7 *Education*: is journalism education a socializing or an individualizing agent?
8 *Curriculum*: how is the balance between practical and contextual knowledge resolved?
9 *Method*: what is the structural or preferred pedagogy, and why?
10 *Management and Organization*: how is journalism education organized?

Each of these issues is a significant area of research and debate, and I consider the decisions made within every category as having a "domino-effect" across the whole spectrum of possible choices.

Motivation

The relevance of journalism education ties in with the ongoing professionalization of journalism (and the discipline of journalism studies), as formal degrees and certificates in some kind of journalism training or education program have become the norm in contemporary hiring decisions made by news media around the world. Weaver (1998, p. 459) indicates that roughly 40 percent of journalists in 21 countries (from all parts of the globe) has a college degree in journalism. A closer look reveals that among those journalists younger than 30 years, college graduates are the vast majority (Deuze, 2002). Considering the growth of higher education, the motivation to start, expand, or innovate a program in journalism education becomes pertinent again. Some kind of training in journalism – coupled with contextual courses – at the university level is offered by a wide range of departments and disciplinary traditions, varying from the humanities, the social sciences up to computer science and library studies. As the average age of journalists in most Western countries is rising steadily, there may be a market for all these graduates when a whole cluster of reporters reaches (early) retirement age during the first quarter of the 21st century. However, such an instrumental motivation for starting or maintaining a journalism education program hardly seems inspiring to its faculty or students. The discussion could therefore be more focused on conceptual arguments for a well-rounded program in journalism, after all: journalism research and education can (or should) help to build and sustain the professional self-organization of journalism, and contribute to the establishment, development, and application of quality assessment tools for journalistic practices. Although many educators insist such lofty ideals are part of their motivation, only rarely are such ideals made explicit, put up for critical reflection or debate. One of the emerging themes in the international debate on journalism education fortunately is to collectively ask the question: "why journalism education"; one can only hope that this reflection goes far enough, beyond instrumental or economic considerations.

Paradigm

The motivation for journalism education is at least partly based on its perceived function as the backbone for the journalistic profession. In its ideal-typical form, and particularly in the eyes of its practitioners and educators, professional journalism is generally considered to be contributing significantly to the functioning and well-being of society. These two fundamental arguments are reflected in the paradigmatic debate on journalism education, as reflected by the choice between preparing journalists for future employment, or rather educating them te become "super" citizens? A focus on the first choice reduces teaching and training to helping young women and men internalize the occupational ideology and practices of journalism, and does not seem to inspire much more beyond that. Shifting the paradigm to the second option, the industry is continuously looked at with a critical eye, instilling historical awareness as well as future perspectives in the mode of instruction. This is not necessarily a debate between practice versus theory; preparing people for immediate employment is a distinctly theoretical exercise as the status quo of the media industry must be gauged and analyzed constantly. A critical perspective on (news) media can be a hands-on program largely based on excessive media use, debate, praxis, and reflection, preparing students to graduate as extremely well-informed citizens – and thus practitioners every employer would love to have. The key here is a reflection on the specific role and mandate of journalism education in today's rapidly converging and globalizing news media market.

Mission

Schools and departments of journalism have to confront a fundamental question when planning and managing their work: how to articulate the relationship of the mode of instruction with the profession of journalism. It all boils down to two basic modes: the "follower" mode, where the mission of the school or program centers on training as a reflection of the actual wants and needs of the profession; and the "innovator" mode, where journalism training is seen as a development laboratory, preparing students for a changing future rather than a static present. Bierhoff and Schmidt (1997) conclude their analysis of these two positions as: "the media industry often says it wants the latter but expects the first" (p. 6). Journalism education tends to be based on a rather traditional and often uncritical understanding of the profession, as defined by its occupation ideology, its history of professionalization, and its self-proclaimed essential role in a democratic society. One could argue that a more differentiated mission might prepare students for an increasingly complex future, if one takes into consideration the combined technological (digitalization and convergence), economical (commercialization and corporatization), and social (multiculturalism and glocalization) changes to the emerging worldwide media ecology. Such developments do not necessarily change the role of journalism in society, but most definitely make the work of journalists more complex, and as I argue elsewhere, introduce an element of permanent "liquidity" to the roles and definitions of the journalistic process in contemporary society. This, for example, means that the core mandate or mission of a journalism program needs to include a critical self-reflective element as to what extent either following the current consensus or spearheading innovative change supports and undermines traditional understandings of what journalism is, or should be. A debate on the mission of a school in this context must also include an analysis or critical awareness of the organization of work in the media industry, especially considering trends such as increasing non-standard forms of employment, (real or perceived) job insecurity among practitioners, and the fast-growing ranks of freelance, part-time, independent, and otherwise temporary workers in the news business. Sennett's "culture of the new capitalism" extends into journalism, and thus begs the question how its educators effectively prepare students for survival.

Orientation

Journalism students generally are trained in sequences, based on the premise that different media – television, newspaper, magazine, radio, Internet – each have distinctly different characteristics, leading to different types of journalism. This is only true if one embraces a strictly instrumental and technodeterminist definition of journalism – an approach that tends to reduce journalists to "button-pushers," media workers who understand *how*, but not *why*. The literature does offer other orientations for journalism education, for example sequencing the program along functions of news – information, opinion, criticism, entertainment – or genres and domains of journalism – "hard" versus "soft" news, human interest versus investigative reportage, the beat system, and so on. There is much to say for each of these orientations, but all suffer from the same problem: they tend to reify and essentialize the existing ideas, values, and practices within the constructed sequence, while ignoring the ongoing hybridization and convergence of such genres, media types, and domains of the media. The recent proliferation of studies and books such as this, offering fundamental overviews and analyses on what the definitions and meanings of journalism and news are (see Löffelholz (2004) in Germany, Deuze (2004) in The Netherlands, and Zelizer (2004) in the United States, for example) clearly suggests as a new orientation for journalism education a critical focus on a perceived "core" set of values, ideas and practices of journalism independent of media, delegating the particulars of possible sequences to the background.

Direction

Contemporary studies in the field of media labor, work, and occupations suggest the direction of education and training should move toward the preparation of students for a "portfolio worklife," arguing that the contemporary professional does not build a career within one organization or by doing one thing really well – he or she switches regularly from employer to employer, within and between companies and media, whereas the quality of his or her work tends to be defined by the diversity and richness of their collection of skills and achievements (Deuze, 2007). This pattern of career-building and employment is typical for today's economy and especially its knowledge and information workers, and indeed is already visible among newcomers in journalism around the world: they switch between newsrooms, departments, and media more in five years than their senior colleagues have done in twenty years. This brings new life to the debate between whether a school or program of journalism education should train specialists or generalists. This debate needs specification: a practitioner may be specialized in a "hot" topic (such as foreign policy, movie celebrity, lifestyle economy), a medium (print, electronic, online), or even a genre. Again, the range of answers to these questions should be considered in the context of the previous issues. If the orientation of a school of journalism is the medium, the graduating student is more likely to be a good newspaper or television reporter (as radio tends to be an underserved sequence, while the Internet still is an underdetermined track), rather than a news worker who has the skills, knowledge, and critical-reflective attitude necessary to survive in today's converging and competitive media market. Yet someone who knows a little bit of everything while not being particularly skilled in any medium, may find it equally hard to find employment – as most media organizations seem to be looking for an excellent person in one medium who understands and can work together with colleagues from other parts of the company (including but not limited to marketing and acquisition). Research in journalism education should identify different ways to translate global trends in the industry with local particulars – such as the mission, orientation, and direction of the school or program in question.

Contextualization

A discussion on issues facing journalism education is not so much a debate on curricular matters – *what* to teach – or pedagogical matters – *how* to teach. Issues common to journalism education on a global level, for example, should include an analysis and discussion of how the various ways to organize the training of journalists can be linked with developments in society on a local as well as transnational level. This understanding is based on the assumption that journalism cannot exist independent of *community*; it is a profession interacting with society in many – and not wholly unproblematic – ways, and should therefore be seen as influencing and operating under the influence of what happens in society (Kovach and Rosenstiel, 2001). Community in this content must be understood as a source of diversity, difference, and "strangehood," rather than in its more common application as a place characterized by an absence of difference. Just as the news organization cannot maintain itself completely distanced or independent from society, a school of journalism also has to define ways to culturally and thematically contextualize its program. In terms of this book a meaningful context could be the global-local nexus, including a distinctly international teaching agenda. Students would be confronted in all matters by the cross-cultural or transnational nature of what they are learning. Contextualizing journalism education can go into many different directions. Next to globalization, one could also think of the multicultural society, featuring themes such as social and cultural complexity, inclusivity, and diversity awareness. Digitalization of media is another possible context, with possible themes like computer-assisted reporting, multimedia news production, desktop publishing, tactical media use, and what Atton (2004, p. 25) calls "radical online journalism." Finally, a focus on the ongoing corporate colonization of newsrooms opens up curricular possibilities for issues like infotainment, tabloid journalism, and the commodification of news. Delegating such contexts to elective coursework or ignoring them altogether may not be a feasible strategy if one's goal is to adequately prepare the student for a professional role in contemporary society.

Education

Paraphrasing Rorty (1999 [1989], p. 117), education refers to two entirely distinct, and equally necessary processes: socialization and individualization. Before students can be educated for freedom, Rorty argues, the constraints of the consensual knowledge of the day have to be imposed. Freedom in this context means self-creation through a cultivating of imagination, doubt, and critical self-reflection. In journalism education, authors as diverse as Glasser (1992) in the United States, Blöbaum (2000) and Weischenberg (2001) in Germany, and Rhoodie (1995) in South Africa, have made similar claims in the past, advocating the training of "reflective practitioners" and an integration of theory and practice in the journalism curriculum. However, influential arguments have been made in the UK by Herbert (2000) or in the United States by Medsger (1996) for a more professional and vocational focus on journalism education, preferably supported by the media industry. The latter view continues the role of education as a socializing agent from secondary into tertiary education, whereas the first sees teaching as a way to help students to develop their own voice in the field – much in line with philosophical notions of journalism as an act of individual freedom and responsibility, rather than a social system located in and managed by corporate media. Ultimately, Rorty calls on colleges to offer a blend of specialized vocational training and provocation to self-creation. The particulars of such a mix are our key concern here: where does the socialization into media sequences (each with their own historically grown and carefully cultivated formulas and legends) stop, and does the individualization of the "free minds" that journalists are supposed to be (in their self-image and shared definitions of legitimacy) begin? It could be argued that much of the decision-making on such issues is determined by cultural and historical factors – and thus should become a prime venue of careful and considered journalism education research.

Curriculum

Most of the literature on journalism education starts here: the curriculum. Many scholars, educators, and media practitioners thus conveniently ignore the forces and decisions that defined the parameters within which any discussion of curricular matters takes place. This also means that there are plenty of tools available for conceptualizing and theorizing the journalism curriculum. As mentioned earlier, most of the literature draws a clear line between practical and contextual knowledge. But this seemingly clearcut distinction is questioned by many, if only because of the impossibility to articulate where "context" stops and "practice" begins. Kovach and Rosenstiel (2001), for example, effectively argue that newsgathering is meaningless without putting the "facts" in a more or less coherent or at least thematic context. Morgan (2000) rephrases this dichotomy as a combination of procedural and propositional knowledge plus a professional capability to enact this knowledge, thereby solving the problem of drawing boundaries between two interconnected sets of values, idea(l)s, and practices. Weischenberg (1990) offers one of the most complex and articulate approaches to what he calls the ideal-typical journalistic competence, defining three particular domains: *Fach-Kompetenz*, *Vermittlungs-Kompetenz*, and *Sach-Kompetenz*. The first domain consists of instrumental skills (such as reporting, writing, and editing), and knowledge about journalism: media economy, law, and history. In the second domain the student learns articulation skills: how to present information and news (genres, formulas, conventions, design, and so on). Third, the curriculum includes elective and required courses on a variety of special topics like sociology, political science, financial economy, but also social-scientific research methods. To this mix, Weischenberg adds what he describes as *Nachdenken über journalistisches Handeln*: reflection on role and function of journalism in society.

Beyond such a theory versus practice set of considerations, one must consider the purpose, form, and content of the curriculum. Carr (2003, p. 133) identifies three core issues in the debate about curriculum: purpose, form, and content. In terms of purpose, a delicate balance must be achieved between more or less objective criteria for inclusion of courses, approaches, or topics, and taking into consideration the cultural, historical, and geographical factors that determine educational value. Regarding the form of the curriculum, the literature generally takes issue with teaching as a way to coherently build up knowledge about a subject, as reflected by moving groups of students through increasingly advanced courses featuring roughly similar topics and skills. Another approach is the more progressive ideal of allowing students to chart their own path through the curriculum, including an emphasis on doing coursework outside of journalism. All over the world, a second debate can be identified on the uses and merits of experiential education, or "learning by doing": stimulating or even requiring students to take internships and apprenticeships in mainstream news media organizations, and engaging them in the production of campus media (maintaining a newspaper, web site, radio and television broadcasts intended for students, faculty and staff). For Blöbaum (2000) the in-house production of campus media is the ideal meeting place for theory and praxis, for others it is a costly waste of faculty time and resources, taking time and money away from teaching and research.

Finally, decisions regarding the curriculum also bear on the conceptualization of journalism education in terms of evaluative assessments of the students' process and performance. Standards have to be matched by those maintained in the industry (which are never exactly the same), the academe (where learning goals and objectives must be identified), and those implicated by a choice for either formal standardization across cultures and media, or course-by-course or even individual case-by-case assessments.

Method, management and organization

Because of the delicate balance between practical and contextual knowledge offered in journalism education worldwide, each school and program tends to combine different methods of teaching. Considering the proliferation of schools and the professionalization of the discipline, debates on pedagogical matters in journalism education seem to get more attention. One important discussion involves tensions between advocates of standardized methods (including testing, coursework, and pedagogy) and those who emphasize a culture of learning rather than teaching (emphasizing the importance of individual expression, exposure to much more than just the consensual knowledge of the day). The first kind of mindset seems to be on the upper hand – which indeed stems in part from the increasing commodification and massification of higher education. As enrolment in journalism programs continues to rise and the number of schools is growing, one should critically investigate the consequences this has, as systems of mass education tend to promote a product-oriented teaching culture instead of a process-focused learning culture. If the structure of higher education reinforces a focus on product rather than process, on student output rather than input, something might be lost along the way. The teaching and pedagogy debate also becomes more salient because of the convergence of media technologies, formats, genres, and structures of ownership in the industry (and thus the corresponding training and educating models). Several studies show how a shift toward a "converged" curriculum challenges the existing ways of doing things in schools of journalism, in particular breaking down the boundaries between formerly distinct departments, sequences, or tracks (Bromley and Purdey, 2001). A third important trend is the growing UK and US influence on higher education worldwide (Daun, 2002). Again, an in-depth study of journalism education must interrogate the profound consequences this has – in terms of opportunities as well as threats. If one links ongoing standardization with increasing Anglo-American influence, a picture of globalized and standardized education emerges that begs research as well as a fundamental critique of its premises regarding the role and function of journalism in society.

Conclusion

In an earlier research project on the various ways in which new media and journalism schools in Europe addressed innovation, we concluded that educators in different countries need to engage in a dialogue – with each other as well as the industry (Bierhoff et al., 2000). Although this advice has been voiced in the past, we identified two significant problems for doing so: the general lack of vision and systematic investigation of (old and new) training models. It certainly seems schools and programs of journalism education all over the world are changing fast, trying to keep up with the at times conflicting wishes of industry and academy, accommodating increasing student numbers with widely varying expectations, while at the same time trying to develop some kind of coherence in the curriculum. There can be no doubt that the world of journalism education faces critical issues in this process of adaptation and change. The biggest threat to any meaningful consideration of the issues outlined in this chapter is twofold. First, as journalism scholars, students, and administrators alike we tend to implicitly assume that whatever changes and challenges are confronting the discipline, these will at some point in the near or distant future crystallize, at which time some kind of new equilibrium can be established. This false assumption creeps in to most discourse surrounding the policies of change in journalism education, as it offers the comfort of "all will be well" in the future as long as "we keeping doing what we do best," which is exactly the same as we did yesterday. The second fallacy is the assumption that the various tension points in the conceptual approach to journalism education outlined in this chapter can be easily resolved by claiming that "we do all of that already," which not only is impossible (as different answers to these questions lead to vastly different kinds of programs), but would also be testament to the criticism that in our society our critical self-reflection does not go deep enough. The fallacy of much work in journalism education is that it uses critical interrogation to reinforce existing, consensual, and praxeomorphic ways of doing things, assuming that the status quo is, all things considered, the ideal one.

Journalism has professionalized to the extent that it has its own body of knowledge as exemplified by this book; so, paraphrasing Reese and Cohen (2001), the scholarship of journalism education has to professionalize accordingly. This chapter should therefore be seen as an attempt to chart salient issues for an agenda of research and discussion on journalism education in globalized era.

Note

1   A note on the history of this conceptual model for analyzing and rethinking journalism education must be made. I was invited to present a first version of this model under the title "Educating new journalists" at the AEJMC Convention of August 9, 2002 in Miami; an abbreviated version of that talk was published that same year in *Ecquid Novi*, 23(1), pp. 89–93. Encouraged by the feedback I received from several colleagues around the world, I kept on working on the model and on its assumptions about the foundations of a "global" journalism education debate, which lead to an extended paper that was included in the 4th edition of J. C. Merrill and A. S. De Beer (eds.), *Global journalism: Survey of international communication*, pp. 145–58, New York: Longman. For the current volume, I decided to further explore the implications of the model, while adding analyses on the changing nature of newswork and the professionalization of higher education around the world. A first draft of that work, titled "Global journalism education: A conceptual approach," was published in *Journalism Studies* 7(1), pp. 19–34, and parts of that paper are reproduced here with kind permission.

References

Altmeppen, K.-D., and Hömberg, W. (eds.) (2002). *Journalistenausbildung für eine veränderte Medienwelt* [*Journalism education for a changing media world*]. Wiesbaden: Westdeutscher Verlag.

Atton, C. (2004). *An alternative Internet: radical media, politics and creativity*. Edinburgh: Edinburgh University Press.

Bierhoff, J., and Schmidt, M. (eds.) (1997). *European journalism training in transition: The inside view.* Maastricht: European Journalism Centre.

Bierhoff, J., Deuze, M., and de Vreese, C. (2000). *Media innovation, professional debate and media training: A European analysis.* Maastricht: European Journalism Centre.

Blöbaum, B. (2000). *Zwischen Redaktion und Reflexion: Integration von Theorie und Praxis in der Journalistenausbildung* [*Between news editing and reflection: Integration of theory and practice in journalism education*]. Munster: LIT.

Brennen, B. (2000). What the hacks say: The ideological prism of US journalism texts. *Journalism*, 1(1), 106–13.

Bromley, M., and Purdey, H. (2001). Chilling out: but not yet "cool." New media training in a UK journalism school: a further report on "journomorphosis." *Convergence*, 7(3), 104–15.

Carr, D. (2003). *Making sense of education.* London: Routledge.

Cottle, S. (2000). New(s) times: towards a "second wave" of news ethnography. *Communications*, 25(1), 19–41.

Daun, H. (ed.) (2002). *Educational restructuring in the context of globalization and national policy.* London: Routledge.

Deuze, M. (2002). National news cultures: Towards a profile of journalists using cross-national survey findings. *Journalism & Mass Communication Quarterly*, 79(1), 134–49.

Deuze, M. (2004). *Wat is journalistiek?* [*What is journalism?*]. Amsterdam: Het Spinhuis.

Deuze, M. (2005). What is journalism? Professional identity and ideology of journalists reconsidered. *Journalism Theory Practice and Criticism*, 6(4), 443–65.

Deuze, M. (2006). Global journalism education: A conceptual approach. *Journalism Studies*, 7(1), 19–34.

Deuze, M. (2007). *Media work.* Cambridge, UK: Polity Press.

Dickson, T. (2000). *Mass media education in transition: Preparing for the 21st century.* Mahwah, NJ: Lawrence Erlbaum Associates.

Fröhlich, R., and Holtz-Bacha, C. (eds.) (2003). *Journalism education in Europe and North America: A structural comparison.* Cresskill, NJ: Hampton Press.

Gaunt, P. (1992). *Making the newsmakers: International handbook on journalism training.* Westport, CT: Greenwood Press.

Glasser, T. (1992). Professionalism and the derision of diversity: The case of the education of journalists. *Journal of Communication*, 42(2), 131–40.

Herbert, J. (2000). The changing face of journalism education in the UK. *Asia Pacific Media Educator*, 8, 113–23.

Holm, H. (1997). Educating journalists for a new Europe. In J. Bierhoff and M. Schmidt (eds.), *European journalism training in transition* (pp. 47–50). Maastricht: European Journalism Centre.

Holm, H. (2002). The forgotten globalization of journalism education. *Journalism and Mass Communication Educator*, 56(4), 67–71.

Kovach, B., and Rosenstiel, T. (2001). *The Elements of Journalism.* New York: Crown Publishers.

Löffelholz, M. (ed.) (2004). *Theorien des Journalismus* [*Theories of journalism*]. Opladen: Westdeutscher Verlag.

Lowe Morna, C., and Khan, Z. (2001). *Media training needs assessment for Southern Africa.* Amsterdam: Netherlands Institute for Southern Africa.

Medsger, B. (1996). *Winds of change: Challenges confronting journalism education.*

The Freedom Forum Report. Retrieved July 14, 1999, from www.freedomforum.org/freedomforum/resources/journalism/journalism_edu/winds_of_change/

Morgan, F. (2000). Recipes for success: Curriculum for professional media education. *Asia Pacific Media Educator*, 8, 4–21.

Reese, S., and Cohen, J. (2000). Educating for journalism: The professionalism of scholarship. *Journalism Studies*, 1(2), 213–27.

Rhoodie, D. (1995). News-editorial journalism education at higher education institutions in the USA and the RSA. *Ecquid Novi*, 16(1/2), 136–45.

Rorty, R. (1999 [1989]). Education as socialization and as individualization. In *Philosophy and social hope* (pp. 114–26). London: Penguin.

Shoemaker, P., and Reese, S. (1996). *Mediating the message: Theories of influences on mass media content.* New York: Longman.

Weaver, D. H. (ed.) (1998). *The global journalist: News people around the world.* Cresskill, NJ: Hampton Press.

Weischenberg, S. (1990). *Journalismus und Kompetenz. Qualifizierung und Rekrutierung für Medienberufe* [Journalism and competence. Education and "recruitment" for media professions]. Opladen: Westdeutscher Verlag.

Weischenberg, S. (2001). Das Ende einer Ära? Aktuelle Beobachtungen zum Studium des künftigen Journalismus [The end of an era? Contemporary observations of the study of future journalism]. In H. Kleinsteuber (ed.), *Aktuelle Medientrends in den USA* [Contemporary media trends in the USA] (pp. 61–82). Opladen: Westdeutscher Verlag.

Zelizer, B. (2004). *Taking journalism seriously: News and the academy.* London: Sage.

Part VI

Conclusions

Chapter 22

Global Journalism Research
Summing Up and Looking Ahead

David Weaver and Martin Löffelholz

It is clear that scholars of journalism in these early years of the 21st century have a wide array of choices when designing and carrying out journalism research. The chapters in this book have introduced various theories and approaches, methods, findings, and future considerations for studying journalism and journalists in this age of increasing globalization. We have mapped the terrain of journalism studies and provided some specific examples, not only for scholars of journalism but also for those who are merely interested in how journalism has been studied in different areas of the world.

Theories

The structures and functions of journalism as a social entity, and the opinions and behavior of individual journalists, can be explained on several different levels ranging from the societal and cultural to the organizational and individual, and also in terms of key characteristics of journalists such as gender. It should be emphasized that these are not necessarily mutually exclusive theoretical approaches. Rather they complement and influence one another. The psychological characteristics of journalists may interact with organizational, societal and cultural variables to influence the practice of journalism in any given cultural, societal or organizational setting.

In his overview on journalism theories, Martin Löffelholz describes journalism studies as a pluralistic, differentiated and dynamic field of research in the broader area of communication science. The theoretical perspectives used in journalism research across the globe range from normative approaches and middle-range theories, to organizational and integrative social theories as well as gender and cultural studies. Overall, Löffelholz identifies and describes six basic theoretical concepts of journalism: normative individualism, analytical empiricism, theories of action, systems theories, integrative social theories, and cultural studies.

Based upon the large number and heterogeneity of the theoretical approaches that developed due to the growing relevance of communicator research worldwide, Löffelholz concludes that the current theoretical discourse on journalism is multidimensional as the development of journalism theories follows neither the linear-cumulative understanding of theoretical emergence introduced by the English philosopher Francis Bacon, nor the regular sequence of normal and revolutionary phases proposed by Thomas Kuhn. Since the progress of journalism theories is not based on the substitution of "outdated" theories, but on the gain in complexity through the emergence of new theories and modification of older theories, Löffelholz sees journalism studies rather as an intermittent development of a multiple perspective.

Accordingly, Manfred Rühl mentions in his chapter that some theoreticians believe that older journalism theories are obsolete in the era of the globalization and the Internet, but the truth is: "Quite the reverse!" Particularly theoretical macro conceptions derived from classical sociological approaches developed by Émile Durkheim, Georg Simmel, Robert E. Park, Talcott Parsons, and Niklas Luhmann are helpful to understand better the function of journalism in an increasingly globalized society. For the purposes of his chapter, Rühl focuses primarily on the ideas of the German sociologist Niklas Luhmann, who is not known as a journalism researcher but has a growing impact on present day journalism research.

Rühl, who is considered the pioneer in introducing societal system theories to journalism studies, describes systems theories as an invitation to open up the study of journalism as a system of society and as decision-making organizations. Unlike approaches focusing entirely on journalists as individuals, societal system theories are analyzing journalistic producers and journalistic recipients as social role structures in world society's journalism. From this point of view, journalism cannot be reduced to single journalists but needs to be analyzed as a social system. The basic elements of social systems are neither actors nor specific individuals but communications. Therefore, journalists are not constituents of social systems but "important external co-performers for communication systems" such as journalism.

Societal as well as cultural approaches to journalism are based on the assumption that journalists as individuals are somehow connected to macro aspects of journalism such as economic or political factors. John Hartley argues in his chapter on the cultural approach to journalism that we need to analyze the subjectivity of readers and audiences in order to assess "the ideological, political, and economic impact of news media, as part of the apparatus of global corporate communications." Specifically, the cultural approach to journalism is trying to describe the textual relations between media corporations or government agencies with "emancipation-seeking addressees" such as audiences or readers.

After opening his chapter with an account of how cultural studies have approached journalism as an object of study, Hartley proposes that "journalism should not be seen as a professional practice at all but as a human right." Contrary to the actual state of journalism research as well as to the self description of the journalistic profession, he argues that following Article 19 of the Universal Declaration of Human Rights everyone has the right not only to seek and receive but to communicate information and, therefore, may be considered a journalist. Hartley believes that what he calls "user-led innovation" will reinvent journalism "bringing it closer to the aspirational ideal of a right for everyone."

Undoubtedly, journalism as a professional practice is challenged by the Internet as a platform for everyone to exchange information, express opinions, and participate in the production of knowledge. Nevertheless, the reasons why modern journalism and its specific organizational forms (e.g. editorial offices, journalistic roles or professional standards) were developed in the 19th century are still not outdated. Organizational forms are helpful to reduce the complexity of news production, enable editors and reporters to work jointly under the same roof, and allow audiences to assess the quality of information by referring to the credibility of media organizations. To better understand journalism, therefore, the organizational approach described by Klaus-Dieter Altmeppen in his chapter on the structure of news production is fruitful since news coverage is not simply the result of the work of individual journalists but depends on the specific organizational details in the newsroom, the different occupational roles, and the influences of various technologies and the repercussions of media markets. The activities of individual journalists are embedded in organizational patterns which influence the journalists' work and behavior. So, the organizational approach to journalism focuses on the relationship of organizations and individual journalists, the relationship between the newsroom and other organizations, and the relationship between journalism and society. With organizational studies, both the internal structure of the newsroom and the environmental structures could be analyzed. Altmeppen argues that one advantage of organizational research into journalism lies in the comparability of the underlying terms (e.g. organization, structure, management). "This especially facilitates international comparisons that are missing for the journalistic organization whereas other global aspects of media organizations have already been analyzed . . . The organizational approach understands the use of a large range of methods and theories for designing a differentiated picture of the worldwide differences and similarities in journalism."

One useful attempt at developing a more theoretical approach to explaining news decisions is Wolfgang Donsbach's chapter on a psychological approach to journalism research. He attempts to use psychological theories of social validation and selective perception and attention to explain news decisions. Some studies that try to link journalists' attitudes with actual reporting are cited in this chapter, as well as studies asking journalists about their perceptions of the influence of subjective beliefs of journalists and the forces determining agendas of news reporting.

It is possible to aggregate individual level data from surveys of journalists into the organizational level, if one has enough cases from each organization, but studying extramedia factors such as the economic and political environments and societal/cultural ideologies is more complicated than surveying individual journalists in one country or culture. Comparative studies across national and cultural boundaries are necessary to assess these influences, as Thomas Hanitzsch's chapter in this book on comparative journalism research makes clear.

We should also make more attempts to link what we know about journalists with what kind of reporting they produce. We already have a great deal of research on media uses and effects, and a number of theories of such effects, including agenda-setting, framing, priming, cultivation, third person, etc. If we could be more successful in linking our studies of journalists and journalism with this research, we would stand a better chance of developing theories of journalism that could explain the entire complex process more thoroughly than has been done so far. But because journalism and journalism research no longer operate within national or cultural boundaries, journalism researchers will have to set up international cooperation if they want to more accurately describe and explain journalism and journalists. Comparative research and theories of wide scope are needed that take into account these developments and include cultural and societal differences as factors influencing journalists and journalism.

The theories that are needed include those at different levels of analysis (psychological, organizational, societal, and cultural) and also those that focus on different key characteristics of journalists, such as gender, which Gertrude Robinson in her chapter considers to be a constituting element of human society. As all interaction is influenced by it, journalism research needs to analyze systemic gender biases within the journalistic profession as well. However, as Robinson points out, "gender theory must be combined with organization and actor analysis, as well as a hermeneutic approach, which is able to explore the meanings people attach to their experiences." The study of journalism needs to take into account all levels of analyses including individual, organizational, societal, and cultural aspects.

Methods

Empirical journalism research is using specific tools. The classics among them are survey, content analysis and observation, so this book has included chapters on each of these by scholars who have done journalism research using them. We have integrated a chapter on the methodology of comparative research as well, given the increasing need to do more studies of journalists across national and cultural borders to assess the influences of culture and society and to search for similarities and differences in the theories and practices of journalism in different settings.

Thomas Hanitzsch's chapter on comparative research emphasizes that cross-cultural research is indispensable for establishing the generalizability of theories and the validity of interpretations derived from single-nation studies. He notes that empirical inquiry into newsmaking has generated a vast quantity of data, yet the more fundamental questions in journalism research remain largely unresolved: What shapes the news and the structures of journalism most? Is it politics, economy or culture? How do the conventional Western values of objective journalism fit with non-Western cultures? Does the increasing dissociation of journalism from the political system in all cultures lead to reliance on economic rationalities?

Hanitzsch advises that journalism scholars who intend to engage in comparative research would be well advised to take advantage of conceptual and methodological progress made in other disciplines which have a long tradition in comparative research, such as political science, sociology or psychology. As he puts it, "Journalism researchers do not have to reinvent the wheel. They must, first, always ask themselves whether a cross-cultural comparison will *extend the scope* of their interpretations enough to make the venture worthwhile." If the answer is yes, then the equivalence of constructs, methods, administration, language and meaning have to be addressed in every publication of cross-cultural comparative studies. He concludes that comparative journalism research is growing in importance as many scholars engage in multinational networks and funding agencies increasingly support such work, but he cautions about the need to carefully define the concepts used in such studies.

In the chapter on survey research, David Weaver argues that surveying journalists is both similar and dissimilar to surveying the general public, and that surveys are strongest for generalizing about journalists' characteristics, opinions, attitudes and beliefs. He discusses other advantages of surveys (gathering information about a large number of variables in a relatively short time across geographical boundaries and facilitating comparisons across time and space) and also some weaknesses (measuring actual behavior of journalists, addressing "why" or "how" questions, determining causal relationships, and difficulty of conducting). He addresses the need to carefully define the population of journalists before attempting to draw samples.

This chapter also discusses recommended practices for constructing questions and questionnaires (open-ended questions are recommended), drawing samples of journalists (especially when there are no accurate lists of journalists), interviewing journalists (telephone is recommended), and analyzing survey data. In the end, Weaver concludes that the survey remains one of the most common and efficient methods of gathering representative information on the characteristics, opinions and attitudes of large groups of journalists, but is less appropriate for measuring actual journalistic behavior than are observations. He argues that ideally surveys should be used in combination with other methods, such as content analysis and observation, to produce a more complete and accurate picture of journalists and their work.

In the following chapter on content analysis, Christian Kolmer points out that content analysis has become an important method for analyzing the products of journalistic activity, and that without it we cannot measure the influence of various factors on news production, including cultural, political and economic structures. He points out that the issue of media bias cannot be discussed in any meaningful way without reference to the actual content that journalists produce, even though many surveys of journalists have established the political leanings of journalists. He emphasizes that coder training and quality control are essential for intercoder reliability and also for the internal validity of any content analysis study, and this is especially true for cross-national studies where the wording of the category definitions is shaped in a national context and where translation into other languages and other cultural environments may change these definitions.

Observation of journalists is another important method in journalism research, and Thorsten Quandt points out that it must be done systematically and be related to more general propositions if it is to be considered "a scientific technique." There are different kinds of observation (participant and non-participant, open and concealed, natural and experimental, etc.), different settings for observations (newsroom, input-output, audience uses), and also a variety of criticisms and problems with it.

But in the end, observation allows for direct insights into observed phenomena in a natural setting. It also often produces unexpected findings and insights into complex interrelations in real life conditions. It is particularly appropriate for observing actual behavior of journalists – more so than surveys and even content analyses that study only the final product, but not how that product was created. But as Thorsten Quandt observes, this does not mean that observation should serve as a substitute for other methods. As with other methods, it can be used to best advantage when combined with one or two additional methods, such as surveys, content analyses or qualitative methods. Besides methods for collecting data on a large scale, tools such as discourse analysis, qualitative content analysis, ethnographic methods, focus groups, or in-depth interviews contribute substantially to the exploration and theory-building in the field.

Findings and Paradigms

The findings that are reported in the overviews of journalism research from various areas of the world suggest that there are a number of similarities that cut across national and cultural boundaries, but there are also differences not only in findings, but also in theoretical and methodological approaches that greatly influence the conclusions drawn about journalists and journalism in different settings.

Jane Singer argues in her chapter that "conventions and categories that have served US scholars for eight decades are becoming restrictive as borders of all kinds disappear." She writes that journalism scholarship in the United States sprang from both the social sciences and humanities in the early 20th century, but there has been a steady narrowing of analytic focus often through a single conceptual or methodological lens, with little synthesis of various theories and topics. She describes the intellectual roots and research categories (form, function, finances, and fiduciaries). She argues that the term "mass communication" has lost most of its conceptual value today, and that journalism needs to be studied "in the rich and multifaceted context it demands." She advocates a combination of traditionally disparate approaches, such as combining scientific methods for gathering data with a more culturally informed and holistic analysis of the data. She sees journalism as "inherently an interdisciplinary undertaking and increasingly cross-cultural" that may serve as an ideal intellectual setting for studying converging forms and functions of communication.

Likewise, Siegfried Weischenberg and Maja Malik see German journalism research as facing theoretical and empirical challenges that arise from new communication technologies and trends. They argue that such research has struggled with the distinctions between journalism and other forms of public communication, using a variety of theories (e.g. systems and action theories or constructivism) and embracing a wide variety of questions. They describe German journalism research as "inevitably interdisciplinary" and "oscillating between sociology, science of history, linguistics, political science and cultural studies." They trace its development from early historical studies to empirical studies of journalists, to viewing the newsroom as a complex social system, to the development of macro-level systems theory. They conclude by observing that even though the current theoretical debates in German journalism research are at the macro level, many empirical studies still employ an individualistic definition of journalism, a contradiction that seems true in the United States and other places as well.

Karin Wahl-Jorgensen and Bob Franklin, in their chapter on journalism research in the United Kingdom, note that even though the UK boasts one of the oldest and most prestigious traditions of journalism in the world, research about journalism has been slow to develop and has been scattered across a variety of fields, largely because journalism education or training has been located outside the university system until very recently. They trace the development of journalism education in the UK and describe the types of journalism research that have largely originated in sociology departments, including production studies, cultural studies, political economy research, and social demography of journalists, as well as the history of the press and broadcasting, and studies of the language of journalism. They argue that although UK journalism research "has taken shape in relative isolation from scholarship in other countries," they see the field as becoming increasingly internationalized and predict that journalism scholars in the UK will take part in these developments.

Arnold de Beer describes journalism research in South Africa as "perhaps not very different from that of any other Western democracy with a successful media system," but he fears that it has become complacent and that many potential academic journalism researchers have turned their attention to public relations, marketing and other forms of corporate communication. He argues that serious journalism research was severely lacking during the apartheid years, but that there were clear schools of thought regarding scientific and critical research. Globalization and postmodernism has reduced the boundaries between these schools, in his view, but not eliminated the context of racism in which this research developed.

De Beer describes the history of journalism research in South Africa and notes that one of the greatest challenges for present-day journalism research in South Africa is "finding its foothold within the world of often conflicting paradigmatic research approaches" including structural functionalism, critical theory and cultural studies. He identifies some journalism topics in need of research, such as journalism education, African journalism in general, and issues of plagiarism, race, language, culture, and media coverage of AIDS. He concludes that new paradigms for journalism research in South Africa will be heavily influenced by the country's racial past and also by how much researchers will be able to move across borders to find new approaches in this age of increasing globalization.

In mainland China, Zhongdang Pan, Joseph Man Chan, and Ven-hwei Lo describe journalism research as "severely underdeveloped," but they are quick to point out that only 25 years ago there was no journalism research other than "pure policy annotations." They note that modern social scientific methods began to be introduced into China's journalism research only in the 1980s and were not widely taught until about ten years ago. In Hong Kong and Taiwan, however, journalism research has had a longer history and "has covered a broad range of topics and has been genuinely interested in theory developing and testing." They cite the effective use of archival analysis and content analysis to address broader theoretical issues in Hong Kong as a valuable model for journalism research in other parts of the world. They argue that journalism research in Hong Kong and Taiwan helps to broaden the literature that has been based largely in the West, and that it will have a substantial influence on the journalism research carried out in mainland China and other parts of the world as globalization and internationalization increase.

María Elena Hernández Ramírez and Andreas Schwarz write that journalism studies began to be established in the 1990s in Mexico – before that it was a subsidiary subject of communication research, a "marginal" field. The literature related to journalism and the press before the 1950s is mostly historical or legal within very specific contexts. They conclude that Mexican scholars "seemed to lack a strong interest in journalism as a clearly defined object of study." They also write that Mexican research on journalism has been influenced by approaches from foreign countries, including the critical perspectives of Latin American scholars, the empirical research tradition of the United States, and influences from earlier British journalism studies. In addition, the development and communication emphasis of UNESCO has had considerable impact on journalism research in Mexico. The authors conclude that all these influences have inspired journalism-related research in Mexico, but also probably hindered the emergence of originally Mexican theories or approaches. They see contemporary journalism research in Mexico as still emerging, with the influence of the socio-political environment remaining strong and with academic efforts "to consolidate a specific trend of study" remaining isolated for a long time.

Future of Journalism Research

The four chapters in this section of the book discuss the problems of describing and defining journalism and who is a journalist in future studies, especially given the emergence of numerous web sites and blogs. As Ari Heinonen and Heikki Luostarinen write in their chapter on reconsidering "journalism" for journalism research: "We suggest that while journalism as a common form of communication is still a vital element of democratic societies, its locus may be moving – at least partially – from the sphere of institutionalized profession and specialized organizations toward wider communication spheres that are not well established nor easily defined." They recommend that journalism research pay more attention to "journalism outside journalism" – that is, the public's journalism as practiced by ordinary citizens on their blogs and web sites, which they argue is "semi-public" and which is often in interaction with the more traditional journalism by institutionalized media. They think that studying the interfaces between the different modes of journalism "may tell us something important about the emerging forms of public communication."

Likewise, Stephen Reese cautions in his chapter about the inadequacy of the local, national and international levels of analysis in studying a more globalized journalism that "increasingly must navigate between its traditional 'vertical' orientation within whatever nation-state it is carried out and a 'horizontal' perspective that transcends national frameworks."

He recommends that journalism researchers become more creative in identifying new study sites, concepts, empirical strategies, and relationships that are more appropriate to global journalism than to national journalism. Reese argues that it is important to ask the extent to which journalists and their audiences begin to take on a sense of a coherent global professional identification with such ideas as objectivity and fairness and neutrality, regardless of national origins. Another topic of research is the extent to which international news organizations standardize the news agenda and frames of news coverage in a way deemed acceptable to clients in many different countries.

Barbie Zelizer begins her chapter by stating that one of the biggest problems facing journalism researchers is lack of accurate communication among journalists, journalism educators, and journalism scholars. She describes five main lines of academic inquiry into journalism as alternative ways of thinking about journalism – sociology, history, language studies, political science, and cultural analysis – and advocates adopting multiple views in future journalism studies "because existing journalism scholarship has not produced a body of scholarly material that reflects all of journalism." She maintains that in trying to establish a model of the global journalist no single disciplinary frame will suffice, and taking an interdisciplinary approach may point scholars in new directions "that resonate more broadly with the global concerns that face us."

And finally, in his chapter on journalism education in an era of globalization, Mark Deuze advocates more theoretically informed and empirically driven studies of journalism education, especially those that take a more global approach than a national approach, to complement the research on journalism that is more global in nature. He maps an agenda of global journalism education research based on ten fundamental questions and urges the development of body of knowledge about journalism education that complements that about journalism.

Conclusions

Thus, the future of journalism research advocated by these scholars is one which will not be restricted to traditional news institutions, traditional geographic locations of countries or states, single disciplinary traditions, or only to the practice of journalism without considering the education and socialization of journalists. All of this research should take place in increasingly global settings and frameworks that transcend national and cultural boundaries. The theories used to explain journalism should not be restricted to a single level of analysis, the methods used to study journalism and journalists should be used in combination with one another and especially comparatively across national and cultural boundaries wherever possible, and the conventions and categories of journalism research should be re-examined in light of increasing globalization. In addition, because studying journalists and journalism is "an inherently interdisciplinary undertaking" in nearly every part of the world, the insights of other fields such as sociology, history, linguistics, political science and cultural studies should be brought into journalism research whenever possible, as the field becomes increasingly internationalized as well as interdisciplinary. This is a very tall order, we realize, but one worth striving toward if we are to have a more complete and holistic understanding of the complex processes of contemporary journalism and the journalists who produce it. We hope that the chapters of this book have suggested some useful ways of doing this and, at the same time, have provided some examples of how to do it.

Subject Index

Name Index